ARRESTED HISTORIES

ARRESTED HISTORIES

TIBET, THE CIA,
AND MEMORIES OF A
FORGOTTEN WAR

Carole McGranahan

Duke University Press   Durham and London   2010

Printed in the United States of America on acid-free paper ∞

Designed by Heather Hensley

Typeset in Arno Pro by Keystone Typesetting, Inc.

Library of Congress Cataloging-in-Publication Data appear
on the last printed page of this book.

Duke University Press gratefully acknowledges the support of
the Association for Asian Studies for providing funds toward
the production of this book.

CONTENTS

ILLUSTRATIONS

NOTE ON TRANSLITERATION, NAMES, AND PHOTOGRAPHS

Tibetan is a difficult language to transliterate. Several transliteration systems exist, but each has problems in rendering the language pronounceable for non-Tibetan speakers. In this book, I use a combination of the Wylie system of transliteration and my own pronounceable rendering of Tibetan words for English speakers. For example, for the Tibetan word for stupa, a commonly used Sanskrit word for Buddhist monuments, I give both the Wylie (*mchod rten*) and a pronounceable spelling of it ("chorten").

When transliterating Tibetan names, I use either the version preferred by the individual themselves or the most common transliteration for that name. In each instance, I give only the pronounceable transliteration rather than the Wylie; for example, I use "Tashi" rather than *bkra shis*.

I use both pseudonyms and real names. Following anthropological convention, I use pseudonyms or subject positions (for example, a "veteran" or an "official") in connection with ethnographic information and political opinions and, following history protocols, I use real names when presenting historical material. In those instances in which ethnographic and historic contexts converge, my use of pseudonyms or real names is based on political context.

Finally, Tibetans have two personal names, often do not have a family name, and sometimes are referred to by a combination of personal names and titles (kin, geographic, honorific). Some examples are Kesang Tsering, a personal name; Lithang Athar, a geographic qualifier preceding a personal name, that is, Athar from Lithang; Andrug Gompo Tashi, a family name prefacing a personal name, that is, Gompo Tashi of the Andrugtsang family; and Gen Lobsang Jampa, an honorific title prefacing a personal name, that is, "respected" Lobsang Jampa (*gen* is a shortened form of "teacher," which is properly spelled as *dge rgan*). For those familiar with Tibetan names, this system is easy to interpret and use. To help readers follow those whose names appear more than once in this book, I have included a Who's Who in the appendix.

All photographs were taken by the author, unless otherwise identified.

ACKNOWLEDGMENTS

With a deep sense of gratitude and humility, I offer thanks to the many Tibetans whose histories and memories comprise the heart and soul of this book. I have written this book with and through the generosity of each of the following people: Adhe Tapontsang, Aga Thubten, Adho Chodak, Anyetsang Pema Gelek, Athar Norbu, Baba Lekshey, Baba Yeshi, Bachung Pön, Beri Lhaga, Chamdo Dronyik, Chatreng Wangyal, Chodak, Dawa Dhondup, Dogah, Dorje Yudon, Gedun Phuntsok, Gedun Rinchen, Gyalo Thondup, Gyari Nyima, Gyato Kalsang, Ibila, J. Paljor, Jagod Se Dhonyod, Jampa Kalden, Jampa Wangdu, Kalay Jampa, Kargyal Thondup, Karma Tashi, Kesang Norbu, Khedroob Thondup, Khyen Rinpoche, Jamyang Nyima, Lingstang Kamphel, Lobsang Jampa, Lobsang Palden, Lobsang Tinley, Lobsang Tsultrim, Namgyal Tsering, Namkha Dorje, Ngatruk, Ngawang Dadhag (Lithang), Ngawang Dadhag (Sog), Ngawang Lhamo, Norbu Dorje, Norsang, Nyarong Aten, Nyarong Gyurme, Oga Toptsang, Palden Wangyal (Wangyal Lama), Pema Choonjoor, Pema Ngabo, Phupa Tsetop, Phurpu Tsering, Potsa, Ratuk Ngawang, Rinchen Dharlo, S. Khedup, S. G. Tharchin, Sadhu Wangdor, Sonam Gelek, Sonam Tsering, Surkhang Lhachem, J. T. Surkhang, Tachen, Tashi Choedak, Tenchoe, Tenpa Dorje, Tenpa Gyaltsen, Tenzin Tsultrim, Thubten Gyaltsen, Thubten Thargy, Trindu Pön Chime Wangyal, George Tsarong, Tsatultsang Wangchuk Dorje, Tseten Tashi, Tsewang Youngdon, and Tsewang Paljor. In many instances, to my delight, spending time with these individuals meant spending time with their families, and so my thanks and greetings also to the children, spouses, and extended family members who were such good company and often a great help during my research.

Lodi Gyari Rinpoche introduced me to the intricacies of Khampa history in 1992. I am indebted to his insights and experience, his long support of this project, and his willingness to discuss history and politics with me in taxis and offices around the world. In Dharamsala, Tashi Tsering was a mentor and guide beyond compare; his knowledge of Tibetan history has no match, and I am grateful for all he so generously shared with me; he is truly one of the national treasures of the exile community. I first met Dawa Norbu on the stairs of the library in Dharamsala, and before I knew it we were engrossed in a discussion of Marxism, nationalism, and exile politics over momos; his premature death is a loss for us all. Jamyang Norbu always cuts to the heart of the politics involved in any issue and does so with his characteristic passion and eloquence; in a community where speaking out is discouraged, Jamyang's public voice is invaluable as both critique and inspiration.

Many retired CIA officers spoke with me in person and over the phone about their work with the Tibetans. My thanks to Clay Cathey, Frank Holober, Joan Kiernan, Ken Knaus, Roger McCarthy, Tony Poe, Mr. Ray, and Bruce Walker. The time I spent with these individuals revealed the layers of the U.S. relationship with Tibet and the deep personal commitments held by many of the Americans involved. In San Diego and Scotland, George Patterson warmly shared memories about his time in Kham in the 1940s and in exile Tibetan communities in the 1950s and 1960s. Dating from our days at Cultural Survival in 1990, Warren Smith encouraged my study of Tibet and also generously shared U.S. government archival documents about Tibet with me. Also at Cultural Survival, Ann Armbrecht was one of the first to send me off to the field and remains a cherished anthropological didi to this day. I have long appreciated Jigme Ngapo's insights on Tibet and am grateful for the help and introductions he provided. Paljor Phupatsang helped me navigate Dharamsala life and politics as well as Chushi Gangdrug history from the perspective of the next generation.

Tenzin Bhagentsang has read and discussed Khampa history with me for hours on end. His participation in this project as research assistant, translator, and friend has been a gift for which I would not have dared to ask. His contributions, care, and questions have enriched this project in important and innumerous ways. I also extend my deep appreciation to Tinley Dhondup, my first Tibetan language teacher and invaluable resource in the Kathmandu Tibetan community. Tinley helped me start this research project in 1994 by introducing me to many people, including the Tibetan family with whom I lived over the next five years and for which I am beyond grateful. Also in Kathmandu, I was honored to have the translation assistance of Samten and hope to someday reciprocate on a research project of his. It has been a joy and an honor to work with each of these three teachers.

Research in India and Nepal between 1994 and 1999 was funded by dissertation research grants from the American Institute of Indian Studies and the Social Science Research Council as well as generous support from the National Science Foundation and, at the University of Michigan, the Program in Anthropology and History, the International Institute, and the Rackham Graduate School; at the University of Colorado, the Department of Anthropology funded a return trip to Nepal in 2003, and both the Department and the Center for Asian Studies provided invaluable funding for research assistance. Thanks also to numerous offices, institutes, and individuals who provided crucial assistance during my research, including the Library of Tibetan Works and Archives, especially Lobsang Shastri and Pema Yeshi; Tashi Namgyal, the former representative of the Dalai Lama in Nepal; the Department of Anthropology at Tribhuvan University; E. Gene Smith and all at the Himalayan and Inner Asian Resource Center; the staff at the India Office Records of the British Library; and staff of the Beinecke Rare Book and Manuscript Library at Yale University and the Hoover Archives at Stanford University. For images, my thanks to Bruce Walker, who donated the cover drawing to DePauw University, to Kaytie Johnson, Director and Curator of University Galleries, Museums and Collections at DePauw University, Jigme Deden Shakabpa and all at the Center for South Asia at the University of Wisconsin, Lauran Hartley at the C. V. Starr East Asian Library at Columbia University, and Eugene Louie of the San Jose *Mercury News* and istoryteller.net, and in connection with the CIA Museum, Toni Hiley, Carolyn Reams, Bruce Walker, and Keith Woodcock. For his deep sense of the cultural politics of geography as well as for the maps in this book, my thanks to John Isom. Rapten Dahortsang introduced me to Wangpo

Tethong's German-language book about the Tibetan exile community, and Chris Morris translated relevant parts for me; my appreciation to both. Thanks also to Champa Tenzin Lhunpo and Kunga Tsering for their friendship as well as assistance with Tibetan translations.

For their hospitality and help in India, a very special thanks to, in Kalimpong, Kazi Lhendup Dorje, Namgyal Tsering, Ola of Shangri La Services, Tempa at Deki Lodge; in Delhi, Gyato Kalsang, the Gyaritsang family, the Ratuktsang family, and the family of Athar Norbu; in Darjeeling, everyone at Hotel Dekeling; and in Dharamsala (and also Toronto), Paljor Phupatsang and family. For friendship, guidance, and inspiration in Nepal, I thank Ian Baker, Dor Bahadur Bista, Chophel, Dilli Dahal, Deepak Gurung, Kamala Joshi, Tom Laird, Kim Luce, Bishnu and Kiran Ranjitkar, Sonam Dolma and family, Tharchin, Tsering Choeden, and the family of Shambhu Sharan Prasad and Bina Verma.

Students in my courses on Tibet, history and memory, and anthropological theory at the University of Colorado have long been some of my most valuable interlocutors. To undergraduates, graduate students, and those on my Tibet study abroad course in summer 2005, my heartfelt thanks for your feedback, questions, and provocations over the years. I am especially grateful to those in my history and memory graduate seminar of fall 2008 who read and engaged with this book in draft form: Rachel Fleming, Kate Fischer, Keith Kloor, Meryleen Mena, Ricardo Moreno-Contro, Colleen Scanlan Lyons, Marnie Thomson, and Crystal Watson. Kate Fischer and Marnie Thomson provided excellent assistance in getting the book into final shape, and Eileen Stack was a brilliant early reader of the manuscript.

Friends, colleagues, and teachers around the world contributed to this book; to my thinking about anthropology, history, and Tibet; and to my well-being in ways for which I will be forever grateful. My thanks to John Ackerly, Vincanne Adams, Ann Anagnost, Lisa Barbash, Robbie Barnett, Jane Baxter, Pam Cannon, Fernando Coronil, Tenzin Dazie, Keila Diehl, Heidi Fjeld, Carina Frantz, Sumit Ganguly, Mel Goldstein, Losang Gyatso, Kira Hall, Rachel Heiman, Isabelle Henrion-Dourcy, Toni Huber, Sandra Hyde, Lynne Johnson, Karen Kim, Julie Klein, P. Christiaan Klieger, Laura Kunreuther, Elsa Lechner, Veve Lele, Donald Lopez, Alex McKay, Mary Moran, Javier Morillo-Alicea, Laurie Mullin,

Amy Oberkircher, Penelope Papailias, Michael Peletz, Losang Rabgey, Tashi Rabgey, Rachel Reynolds, Matt Rudolph, Lucie Schmidt, Tamar Scoggin, Kathryn Selig-Brown, Tsering Shakya, Jen Shannon, Elliot Sperling, Tenzin Tethong, Gina Ulysse, Stacey Van Vleet, Cairn Verhulst, Amani Weusi-Williams, Terry Woronov, Sonam Yangzom, Abe Zablocki, and my colleagues in the Department of Anthropology at the University of Colorado.

This book began as a portion of my Ph.D. thesis in anthropology and history at the University of Michigan, and I remain grateful for the opportunity to learn from an exceptional group of scholars on my dissertation committee: Larry Epstein, Erik Mueggler, Leslie Pincus, and my two co-chairs Nick Dirks and Ann Stoler. My intellectual debts to Nick and Ann are great; it has been a privilege and a pleasure to work with each of them. Nick changed the way I saw anthropology and led me to get a Ph.D. in history as well as in anthropology; his work has been foundational for my own in all areas. Ann inspires and challenges me in ways that shake the roots of my thinking, providing me with an exemplary model for critical scholarship, generous mentoring, and academic parenting.

Over the years, treasured friends and colleagues have read, commented on, and critiqued chapters of this book at various stages, often several times over. For this gift of their critical engagement, my thanks to John Collins, Val Daniel, Nick Dirks, Sondra Hausner, Wynne Maggi, Charlene Makley, Meg McLagan, Ann Stoler, and Lucien Taylor. At the University of Colorado, I am blessed with colleagues—Donna Goldstein, Carla Jones, Mithi Mukherjee, and Kaifa Roland—who not only read successive drafts of various chapters, but who are also dear friends.

A final brave group read and commented on the entire manuscript, for which I am truly humbled. Some pushed me to be bolder, some asked me to be gentler, some encouraged me to be a little bit of both; each made invaluable contributions. My deep thanks to Ann Armbrecht, Yu-shih Chen, Rinchen Dharlo, Lodi Gyari, Jamyang Norbu, Kunga Tsering, and Emily Yeh as well as to the excellent and incisive reviewers for Duke University Press, one of whom later revealed himself to me as Martijn van Beek. While many people participated in my research and commented on this book in draft form, sole responsibility for the book's arguments and interpretations as well as any errors is mine. In light of the political nature of the histories I discuss here, this is not the usual academic disclaimer, but a recognition that not all of those with whom I worked on this study will agree with my conclusions.

Writing goddess Cat Altman worked her magic with me, posing thoughtful and smart options, phrasing suggestions in ways that revealed things I could not see on my own, and doing it all with an understanding of the importance of true love (as well as of giants, monsters, chases, revenge, and miracles) to all good books. Heartfelt thanks also to Ken Wissoker, my editor at Duke University Press. I am ever grateful for Ken's patience, his keen editorial eye, and his unwavering support for this book during the review and revision process. My sincere gratitude to all who made publishing with Duke such a pleasure.

One special group of people was instrumental in the writing of this book: Jessica Gomez-Noguez, Lyn Mead, and Brenda Smith. From the bottom of my heart, my thanks to each of you for providing loving, stimulating, and safe care for my children while I wrote.

This book is dedicated to my family around the world—through birth, through marriage, and through anthropological kinship. My life changed in so many wonderful ways the day I met Lobsang Tinley, Kesang Tsering, and Tenzin Peldon in 1994. They welcomed me into their home in Kathmandu, not knowing that for better or worse our lives would become entangled. My perfect day on this earth would start with them: Pala's prayers followed by a simple breakfast of tea, Amala's homemade bread, and their always delightful, always lively conversation. I was delighted to inherit the academic position in my husband's family from Yu-Shih Chen and Tsu-lin Mei and am happy to be able to include my husband's grandfather, Y. P. Mei, in the notes of this book. Many thanks to the Chen, Chow, Jiang, and Mei families for their support, including culinary delights too numerous to name. Estranged from my late grandfather for decades prior to my birth, my great-uncle Donald McGranahan unexpectedly appeared in my life while I was conducting research for this book. I remain deeply grateful for his olive branch across the generations and for his support of my academic career. My grandparents, Ann and Walter Camuso and Harvey and Marjorie McGranahan, were early advocates of my education and travel; I am glad to be able to share this book, the result of so much time so far away from them, with my Nana Camuso. Eric McGranahan and Lynne Banach have long shared in the joys of this research in their own unique and creative ways, and I thank them for their many gifts, including bringing Ellie, Eric B., Gus, Jai, Jesse, and Teja into our collective lives.

My two children, Riley and Liya, disrupted my writing in all the right ways. Their arrivals delayed the book and, I hope, matured the arguments I make here. More importantly, however, they have made the world new for me, bringing a deep sense of contentment, joy, and wonder to each day. Eugene Mei has kept much afloat while I tended to this book, and I thank him for his love, encouragement, endurance, and laughter over the years. Finally, I thank my parents, Dean and Eileen McGranahan, for allowing me to first travel to Nepal in 1989, for shortening the distance between here and there in meaningful ways, for their constant support and faith, and for the models they embody of an active, loving, and grounded life. To all, I bow before you with thanks: *thugs rje che.*

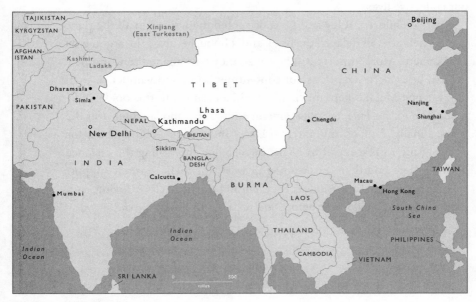

MAP 1 Tibet (Chol Kha Gsum / Three Regions model)

MAP 2 Tibetan Areas of the Peoples' Republic of China

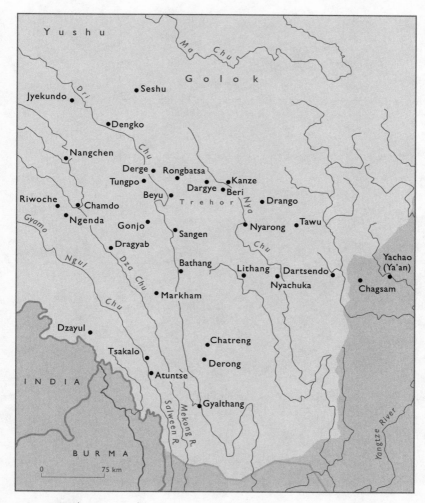

Y u s h u

Ma Chu

G o l o k

Dri

Jyekundo •

• Seshu

• Dengko

Chu

Nangchen •

Derge • • Rongbatsa
Tungpo • • Kanze
Dargye • • Beri
Beyu • T r e h o r • Drango

Riwoche • • Chamdo
Ngenda •
Gonjo • • Sangen
Dragyab •

Bathang •
Gyamo
Ngul

Markham •

Dza Chu
Chu

Nya Chu

• Nyarong • Tawu

• Lithang • Dartsendo
Nyachuka •

Yachao
(Ya'an)

• Chagsam

Dzayul •

Tsakalo •

I N D I A

Atuntse •

Chatreng •

Derong •

Gyalthang •

Salween R.

Mekong R.

Yangtze River

B U R M A

0 _____ 75 km

MAP 3 Kham (eastern Tibet)

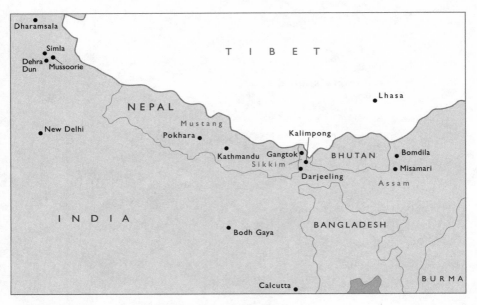

MAP 4 The Himalayas: Selected Tibetan Refugee Communities

There was no turning back once the monasteries were bombed. In the beginning, things had seemed different. The first Communist Chinese soldiers who came to Tibet in 1949–50 were polite and generous. They showered silver coins upon the Tibetans and spoke of the glorious society they would jointly construct. While most Tibetans felt no need for a new society, they appreciated the coins and the respect the soldiers showed to Tibetan Buddhism. "How naïve we were!," Tibetan refugees now exclaim, for this period of benevolence and restraint was short-lived. In its place, the Chinese instituted drastic reforms that violently targeted revered Tibetan religious and lay leaders. In response, ordinary Tibetans took up arms to defend their leaders, religion, and country. Using the anti-quated rifles they had on hand, farmers and monks and nomads and traders spontaneously rose against the infinitely larger People's Liberation Army (PLA). Once the Chinese began aerial bombing of Tibetan Buddhist monasteries in 1956, there was no turning back; this was war.

But if this period was a time of war it is not remembered as such. Begun in the eastern Tibetan region of Kham (*khams* or *mdo smad*) in the mid-1950s, this war continued for almost two decades. In addition to bombing monasteries, the PLA flooded Kham with troops, vastly outnumbering the Tibetans. Many fled west to Lhasa, Tibet's capital, where they formed an all-volunteer resistance army. They named the army Chushi Gangdrug (*chu bzhi gangs drug*), meaning "four rivers, six ranges," an ancient name for Kham. In

1959, this civilian army provided safe escort to the Dalai Lama when he fled into exile in South Asia. Once in India, both the resistance army and the Tibetan government reconstituted themselves. The army continued fighting until 1974, when the Dalai Lama convinced the soldiers to lay down their weapons. Yet despite the bombings and the mass uprisings, despite the citizen-initiated army and its struggles, the history of this period is not told as one of military battle. In the Tibetan refugee community, war is forgotten and other histories are told in its place, histories focused primarily on the Dalai Lama's diplomatic and nonviolent efforts to regain Tibet. This book is about the grassroots Tibetan militia, the war they fought, and how and why it was forgotten.

Three explanations are called for immediately. First, this was a guerrilla war, covertly supported by four governments—those of India, Nepal, Tibet, and the United States primarily through the Central Intelligence Agency (CIA). Aspects of such wars are necessarily secret, and it follows that much about the Tibetan resistance remains secret (and not just forgotten) today. Second, under the leadership of the Dalai Lama, the Tibetan struggle against the People's Republic of China (PRC) is a nonviolent one. Reconciling violence with a philosophy of nonviolence is not easy and is another reason the guerrilla war rests uneasily within current history. And, third, the guerrilla war did not succeed in regaining political control over Tibet for the Dalai Lama and the Tibetan government. Having failed, it has not been highlighted in Tibetan histories of this period. In this book, I argue with and against these three reasons and offer a fourth, overlooked, reason: histories of the Tibetan resistance army challenge the expected order of things, that is, they challenge the Tibetan social and political status quo. The resistance army contested not just China, but also long-standing power structures and cultural hierarchies within the Tibetan community itself.

Arrested Histories is both a subaltern history of war and an ethnography of how histories and communities are made in troubled times. Central to this intertwined story are the Chushi Gangdrug resistance army veterans in India and Nepal. Veterans live throughout the Tibetan refugee community but are not marked in any special way. Young and middle-aged men in the 1950s and 1960s, they are now elders, anonymous in their communities, old men one would see out buying vegetables and meat in the market, or praying at Boudha or Swayambhu in Kathmandu, or with the crowds in the streets welcoming the Dalai Lama "home" in Dharamsala, India. Since the end of war in 1974, they have lived mostly quiet lives, raising families, selling rugs, working the fields, participating in political protests, conducting petty business, praying to the gods, and paying close attention to everything the Dalai Lama says and does in regard to the resistance. If, as veterans estimate, there were over ten thousand soldiers based in exile—and tens of thousands more inside Tibet, including many who were jailed or killed by the Chinese—their numbers have dwindled as the years passed. As veterans turn the leadership of Chushi Gangdrug, which currently exists as a refugee social and political welfare organization, over to the next generation, they feel certain aspects of history slipping away.

Historical truths are always also social truths. The making of history is a social and political process, not a neutral rendering of what happened in the past.[1] To make history is to historicize, to socially and politically legitimate a particular happening or version of what happened as true. How is it that certain pasts are converted into histories while others are not? How is this process both reliant on and generative of categories of difference within a community? Answering these questions requires disentangling social and historical truths; it requires asking *how* histories are made and lived, rather than asking only which ones are and why. As veterans would learn, history is as much about organizing the present and working to secure certain futures as it is about the past. I argue that veterans experience the forgetting of resistance history as part of the social politics of belonging. Forgetting creates not just a narrative absence for this past, but also a specific social presence for the veterans. Despite veterans' sentiment that they were and still are in service to Buddhism and Tibet, they are socially categorized as problematic, as inhabiting subject positions and embracing political projects at odds with Tibetan society. As I show in this book, veterans' experiences confirm Veena Das's observation that societies hide the pain of belonging.[2]

Belonging, or alignment with and acceptance by a community, is a process subject to constant negotiation and change. The era of the Tibetan resistance, for example, was not just a time of war, but one in which important changes in historical consciousness and civil society were underway. These transformations affected the soldiers in many ways, among them their understanding of what it meant to be a good, contributing member of society, including how one might participate in the transformation of national community. Veterans narrate their war experience as such participation, specifically as a new opportunity for Khampas, or people from the region of Kham, to contribute to the nation. In its strong identification with Kham, the resistance army embodies one of the key categories through which Tibetan identities are grounded, that of region. In Tibet before 1959 and in exile society after 1959, region serves as a central marker of difference. Central Tibetan social and political forms before 1959 were privileged over those from other regions; after 1959, these same central Tibetan norms were recast in exile as a shared, pan-Tibetan identity. This conversion of the particular to the general, of a specific regional identity to a homogenous national identity, is one means by which regional identities were criticized and devalued. Yet if regional identification is categorized as a problem to be disciplined, and the resistance veterans are associated with a specific region, then—to paraphrase W. E. B. Du Bois—what does it mean to live life as a problem?[3] One tangible result is that veterans quietly abide the lack of recognition they receive for their wartime efforts. The pains of belonging involve important cultural contradictions and compromises, chief among them Tibetans' relationships to the Dalai Lama.

In exile, Tibetans are dislocated from the land that for generations anchored and animated their histories, identities, and memories. However, if refugees no longer have access to the land, they do have access to the Dalai Lama. The fourteenth Dalai Lama is the leader and symbol of Tibet in exile, a tangible and physical moral presence in the refugee community. It is next to impossible to overestimate his importance to Tibetan refugees or the respect they have for him. His leadership endows this story of the Tibetan resistance with a meaningful difference from much of the literature on suppressed histories.[4] This is not a case of an authoritarian state or a situation of "dominance without hegemony," but instead one in which authority, in the form of the Dalai Lama, is deeply hegemonic.[5] In the exile Tibetan community, governance is composed of hegemonies in that political rule is secured through consent.[6] However, the Dalai Lama receives not just Tibetans' collective consent, but also their collective devotion. His is a highly visible power paired with consent consciously rooted in belief and faith. For veterans, therefore, to request recognition of the resistance war is risky in that they challenge the status quo and thus the Dalai Lama by articulating not just a suppressed past, but also an alternative vision of community (albeit one under his continued leadership). They do so under conditions that are not static. For example, in 1987, when the Dalai Lama first publicly articulated nonviolence as the entirety of the Tibetan struggle rather than as a component of it, the conditions of possibility for resistance histories shifted. Constant throughout, however, has been veterans' belief that military defense of Buddhism is service to the Dalai Lama. Remembering war enables veterans to demonstrate dedication to the Dalai Lama in that they fought to defend him, their religion, and Tibet. Living with such tensions is to embody and embrace contradictions in one's everyday life.

In this book, I theorize the space between resistance and deference as a site of lived impermanence. This is where contradiction resides, a space of both epistemic murk and clarity in which the world and one's place in it are constantly being reconfigured. Lived impermanence signals simultaneous states of fixity and mobility. One sees this clearly with the veterans in exile: geopolitically displaced from their homes, socially marked as problematic, and historically placed on hold, veterans are fixed in certain subject positions that do not neatly align with the ones they claim for themselves. Veterans neither actively resist nor passively accept the forgetting of war. They bear the social politics of history alongside the religious burdens of their military past, working individually to accumulate the merit needed to transcend past transgressions and working collectively to carve out future spaces for telling war as a part of contemporary Tibetan history. They endure the pains of belonging through the reassurance of consent. Contradictions and tensions are mitigated through consent, through the promise of community and of eventual recognition by leaders, peers, and the gods. Theirs is a belief, a mostly patient belief, that the time will come for the story of bombed monasteries and the war they fought against the Chinese to be told.

There is not just one way to suppress a history, fashion a community, or live with contradiction. I present here specific ways to accomplish each of these, grounded in the cultural, historical, and political contexts of contemporary Tibetan life in exile. Consonant, for example, with Tibetan religious history, I contend that histories of the resistance war are not suppressed indefinitely, but are instead arrested or delayed until a time in the future when it will be deemed appropriate to tell them. This history and its suppression take place in dialogue with the world beyond Tibet, with the CIA and the politics of the Cold War, with Asian forms of nonviolence, and with imperial formations at work in the era of and beyond decolonization.[7] Tied into globally hegemonic discourses such as those of sovereignty and rights, the particularities of historical arrest in exile Tibet open to broader, shared questions about the production and suppression of history around the world. As the lives and narrations of Tibetan veterans reveal, to live with forgetting is to accept a delayed form of historical time and, in solidarity with others elsewhere, to wrestle individually and collectively with the pains of belonging.

A Khampa History of Tibet

"If we weren't boiling water for tea, we were fighting the Chinese," said Baba Lekshey, conjuring up a world familiar yet distant to contemporary refugee life. While refugees still boil bottomless pots of water for tea, they now fight China with protest signs and chants rather than with guns and knives. The day Baba Lekshey said this to me, musing out loud about what life had been like in Kham in the 1950s, we were sitting in his room in Kalimpong in 1995. I was hurriedly jotting down his words as natural light receded at the end of the day, and he was occasionally sticking his head out the window to call down to the folks below, "Oh-ooh. Oh-ooh. Bring up two teas for us. And some biscuits. That American girl has come back." His punctuated conversation with those below contrasted with the vivid worlds he called forth in narrating to me a history of the resistance. That day and over the course of four years of conversations and interviews Baba Lekshey told me stories of his transformation from young trader to politically active resistance soldier. Four decades later, he was now elderly, a refugee and a monk, spending most of his days in prayer to best atone for his battlefield sins. As he spoke, the Tibetan curtain hanging in his doorway was pulled back, and in came a girl from the family downstairs. With a shy smile, she placed two cups of chai and a pack of biscuits on a small table next to the bananas I had brought and then slipped out of the room as quietly as she had entered. Taking a sip of the scalding tea, Baba Lekshey returned to explaining how and why he and his fellow soldiers had fought the Chinese.

Living on the eastern border with China, the people of Kham were in many ways the first line of defense for the Tibetan state. The Tibetan

FIGURE 1
Baba Lekshey.

army was small, based in faraway Lhasa, and had only a portion of its troops stationed in Kham. Defense was usually a local affair. As another Khampa veteran explained to me, "The Chinese were more scared of my monastery, Dhargye Gonpa, than they were of the Tibetan government." Encouraged by a strong sense of independence, such Khampa bravado was tempered by loyalty to the Dalai Lama as religious and political leader. Yet, political allegiances were never singular. Baba Lekshey's area of Bathang had a series of layered and sometimes conflicting relationships with Lhasa, with neighboring areas, and with successive Chinese powers. When the Communists came to Kham and bombed the monastery in Bathang, he and his relatives and friends were appalled, frightened, and angry. There had always been fighting, but this was different.

In Tibet and elsewhere these were unsettled times. Massive political shifts were taking place around the world, including in neighboring India and China. In 1947, Great Britain's departure from India left the Tibetan government without its primary international ally, while to the east the civil war in China raged on much longer than anyone had anticipated. The fighting between Chiang Kai-Shek's Nationalist army and Mao Zedong's Communist army was taking place far from Tibet, and most Tibetans were somewhat oblivious to what was happening in China. Baba Lekshey and other Tibetans, for example, usually made only minor distinctions between the different Chinese armies; for them, both were Chinese, were fighting each other far away, and and had little to do with Tibet. They could not have been more wrong.

One person who was aware of the threat the Communists would pose to Tibet was the thirteenth Dalai Lama. In 1931, two years before his unexpected, premature death, he wrote his *Final Testament*, in which he warned his subjects of the difficult times that lay ahead:

> It will not be long before we find the red onslaught at our own front door. It is only a matter of time before we come into a direct confrontation with it, either from within our own ranks or else as a threat from an external nation. . . .
>
> Therefore, now, when the strength of peace and happiness is with us, while the power to do something about the situation is still in our hands, we should make every effort to safeguard ourselves against the impending disaster. Use peaceful methods when they are appropriate, but when they are not appropriate, do not hesitate to resort to more forceful means.[8]

His warning went unheeded, was set aside and then forgotten in the confusion and contention that came after his death.[9] As he predicted, the Communist Chinese came to Tibet, but it was not until their policies grew violent that Tibetans finally heeded his advice to use "more forceful means."

Baba Lekshey described the 1950s as a period in which everything was turned upside down. Communist policies were directed at changing, if not eliminating, multiple aspects of Tibetan culture: religion, politics, social relations, and more. Former leaders were stripped of their power and wealth, and former peasants given high office. Monks and nuns were publicly humiliated. Under such conditions, nationalist sentiment grew throughout Kham and Tibet in general, and people began to take up arms in new and collective ways. Tibetans who were serving in the Chushi Gangdrug army believed the resistance signaled to the world the political sentiment of the Tibetan people, to the Chinese their independence, and to the gods their defense of Tibet, Buddhism, and the Dalai Lama.

Over the decades, the resistance army received support from multiple governments. The Tibetan government gave moral and strategic support in Tibet and in exile. The government of India provided training and funds and created Tibetan military units within its own forces, while the king's government in Nepal allowed the resistance to use Mustang, an ethnically Tibetan kingdom within Nepal's borders, as a base of operations. Through the CIA, the United States provided training, funding, and logistical support. Chushi Gangdrug forces, as noted, registered at least one major victory: the safe escorting of the Dalai Lama to India during his undercover escape from Lhasa in 1959. The CIA withdrew support in 1969, and, as mentioned above, official Tibetan military operations ceased in 1974. Some soldiers joined Tibetan forces in the Indian militia but most simply became refugees in one Tibetan community or another throughout South Asia.

The dominant narrative of Tibetan history for this period tends to sound something like this: the Chinese Communists invaded Tibet; the Tibetans tried unsuccessfully to cooperate with the Chinese for several years; individuals in Lhasa rose in protest against Chinese rule on 10 March 1959; immediately afterward, the Dalai Lama escaped from Lhasa to India; in exile, he and the reconstituted Tibetan government began the process of securing international support for their political struggle against China; this struggle, ongoing at present, has primarily been a diplomatic, nonviolent one. While some Tibetans and some histories of Tibet do recognize the Tibetan resistance army as part of this history, the standard history of Tibet that circulates both inside and outside of the Tibetan community tends to include the resistance as only a brief, unfortunate, and unsuccessful undertaking. As a result, the Tibetan mirror of history has turned increasingly clouded with time.

Most of the veterans with whom I spoke were well versed in the politics of historical production. The histories they desire are national ones, not those relegated to the category of personal experience. Collectively, veterans want resistance history to enter the registers of national history, to be socially known and widely taught, to be officially endorsed and publicly recognized. As they and the refugee community understand it, the transformation of this past into national history requires the action not of historians, but of the Dalai Lama. As Baba Lekshey might explain, what really matters is not only that their histories be written down, but also that they be approved by the Dalai Lama. Resistance as national history hinges on the Dalai Lama's acknowledgment of the Chushi Gang-drug army's political contributions and religious service in a time of war. Veterans desire this but for the most part do not act on it. Theirs is a desire borne with patience and Buddhist detachment. Theirs is a resistance driven by respect.

Khampas like to describe themselves as straight talkers—*kha ri kha thug*. Baba Lekshey fit this mold. "You're back," he would say when I appeared at his door without notice after several days or sometimes months, and he would immediately launch into the past, skipping social niceties until he had satisfactorily recounted a story he wanted to tell me. His histories of Kham and of war call attention to the way history unfolds and is remembered outside of, but often in compromised relation to, centers of power. Narrated from an unprivileged location in exile and from a forgotten historical moment, a Khampa history of Tibet supplements and gently challenges histories of Tibet that homogenize and whitewash the past. To be clear, history is always in tension with histories. Any history that claims to be singular makes that claim at the expense of multiple other histories, of many other ways of explaining the past. Following the lead of Baba Lekshey and his fellow veterans, this book is a Khampa history of Tibet that remembers war while respecting and yet questioning the reasons it was forgotten in the first place.

Lived Impermanence and Public Secrets

Scholars do not know how many people were killed in Tibet during the 1950s and 1960s.[10] Neither do we know well the story of their struggles. What might be called common or popular knowledge is woefully short and specifically situated. Whatever each person knows about the resistance is stratified by nationality, politics, gender, regional origin, and age. Some know about the Tibet–China struggle in general terms, whether those of the Free Tibet movement or those of Chinese government discourse (neither of which highlights the resistance war). Others know that an actual decades-long war was fought. Still others know the details of this war, perhaps through its connection to Kham or the CIA or someone known to them. And, finally, a small group fought in it themselves. Within the Tibetan exile community, the story of the Tibetan resistance is what the anthropologist Michael Taussig calls a "public secret."[11]

The public secret is not (just) what you think it is. The resistance is somewhat of a literal public secret, that is, something quietly and publicly known, but known not to be made much of. Taussig's understanding of public secrets takes one to an additional place, a place just as important for making sense of the resistance war. As he explains it, public secrets are about convention and compromise, about making one's way in a world organized by arbitrary cultural structures of meaning. It is about that which makes humans social beings and about a process of dissimulation whereby "we act and have to act as if mischief were not afoot in the kingdom of the real and that all around the ground lay firm."[12]

In terms of Buddhist philosophy, such engagement with the nature of perception and impermanence—that is, with the mischief afoot in the kingdom of the real—is fundamental and ongoing. For Tibetan laypeople, however, actually *living* impermanence is something else altogether. As one makes his or her way through each day, philosophy and practice may or may not converge. The arbitrariness of culture and the impermanence of existence are sometimes felt deeply, at other times fleetingly, and at still others not at all. Public secrets traverse the gap between hegemonic norms such as the status quo or what is considered natural or normal and other ways of being in, seeing, and explaining the world. Minding this gap has become for Tibetan veterans a way of simultaneously demonstrating respect and embodying resistance. For those veterans who lived the resistance and who thus inhabit a public secret, knowing what not to know or what not to articulate is crucial.

Pain is involved. The pain incurred through subjugated or marginalized identities cannot be forgotten away.[13] Building on Friedrich Nietzsche's politics of *ressentiment*—and his contention that "only that which never ceases to hurt stays in the memory"—the political theorist Wendy Brown suggests that pain is at the heart of many contemporary political demands.[14] Recognition, acknowledgment, release, and eventual dissolution: these, not revenge or therapy or memory, are what drive contradictory politics in late modernity. Many veterans would agree with her; the

FIGURE 2 Tibet Memory Restaurant, Boudha.

FIGURE 3 Tibet Memory
Restaurant, Dharamsala.

forgetting of the resistance hurts. What they seek is not memory (they have that) but recognition in the Hegelian sense of social consciousness. Recognition from their community, from the U.S. government, from the Tibetan government-in-exile, and especially from the Dalai Lama. Recognition in the sense of being acknowledged participants in social and political life.[15]

To be a refugee is to hold a subjugated subject position, one of lived impermanence vis-à-vis the world. Tibetans are refugees in a collective sense; that is, they are not refugees on individual terms but as part of a nation-state community or, more accurately, a nation-state in exile. Exile on a national scale began in 1959, when thousands of Tibetans followed the Dalai Lama to India, and today the Tibetan refugee community numbers over 130,000.[16] The Tibetan government-in-exile, based in Dharamsala, has sole administrative responsibility for Tibetan refugees in South Asia. Everything from voting to taxes and from social protocol to social repairs falls under its administration. Public secrets are understood to emanate from these offices, as does social or political injury. As in the case of the liberal state, redress of injury or acknowledgment of public secrets (such as the excommunication of community members or arrest of resistance history, both of which tear at least portions of the exile community apart) is linked to the exile state. Expectations are that the Dalai Lama will address, if not alleviate, such problems, for example, by privately meeting with an individual who fell out of favor with the Tibetan government-in-exile. The alleviation of political grievances ironically rests with the same state apparatus responsible for creating them.[17]

The Dalai Lama and the Nation-State in Exile

As I heard so often during my research, if you don't have your own country things are difficult—*so so'i lung pa med na dka' las khag po 'dug*. Such comments were usually followed by proclamations about how lucky Tibetans were to have the Dalai Lama. "Without him, I don't know what we would do," people said. The lives of Tibetans in exile revolve directly around the Dalai Lama. The faith, *dad pa*, that Tibetans have in him grounds their actions, identities, and memories, their claims to knowledge, and their productions of history. Much of this book therefore rests on navigating the rough waters of Tibetans' relationships to the Dalai Lama.

Of all the things that bind the Tibetan community in exile—for example, culture, religion, heritage, and loss—the Dalai Lama is supreme. The Gelug sect's Dalai Lama lineage was installed as rulers of Tibet in 1642, and since then their power has grown so that national (rather than just sectarian) genealogies of religion and politics now validate their rule. In exile, the power of the Dalai Lama lineage has only become stronger.[18] Respect and devotion to the fourteenth Dalai Lama are proffered on both sacred and secular terms, but primarily because he, like all previous Dalai Lamas, is understood to be an incarnation of Chenrezig (in Sanskrit, Avalokiteshvara), the deity who embodies wisdom and compassion.

While each Dalai Lama has been important to the Tibetan people and history, perhaps none has been so called upon to lead as the current Dalai Lama, Tenzin Gyatso. Born in 1935 in the northeastern region of Amdo and recognized at the age of two as the Dalai Lama, he has faced the formidable tasks of inheriting a politically troubled government, of coming to political age at the time of the PRC's invasion and takeover of Tibet, and of guiding the Tibetan community in exile, including leading their international effort to regain Tibet.[19] As both person and institution, the Dalai Lama is the twentieth-century symbol of Tibet, a unique merger of religion and politics, of the sacred and the secular.[20] In terms of understanding the Tibetan refugee community in general and veterans' experiences in particular, the Dalai Lama's position as head of the exile Tibetan state is crucial.

From its earliest days, the exile community operated in the belief that they would be returning to Tibet. By definition, exile embodies a notion of impermanence, a yearning for somewhere else, a displacement from home. Exile holds no generic form but is always situated in a unique context.[21] Tibetans in exile, for example, are not independent or unorganized groups of refugees but a coherent group administered by the Dalai Lama and the Tibetan government-in-exile.[22] On 29 April 1959, soon after crossing the border into exile in India, the Dalai Lama reconstituted the government. The Tibetan exile state is a combination of old and new organizational principles—grounded in the Charter for Tibetans in Exile and administered by the democratically elected Assembly of Tibetan People's Deputies and the Council of Ministers (the Kashag), which is elected by the Assembly, and headed by the Dalai Lama. The exile government provides crucial services to the Tibetan refugee community, including education, health care, political advocacy, spiritual guidance, an independent judiciary, community administration, tax assessment, and more. Among refugees, service to the state is highly valued.

Tibetans from all regions, sects, and socioeconomic classes—from former nomads, farmers, and mule herders to chiefly families, royalty, aristocrats, and the few groups that were in between, such as traders, intellectuals, monks, and nuns—are represented in exile. Refugees can be divided into two groups, those who escaped from 1959 through the early 1960s and those who escaped from the early 1980s to the present. The exile Tibetan state governs this population rather than a territory. Specifically, the Tibetan government-in-exile has responsibility for the more than one hundred thousand Tibetans who live in India and Nepal as refugees as well as some authority (for example, via taxation) over Tibetans living in other countries around the world. As a transnational state centered within the territorial boundaries of another state (India), the exile Tibetan state departs from geographic expectations of statehood but meets other norms. In terms of political anthropology, Thomas Blom Hansen and Finn Stepputat explain the dimensions of the state as follows: "*Technologies of governance* encountered in the guise of classifications: forms to be filled in, rules to be obeyed, epistemologies learned, and so on; *symbolic representations* of the state as a locus and arbiter of justice and a symbol of larger society; [and] the invocations of the state as a *set of institutions* that can recognize, adjudicate, and authorize, that is, invest its authority in and give legitimacy to certain representatives, forms of community, public symbols, and also become loci of resistance and contestation."[23]

The legitimacy of the exile state rests in and with the Dalai Lama. Initial and continuing support from India, respect from world leaders and citizens, and consent from Tibetan refugees all hinge on his leadership. Within the Tibetan refugee community, the Dalai Lama's authority is unchallenged. It is through him that the state's technologies of governance, symbolic representations, and sets of institutions are all validated by the Tibetan people. Outside the refugee community, the coherence of the Dalai Lama's leadership often results in the Tibetans being considered a successful refugee community despite the fact that they have not accomplished their primary political goal of regaining Tibet. In 2009, the Tibetan community in exile marked fifty years as refugees, a duration far longer than was expected as well as out of balance with the often presumed temporality of refugee situations. As refugees in rather than citizens of India and Nepal, Tibetans in South Asia strongly assert a political, not just a cultural and religious, base to their community. However, while this strategy validates the Dalai Lama's continued rule as head of state, it also holds drawbacks for Tibetans in exile.

In India and Nepal, Tibetans have few to no rights guaranteed to them under either national or international law in that neither country has signed the Geneva Convention Relating to the Status of Refugees (1951) or the protocol of 1967 that updated the convention.[24] As a result, the Dalai Lama and the Tibetan government negotiated individual arrangements with each country (at times through third parties such as the United Nations High Commission for Refugees and the International Committee of the Red Cross). The exile government has official, longstanding agreements with the government of India, their primary host, and less official and much less secured agreements with the government of Nepal. While socioeconomic statuses of Tibetan refugees differ widely according to a range of historic and contemporary factors, their political situations differ depending on the country in which they live. India, the world's largest democracy, has been a relatively stable home for Tibetans. By contrast, rapid political changes in Nepal over the past two decades, including a violent civil war, have resulted in important shifts for Tibetans living there.[25] As one of the world's poorest countries, Nepal is caught between India and China, and one result of recent politics is heightened influence from China, including tightened restrictions on Tibetans. In general, Tibetans' reliance on the exile state as advocate signals a new aspect of Tibetan practices of political belonging.

Reconstituting community in a time of national trauma and in new and scattered locales is never an easy or singular task. Nonetheless, the Tibetan diaspora presents a coherent Tibetan refugee identity to the world. This homogenized identity is cultivated at the expense of identities based on regional and sectarian affiliations. As Liisa Malkki has argued, such flattenings of identity and ethnicity are widely documented international phenomena generated in part by post–Second World War perspectives on refugees.[26] In exile Tibet, a nationalist identity both flourishes and flattens. The perceived need for internal cohesion, given the current political state of Tibet, resulted in the devaluing of diversity in the exile community. A homogenous and hegemonic Lhasa-centered identity critiques regional and sectarian identities as backward, divisive, and harmful to the Tibetan cause. Favored are central Tibetan styles of language and dress, general senses of propriety and comportment, and ideas of class, hierarchy, and prestige directly correlated to central Tibetan sociopolitical worlds.

However, at the same time that national discourses highlight homogenized rather than divergent features of the community, regional identities remain practically and symbolically important in the exile community. For example, the election of representatives to the Assembly of Tibetan People's Deputies is based on regional and sectarian affiliations.[27] Tibetans from all regions of Tibet, including Kham, currently serve in very high positions in the exile government.[28] Perceptions and performances of regional identities in relation to a shared refugee identity are often highly politicized. Yet, as the Tibetan scholar Matthew Kapstein explains, "local, tribal, and sectarian identities" have long played "a divisive role in the Tibetan world, [and yet also] presuppose, and so in some aspects also maintain, the very fabric of that world."[29] In exile, regional and sectarian identities—such as Khampa or Amdowa, Kagyu or Sakya—persist as chief organizing features of the refugee community. The slippage between regional and hegemonic identities is an everyday tension many Tibetans live with. Senses of lived impermanence dwell in such contradictory spaces, in the cracks and fault lines of hegemony's "ground laid firm."[30] As points of rupture in an otherwise smooth sociopolitical formation, certain categories of difference are marked as potentially signaling dissent.

Hegemonies, Memories, Transformations

Life in exile includes a range of practical and epistemological community dilemmas: governmental debates regarding what to do vis-à-vis the Chinese; political disagreements over how to reconstitute the government-in-exile; social troubles concerning the organization of the refugee community; economic crises about funding life and war in exile; communal disputes over recognition, participation, and action; and everyday dilemmas of identification, subsistence, and dislocation. Such dilemmas are manifest in everyday life as contradiction. Consider, for example, Tibetan desires to forge a democratic society without giving up the leadership of the Dalai Lama, or Tibetan service in the militias of other countries despite the current Tibetan policy of nonviolence. How are such contradictions lived and explained? Hegemonic political formations forge and assuage contradiction. Consent to such hegemonies is both active and passive: it involves actively accepting that one is a member of any given community and passively accepting the opportunities and constraints that define that community. Hegemonies are contradictory in that they are never completely closed, in that they silently disappear difference, and in that they extend a "lived system of meanings and values" over the entire population while also dominating and subordinating particular classes.[31]

Raymond Williams describes hegemonies as "a whole body of practices and expectations, over the whole of the living: our senses and assignments of energy, our shaping perceptions of ourselves and our world."[32] As such, they need to be continually "renewed, recreated, defended, and modified."[33] In that hegemonies are never complete or total, they are also continually "resisted, limited, altered, [and] challenged."[34] This history of the Tibetan resistance army is grounded in the simultaneity of alignment and antagonism. Tibetan veterans and their histories align with some social norms at the same time they antagonize others. The social alternatives they propose straddle multiple fault lines—of geopolitics, of identifications, of deference—in living, engaging, and challenging hegemony.

Challenge is compromised in that Tibetans' respect for the Dalai Lama as a religious figure makes it difficult to engage him critically as a political leader. Social prohibitions against critiquing the Dalai Lama extend also to the exile government, such that even secular critiques of the government are controversial and widely avoided. The furthest most individuals will go is to criticize the Dalai Lama's senior advisors, family members, or exile government officials; or, at times, to offer sympathetic critiques such as "the Dalai Lama is too trusting." Individuals or groups who publicly express political critiques are often themselves criticized, if not silenced, by other community members. My field notes include stories of individuals verbally and physically attacked in Dharamsala by other Tibetans for their political views; some of these attacks are at the hands of women, who in Tibetan exile society are often charged with upholding aspects of cultural tradition and propriety.[35] Familiar logics of serving the Dalai Lama undergird such community disciplining of perceived transgressions. If to defend the Dalai Lama is one of the highest forms of religious service, to transgress him is one of the most serious charges one Tibetan refugee can make against another. The risks and tensions inherent in expressing critique or dissent reveal that loyalty to the Dalai Lama is not without its contradictions.

The space of forgetting swallows up contradictions and shelters deferrals. Veterans consider social recognition of their national participation to be deferred rather than denied. Hope invested in deferral is shrouded in difficulty. The anthropologist Michael Jackson contends that state or institutional withholding of recognition causes stories to be "salted away in subjectivity and silence, often becoming marks of insignificance and shame."[36] Insignificance, if not shame, is certainly felt by at least some of the veterans in relation to their collective historical position. With this in mind, in thinking of histories of the Tibetan resistance as deferred, I reference both the Derridean sense of deferral as a mode of difference possessing an inability to reach closure of meaning,[37] and the Foucauldian sense of the deferred as forgotten, as that which did not change the order of things.[38]

History and memory are social practices with a politics. They both work to categorize and organize community in ways that are anything but neutral.[39] The work of history and memory takes place in a social domain that is always already hegemonic and laden with issues of power, representation, and reproduction. As such, history and memory are not just constituted by "social frameworks of meaning," as Maurice Halbwachs postulated in 1925, but are also constitutive of them.[40] They give meaning to experience; they legitimate authority; and they generate and are generated by culturally shifting and politically specific conditions of possibility. They are tactics of social institutions—of resistance armies as much as of exile governments—as well as entities belonging to people. Deployed to certain tactical ends, neither history nor memory is ever only about past and present, but they are also very much about the future. Connected though they are, history and memory are not the same thing.[41] History is narrative, stories with beginnings, middles, and ends. Memory is different in that it has no preassigned genre or form. If history is narrative, memory is what drives historical narratives; that is, memory consists of the stuff and the energy with which histories are forged or forgotten.

Memory propels history forward into specific futures as much as it pulls it back into particular pasts. Both forward and backward movements index a temporal politics of belonging. Such politics often generate an authoritarian fear of history as a clinging to the present, that is, as a fear of losing modernist holds on authority, belonging, and temporality in favor of newly imagined futures.[42] Time works on such relationships so that they are "reinterpreted, rewritten, sometimes overwritten—as different social actors struggle to author stories in which collectivities are created or re-created."[43] Relationships are precisely what are at stake for the resistance veterans. Relations to their selves (in a Buddhist sense), relations to their community in its moments of both creation and re-creation, relations to the Dalai Lama as political and spiritual leader, relations to the deities, and relations to the broader world community in which hope (if not trust) is invested. Time, in this sense, is about process, possibility, and becoming.

Becoming, or what one might become, rather than what one is or where one is from, is a compelling way to understand identity.[44] Thinking of identity as becoming reveals how confrontations between past and future take place in the present as a "tug of war between 'identity' as essential being, locked in (an image of) the past, and 'identity' as open-ended becoming, invested in a future that remains to be struggled over."[45] Resistance soldiers are caught in just such a temporal politics: arguing over past and future in the present, yet holding on tightly to a regional identity at the same time that they want to transform a national identity. In so doing, they focus primarily on becoming rather than on re-creating.

At the end of several days of conversations about Kham, Lhasa, and the resistance army, one veteran in India spoke directly about the need to historicize the past: "I am explaining these things to you so that you will understand. It is not as though I have a preference for feudal systems. In fact, I am among those who have a more progressive way of thinking and want—wanted—to see change. These answers are to explain to you how things were before. They are not nostalgia for the way it was. Things change with time, and they should."[46] The future he envisions is inextricably linked to the past, but not just to the way things were; instead, he and many others desire a future that resembles the past they wish they had had. If, as the Tibetan proverb says, "The wise learn from the past, the brave learn from the future," then veterans' efforts to narrate the past reside firmly in the present, where they have the courage to interrupt the future. Interruptions, of course, are not discontinuous with that which they interrupt. They do not so much stop things as abruptly rupture them, lead them into unexpected transitions in which "things are no longer perceived, described, expressed, characterized, classified, and known in the same way."[47] Change is therefore not absolute but a redistribution and reconfiguration of prior forms of knowing and organizing the world.[48] For the Chushi Gangdrug resistance army, their troubling of the order of things begins, but does not end, with their embodiment of such change.

Chushi Gangdrug in the Tibetan Order of Things

A glance, an examination, a language. Without such things and the cultural grid they create, contends Michel Foucault, humans would not have order.[49] Order in the central sense of the "fundamental codes of a culture" or "scientific theories or philosophical interpretations," but also order in a "more confused [and] more obscure" sense: order unspoken, emancipated, and liberated.[50] Order unspoken is the messy, middle ground of culture, the area where things don't always work as intended, where neither claimed cultural logics nor universal laws hold, but where life goes on nonetheless. Chushi Gangdrug veterans inhabit both of these zones: central and middle. They dwell squarely in the center—the fundamental codes of culture—in ways analogous to Pierre Bourdieu's assertion that "doing one's duty as a man means conforming to the social order and this is fundamentally a question of respecting rhythms, keeping pace, not falling out of line."[51] For example, the resistance army follows both the thirteenth Dalai Lama's advice to adopt "more forceful means" when appropriate and also the fourteenth Dalai Lama's eventual request that violent struggle be abandoned. And yet the veterans also reside in the middle ground in that their existence "makes manifest" and thus calls into question "the modes of being of order" in the Tibetan community.[52]

The order of things in exile is decidedly national. Although the concept of the nation has a long career in Tibet, and progressive Tibetans advocated national views of Tibet in the first half of the twentieth century, it was not until the 1950s and the Chinese occupation that nationalism became a philosophy and practice of the Tibetan people and state.[53] Concurrent with the political embrace of pan-Tibetan national community, national history gained prominence. Across the twentieth century, national histories were cast as modern histories and vice versa: for example, as "one of the most important signs of the modern," history is said to promote notions of order and linear progress, to spur secular thinking, and to work to fix national identities.[54] As scholars from Ernest Renan on have argued, the production and reproduction of the nation rest on social exclusions generated by forgetting.[55] Forgetting organizes community by endorsing specific discourses on community and belonging. National narratives suggest not only who belongs, but also who is excluded, that is, "whose claims [to the nation] were worthy and whose were not."[56] Understanding the politics underlying the recognition of claims to the nation requires a culturally situated historicizing of the categories of exclusions and the structures upon which they play out.[57]

History is a language of governance. Exile histories homogenize the nation in service to the state, specifically to the political struggle of the Tibetan state versus the Chinese one.[58] In doing so, they embody the Foucauldian idea of historiography as a political force, as a tool of and against the state.[59] The polemics of Tibetan political history are those of supposed objective and singular truths associated with modernist claims to power.[60] In many ways, this focus on the state obscures subaltern or nonelite discourses of community, nation, and politics such as those of the resistance army. Subalternity is a "position of critique," a "recalcitrant difference that arises not outside but inside elite discourses to exert pressure on forces and forms that subordinate it."[61] To redirect attention to subaltern experience as Tibetan history is thus, in the tradition of subaltern studies,[62] to challenge elite voices, to think critically about resistance (in its armed and everyday forms), to acknowledge missing narratives in official Tibetan history, and to be "suspicious of any and all forms of national homogeneity."[63] The historian Peter Hansen contends that scholarship on Tibet mostly lacks this critical edge. He asks, "Why is there no subaltern studies for Tibet?"[64] This book is written in dialogue with such critical historiography in that it deconstructs internal myths of Tibet as much as external ones. In the context of the Tibetan resistance, to historicize the subaltern is to write about veterans' war experiences as hegemonic and nationalist.

Chushi Gangdrug histories are nationalist ones.[65] Whether told in 1956 or 1996, in Kalimpong or Kathmandu, they chart a subaltern but nationalist version of past, present, and future. In their relationship to official Tibetan history in exile, Chushi Gangdrug histories pose challenges to normative views of the nation and thereby remain but fragments in both popular and governmental narratives. As Gyanendra Pandey explains, historical fragments reveal, among other things, the partiality of supposed totalities: "The fragment is, in this sense, an appeal to an alternative perspective, or at least the possibility of another perspective. It is a call to try and analyze the historical construction of the totalities we work with, the contradictions that survive within them, the possibilities they appear to fulfill, the dreams and possibilities apparently suppressed: in a word, the fragility and instability of the 'givens' (the 'meaningful totalities') of history."[66] Although the Tibetan exile community presents itself to the world—and to itself—as harmonious, contradictions survive such that history is a quietly contentious topic within the community.[67] In the case of the Tibetan resistance what is acknowledged to have happened as well as what lies below the surface of permissible knowledge is fragmentary and mired in the controversial murk of historical memory, government secrets, and the politics of community in exile.

Nonetheless, each veteran I spoke with situated his narration as a broader story of the nation rather than as a singular tale of the self. Some of this signaled humility in that most of the veterans are individuals who described themselves as ordinary, that is, not big leaders or from important families; they are people for whom the promotion of oneself would be cause for embarrassment, or *ngo tsha kha skyengs*. Some of this was a reflection of a Buddhist sense of the self, in which selfhood and subjectivity are muted, presumed impermanent, and not necessarily grounds for launching societal critique.[68] Some was the oft-expressed belief that their story was collective, that every individual sacrifice was but a piece of a larger, collective experience. Tensions of resistance history are somewhat mitigated by the Dalai Lama's encouragements to Tibetans in general to tell their stories. Veterans commonly interpret this as meaning that a time will come for narrating their version of the nation. In general, the veterans with whom I worked believed that such history and memory work—even in deferred form—constitutes service to the community as well as to the Dalai Lama. However, many histories and memories are kept in check by community politics and fears of critiquing, rather than serving, the Dalai Lama. Some of these histories are told among friends, exchanged and shared over tea, beer, and meals. Some are told orally and some in written form, neither of which is necessarily welcome in public spaces. And some are not told at all.

Historical Arrest: Time Delay as Cultural Practice

In 1997, the Dalai Lama made his first, historic visit to Taiwan.[69] The Tibetan community in Kathmandu was buzzing with talk about it. Some people were hopeful that the Taiwanese government would change its position on Tibet from considering it as a part of China to accepting it as an independent state. However, most people focused on the secret economic and political support some Tibetans in exile had received from the Taiwanese government. Such relations were long subject to public criticism as being anti-Dharamsala or, at the very least, as signaling an individual's falling out with the Tibetan government-in-exile. One day, in the course of an interview about the resistance, I asked a Khampa businessman why relations between Tibet and Taiwan were rarely discussed. "Yes," he said, "talking about it was restricted until this year, and wasn't allowed by either side. Now that His Holiness [the Dalai Lama] went to Taiwan, it is open. The story can be told."[70] He agreed that Chushi Gangdrug resistance histories fit this pattern of restricted histories and offered several other pasts he thought qualified, all of which had to do with internal politics and external perceptions of the Tibetan community. Although I was aware that some pasts were not publicly converted into histories and that time delays structured the narration of Tibetan histories, precisely how and why this happened was not clear to me until that day. Although many Tibetans would speak about the time delay and the public secrets it often engendered, this practice did not seem to have a name. I settled on the idea of historical arrest as a way to talk about it in order to capture the idea of a future time for revealing a history prohibited in the present. The question, then, became one of understanding Tibetans' engagement with histories that could not be told or for which, as they said, "the time was not right."

Historical arrest is the apprehension and detaining of particular pasts in anticipation of their eventual release. Pasts that clash with official ways of explaining nation, community, and identity are arrested, in the multiple senses of being held back and delaying progress but also in the ironic sense of drawing attention to these pasts. Sometimes overtly categorized as secrets, arrested histories are left noticeably unspoken at other times. The halting of such histories in the present to store them away to be told at another time is a conscious act, albeit one not always explicitly stated as such. Arrested histories are thereby not so much erased or abandoned as they are postponed and archived for future use. Certain histories are detained by those with sufficient political or religious power, such as the Dalai Lama or agents of the government, through overt mentions, subtle silences, or meaningful actions. Historical arrest is not a permanent ban, and a time in the future is anticipated, although not guaranteed, when these histories will be released for narration. This practice is more complicated than a sweeping under the rug of inconvenient pasts and politics; it is a delay or postponement of histories for the present only. Arrest is not just for written histories, but also for the many and varied forms history may take and for those ways in which histories are unmade as well as "made and made sense of."[71]

Once arrested, histories inhabit the Foucauldian category of "subjugated knowledge"—existing either (or both) as "historical contents that have been buried and disguised in a functionalist coherence or formal systematization" or as "a whole set of knowledges that have been disqualified as inadequate to their task or insufficiently elaborated."[72] Such prescriptions for history are efforts to control knowledge of the past, to reproduce power structures in the present, and to secure particular futures. In this context, I understand culture not as a category of history but as a condition for history as well as its product.

This conceptualization of historical arrest resonates with a Tibetan Buddhist tradition of the storing away and rediscovery of religious texts and ritual objects. One way Tibetan Buddhist teachings are transmitted is through revelation, that is, through "treasure teachings" (*gter*) that are hidden and later become available at specified times.[73] These may be either texts or sacred objects (*gter ma*) hidden in the ground, in caves, or other places by a trained religious master (*gter bdag*) to be discovered by a similarly trained master (*gter ston*) at a specific time in the future. The time elapsing between when a treasure teaching is hidden and when it is found may be hundreds of years. Arrested histories follow a similar cultural and temporal protocol insofar as their arrest and release are also understood to be in the hands of authority figures, most notably the Dalai Lama. The connection between arrested histories and the treasure teachings is a slightly circular one: scholars believe the treasure teachings were developed out of the early Tibetan political practice of burying "politically sensitive items underground as a means of preventing their destruction."[74] At present, what are metaphorically buried or arrested are exactly such politically sensitive topics.

In its contemporary incarnation, this practice is directed specifically at histories that challenge dominant versions of the nation. These challenges trigger fear in individual and collective registers as well as in karmic, social, and political ones: fears that Tibet will not be regained, the diasporic community will splinter, harm will come to the Dalai Lama or to Tibet, one might be excommunicated from the community or given a bad name, or harmful actions in this life—killing, fighting, causing trouble—will negatively affect one's next life. The social and political limits encouraged by such fears work on renegade pasts in tandem with "delayed" time. Such temporal lags are often associated with modern time-space configurations. Homi Bhabha, for example, suggests that historical revision as the generation of political and cultural agency often takes place through a "discursive time-lag," in which dominant symbols are subject to new signs, meanings, and truths.[75] Similarly, Reinhart Koselleck argues that modern forms of temporality incur new demands on the future, such that novel approaches to and ways of assimilating experience emerge.[76]

Historical arrest fixes the linear truths of official history through nonlinear means. By arresting potentially disruptive histories so that they are "structurally unavailable as history" (in ways similar to other historical contexts, such as the Holocaust), spaces are secured for officially authorized truths.[77] Such truths and their temporal logics are generated in and by specific cultural contexts and practices. New meaning is both assigned and withheld from the discrete memories and histories collected together.[78] In the assimilation of renegade experience to normative story lines, the state—here in the form of the exile Tibetan government—does not so much destroy memory and experience as relocate and refunction them.[79] These acts take place in many domains, often forcing awkward complicities between rupture and continuity, between desires for recognition and obligations to submit to the demands of the present.

Explanations of how people respond to historical arrest require investigation into the ethnographic conditions of possibility for history, into those "processes that make and transform particular worlds—processes that reciprocally shape subjects and contexts, that allow certain things to be said and done."[80] Ethnographic as well as historic processes and contexts transformed Tibetan worlds, shaped new historical subjects and their consciousnesses, and made possible the saying and doing of certain things, while guarding against the saying and doing of other things.[81] In determining how people work with and around the arrest of histories to which they are close and in thinking about which histories slip through the cracks of arrest, one must focus on Tibetan practices of history and memory.

My recognition and development of historical arrest as a specific practice are indebted to the many conversations about history I had with Tibetans in exile. I found that people talk both abstractly and directly of things that are not yet to be spoken of, of those events and peoples whose stories are publicly recognized as not yet historicized. The key is in the "not yet" aspect, in the certainty that a time will come when these histories will be told. An anticipation for a time other than now is built into the conceptual structure of arrested histories. A time when buried political items can be dug up, when treasures can be revealed, when refugees can return home to Tibet, and when histories are no longer drafted in the temporal terms of the modern nation-state (despite exile geopolitical aspirations to just such a polity).[82] The success of such a historical practice requires a view of history not restricted to a progressive or linear unfolding of time, but rather an understanding of history as a series of more erratic movements. Walter Benjamin explains this as the way in which "thinking involves not only the flow of thoughts but their arrest as well."[83] Or, as one Tibetan man mused over tea as we spoke about the resistance, of history as something that moves like water. "History," he said, "doesn't go forward in a straight line. It's like a river. It meanders and moves, disappearing, reappearing, visible, audible, tangible."[84]

Research as *Kora*

In listening to the histories Khampa Tibetans do and do not tell, I take seriously my instructions from one Chushi Gangdrug veteran in Kathmandu: "It is important that you write the truth," he told me, "but the truth can also change." Changes in historical truth, such as the categorical rehabilitation of an individual from traitor to patriot, are triggered by sociopolitical shifts in the terms of the possible. Beginning in the 1950s, the conditions of possibility for imagining national community shifted dramatically for Tibetans. Collecting arrested histories involved tracking their conditions while they were still in motion. For me, timing was crucial, as was my outsider status in the community. As is true of all cultural anthropology, my research was possible owing to the cooperation I received from the community itself, the Chushi Gangdrug veterans.

Explaining their unanimous cooperation is complicated, for it involves varied sets of hopes and dreams, privileges and commitments, senses of obligation and service, skills of narration and writing, and continually negotiated feelings of trust and fear. In some ways, as I was told on several occasions, "you can write this because you are an outsider. We couldn't write this." Politics of critique, literacy, and mobility were all factors, as was the timing of my research during the gradual release of resistance history beginning in the 1990s and continuing erratically into the present. The period of my research involved a split within Chushi Gangdrug, one part of the group being excommunicated by the Tibetan government-in-exile. The split began in June 1994, the summer I began my predissertation research, and therefore colored my research in particular ways.

"With whom have you already spoken?" was a question commonly put to me; there were general attempts to gauge how much I knew or did not know about the split. The more I learned, the better the questions I could ask, the deeper my ability to engage intricate and important historical detail. My decision to talk with people on both sides was widely approved and was thought to be in line with the general belief that one's current political views did not cancel out his or her wartime accomplishments. This recent split in Chushi Gangdrug, evocative of earlier splits in the 1960s and 1970s, gave an edge to a history that had been smoothed over in times of organizational peace.

However, the split did not produce two politically separate versions of history. To my surprise, I found a wide range of narrations, including several whose narrators chose not to participate in the politics of the current split. Many Khampa veterans openly discussed community politics and frustrations with me, whereas others tried to keep history and politics separate. As I traveled back and forth between Tibetan communities in Nepal and India, some of the veterans took an interest in tracking my progress, in seeing what old friend of theirs I had tracked down and what new insights I gained as time went on. Some took pride in the number of veterans I interviewed and in my meeting with individuals whose stories had not yet been recorded (as opposed to those who were more regular spokespersons for the resistance). Others urged me to talk with people who had differing political opinions and coached me on what to ask and not to ask. "Don't ask him about politics," I was told in reference to an elderly veteran who lived in a monastery. "Just ask him about history."

The knowledge veterans shared with me—and my cumulative inter-pretations of it—are examples of situated knowledge, grounded in spe-cific contexts and tied into already existing debates and desires.[85] The histories they told me were located in the particularities of their lives and the hegemonies that govern them. Alongside these specificities, it is im-portant to note that Tibet is not a singular cultural field but a vast and varied territory. In exile, the Tibetan refugee experience may be shared, but it is not singular. The stories I tell here are explicitly situated and stratified within the exile community. They belong to an older genera-tion, to Khampas, to war veterans, and to men more than women. Their stories are neither homogenous nor interchangeable.

The accessing and assessing of arrested histories require research that unravels what is considered normal or natural within a society and why it is so considered.[86] It requires listening, vulnerability, and trust and the challenge of what is never fully possible—"thinking outside dominant systems of thought."[87] The anthropologist Kim Fortun argues that field-work, especially poststructurally informed ethnographic research, is criti-cal to providing the "vocabulary and conceptual models" to engage "with what is not expressible in dominant idioms."[88] Such fieldwork—living within a community, conducting research over an extended period of years, and focusing on everyday interactions with people—is the prin-cipal ethnographic and historic research method I used in this study. The overwhelming majority of people I write about in this book are individ-uals I came to know personally.

My research methods included ethnographic participant-observation, oral history interviews, formal and informal archival research, and a multi-sited approach, that is, research not only in various geographic locations,

FIGURE 4 Boudha chorten.

FIGURE 5 Kora path at Boudha.

but also in differently oriented or scaled communities and institutions.[89] I call this final method research as *kora*—(*skor ba*—circumambulation, a form of walking prayer). Religion saturated my research experience. In almost every conversation I had, religious practice was involved. Someone was always turning prayer beads as we spoke or reading scriptures as they listened or making reference to deities in their narrations. The rooms in which we talked were dominated by immense family altars, images of deities, offering bowls, incense burners, and photos of the Dalai Lama, other high lamas and reincarnations as well as on occasion images of Andrug Gompo Tashi, the lay leader of the Chushi Gangdrug army. But it was kora, circumambulation, that was the most embodied aspect of my research. In my primary research site, Kathmandu, Nepal, I lived with a Khampa Tibetan family near the Boudhanath stupa (in Tibetan, "chorten," or *mchod rten*), a major pilgrimage site for Buddhists, an important Tibetan Buddhist *gter* site, and an enormous, beautiful, white dome monument representing the Mind of the Buddha that is meant to be circumambulated in order to achieve merit. Each morning and evening, hundreds of Tibetans and other Buddhists would go to Boudha (as it is colloquially known) for kora, to circumambulate as well as to see friends and socialize. The family with whom I lived went every afternoon around four without fail.

Research as kora involved many trips around kora paths at Boudha and elsewhere, but much more than that. Research as kora was the idea of being in motion, of being engaged and embodied, and of circling around and through Tibetan communities. Using Kathmandu as a base, I conducted research in five other Tibetan communities—Pokhara in Nepal and Darjeeling, Delhi, Dharamsala, and Kalimpong in India—as well as with Tibetan veterans and retired CIA officers in the United States. I spent extended periods of time in each of these communities in South Asia and circled back through them several times over the course of my primary research from 1997 to 1999. This research model was widely approved of by the veterans, for, as they knew better than anyone, their community was scattered between the two countries. Each community had its own rhythms, its own relationships, and its own issues. These also became part of my research—the difficulty of refugee life in Kathmandu, the isolation of the camps in Pokhara, the politically charged intimacy of the Majnu-ka-Tilla settlement in Delhi, the deep histories and distant

FIGURE 6 Kora path in Dharamsala.

feelings of Darjeeling and Kalimpong, and the constant awareness of the presence of the Dalai Lama in Dharamsala, where the kora path literally encircles his abode.[90]

In Kalimpong one summer, two schoolteachers I spoke with discussed the politics of regional identity in the exile community. They told me that the place "to find out the facts" about history and community—"about things that might be perceived as negative or harmful to the Tibetan government or the Dalai Lama"—was not Dharamsala or Delhi, "where everyone is involved in politics," but "here in Kalimpong" and other places distant from the center.[91] This encouragement to turn to the margins in order to understand the center confirmed and also compelled my embrace of poststructural theory as an analytic framework. Making sense of how and why certain pasts do not become histories, and how this affects peoples' lives in the present required movement in and through the margins of community as well as in and through its center. My focus on Kham and on the Chushi Gangdrug resistance army grounded this inquiry in ways that enabled me to ask what commitments and concessions people make in the name of the nation and why they do so as well as to ask at what point these recede and what happens after the recession, questions that drew me to practice theory's concern with agency, life as lived in the everyday, and the interactive negotiation of social norms.[92] At heart, this is a book about the production of history and about the politics of knowledge and community. It is a story of Khampa loyalty to, yet independence from, the monastic and political institutions of central Tibet and Dharamsala and of the ensuing pains of belonging as experienced in everyday life in exile.

A Caution: How (Not) to Read This Book

I write in a time of protest. In the spring of 2008 Tibet erupted in the largest, most widespread uprisings since the era of the Chushi Gangdrug resistance. Across Tibet, people raised their voices against the Chinese state. Many things appear to have grounded their actions: political disenfranchisement, economic hardship, religious oppression, cultural marginalization, historical grievances, and Tibetan nationalist sentiment among them.[93] As with the uprisings of the 1950s and 1960s, we do not yet know their extent or the range of state repercussions against participants. This book is not about these recent demonstrations or about contemporary Tibet as part of the People's Republic of China. However, as a study of earlier Tibetan resistance to China, it offers background to these latest protests, and as a study of community politics in exile, it serves as a complement to scholarly work on Tibetan communities in the PRC.[94]

Writing about Tibet is political. Writing about a guerrilla army associated with the CIA and labeled controversial even within the Tibetan community is even more political. Given the general polemics of the Tibet–China struggle *and* the heightened political tensions in this new moment of protest, I want to be clear about the politics of this book and its potential interpretations:

1. *The focus of this book is Tibet,* not China, the CIA, or the United States. I do not approach Tibet as a China-centered "Tibet Question" or subsume Tibetan history in that of the Cold War or U.S. imperial politics. As a component of Chinese or U.S. history, the Tibetan story is important but is not my focus here. Instead, in solidarity with subaltern studies' project of telling the history of India as Indian history, rather than as a portion of British history, I situate this history the same way the Chushi Gangdrug veterans did: as Tibetan history.[95]

2. *Tibetans are handicapped by the myth of Shangri-La,* the external view of Tibet as a forbidden, yet desirable land in which lives a peaceful, happy, nonviolent people who will save the world. This unrealistic view denies history and humanity to Tibetans, thereby rendering them "prisoners of Shangri-La," and holding them responsible for the unreasonable expectations such skewed understandings generate.[96] Absolving Tibetans of this responsibility is to recognize their individual and collective complexities in both ordinary and extraordinary times. Deconstructing the myth of Shangri-La is an ongoing, collective project to reveal its effects, to ask why some hold so tightly to this myth, and also to historicize key aspects of it, such as the often essentialized place of nonviolence in contemporary Tibetan history and politics. To unravel a depoliticized view of Tibet as Shangri-La is to replace simplistic views of Tibet with grounded sociohistorical scholarship and analysis.

3. *To push past the myth of Shangri-La is to acknowledge that Tibetans have rights*—rights to hold political opinions, rights to craft political strategies, and rights to have disagreements. Like all peoples, they should not be bound to a neutral or unobtainable political objectivity. They have the right to be complicated, contradictory, and contentious, not just to be compassionate. Tibetans have the right to make decisions, both good and bad, in ways that make sense to them, including in ways they hope will be effective in "molding both national and international public opinion."[97]

4. *The resistance is a specific and fractured community.* The histories I tell belong to the resistance veterans, and I tell them in the knowledge that the veterans are not a united or homogenous group. Axes of difference cut across the exile community in general and yet also pierce the resistance itself, such that experiences, commitments, and dreams in and across these groups vary. So, too, does knowledge of the resistance. Most Tibetans in exile know little about the resistance army. Others participate in highly charged online and face-to-face debates over which is the "real" Chushi Gangdrug, or over who did or did not fight in Tibet or contribute to the struggle (rather than act for personal gain). While I discuss the various political splits within the resistance, I do not take sides. Instead, as scribe and analyst, I seek to understand this history and how the

veterans live it. As such, I consider resistance splits and the passions they generate as commentary on the politics of belonging as much as on the politics of history.

5. *To critique is not to invalidate.* To ask about the production of history is to explore structures of power. For resistance history this means to critically examine the social politics of the refugee community, the Tibetan government-in-exile, and the Dalai Lama. I critique from a point of engagement; with the veterans' guidance, my discussion of the pains of exile, of forgetting and loss, and of specific disputes within the refugee community is designed to show the very real and deeply felt commitments individuals have to their communities and leaders.[98] It is not to invalidate the exile community or the Dalai Lama or the political projects of either, but to show the range of decisions people make in the name of religion, nation, and history.

In critiquing without invalidating, I write against recent Chinese claims—both governmental and popular—that the Dalai Lama is insincere about nonviolence or autonomy. I write against far leftist critiques of Tibet, which in celebrating socialism misrepresent Tibetan history and minimize Chinese excesses in Tibet.[99] I similarly write against the simplifications of Tibetan history encouraged by a romantic view of Tibet and Tibetan Buddhism. I write against those who argue that Tibetan collaboration with the CIA cancels out the validity of their cause. And I write against war and violence in this book that documents both, that documents the complexities, hesitations, affirmations, and pains of the armed Tibetan defense of their country and religion as well as those of the nonviolent struggle the Tibetans have waged since 1974. However, despite these disclaimers, I write mostly *with* rather than against. I write with those Tibetan veterans, scholars, and others who understand that *to critique is not to invalidate history or politics, but to make them interpretable and bearable in the present.*

In the fall of 1959 the Tibetan struggle was globally downgraded from an issue of sovereignty to one of human rights. The Tibetans fought this categorization; from the Dalai Lama on down they argued that theirs was a state struggle, a question of regaining the sovereignty of the Tibetan state. In their opinion, the Tibetan conflict with China was not an issue of individual or even collective human rights, but one of political independence. In October 1959, Gyalo Thondup, the eldest brother of the Dalai Lama, was dispatched to the United States to see to what extent the American government could support Tibet. U.S. officials told him they were not willing to support state sovereignty but instead would act on human rights violations in Tibet. U.S. Department of State records note the following: "Thondup makes extremely favorable impression and is excellent spokesman for Tibetan cause. We were struck by his deep sincerity and by his strong desire to do whatever circumstances here seem to require in best interests of Tibetan people. He recognizes importance of not seeking action on basis which would fail to receive necessary support and which could then be exploited by ChiComs [the Chinese Communists] and others against Tibetans."[1] Despite this advice, Gyalo Thondup remained convinced that a focus on human rights would sacrifice the struggle for independence. He repeatedly but unsuccessfully pressed U.S. officials on the issue. They "reassured him the consideration of violation of human rights in Tibet would in no way adversely affect broader Tibetan aspirations."[2] It was at this historical moment that the case of Tibet as a state, as a people fighting to defend their country, was eclipsed by the political inconvenience other states would undergo by challenging the PRC.

American reassurances about the human rights strategy turned out to be empty. In the five decades since Gyalo Thondup's trip, Tibetans' fears have been realized time and again. The naming of the Tibetan struggle as a human rights issue has prejudiced Tibet's case for state sovereignty. Internationally, Tibetan political accomplishments have primarily been in the realm of human rights. In the 1950s and 1960s, the United States led a behind-the-scenes campaign for Tibet at the United Nations. With encouragement from the United States the politically weak states of Ireland and the Federation of Malaya requested that the issue of Tibet be discussed by the General Assembly. Eventually, under the steward-ship of these two countries, a resolution condemning China for human rights violations in Tibet was passed.[3] Two years later, in 1961, a sec-ond and stronger resolution sponsored by Malaya and Thailand with the support of El Salvador and Ireland was passed by the General As-sembly. Although the second resolution added language regarding self-determination to that of human rights, a third resolution in 1965 deleted the self-determination reference in favor of language referencing "human rights and fundamental freedoms." Since 1965, the UN General Assembly has not issued any resolutions regarding Tibet.

Subsequent efforts by the Tibetans to put sovereignty on the table were not successful anywhere except behind closed doors or in legislative bodies with the power to give only symbolic support.[4] At present, the Dalai Lama states that he is calling not for independence but for genu-ine autonomy in Tibet (including, but not limited to, issues of human rights). U.S. policy on Tibet was crafted in response to Cold War politics, to specific and internally disputed relations with Taiwan (the Republic of China) and China (the PRC), and to earlier British imperial policies on Tibet. If the decade of the 1950s was a period of decolonization for many countries around the world, it was ironically a time when imperialism was doubly asserted in Tibet—by the Chinese and the Americans.[5]

Crucial to the story of modern Tibet are early imperial efforts to delineate the boundaries of the country. In 1913, the British government opened treaty discussions with Tibet and China with the goal of mapping the political boundary of Tibet. At the time, the modern belief that hard boundaries were necessary to determine where one country ended and another began was not in operation in Tibet. Instead of a fixed boundary between Tibet and both China and India there were overlapping zones, open zones, and locally governed territories, both lay and monastic. Efforts in 1913 and in subsequent decades to fix these boundaries were not successful. As a result, when the PRC invaded Tibet in the 1950s, Tibet's boundaries and political status were not defined by modern state-making principles.[6] This does not mean, however, that Tibet did not exist as a state. As in many territories outside of Europe, Tibetan state organization operated under different principles and organizational strategies. The story of the formation of the modern borders of Thailand, for example, is remarkably similar and instructive.

In *Siam Mapped: A History of the Geo-Body of a Nation*, Thongchai Winichakul contends that premodern political space in Thailand was at odds with parameters for the modern nation-state (introduced by British and French officials in the Thai case).[7] He documents five specific differences between Thai and Western concepts of the state, each of which fits the Tibetan case: in the Thai concept, (1) boundaries were determined and sanctioned locally rather than by central authorities; (2) sovereignty and boundary were not coterminous; (3) buffer zones and overlapping zones between polities were allowed; (4) external ratification of rule was not required; and (5) the sphere of a realm was defined not by territorial integrity, but by power relationships of allegiance between local polities and the center. In outlining these aspects of the Thai state, Thongchai demonstrates that the modern relationship between territoriality and nationhood is not a timeless feature of the nation but is of recent and external origin. The "absence of definite boundaries" of premodern Thailand—or of Tibet—is not owing to "some practical or technical reason" but is evidence of a different set of concepts of geopolitical space from those associated with the imperially sanctioned modern nation-state.[8] Differences in state formation are as hierarchical as they are conceptual, and hence, in 1959 and thereafter, as Gyalo Thondup and the Tibetans were to learn, the inviolability of the Tibetan state was not a priority for anyone other than the Tibetans.

Modern political geography posits that nations and states are to be coterminous. Sovereignty must be territorial, not only jurisdictional; that is, in addition to the securing of a people's allegiance, a land must be ruled. Yet state organization has never been consistent across polities or periods. There have always been multiple and changing ways to organize peoples and places under the banner of an overarching community.[9] The twentieth century is notable in its departure from this multiplicity of state forms. Since roughly the end of the Second World War and subsequent European decolonization, the world has been transformed into a system of nation-states represented by the United Nations. This new system allows for different types of governments but assesses them all as modern nation-states regardless of their actual composition. That is, the modern state is presumed to be coterminous with a nation, even in instances where there is not such a relationship, such as in a multinational community. Presented as universal and even natural, the modern nation-state was created out of European historical conditions and interpreted and implemented differently around the world.[10]

This model of the nation-state was introduced to Tibet at the beginning of the twentieth century but without great success. Premodern Tibet was not defined by lines drawn on a map or by the modern logic of a seamless unity between territory and politics. Instead, Tibetan national community was determined through a broad set of connections combined with shifting center–periphery relationships of influence and allegiance. In his monumental study *Civilized Shamans: Buddhism in Tibetan Societies* (1993), Geoffrey Samuel argues that premodern Tibet is best thought of not as a centralized or even a decentralized state, but as a series of societies existing in a continuous social field.[11] There was a wide variety of political and social formations across Tibetan societies: large agricultural states, smaller agricultural states, agricultural populations on the edges of states, and nomadic pastoralists.[12] Some of these groups were subordinate to others, and some were self-governing; many, but not all, of these groups were subordinate to the Dalai Lama's administration in Lhasa. Yet the administrative aspects of rule were not weighted more heavily than the ritual or performative aspects of rule; for example, control of people, which relied on performative practices, was considered more important than control of land, which relied on administrative practices. With this in mind, Georges Dreyfus contends that Tibet should be understood as a semibureaucratic state, one in which the inequalities in bureaucratic administration across Tibetan territory are "typical of any pre-modern state, which is defined not by boundaries but by a complicated network of overlapping allegiances."[13] That is, for premodern Tibet, what mattered was not where or if lines were drawn on a map, but the sentiments and allegiances of people and communities to the central state.

The twentieth-century structure of the Tibetan state had been in place since 1642. From the fifth through the fourteenth Dalai Lamas, with loose variation from regime to regime (including periods of regent rule in between Dalai Lamas or when the Dalai Lama was a minor), the Tibetan state was run by the Dalai Lamas as a joint religious–political system, referred to in Tibetan as *chos srid*. Based in Lhasa, the Tibetan government governed its subjects through a range of hierarchical practices that varied throughout the regions of Tibet. Center–periphery political ties also included monastic relations: the Dalai Lama's government was of the Gelug sect, and the three major Gelug monasteries in the Lhasa area, Sera, Drepung, and Ganden, were intimately involved in government affairs. Throughout Tibet, Gelug monasteries had special and specific relations with the Dalai Lama's government in Lhasa.

Moving from a state-level view to a regional one offers a valuable sense of how the Tibetan state and nation were experienced, organized, and understood locally as well as insight into how local practices would later be deployed and rethought. The region of Kham, for example, consists of some thirty-odd *pha yul*, a term which translates literally as "father land" and structurally as native places, areas, or territories. Each pha yul is composed of a series of villages and monasteries of varying sizes and sects, often separated by massive mountain ranges and the rivers that cut through them. Prior to 1950, Khampa systems of governance varied by area—some were kingdoms, others were chiefdoms, and still others were governed by hereditary lamas.[14] The entirety of some pha yul was one administrative unit, while other pha yul were governed via separate internal units (for example, the north under one chief, the south under another). Pha yul were flexible in form, had no generic or shared administrative format, and were defined as much by social markers as by political ones.[15]

Relations between territories and between monasteries were often tense. Feuding was common, and bandits roamed the mountainous terrain. Differences between pha yul were marked in both secular and sacred ways, through dialect, clothing, and ornamentation as well as through lamas, sects, and the deities associated with local landscapes.[16] Not all areas or monasteries were assumed to be equal, and some were nominally or entirely under the stewardship of other ones. Beyond its internal boundaries, Kham was a distinct part of Tibet, yet this relationship was determined not only by politics, but also through a series of shifting religious, political, and economic relationships with the various power holders in Lhasa. At times, portions of Kham fell under Chinese influence. For the most part, daily life in Kham was regulated not by direct or even absentee Lhasan (or Chinese) authorities, but by local rulers. As in the rest of Tibet, continuity and succession were as structurally important in Kham as fluidity and flexibility.[17]

Under the Dalai Lamas, the Tibetan state was a political and a religious enterprise, one that varied in form and content across Tibet but that nonetheless was a functioning state. In the first half of the twentieth century, the independent Tibetan state entered tripartite negotiations with the British and Chinese. Feeling secure in its independence vis-à-vis its neighbors, the Tibetan government was in no hurry to ally itself with the rest of the world. As one veteran explained to me, "Tibet remained isolated from the rest of the world. Many countries did not know a country called Tibet even existed. If we had had diplomatic relations with other countries, they would have helped us when we were in trouble."[18] In addition, the Tibetan government did not align itself with modern versions of the nation-state—geographically bounded, politically secured, internationally recognized—until the threat from the PRC became clear. By then it was too late.

Imperial Boundaries: Negotiating Tibet's Political Status, 1913–34

In 1907, George Nathaniel Lord Curzon, viceroy of India from 1899 until 1905, delivered a lecture entitled "Frontiers" in the Sheldonian Theatre in Oxford. One passage in his lecture continues to haunt Tibet to the present day: "Frontiers are indeed the razor's edge on which hang suspended the modern issues of war or peace, or life or death to nations. . . .

The integrity of her borders is the condition of existence of the state."[19] In many ways, Curzon was the chief architect of British policy toward Tibet, a policy that focused on establishing the political status of Tibet vis-à-vis both India and China.[20] British efforts to court Tibetan allegiance had begun in the late eighteenth century but took full force in 1904, when Curzon dispatched a mission to Lhasa. The Younghusband Expedition, whose time in Tibet is remembered by Tibetans as the Anglo-Tibetan War, successfully fought its way to Lhasa, forced the Dalai Lama into temporary exile in Mongolia, and secured favorable trade and political agreements with the Tibetan government.[21] With the fall of the Qing dynasty in China in 1911, British officials of British India and of the British Consular Service in China ensured that their "good offices" were involved in all negotiations and governmental interactions between the Tibetans and Chinese.

Central to British interests at the time was the transforming of Tibet into a friendly buffer state between India and China. Tibet was an example of Britain's forward policy, in which imperial agents intervened in polities beyond the colonial domain, that is, in places not colonized by them.[22] For British agents of empire, determining the status of Tibet required determining the boundaries of Tibet. Converting Tibetan frontiers into modern discrete boundaries proved to be a complicated task. On three occasions between 1913 and 1934, the British government tried to delineate the borders between Tibet and India as well as between Tibet and China.[23] Their persistent efforts were ultimately unsuccessful, as the one issue that consistently impeded the passing of any treaty was the delineation of the eastern border between Tibet and China, that is, the border in Kham.[24]

Disputes over boundaries are never solely political but also saturated with cultural and historical significance. For Tibet, the eastern frontier was a key component of the multiregional nation and a crucial extension of the politico-religious state. Kham presented an immediate challenge to British plans by not fitting neatly into their proposed partition of Tibet, which was designed to favor British imperial interests. In Simla in 1913–14 the British colonial official Sir Henry McMahon proposed the terms "inner" and "outer" Tibet, which Sir Charles Bell converted to "ethno-graphic" and "political" Tibet in 1920. Territories—or pha yul—not "directly administered" by Lhasa were categorized as inner or ethnographic Tibet, while those under the "direct administration" of Lhasa were categorized as outer or political Tibet. However, the range of political relations between Lhasa and various Kham territories did not easily fit this model, and in addition the governments of Tibet and China both claimed a number of the same territories. As a result, McMahon and Bell both included a third category for areas in Kham whose political status did not fit their models.[25] Tibetan areas that had been incorporated into British India were not included, despite Tibetan government disputes with the British over several of these territories.

The inability to settle Tibet's boundaries in 1914 at Simla served as a catalyst for a long series of subsequent disputes in and about the Tibet–China border and, later, the China–India border in Tibet.[26] Political intransigence and disagreement are not solely to blame for this inability; just as crucial were the British-directed terms of the negotiations in which specific ideas about boundaries and governments were presented as neutral ones. Although the British presented their proposal as consonant with already existing Tibetan geopolitical practices, it was not. For students of British empire, this is a familiar story of imperial rearrangements of supposedly old aspects of cultures and histories with "new meanings in institutional theaters with major consequences for colonial subjects."[27]

The requirement proposed by the British of direct administration for qualification as outer or political Tibet combined a European model of statehood with a Lhasa-centric view of Tibet. Even if territories in Kham did claim affiliation with the Tibetan state, they were unlikely to be directly administered by Lhasa. Despite this fact, direct administration was the criterion the British used, resulting in a partition of Tibet in which certain parts of the country were ruled to be outside the Tibetan polity.[28] Although this partition was never formally implemented and the border between Tibet and China never agreed upon, over time the divisions suggested by the British came to be seen as traditional and customary. Eventually, the lack of a border settlement would leave the PRC with an all-but-blank map upon which to fix the boundary of Tibet. The lack of a defined border later troubled the Tibetan government-in-exile when it desired to make a series of political and historical claims to Kham territories but was unable to produce any one document that clearly showed the pre-1950s borders of Tibet.

The Tibet–China Conflict

In 1949, two years after the British quit India, the communist PRC was formed from the ruins of Chiang Kai-shek's Republican China. One of Chairman Mao Zedong's first publicly stated goals was what he referred to as the liberation of Tibet. PLA troops arrived first in eastern and northeastern Tibet. In late 1949, as communist Chinese troops massed in eastern Tibet, the Tibetan government asked the United States to support their planned request for membership in the United Nations. The United States turned them down, as did Great Britain, whose new policy was that Tibet was no longer a British issue but one for the independent government of India. Whereas Indian leaders chose not to intervene on Tibet's behalf with the leaders of the PRC, the United States did intervene to a limited extent and in a mostly quiet manner. Cold War discourses and politics of anti-imperialism directly affected U.S. decisions regarding how involved they should be in Tibet, as did one other pivotal event: the Korean War.

On 7 October 1950, the very same day forty thousand Chinese troops marched into territory directly controlled by the Tibetan government, U.S. troops crossed the 38th parallel in South Korea on their way to recapturing Seoul, thereby drawing China into the war on the side of North Korea.[29] With the world's attention focused on Korea, the governor of Chamdo, Ngabo Ngawang Jigme, surrendered to the Chinese on 19 October 1950. In Lhasa, confusion reigned among government officials regarding how to respond. In time, the two state oracles pronounced that the then-sixteen-year-old Dalai Lama should assume the political and religious authority that, under normal circumstances, he would assume at the age of eighteen. The ruling regent, the Kashag cabinet, and the Tibetan National Assembly accepted this pronouncement, and on 17 November 1950, the fourteenth Dalai Lama became the spiritual and temporal head of the Tibetan state. In the month that followed, two important decisions were made: first, to appeal to the United Nations for help and, second, to have the Dalai Lama leave Lhasa for security reasons. On 16 December the Dalai Lama left for the Tibet–Indian border to wait out the deteriorating situation. In the meantime Tibetan officials appealed to the United Nations for help, but their efforts were unsuccessful, and negotiations with China soon began.

Headed by Governor Ngabo, a Tibetan delegation was dispatched to Beijing to start the negotiation process. Ngabo was armed with a list of Tibetan proposals and instructions to contact the Dalai Lama and Kashag before consenting to any Chinese offers. After a month of meetings and arguments, the "Agreement of the Central People's Government and the Local Government of Tibet on Measures for the Peaceful Liberation of Tibet," commonly known as the Seventeen-Point Agreement, was signed by the two parties on 23 May 1951. Governor Ngabo had not sent the terms of the agreement to the Dalai Lama and the Kashag for approval before signing. As a result, the Tibetan government felt that the agreement was signed "under duress" and without necessary approvals.[30] Lacking the international support necessary to defend itself diplomatically or militarily against the PRC and PLA, the government ultimately decided not to renounce the agreement. On 23 July 1951, the Dalai Lama began his return journey to Lhasa from the Tibetan border.

U.S. Department of State archives from the early 1950s reveal numerous plans to help Tibet if only the Dalai Lama would renounce the Seventeen-Point Agreement and proclaim Tibet's independent status. However, just as U.S. memos repeatedly refer to a desire not to anger Mao (or Chiang), so the Dalai Lama did not want to incur the further wrath of his much larger neighbor. He cooperated with the Chinese for several years but also remained in discussions with other governments over how to regain independence. In 1956, the Tibetans asked the United States for military aid as uprisings flared in Kham; the United States assented, and CIA training of Tibetan civilian soldiers commenced.[31] Over the next several years, as I will detail in chapter 4, the political situation disintegrated. By March 1959, the situation in Lhasa was grim. Chinese political restrictions grew worse by the day, and Tibetan government officials began to fear the Chinese were planning to kidnap the Dalai Lama. As Tibetans rose in protest over Chinese plans and policies, the Chinese bombed Lhasa, and the Dalai Lama escaped in disguise to India. He traveled for three weeks on horseback before reaching the Tibet–India border, where he was welcomed into India and granted refuge. Over the course of the next year, tens of thousands of Tibetans followed him—aristocrats and peasants, monks and laymen, and whole families from villages and towns throughout Tibet. Soon after his arrival in India, the Dalai Lama repudiated the Seventeen-Point Agreement and reconstituted the Tibetan government.

Beginning in 1949 and continuing to the present day, the Tibetans have appealed for and received international aid for their political efforts.[32] While the aid they received was not large enough to achieve their goals, it did signal the inauguration of the international support network that plays an important role in the Tibet–China conflict. Vital to this global network is the United States, which began its imperial shepherding of Tibet—and of the world at large—following European decolonization.[33]

In the 1970s, the Dalai Lama began to travel around the world, initiating a new strategy of personally visiting and appealing to heads of state and parliamentary and legislative bodies and speaking to public audiences. The Tibetan government-in-exile established offices in cities in fourteen countries around the world, including Washington, Geneva, and Taipei.[34] Many countries' parliamentary and legislative bodies have passed resolutions dealing with Tibet.[35] Some of this political activity is strident in tone, but much of it is cautious so as not to anger China. State leaders who meet with the Dalai Lama, for example, overwhelmingly recognize him publicly as a religious leader rather than a political one. No state recognizes the Tibetan government-in-exile as a legitimate political entity. At the United Nations, where China holds a seat on the Security Council, there is a very low probability of Tibet reappearing on the General Assembly agenda.

In bilateral relations, the Chinese and exile Tibetan governments have had two periods of extended discussions. The first followed the Cultural Revolution, when four Tibetan fact-finding delegations traveled from India to China and Tibet between 1979 and 1985, and two political delegations traveled to Beijing in 1982 and 1984. Relations cooled dramatically for the next two decades until September 2002, when a Tibetan exile delegation returned to China for the first time in twenty years. Eight more rounds of talks have taken place since that time, seven in China (in 2003, 2004, 2005, 2007, three in 2008, and 2010) and one in Switzerland (in 2006). Tibetan hopes for reaching a negotiated solution to the conflict rest in both bilateral talks and in the Dalai Lama. Members of the

Tibetan delegations have included individuals from all regions of Tibet, including most prominently Lodi Gyaltsen Gyari, special envoy of His Holiness the Dalai Lama, a Khampa who served on the delegations in the 1980s and has led them in the 2000s. In the wake of the Tibetan protests in China in 2008, a new urgency was found in these discussions and in global concern over conditions in Tibet.

What Is Tibet?: Clarifying Contested Terrain

A recurring concern of the Tibetan government-in-exile is the broader Tibetan region in China, not just the smaller area named the Tibet Autonomous Region and given provincial status by the PRC in 1965. The PRC government split Tibet into multiple administrative zones: the Tibet Autonomous Region and smaller Tibetan Autonomous Prefectures and Counties, which were placed in the Chinese provinces of Gansu, Qinghai, Sichuan, and Yunnan. Amidst this current fragmentation, the Tibetan government-in-exile consistently expresses its desire to reunite the Tibetan regions in China under one administrative unit, either through an enlarged Tibet Autonomous Region or through a Tibet that is politically distinct but not separate from China. Differences in Tibetan and Chinese opinion over what constitutes Tibet are an important disagreement between the two governments and peoples.

The question What is Tibet? is as difficult to answer today as it was during Tibetan, Chinese, and British negotiations in the first half of the twentieth century. At present, two competing versions of Tibet circulate. The first is derived from British imperial practices of state making and currently exists as the geopolitical boundaries of Tibet as part of the PRC. The second version overlays premodern Tibetan views of community onto modern forms of the state. Conceptual differences between these two ways of understanding Tibet are not just disagreements about political geography but are more deeply rooted differences in terms of staking claim to community. Clarifying what one means in referring to Tibet is a highly contested but crucially important exercise.

Consider the following statements by two respected scholars of Tibet:

Melvyn Goldstein, Director, Center for Research on Tibet, Cleveland, Ohio:
I use "Tibet" to mean the political entity that was equivalent to Tibet

in the 1930s and 1940s, that is, to today's Tibet Autonomous Region, and not the artificially conceptualized "greater Tibet" that Tibetans in exile would like to see created.[36]

Tashi Tsering, Director, Amnye Machen Institute, Dharamsala, India: On my part, when I refer to Tibet, I mean the greater cultural and racial Tibet comprising of Mngar'-ris, Dbus-gtsang, Khams, and A mdo. This is the Tibet which corresponds to the political Tibet of the Tibetan imperial age of the Yar-lung Dynasty and chol-kha-gsum of 'Gro-mgon Chos-rgyal 'phags-pa.[37]

The discrepancy between these two positions is stark. The first dates Tibet to the 1930s and 1940s, the second to the eighth and thirteenth centuries. The first corresponds to present-day geopolitical reality, the second to much deeper cultural and historical realities. Each has important implications for how Tibet is governed, criticized, and imagined.[38] The stakes involved extend past temporal as well as geographic boundaries: how Tibet is understood in the present affects how one plans for the future. This matters at all levels, from individual Tibetan decisions to escape from Tibet to India, or perhaps to return to Tibet from India, to governmental (and nongovernmental) decisions in Beijing, Dharamsala, Washington, and elsewhere on how to set policy and programs for an unknown but desired future.

In this book, I follow the lead of those Tibetans with whom I worked on this project in using the term "Tibet" to refer to the broader Tibet spoken of in Tashi Tsering's quote above, and I use "Tibet Autonomous Region" to refer to those areas included within that Chinese-designated region. Baba Lekshey's home region of Bathang, for example, falls outside the Tibet Autonomous Region, but to him Bathang is a part of Tibet. My following of Baba Lekshey and other Khampa veterans consciously aligns this book with a particular version of Tibet. With this in mind, I openly discuss and deconstruct these two predominant ways of understanding Tibet. As I see it, the histories and politics involved in each of these ways of approaching Tibet are "models for" and not just "models of" Tibet.[39] As models for, they work to fashion Tibet as much as (or more than) to represent it. To acknowledge this is to set both models in their relevant historical and political contexts.

British efforts to affix territorial boundaries to the Tibetan nation and state remain one of the predominant explanatory models for Tibetan political status. McMahon's and Bell's dividing of Tibet into three parts—inner or political, outer or ethnographic, and an in-between zone—is still operative today, at least in terms of a dual divide. Following the Chinese reorganization of Tibet in the 1950s and 1960s, Hugh Richardson, former head of the British and later the Indian Mission in Lhasa, revised the earlier British models to align precisely with the new Chinese political divisions. Gone were the in-between zones of the McMahon and Bell models as well as any acknowledgment that the borders were contested. Political Tibet was now equivalent to the Tibet Autonomous Region; all other areas were ethnographic Tibet. Revisions of the British model simply followed the Chinese partition of Tibet into administrative regions.

The political and ethnographic model does not sufficiently capture the complexity and range of Tibetan political forms. This model glosses over territories that had significant political relations of affiliation and subordination with Lhasa as ethnographically Tibetan. The advent of Chinese rule in Tibet has resulted in a definitive demarcation and labeling of Tibetan territories, yet these boundaries are as arbitrary as any others that might have been chosen. Administratively, conceptually, and disciplinarily they may order peoples' lives, but the histories and politics involved in their establishment are contingent rather than indisputable. They are but one way, one specific way, to organize Tibet.

THE CHOL KHA GSUM (OR THREE REGIONS) MODEL

Bod chol kha gsum red ("Tibet is three regions"). From Baba Lekshey to the family with whom I stayed and everyone in between, this deceptively simple statement is how many Khampas began their explanations of the past to me. Continuing, they would add, *dbus gtsang chos kyi chol kha mdo smad rta'i chol kha mdo stod mi'i chol kha*, which colloquially translates as "U is the place of the best religion, Amdo of the best horses, and Kham of the best people." Dating back to the period of Tibetan empire in the seventh century and the eighth, this depiction of Tibet as the three regions of Kham, Amdo, and U (with Tsang and Ngari implicitly attached to U) is operative today in exile and inside Tibet as a cultural and political organizing force.[40] The model unites U-Tsang, Amdo, and Kham as Tibetan nation and state and in the present is supplemented by modern political arguments about self-determination.[41] In the political moment from the 1950s to the present, self-determination has become a global issue. At times, contemporary arguments for self-determination rest uneasily with historical arguments that Tibet has always been three regions (in that the former is based on political will in the present and the latter references a unity in the past). For the most part, however, this contradiction is bypassed in favor of articulating a strong, united front.

The Tibetan government-in-exile uses the *chol kha gsum* ideology in their administration of the refugee community. Tibetans from all regions of Tibet fall under their domain, yet in terms of the political boundaries of Tibet, the government-in-exile is not always as clear. In general, the Dalai Lama long refrained from making direct statements about what constitutes Tibet. In 1996, for example, he explained that the composition of Tibet needed to be assessed in terms not just of international expectations but also via the complexity of Tibetan sociopolitical forms, specifically rejecting the notion that areas not directly under Lhasa were governed by China.[42] More recently, however, in a memorandum of 2008 addressed to the PRC, he proposed that all Tibetan areas in the PRC be administered as a single unit: "The entire [Tibetan] community, comprising all the areas currently designated by the PRC as Tibetan autonomous areas, should be under one single administrative entity."[43] This proposal was immediately rejected by the Chinese.

In exile, as in Tibet earlier, that which boundaries enclose—peoples, territories, ideas, and so on—are as important as the actual boundaries themselves. The absence of an internationally recognized border between Tibet and China, for example, did not mean that local people were unaware of boundaries or that such boundaries were not important. They were. Their meanings, however, were manifest in different ways, they enabled diverse sorts of interactions, and they generated varying responses to the notion of the state (among other things). If the boundary between Tibet and China, or Kham and Amdo, or Lithang and Bathang was known locally rather than approved internationally and understood in flexible or even blurred terms, that did not mean they did not at times have very real implications for how people lived their lives, then as well as now. Political status is never only about the state. Political statuses reach deeply into people's lives, affecting how their communities are organized and how they move themselves, their bodies, and their histories through the world. For Tibetan refugees, the experiences of empire and exile involve learning how to live their lives under multiple and often contradictory sets of rules.

What does it mean to belong to a community? How is belonging accomplished? Traced through the body, through social allegiances, and through incorporating and disciplinary practices of state and nation, belonging is never a disinterested process. In the context of post-Partition India, Veena Das suggests that societies "hide from themselves the pain which is inflicted upon individuals as [the] price of belonging."[1] Such pains of belonging are well hidden in the Tibetan exile community. Belonging involves muting certain aspects of being and knowing so that one's public self is aligned with expected social norms. Lobsang Tinley, a veteran of Chushi Gangdrug, bore those pains quietly and unquestioningly, working through them daily in his rituals, working through them constantly through his faith.

Each morning he rose before the sun and in the still darkness filled his kettle at the tap. Leaving the kitchen, he would enter the altar room to fill the offering bowls with water from the kettle. Carefully turning each bowl over, he filled all seven, praying audibly but quietly the entire time. Next he turned to the incense. Preferring long sticks of special blends hand carried from Kalimpong, he would pull out the longest unbroken sticks and light them. Circling in the air three times with the lit incense, praying all the while, he would then lay them in the burner. Bowls filled and incense lit, he would turn to a different sort of offering, a physical and mental offering of the self through prostration.

As the rays of the sun began to poke through the vertical depths of Jorpati, his densely packed Kathmandu neighborhood, Lobsang

FIGURE 7 Lobsang Tinley.

Tinley offered his body as an instrument for prayer. Palms together, hands up, on the head, to the forehead, at the heart, down to the ground and out in front, his body following, knees to the carpet, then stomach, chest, and head, hands up, then back down to propel the body up to standing and then starting all over again. Once, twice, ten, twenty times and beyond, until the body was primed, the offerings made, and the day had begun. This ritual led to others throughout the day, throughout the community, and throughout Lobsang Tinley's life. It was as sedimented in his body as it was in his sense of self, culture, and religion.[2] It grounded a life of reflection and hope amidst the chaos and upheaval of refugee life.

Political Status and Everyday Life

How is political status relevant in everyday life? When is it meaningful and when does it slip away, unfettered to mundane activities like buying vegetables or bus tickets or visiting friends and sharing bowls of home-brewed beer? There is no single answer to this question, just as there is no single way to experience exile or be a refugee. The answer I offer is linked specifically to the lives lived in exile by Tibetan veterans such as Lobsang Tinley.

As a boy, Lobsang Tinley joined the Lithang Monastery as a monk, later setting out for Lhasa's Sera Monastery, where he devoted himself to his studies and religious practice. In 1959, when the Dalai Lama fled Tibet, Lobsang Tinley and several of his fellow monks—and many more from Sera and other monasteries—decided to follow, setting off for India on foot. The journey took several weeks and was full of anxieties about food, safety, and the status of the Dalai Lama. Once they were safely on the other side of the border in hot, steamy Misamari, the site of a former Allied military base in Assam during the Second World War, they found themselves in a classic situation of refugee limbo: out of place, insecure, uncertain, and experiencing growing political, economic, and health problems. Conditions remained difficult for months. Little grounded the community save the belief they would be returning home soon, the comfort of knowing the Dalai Lama was safe, and the familiarity of those daily religious and cultural rituals they carried with them in their bags, their bodies, and their minds.

As months turned into years, Lobsang Tinley found himself unsure of what the future held. Upon hearing that Chushi Gangdrug was organizing a military base in Nepal, he joined the hundreds of men who traveled from India to Nepal to join the army. This gentle former monk was not cut out to be a frontline soldier, so he held a supply position within the army. Traveling along the Kali Gandaki river trade route that ran from Mustang to Pokhara, Lobsang Tinley donned a Nepali *topi* (hat) and, while engaged in the dozens of buying trips he made for the troops, learned to speak Nepali. Passing as a Nepali—so as not to give away the Tibetans' secret location in Mustang—became easier with each trip up and down the Kali Gandaki. Starting in Mustang at 12,500 feet in altitude and heading south through Kagbeni, Jomsom, Marpha, and Tukche, communities shifted from mostly Buddhist to mostly Hindu as he passed through Ghorepani, Birethanti, and Naudanda all the way to lowland Pokhara at 2,700 feet to shop, barter, and reload his bags and animals for the trip back to Mustang. Religions, languages, foods, livelihoods, climate, fauna, and more shifted as he made these trips along the river. For years to come, Lobsang Tinley held fondly the intimate knowledge of Nepali peoples and places he gained through this work.

During his years in Mustang, Lobsang Tinley's Tibetan social worlds expanded just as much as his Nepali ones. If in the monasteries he spent most of his time with other men from his *pha yul* of Lithang and from neighboring areas in Kham, in the army he was exposed to Tibetans from around Tibet. For while the Chushi Gangdrug army was dominated by Khampas, and among them by men from Lobsang Tinley's area of Lithang, the men based in Mustang were from all over Tibet—Kham, Amdo, central Tibet, and increasingly from the Tö area of southern Tibet that stretched along the Nepali border. Like many soldiers, Lobsang Tinley found that his military identity cut across other Tibetan identities. Such multiple identities and subjectivities would come to define the Tibetan diaspora.

Following the dramatic end of Tibetan military activities in Mustang in 1974, many of the soldiers, including Lobsang Tinley, were imprisoned. After their release from prison, these men dispersed into camps in the Pokhara area, into settlements in and around Kathmandu and other areas of Nepal as well as in India, causing the Chushi Gangdrug force itself to become a diaspora of sorts. In this way, a portion of the Tibetan community in exile reconstituted itself. Locales dotting the South Asian subcontinent became sites inhabited by people one knew personally. Travel between these places was limited. Most Tibetans and certainly most resistance veterans had little income. They lived on the margins of society, generating as much sufficiency within their own communities as possible but still relying on local markets and services as well as on services provided by the exile government or by India, Nepal, and foreign sources of aid. Having neither money to travel nor the security of citizenship if they did travel, they received updates about friends in other towns and countries only when someone did travel between communities. Should someone be departing from Kathmandu for Pokhara or Dehra Dun or Darjeeling, an informal message and delivery service would be activated by Lobsang Tinley and his friends. Common requests and questions for travelers went as follows: Please check in on so-and-so. Say hello to this old friend. I've heard that Tashi has been sick. Did you see Thubten and did he send a message for me? And could you please bring some incense from Kalimpong? From that shop at Tenth Mile?

The Pains of Belonging

For many veterans, political status is felt deeply even in the most banal of situations. Refugees in Nepal and India are not allowed to own property or to open bank accounts, and they do not qualify for government work or often for other jobs either. Rights guaranteed to citizens in these countries are not guaranteed to refugees within them. While the Tibetan government-in-exile does guarantee some rights to Tibetan refugees through its Charter of Tibetans-in-Exile, neither India nor Nepal does, meaning that Tibetans in South Asia must navigate dual governments everyday—that of the Tibetan government-in-exile and that of either India or Nepal. While all states make exceptions to their own rules, refugees like the Tibetans often exist outside even expected exceptions.[3]

Class matters here. Disproportionate local and global attention is focused on Tibetan elites in exile, on those who might possess passports, who drive big cars, are successful businessmen, or who are accomplished women within the refugee community. The elite strata, whether they are from older aristocratic families or newly successful families, are a small but highly visible part of the community. The majority of Tibetan families are not elite. They struggle to get by, coexisting in a Tibetan-focused world of schools, social gatherings, prayer, and politics and either an Indian- or Nepali-oriented world of daily necessities, media (especially beloved Hindi films), and bureaucratic systems through which they must maneuver.

Most of the Tibetan veterans with whom I spoke and visited over the years are poor: getting by, helping each other, having food to eat, clothes to wear, and roofs over their heads, but poor. Many of these elderly men, Baba Lekshey for one, live (or lived) alone. The loss of Tibet often meant the loss of family, through death or separation either in the 1950s or 1960s or in the decades since. It is an impermanence they live and bear, but also one they anticipate transforming in their lifetimes. Political status haunts not just their categorization by the state, but where and with whom they live, the languages in which they communicate, and the ways in which local Indian and Nepali communities interact with their Tibetan neighbors, who are still, after almost five decades, considered foreigners.[4]

Categories of not belonging pervade all levels of life within the exile community, the host community, and the global community. If the pains of belonging are hidden, as Das argues, then those of not belonging are more obvious. To be dissociated with the exile Tibetan government (as some refugees are by choice or by disciplinary action), to be a refugee in India or Nepal, to be a stateless community in a world of in-place, intact nation-states all offer more easily accessible, interpretable, and diagnosable pains. In the twentieth century, being out of place and not belonging has become an almost common condition.[5] To inquire instead about the hidden pains of belonging is a different project, but not an unrelated one. Tibetan politics of inclusion in exile are directly related to multiple politics of exclusion. As the work of Ann Stoler has demonstrated, belonging is always intimately entangled with simultaneous experiences of not belonging.[6]

The public pain of the exile Tibetan community is the loss of Tibet. The hidden pains are those involved in reconstituting community and addressing internal conflicts or what some might call dirty laundry. These pains are generated as much in-place—in the refugee communities themselves—as they are built upon the sense of being out of place, that is, not in Tibet.[7] These are the pains of being a good Tibetan, of not being the proverbial nail that sticks up or one who challenges normative story lines even when one's story and being do not squarely fit with prescribed norms.[8] Such tensions between social reproduction and social transformation lie at the heart of everyday problems of political status for Tibetans like Lobsang Tinley. Region and resistance are intimately involved. Region occupies a tenuous place within the nation, but a primary place within the resistance. The Khampa Tibetan identities and veteran status of men like Lobsang Tinley are aspects of their being and of their Tibetan-ness that are as indisputable as their commitments to the Dalai Lama and to Tibet in general. If the public pain of belonging is simply being in exile, then the hidden pain for refugees like Lobsang Tinley involves rectifying the various aspects of their identities and commitments, accepting, for example, the historical arrest of resistance history while simultaneously rejecting a full-fledged homogenization of community. This simultaneous personal and communal aspect of political status and of the complications of belonging is always lived and understood in relationship to the Dalai Lama.

FIGURE 8 Schoolchildren at Boudha on Losar, Tibetan New Year.

The Dalai Lama and Middle-Way Modernity

For much of the outside world the Dalai Lama represents a culture and civilization that offer an antidote to modernity. However, for the Tibetan community in exile the Dalai Lama symbolizes ways to be both Tibetan and modern. His predecessor, the thirteenth Dalai Lama, supported the cautious introduction of modern ideas into Tibet. Together, the thirteenth and fourteenth Dalai Lamas have charted a middle way for Tibetan modernity. This middle-way modernity, a controlled nod to secularism, reflects long-standing Tibetan ways of being in the world.

Madhyamaka, the Middle Way, is the central tenet of Buddhism. The Middle Way was the Buddha's name for the path he advocated, one that avoids both worldly and ascetic extremes. All Tibetan Buddhist sects (that is, the Mahayana tradition) base their practice and philosophy on Middle-Way notions of emptiness and dependent arising.[9] In lay terms, emptiness and dependent arising are about the relativity of existence. In exile, the Dalai Lama titled his political strategy vis-à-vis China the Middle-Way Approach. This approach is an effort at compromise, including the move from a platform of independence to one of autonomy.[10] As explained on the exile government's website: "The Middle-Way Approach [is] a non-partisan and moderate position that safeguards the vital interests of all concerned parties—for Tibetans: the protection and preservation of their culture, religion and national identity; for the Chinese: the security and territorial integrity of the motherland; and for neighbors and other third parties: peaceful borders and international relations."[11] Rooted in a recognition of the dependent benefits to all parties involved, the Middle-Way Approach directly indexes religious thought and practice in a political realm. Within the refugee community, ideas of the Middle Way appear in terms of how Tibetans understand and practice the modern in social and cultural terms.

Middle-Way modernity charts a moderate path between old and new, between cultural preservation and political change. Loss of culture is widely assumed to be a general danger for refugee communities; this profile fits the Tibetan exile community well, such that traditional elements of culture are kept strictly separated from the modern influences of India and the West.[12] Middle-Way modernity preserves a distinction between the two categories, labeling tradition precious and considering the modern something worthy of cautious exploration.[13] Despite, for example, recent efforts of the Dalai Lama to democratize the exile Tibetan government and reduce the political power he holds, he is still considered the primary center of power within the community.[14]

Tensions over how to express critique or dissent are reflected in community responses to Middle-Way modernity. People often find gentle ways to transgress restrictions of certain memories, experiences, and narratives. Resistance veterans, for example, are often torn between voice and silence, between publicly proclaiming their service to the Dalai Lama and to Tibet and honoring the arrest of their histories. In that most of the veterans are Khampas, this relationship to the Dalai Lama as head of state holds another layer of complication.

Kham in the Tibetan Imagination

The most important part of Tibetan history is the relation of the east and northeast with Lhasa. The Chinese have now made Tibet into Inner and Outer Tibet. Kham was cut off. Most people have misunderstood this. Central Tibet, for example, didn't have the same problems as Kham. Foreigners all went to Lhasa, so there is little written about Kham. Everything is written from the point of view of the aristocracy—the U-bas. The history of Kham is found only in religious books.

There are no separate books for it. What they ate, the religious festivals. . . . all these are found only in the religious books.

INTERVIEW WITH KHAMPA GOVERNMENT OFFICIAL, NOVEMBER 1997

Kham occupies a specific place in the Tibetan imagination.[15] As Tibetans from other regions and Khampas themselves might tell you, Khampas are stereotypically known to be honest, straightforward, loyal, hot-tempered, uncouth, and even dangerous. As is true of all stereotypes, the images of this one both do and do not fit the Khampa community but nonetheless capture the broader Tibetan imagination in ways that matter. These descriptions apply across genders but are also specifically marked as masculine, as is the Tibetan nation in general. One veteran referred to his area of TreHor, where Dhargye Gonpa is located, as the Texas of Kham where Khampa cowboys are from. "Real *Khampa's* Khampas," he emphasized. Other veterans threw up their hands at the stereotype. As one complained, "They say Khampas are the bravest Tibetans. In my opinion, Khampas are arrogant and headstrong. They don't think before they act. If they are provoked, they don't hesitate to stab others. They don't bother [to think] about the consequences of their actions." Kham's place as home to the legendary King Gesar of Ling, the great warrior memorialized in one of the most widespread epics in all of Asia and the longest epic in the world, further compels such ideas.[16] Gesar is renowned for his defense of Buddhism, his heroic bravery, and his ascension into the realm of the deities as a warrior god. His legacy continues today in the idea of Khampas being warriorlike, a notion embodied in the Khampa-dominated Chushi Gangdrug army. Above all, the people of Kham are noted for their fierce spirit of independence.

Khampa independence was perhaps as geographic as it was political. During the first half of the twentieth century, travel in Tibet was solely on foot or horseback. To reach Lhasa from Kham took a journey of several months. Distance reinforced autonomy, and local rather than national affairs were often paramount in Kham. Local power struggles included appeals to Lhasa as well as to regional Chinese leaders for military and financial support. If some Khampas were like Baba Lekshey, fighting against the Chinese, others were aligning themselves with the Chinese. A proverb from this time mocks the self-interest of such political associations: *rgya mgo thug dus rgya bod mgo thug dus bod*: (Side with China when China is in power, side with Tibet when Tibet is in power).

To "side with" or seek support from Tibet or China did not at that time imply the same thing it might today in the current highly charged political climate. In Kham the pressing issues were about local rather than state power, about autonomy within one's own domain, and about maintaining relations with as well as distance from one's neighbors. Identities were not easily broken down into discrete categories. Instead, they were cultural, geographic, political, and religious all in one: for example, as Baba Lekshey explains, he is a Baba, that is, from Bathang, and also a Khampa, a Tibetan, a Gelugpa, and so on. He ties his belt a certain way, he speaks Tibetan a certain way, and he eats *tsampa* (roasted barley flour) a certain way, each a relational marker to other Tibetans of who he is in this world.

Kham was the most populous and prosperous of Tibetan regions. Khampa families controlled most of Tibet's tea and wool trade with China, India, and neighboring countries. Inhabited by both large-scale and petty traders, Kham was also home to farmers, shepherds, nomads, and a very large monastic population. Kham did not have the aristocratic and monastic estates that dominated the economy and society of central Tibet. Central Tibetan aristocratic ways of organizing sociopolitical worlds were (and still are) dominant but never the only way of imagining Tibet. Other areas of Tibet had different rules, logics, and traditions. In a conversation one day at Nirula's restaurant in New Delhi, the Tibetan scholar Dawa Norbu and I discussed Khampa society and Tibetan history. I mentioned that one of the recurring themes in my research was allegiance and loyalty, and Norbu agreed: "Khampas are incredibly loyal, even today. If they say they are with you, they are loyal for life."[17] In his view, such loyalty sprung from the political history of Kham as being linked to the Tibetan government, even though most of Kham was quite independent of actual centralized control. As a result, he stated, one sees in Kham "the assertion of civil society in a stateless area."[18] Norbu explained, "Flexibility came from the Khampa lifestyle. They didn't have the bonded labor found in central and western Tibet. People were freer in their own lives to make decisions, choices, to be more independent. We see this with the successes of Khampa traders and Khampa lamas in the West, and the mobility of Khampa groups in general."[19]

Kham is also marked by its religious history. Kham was the home of the nineteenth-century *ris med*, or nonsectarian movement, which advocated drawing from the teachings and precepts of each of the four main Buddhist sects (Gelug, Nyingma, Kagyu, and Sakya). Gelug attempts throughout Tibet to convert Nyingma, Sakya, and Kagyu monasteries to Gelugpa ones were not as successful in Kham as in other areas. One result of this is that Kham was not as politically dominated by the Gelug sect as central Tibet. However, in terms of religious practice, as opposed to political rule, many of the Chushi Gangdrug soldiers were Gelug, including those from Lithang, Bathang, and Dhargye Gonpa, each of which contributed large numbers of men to the army; perhaps just as many, however, were Kagyu or Nyingma practitioners. As a result, some Khampas had sectarian as well as regional differences with central Tibetan political leaders.

Differences are sometimes made to appear as dissent. Logics for this equation are dual, drawing, first, on Buddhist hierarchies of authority and subordination, which are very much part of Tibetan social worlds, and, second, on notions of the modern, specifically, the idea that Tibetans are now global citizens who should be able to transcend such internal and anachronistic divisions as region and sect.[20] Homogenizing efforts, especially those that mark difference as dangerous, do not go unnoticed. One resistance veteran fumed as he and I talked about history that the problem is not contained within the Tibetan community but also influences how others perceive it: "Kham and Khampa history is important for Tibetan history. Films like 'Kundun' and 'Seven Years in Tibet' don't help with this. They either entirely ignore Kham and Khampas, or portray all Tibetans generically as U-Tsangpas, even when they're wearing Khampa clothes!" Internal and external acknowledgement of belonging (or not) matters. Audiences for and arbiters of identity are not only those close to home, but ones imagined around the world.

The Price of Pain

As Lobsang Tinley's story illustrates, Tibetan worlds both expanded and contracted in exile. They expanded in the sense that a once-imagined in situ community was now newly imagined as a displaced community, albeit one in which a newly arranged face-to-face component was present.[21] Lobsang Tinley's experience in the resistance army and in exile in general opened his world to a Tibet beyond his area of Lithang. The insularity of Tibet prior to the Chinese arrival weighs heavily on the minds of some. As one Khampa government official in India explained it, "The worst thing was that we Tibetans had no means of transport and communication. We had to travel from one place to another on horseback. We had to carry our food and clothes. *We did not know each other.* So we behaved like strangers with one another. Hence there was no question of trusting each other. When the powerful Chinese came, we could do nothing. Now everything is all over. The intervention of you foreigners is a belated effort. Everything is late now. We Tibetans did not see the outside world. Similarly the world did not see Tibet, hidden behind the Himalayas." As he explains, what matters is not just that the world did not see Tibet or that Tibetans did not clearly see the outside world, but that they did not see each other. In exile, individuals from across Tibet were now neighbors, if not friends and colleagues. Dialects were broached, songs and food shared, different styles of dress and bodily comportment became a part of everyday reality, of lived reality rather than something known in the abstract or in passing. In the army and elsewhere, new needs for cooperation fostered this development.

At the same time, community also contracted in a classic anthropological sense. As Fredrik Barth argued in the late 1960s, identities form in relational ways through the ongoing negotiation of boundaries between groups.[22] That is, people define themselves as much by who they are not as by who they are. Khampas who were now in everyday contact with other Tibetans found that despite, and as a result of, a newfound homogenized refugee identity, older regional identities persisted, hardened, and became newly meaningful. One way identities translate into social practice—and that pains of belonging are lessened—is through mutual aid groups called *kiduk*, organized usually by pha yul but sometimes by region, sect, or school.[23]

Kiduk groups are found throughout the refugee community and collect money through individual donations, membership fees, and parties that last for days and include dancing, singing, eating, and drinking as well as card games and mahjong, from which kiduk funds are generated. The monies collected are used to help *pha yul gcig pa'i mi*, or "people of the same territory," in times of financial hardship. Aid is provided to care for indigent elders, to help families arrange funerals or pay hospital bills, to assist with school fees, and the like; in 1996, the Markham kiduk organized two buses for Chushi Gangdrug veterans to attend the Dalai Lama's Kalachakra teachings in Siliguri, India. Kiduks also make donations to monasteries on behalf of the pha yul, thereby securing merit for members of the kiduk beyond what they could accrue on their own. Along with territorial, regional, and sectarian affiliations carried over from Tibet to exile, Tibetan refugee identities include new associations organized around residence and education (for example, what refugee camp, town, and country one lives in or what school(s) one attended, and so on) as well as divisions between first-wave refugees and second-wave refugees, colloquially—and pejoratively—referred to as *sanjorba*, or "newcomers."[24] Such differences, of course, foster not only associations but also divisions that are incorporated into existing hegemonies.

In Manali and Mussoorie, Jampaling, Jorpati, and beyond, internal and external problems of political status plague the exile community. Internally, the precariousness of calling attention to divisions within the community is a constant issue. Externally, the precariousness of stateless refugee status is felt in everyday situations within host countries as well as in the broader political struggle. All of these are daily realities for individuals such as Lobsang Tinley, his friends, and family. Politics, especially the subject of regaining Tibet, is always a ready topic of conversation. In the late 1990s, as more Tibetan families received remittances from family members overseas, television sets became the commodity of choice for families who could afford one.[25] Most veterans, it turned out, wanted to watch just one type of show: the international news, either the British Broadcasting Corporation (BBC) or Cable News Network (CNN). Both of these programs are in English, a language the vast majority of veterans did not understand; but they watched the program nonetheless in the hope there would be a story about Tibet or the Dalai Lama or some sign of global action on Tibet.

Lobsang Tinley preferred the BBC. Watching it, however, was not a regular activity for him. Not regular like his morning offerings and his afternoon kora at Boudha. Not regular like his reading of scripture after breakfast or his visiting with friends over lunch or afterward. His everyday political struggles were not televised. Instead, they were lived and embodied; they were a part of prayer, a part of ritual, a part of friendship, and a part of life. His work to belong, that is, to be a good person and a good Tibetan, was not without pain. The pains of belonging rival those of not belonging. One price of such pain is consent to the arrest of resistance history, consent to publicly suspend a key part of one's being. Lobsang Tinley felt this pain and its price most acutely in the form of the resistance's collective relationship to the Dalai Lama, but also through community disparagement of the resistance and through current divisions among the Chushi Gangdrug veterans themselves, divisions that separated men who had long been friends, neighbors, and colleagues. Yet, as he might remind us from his experiences as a trader during the war, market prices in the Himalayas are negotiable. Bartering and bargaining are always involved. And so the price as well as the pains of belonging are neither fixed nor permanent but open to change in the future.

Almost without exception Khampa Tibetans in exile claim they were just living their lives during the initial years of Chinese occupation in the 1950s, getting by day to day, thinking about family, food, the gods, and so on. While they might have hoped that the Chinese would go home soon, the thought that their lives were about to be radically disrupted was not a reality. Uprisings against the Chinese began in 1955–56, although in areas such as Gyalthang there were battles as early as 1952.[1] In exile, many Tibetans feel compelled to explain the gap between the communists' arrival and the Tibetans' revolt. The lapse, many people told me, was attributable to a combination of Tibetan naïveté and Chinese duplicity. It was also about money: when the PLA first came to Tibet, the soldiers and civilian officers not only paid for their food, lodging, and animal transport, but also gave presents, clothing, and generous bags of silver coins, called *ta yang* in Tibetan, to the Tibetans.

According to one Khampa veteran, cooperation and coexistence with the Chinese seemed possible: "I lived for one year in Chamdo after [the Chinese] arrival. In the beginning they were really nice. They paid for fuel and water. They helped us when we harvested. They said that they had come to help us. They carried their own luggage. They bought firewood from us. People went to the extent of saying 'The Chinese are our kind parents, the silver dollars are raining down on us' [*rgya gung bran drin chen pha ma red dngul dayang char pa 'bab 'bab red*]."[2] Not long after, however, things drastically changed.

Tibetans abandoned their hopes for a peaceful coexistence when the Chinese introduced a new political program of alleged democratic reforms. The reforms turned society upside down by dismantling Tibetan systems of authority, reversing class privileges, and working to eliminate religion entirely. Upon realizing the nature of the reforms, the Tibetans gave a new name to the Chinese: *bstan drga*, or "enemy of the faith." While Tibetans considered the attacks on their sociopolitical structures unwelcome, the attacks on their religion were unbearable. Throughout Kham, people rose in spontaneous, independent uprisings that over time coalesced into the united Tibetan resistance movement.

In numerous places Tibetan uprisings were met with Chinese airstrikes. Villages and monasteries throughout the region were bombed. International news coverage of these events was spotty and discouraged by Chinese claims that the skirmishes were in Sichuan, not Tibet, and were defeated quickly by the PLA. Khampa responses to Chinese reforms and military action were independent and localized; these uprisings were not orchestrated by Lhasa. At the time the Tibetan government was still cooperating with Chinese authorities, and while it was quietly supporting some dissident activity in Lhasa (for example, the formation of an independent political party), it was not involved in the popular revolts taking place in Kham. From these localized beginnings a nationalist movement grew. Battles begun in 1956 also mark another important development: that of a new historical genre based on testimony.

Khampas' frustration at their inability to match the firepower and manpower of the PLA resulted in pleas for help to the Tibetan and outside governments. There were few opportunities to speak publicly about what was happening in Kham. In 1956 there were no newspapers in Tibet, and in China the media downplayed the uprisings in Kham. The only option for Tibetans to speak to the press was to go to India. As one Khampa testified there, the situation in Kham was dire: "The people of Kham were killed by guns and bombs. Every monk and man sighted by the Chinese was to be killed. It was as if the Khampas were wild animals and the Chinese were hunters. The Kham areas were wiped out like a broom sweeping clean a floor."[3]

The Eyes of the World: Testimony as Historical Genre

In India, as Tibetans began to tell their stories, testimony as subaltern historical practice became a new weapon for seeking change. Khampa traders had long gone to India, specifically to the mountain town of Kalimpong at the end of the China-Tibet-India trade route. Beyond trade, Kalimpong was a center of international politics—a "den of spies," as Jawaharlal Nehru infamously called it. Home to Tibetan aristocrats, European Tibetophiles, wealthy Khampa traders, British missionaries, Mongolian Buddhists, Indian intelligence officers, CIA agents posing as tourists, Bhutanese royalty, Burmese royalty, and more, Kalimpong was also home to the Reverend Gegen Dorje Tharchin's *Yulchog Sosoi Sargyur Melong (Tibet Mirror)* newspaper.[4] In response to the violence of the Chinese democratic reforms, some Khampas made the long journey to Kalimpong to tell their stories to Reverend Tharchin in the hope that imagined local and global communities of *Tibet Mirror* readers might intervene.

The Reverend Tharchin, or Tharchin Babu as he was known to Tibetans, was an ethnic Tibetan from the Indian Himalayas who had built a strong connection to the Tibetan community in Kalimpong.[5] He was trusted by them, and he in turn worked diligently on their behalf, publishing many Tibetan religious texts, including a copy of the thirteenth Dalai Lama's political testament, and printing any and all information about Tibet he could uncover in the *Tibet Mirror*. Although Tharchin was a Christian and came from a family of missionaries, his preachings in the *Tibet Mirror* were not about religion. Instead, Tharchin used the newspaper to disseminate news in and about Tibet (and the world in general), and also to advocate his sense of what Tibet could and should be: a united, modern self-governed country. To Tibetans such as Baba Lekshey, Tharchin Babu was a respected teacher. "I only know a little about Westerners," Baba Lekshey told me one day, "but everything I know I learned from Tharchin Babu. I was like you. I worked for the newspaper; whatever information I found out, I told him."[6]

In 1957, illustrated articles about the bombings of monasteries in Kham ran in the *Tibet Mirror*. Drawn by Kargyal Thondup, an eyewitness to the Chatreng bombing who traveled to Kalimpong to tell the story, the drawings are an excellent example of the new testimonial style. A brief explanation accompanied each drawing: "Drango Monastery had 1,000

FIGURE 9
The *Tibet Mirror* newspaper.

monks. Not a single one is left now. Lobsang Yonten fought heroically"
(figure 10);[7] "Bathang Chode Monastery had 700 monks. None are left
now. Half of the monastery is destroyed" (see figure 14);[8] "Lithang Monastery used to have 3,700 monks. I've heard that now there are no more
than ten" (figure 11);[9] "At Chatreng Sampheling Monastery, there were
1,800 monks. Now it is said there are only seven. Thirty-five monks were
killed, thirty-one women and children were killed, and 600 Chinese soldiers were poisoned" (figure 12).[10] Alongside the articles ran a "reminder
song" exhorting the Tibetans to "stand up!":

> Don't be fooled!
> Young friends of Ba, what are you doing?
> Don't let silver coins lure you!
> Stand up, stand up the tsampa eaters!
> Stand up the Titos of Kham and U-Tsang![11]

の中 Tibetan text in the illustration

FIGURE 10 The Bombing of Drango Monastery (from *Melong*, 1 July 1957, 4).

Passionate and political, articles in the *Tibet Mirror* combined testimony with imperatives and, at times, indignation. In October 1956 an article by "a knowledgeable person from Kham" directly addressed Chinese claims that there was no conflict in Tibet and that fighting in Sichuan was over. Speaking to fellow Tibetans and to the world, the author stated, "This is an unbelievable lie. It looks down on us, the Tibetan people. The ones who are fighting are Tibetans. They say 'Sichuan' because they have cut Tibet into pieces in an attempt to destroy the unity of the Tibetan people. The Chinese plan to destroy Tibet without the world even knowing about it. . . . They are covering the eyes of the world with the dust of their lies."[12]

Tharchin's fostering of testimony as a legitimate historical genre recalls Benedict Anderson's emphasis on the importance of print media to national political projects.[13] Anderson stresses the regular production, circulation, and consumption of newspapers as important components of print nationalism, although none of these things was regular in the case of the *Tibet Mirror*. It was produced only irregularly, circulated erratically beyond Kalimpong, and was read only by the minute portion of the Tibetan population that was literate at the time. Likewise, the calendrical time of production and the simultaneity of ritualized, yet anonymous reading so associated with print nationalism were not a part—or at least not a regularized part—of the *Tibet Mirror*'s role in Tibetan society. Nonetheless, like other forms of print media around the world and as read and known by Tibetans, the *Tibet Mirror* "made it possible for rapidly growing numbers of people to think about themselves, and to relate themselves to others, in profoundly new ways."[14] In publishing his newspaper, in encouraging ordinary Tibetans to tell their stories, and in fostering the belief that telling these stories might effect change, Tharchin and his *Tibet Mirror* newspaper were crucial in developing Tibetan testimony as a form of *testimonio*.

Testimonio is a first-person eyewitness narration in which the "unit of narration is usually a 'life' or a significant life experience."[15] Commonly associated with the armed liberation struggles of the 1960s in Latin America, testimonio, as John Beverley describes it, is subaltern claims to politics and the nation, that is, stories that "*need* to be told, that involve some pressing and immediate problem of communication."[16] Tibetans who traveled to Kalimpong to tell their stories in the *Tibet Mirror* were compelled by such needs. They believed the world needed to know what was happening to them in their country. In this early period of resistance, Tibetans were not restricted by practices of historical arrest begun later in exile. Instead, their testimonies were textual and, they hoped, transformative. As Beverley explains, the point of testimonio is transformation: "To recall Marx's well-known distinction, testimonio aspires not only to interpret the world but also to change it. Nevertheless, how one interprets the world also has to do with how one seeks, and is able, to change it."[17]

Testimonies by ordinary Tibetans—that is, Tibetans who were not aristocrats or religious or political leaders—constitute a crucial new literary genre in the exile community. They have been widely embraced in general as a needed and valued part of the Tibetan historical record and claim important discursive space and authority. Over time, however, community authorities would mark narrations of certain histories as problematic by arresting them. Testimony of these histories would not disappear but would be put on hold during the period of arrest, waiting until the time was right for them to be told. Such struggles over history are examples of deference to authority that authors from Milan Kundera to Giorgio Agamben have contended are no less than struggles over life. Agamben argues that twentieth-century power structures sought to make individuals survive, that is, to not produce life or death per se but instead a "mutable and virtually infinite survival."[18] Testimony, as Agamben sees it, rejects mere survival: "With its every word, testimony refutes precisely this distinction of survival from life."[19] To testify is to claim life. It is to claim a new stake in one's community.

Lithang: When the River Ran Red

In narrations of the siege of Lithang, the Tibetan nation stretches from village, *pha yul*, and region all the way to Lhasa and His Holiness and back again. For many Khampas, the revolts of the 1950s energized their identities as Tibetans and gave impetus to new connections across Tibetan communities. What makes the story of Lithang so important is the drama with which the story unfolds and the centrality that some claim for Lithang within the Tibetan resistance (as men from Lithang would go on to lead the united Tibetan resistance army). As a result, the story of the fighting in Lithang in 1956 is one of the few Khampa histories told widely, including in written and theatrical forms.[20] The version I tell here is a composite of the histories told to me by six Lithang veterans in Nepal, India, and the United States: Athar Norbu, Chodak, Dadhag, Gyato Kalsang, Lobsang Jampa, and Lobsang Tinley.[21]

"In 1945, the first Communist Chinese [*rgya gung khran*] came to Lithang. It was peaceful then. The Chinese were nice and polite, and spent lots of silver coins. They gave away so many it was like it was raining silver coins. Lithang monastery officials sent letters to Lhasa to tell them about the Chinese civil war and to emphasize the fact that the Kuomintang were losing to the Communists. They suggested to Lhasa that now was the time to mobilize in preparation for a Communist threat. This was in the 1940s. The response of the Lhasa government was to pray. They said, 'You should pray. Pray to the gods.'

"Some Khampa leaders helped the Kuomintang to turn back the Communists. Kuomintang troops stored arms and ammunition in the Lithang

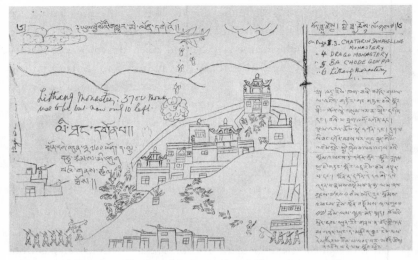

FIGURE 11 The Bombing of Lithang Monastery (from *Melong*, 1 July 1957, 6)

monastery. Eventually, they were defeated by the Communists. When the Communists reached Dartsendo, Khampa leaders gathered in Lithang to discuss what to do. Following the advice they had received from Lhasa, they decided to appeal to the gods for direction. They made two *tshe ril*, or dough balls, and inserted pieces of paper into the balls, [and put them into a cup.] On one piece of paper they wrote, 'Fight the Communists,' and on the other they wrote, 'Stay peacefully.' The lamas all prayed; one ball jumped out of the cup. It was the 'Stay peacefully' ball. This was in the beginning of 1950. In June of that year, Phuntsog Wangyal [from Bathang] came to Lithang with the Chinese Communist army [as a translator]. We didn't fight, but surrendered to them. If we had fought then, things might have been different, for we had all of the ammunition and arms left behind by the Kuomintang in the monastery. But the gods had said not to fight.

"The violence didn't start until 1955. The Chinese began saying all people were the same, all were equal. They wanted to distribute the property of the rich people to everyone in the village. People threw their valuables into the river at night. We were not ready for the liberation the Chinese insisted we accept. The monks protested, and local Tibetan authorities could not do anything because they had accepted money from the Chinese. From Lithang, the chieftains sent messages to the other Khampa leaders. War broke out and many people sought refuge in the Lithang monastery. The monastery was bombed, although the bombs fell to the side. The Chinese arrested many monks and lamas. They rode them like horses with saddles and bridles.

"One of the chief leaders of Lithang was Yonru Pön.[22] He was about twenty-five years old. Together with another chief, Dhago Pön, he came out of the monastery and told the Chinese soldiers he wanted to surrender to their leader. The Chinese leader was summoned. Before the leader arrived, Yonru Pön gave his two guns to the Chinese soldiers. The leading Chinese officer arrived and was seated, and the two Lithangba chiefs were made to kneel in front of him. He berated them for their behavior against the Chinese. While he was scolding them, Yonru Pön pulled a pistol out from inside of his chuba (robe), and shot the Chinese officer dead. In response, Chinese soldiers shot and killed Yonru Pön. They hung his dead body from one of the monastery's eight gates.

"Massive fighting commenced between the Tibetans and Chinese. Many monks died; bodies were scattered all along the roadside. The river turned red with blood. The sky wore a new shade of yellow from all of the explosions and gunshots. People were very scared, but were also angry and were united in opposition against the Chinese. The monastery was entirely destroyed. The monks and people of Lithang fought hard against the Chinese. Even the Tibetan government could not have fought such a war."[23]

The devastation in Lithang was immense. More than one veteran told me the river ran red, and they all told me about the unthinkable number of monks who died. They told me about how they visited with their families before they took to the hills or to Lhasa, about how one family would burn incense on their roof to alert those in the hills that Chinese troops were not in the area and would place a white flag on the roof if they were, and about how the head of Lithang monastery, Khashak Ngawang Tenzin, never accepted a single silver coin from the Chinese.

In this abbreviated history of Lithang, the feeling of disenfranchisement vis-à-vis the Tibetan government is tempered by a sense of local pride. This back and forth between seeking help from Lhasa and taking independent action within one's area is a common theme in local Khampa histories. Specific to Lithang, however, are two factors: (1) the aforementioned leadership role men from Lithang would have in the pan-

Tibetan resistance army, and (2) Lithang's connection to the seventh Dalai Lama. Lobsang Tinley, for example, prefaced his initial comments to me about Lithang in the 1950s with the statement "Kalsang Gyatso, the seventh Dalai Lama, was born in Lithang in 1708." Veterans frequently mentioned this special connection and saw it as a grounding force in demonstrating their allegiance to Lhasa. At the same time, however, most veterans did not mask the tensions present in these histories of 1950s Kham.

The following individual narrations highlight the "tense and tender" ways in which Lithang veterans identify with Lhasa, the Tibetan government, and especially the Dalai Lama:[24]

> The Lithang monastery was destroyed. No Tibetan armies came to help. Chamdo was also occupied at the time. The Lithang side was independent but was under the Tibetan government. It was very far from Lhasa. The seventh Dalai Lama was from Lithang. We Chushi Gangdrug soldiers went to the Norbulingka and rescued the Dalai Lama to escort him out of Tibet. From Lithang there were thirteen soldiers who accompanied His Holiness the Dalai Lama, out of sixty total. The rest were mostly from Bathang, Markham, and Chamdo.[25]

> In 1956, there was a battle in Lithang. Before we fought in Lithang, we sent letters to many places. We also wrote to the Tibetan government that we did not need men, but did need arms and ammunition. The Tibetan government did not respond. We did not receive any assistance from them. We also informed the people of Dhargye Gonpa, Markham, Tsawa Pondha, and Chatreng about our plan. Our most important achievement was that we were able to provide security to His Holiness the Dalai Lama during his flight from Tibet.[26]

As is evident in these excerpts, native place is a key ground for history, the category around which relations to other Tibetan entities are framed. "Lithang," therefore, is an example of how histories are mediated through local frameworks. At the same time solid connections are made to other territories in Kham and to the Tibetan government in Lhasa, a locally grounded focus remains. The seventh Dalai Lama was from Lithang. More men from Lithang were in the Dalai Lama's escape escort group than any other. And, tellingly, no Tibetan armed forces came to help.

Chatreng: 167 Bombs

One of the first people I met when I began this project was Kargyal Thondup. I was introduced to him as the one person who could tell me the true story of the history of the area of Chatreng (*cha phreng*). Over the course of several days at his home in Kathmandu, he told me what he knew, both from his own experience and from the informal interviews he had conducted to collect information for his book on Chatreng history.[27] Pausing for occasional verifications from his wife, Kargyal Thondup introduced me to the story of Chatreng told as collective testimony. His story of the bombing of Chatreng is as follows:

> It was normal in Chatreng to be fighting with the Chinese. During the Kuomintang period, the Chatrengbas skirmished with the Chinese many times. Although the Chinese would lose, they would keep coming back. Nine times we fought with the Chinese, and then they were defeated by the Communists. The first Chinese Communists who came to Chatreng weren't soldiers. This was in 1950, and they came disguised as merchants and doctors. They gave us brocades, money, medical services, all freely. After we grew comfortable with them, the military came, with many guns, boxes and boxes of guns. They built hospitals and houses, and we weren't sure if they were doctors or soldiers because they had so many guns stockpiled in their hospitals. We only learned [that they were really soldiers] after six years had passed and the Chinese "doctors" went to Yunnan to create a seven-point document for revolution in Yunnan. While they were away, we held a secret meeting and decided to fight. The doctors were soldiers after all.
>
> We fought for nineteen days. Many Chinese were killed, their houses burned down. The fighting went on and on until we were able to stop water supplies to the Chinese and thought they would have to surrender. We didn't know they had telegraphed their superiors in China, who had replied that there would be airstrikes the next day. The Chinese celebrated inside the monastery where they were trapped. There was a Tibetan woman also trapped inside who sang a song about the need to make "fire offerings"—telling us to burn down the monastery. She sang this loud enough so that people outside could hear, but

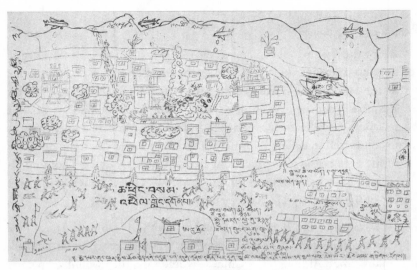

FIGURE 12 The Bombing of Chatreng Monastery (*Melong*, July 1, 1957, 3)

no one listened. The next day, three Chinese airplanes came, dropping water and supplies to the Chinese, and dropping bombs on the village. This lasted for ten days. They dropped 167 bombs throughout Chatreng. This was 1956.

We could no longer stay in the village, so escaped with guns in hand, going first to Markham, then to Tsawarong, and next on to Lhasa. From Lhasa we went to India. In India we had a meeting and decided to go to Delhi. I was interviewed by the BBC and by Jawaharlal Nehru himself. I told them everything. Tharchin Babu was my translator. The Chinese denied the bombing and said that the Chatrengbas were lying. I told the newspaper reporters that we could go to Kham together to witness things. "If the Chinese did not bomb Chatreng," I told them, "then you can kill me. If they did bomb Chatreng, then kill them." The newspaper telephoned China, but they got no reply. The journalists kept waiting, but no reply ever came.[28]

After Kargyal Thondup left Chatreng for Lhasa, the fighting continued:

Most of the men fled into the mountains, into both wooded and rocky areas, where they hid and waited for the Chinese troops. The women, children, and old people stayed in the village. The Chinese tried to trick them, claiming that the bombing was a mistake and saying that in the future, there would be no more fighting. Airplanes dropped letters saying that the people should not listen to a few reactionary [*log spyod*] individuals. The Chinese invited people to make religious offerings for their relatives who had been killed. The Chinese troops gave the appearance of withdrawing in an effort to get the men to come back to the village. The villagers grew bolder, and started venturing out to rescue men who were trapped under collapsed buildings. While many had died, some were still alive. As rescue attempts began, the Chinese again dropped bombs on the village; the people trying to save the trapped and injured men were themselves killed.

When it was finally safe for the women, elders, and children to search for the bodies of their men, they could not find the bodies in one piece. The pieces were scattered about. Some found their father's head only, went into shock and died. Others recognized their family member's hands and arms and fainted. The whole village was filled with the smell of dead bodies. The Chinese told the Chatreng people to clean the village. People had to drop the bodies and body parts into the river below the monastery. Not all the homes of the village were destroyed, and the Chinese came to stay in these houses. Women took their children from these homes, and left. Some jumped in the river and others hung themselves. People lost their ability to cherish life and decided to fight until death. Many of those still alive, left the village to join the resistance to fight against the Chinese troops.[29]

In exile, Kargyal Thondup devoted himself to the Tibetan government-in-exile. He worked in Dharamsala, Dehra Dun, and Mussoorie for several branches of the government, including the Tibetan resistance. When the Dalai Lama told him to write a book about Chatreng, he readily agreed. It took him seventeen years to write it. In order to write the book, he said, "I had to think a lot and ask about many things. I read many books and documents and spoke with many people." As a result, his knowledge of what happened in Chatreng extends well beyond his personal experience. After Tibet was opened in the 1980s following the Cultural Revolution, Kargyal Thondup traveled to Chatreng from India. He was surprised to find that the local police had a copy of the Indian newspaper from 1959 with his interview and photo. The police gave him sixteen days to leave his hometown. Kargyal Thondup's book embodies his commitment to document history through this period of loss and terror.

Nyarong: Dorje Yudon's Story

In the territory of Nyarong uprisings against the Chinese in the 1950s unfolded in a manner similar to those in other areas in Kham, but with one twist: the leader of the revolt was a woman, adding a gendered difference to both history and historical production (see chapter 5). Dorje Yudon told me her story one morning in her home in Delhi, quietly and steadily calling the mountains of eastern Tibet into that hot and dusty day in India. In retelling her history here, I draw primarily on our conversation that day, supplemented by two later interviews I conducted with her husband, Gyari Nyima, chieftain of the Gyaritsang family.[30] The Gyaritsang were one of four chiefly families who controlled the upper region of the vast, spectacular pha yul of Nyarong.

Dorje Yudon and Gyari Nyima tell their story as follows: at the time of the Chinese Communist invasion, Gyari Nyima was the head of the Gyaritsang family. He had two wives, Norzin Lhamo and Dorje Yudon, sisters from the Miloktsang family who were seven years apart in age. One day, the Chinese called the local chiefs to a meeting in Kanze. At this meeting Gyari Nyima was shocked to hear that a series of democratic reforms were about to be initiated. These included political "struggle sessions" ('thab 'dzing or "thamzing" in colloquial Tibetan) in which people were made to publicly criticize others, the establishment of communes, the elevation of common beggars to high positions, and the recording of the wealth of each family. The more Gyari Nyima heard about these drastic changes, the more convinced he became the time had come for revolt. He rushed home from Kanze to tell his wives the news. Together, the three of them sat down to discuss strategy.

Gyari Nyima's chieftain status meant he was often under Chinese military surveillance. His senior wife, Norzin Lhamo, had a similarly high profile with the Chinese. Dorje Yudon, however, was less of a public figure and not watched as closely, so they decided she should be the one to organize the rebellion in their area. They chose eighteen men to protect the family and named this group the *stag phrug*, or "tiger cubs." If their rebellion was unsuccessful, their back-up plan was to flee to Lhasa.

FIGURE 13 Dorje Yudon, Gyari Nyima, and Norzin Lhamo. Photo courtesy of Gyaritsang family.

Meanwhile, chieftains in Lithang decided to organize a regionwide rebellion to protest the reforms. They sent letters by messenger to the Gyaritsang family and other chieftains throughout Kham. The letter proposed a simultaneous revolt throughout Kham on the eighteenth day of the first month of the Tibetan year. This group called itself *bstan srung dang blangs dmag* (Volunteer army to defend religion). In her reply, Dorje Yudon confirmed that the Gyaritsang family and the people of Upper Nyarong would participate in the coordinated rebellion. Soon after, Chinese officials summoned Gyari Nyima to Dartsendo for a meeting, which turned out to be a ruse to draw the chiefs to Dartsendo, where they were captured by PLA troops. While Gyari Nyima was away, Dorje Yudon received word from Lithang that twenty-three Khampa chiefs had agreed to participate in the simultaneous revolt.[31] Norzin Lhamo rushed to Dartsendo, a journey of several days, to tell Gyari Nyima the news about the revolt so that he might try to escape. In Dartsendo, however, he and the other Tibetan chiefs were guarded by sixty to seventy PLA soldiers at all times, making escape impossible, so Norzin Lhamo returned to Nyarong alone. Two days later, along with twenty-two other local leaders, the Chinese summoned her to the Nyarong town of Renuk for a series of meetings.

Since the most important chiefs and leaders were away at the meetings in Dartsendo and Renuk, Dorje Yudon called the community together for a meeting of their own. She gathered one hundred of the remaining Upper Nyarong leaders together and told them about the Chinese plans to institute reforms and the Tibetan plan for rebellion. The community supported the rebellion plan and sealed their commitment to it by putting their guns together and making a solemn oath to join Dorje Yudon in revolt. The members went to spread the news of the planned revolt in their villages. Each family in Upper Nyarong who could afford to donated one gun and one horse to the Gyaritsang family for the rebellion army. Dorje Yudon sent messages to other Khampa leaders to inform them of her preparations. En route to Drango Monastery, her messenger was followed and her letter intercepted by the Chinese officials. They uncovered the plans for the rebellion and assassinated the head of the monastery. Word of this turn of events did not reach Upper Nyarong in time.

In anticipation of the democratic reforms, the Chinese had invited five hundred poor Khampa families to Kanze and, solely because they were from the lowest classes of society, bestowed the title of model citizen upon them. These families were to be the leaders at the struggle sessions and were intended to eventually replace chieftains such as Gyari Nyima. After discovering the Tibetan rebellion plans, the Chinese set the Tibetan model citizens into action, sending them out to the various regions of Kham with instructions to kill the chieftains and confiscate all of their weapons. One group entered the palace of another Nyarong chiefly family, the Gyarishiba, and killed six people. Another model citizen tried to assassinate Dorje Yudon with a grenade but was stopped by her servants. Assassination attempts took place throughout Nyarong. The local people were shocked and realized there was no longer time to wait for the coordinated rebellion; they needed to act immediately.

Dorje Yudon ordered the Tiger Cubs bodyguards and the one hundred community leaders to arrest all model citizens in Upper Nyarong. These individuals were brought to the Gyaritsang castle in Ralong, where Dorje Yudon spoke to them about the divisions the Chinese were trying to forge within the Nyarong community. She told them that if they pledged to support the revolt rather than help the Chinese, she would release them. Each model citizen who promised to work for Nyarong was therefore released.[32] Meanwhile, Dorje Yudon's troops arrested or killed all Chinese troops in the area. Upon hearing about these events in Nyarong, the Chinese leaders in Renuk brought Norzin Lhamo to Ralong to convince Dorje Yudon to cease fire.

The two sisters met twice. At their second meeting, Dorje Yudon devised a plan to rescue Norzin Lhamo and to capture forty Chinese soldiers. She received the Chinese troops in the castle with great hospitality. She also arranged for a large group of monks to be praying inside the castle, a common sight in wealthy Tibetan homes. During their meeting, the Chinese set up two machine guns, one aimed at the Tibetan chiefs and one aimed at the monks. Under the pretense of going to relieve himself, a monk rose from his seat and surprised one of the machine gunners, quickly overpowering him. The other monks followed him and were able to disarm the rest of the soldiers. Dorje Yudon then negotiated the exchange of her captives and their weapons for the twenty-two Nyarong leaders held at Renuk. Renuk was now the only area in Upper Nyarong that still had a Chinese presence.

The Chinese stationed themselves in Drukmo Dzong, the Castle of the Female Dragon, which had formerly been the Gyaritsang family palace. After all of the chieftains were safely released, Dorje Yudon led an attack on the castle. Her troops, which numbered fourteen hundred, did not have sufficient artillery to destroy the thick walls of the castle, so they surrounded it, intending to cut off supplies to the Chinese soldiers inside. Before long, one thousand troops from the Eighteenth Division in Kanze arrived to assist their fellow PLA soldiers. Dorje Yudon's troops killed all but forty-three of these troops and lost twenty-six of their own soldiers in battle.

Dorje Yudon told the Chinese she would agree to a cease-fire if they would meet two conditions. She first asked that Gyari Nyima and the other Khampa chieftains captive in Dartsendo be released. Her second request raised the stakes: she demanded that the Chinese stop their democratic reform program. In time, the Chinese brought Gyari Nyima and six other chieftains to Nyarong under heavy guard. Dorje Yudon and her troops were not allowed close contact with them, and she decided to end negotiations with the Chinese. All the captured chieftains were taken back to Dartsendo.

Four thousand Chinese troops soon arrived in Nyarong to fight against Dorje Yudon's troops. The ensuing battle was long and hard, and eventually the Tibetan troops had to retreat because they were greatly out-numbered. In the battle, however, they were able to capture two hundred Chinese weapons that were greatly superior to the antiquated weapons of the Nyarong troops. By this time, approximately fourteen hundred Chinese troops had been killed in Nyarong. In Dartsendo, the Chinese decided to release Gyari Nyima and the other chieftains. However, after they released them, they publicly announced that the chieftains had escaped. Calling their release an escape legitimated the next Chinese move: sending out teams of model citizens with instructions to hunt down the chieftains and kill them. The model citizens of Upper Nyarong remained true to their pledge to Dorje Yudon. They pretended to go in search of Gyari Nyima but killed another person and claimed they thought it was Gyari Nyima. As a result, Gyari Nyima was able to make it back to Ralong safely to join Dorje Yudon and Norzin Lhamo.

The situation changed drastically with the next battle. Thirty thousand Chinese troops surrounded Nyarong. Dorje Yudon's troops were only one thousand strong at the time. As they retreated, they split into two groups, one led by Dorje Yudon and Gyari Nyima and one by Gyari Nyima's uncle and brother. The two sides were never to see each other again. The Gyaritsang family salvaged all they could from their home and set off for the mountains with two hundred troops. They joined forces with several other families to increase their numbers to two thousand. They lived like nomads, moving frequently to evade the Chinese troops who were constantly hunting them, often engaging in battle, and always suffering shortages of food and other supplies. This situation continued for months, and as many as eighteen battles were fought in one month. After a year had passed, Dorje Yudon's and Gyari Nyima's group found themselves surrounded by forty thousand Chinese soldiers. Their battle against these troops was devastating, as many of the Tibetans were arrested or killed and those remaining were separated in their escape. The Gyaritsang group was reduced to two hundred individuals, including a baby girl that was born soon after this battle. Four of the Gyaritsang children had been traveling with the family since they had taken to the mountains, and two others were staying in a local monastery. Dorje Yudon had one final secret visit with the two in the monastery before the family left for Lhasa and eventually made their way to India as refugees.

Like communities throughout Kham and other areas of Tibet, Nyarong was ravaged by both war and the reforms at the cost of great loss of life, disruption of everyday routines, political order, and religious practice, and the often permanent fragmentation of families. Dorje Yudon repeatedly emphasizes loyalty across classes; in her narration, the people of Nyarong are a stratified but unified group: together they fought; together they suffered.

Bathang: Never Before in This World

As Baba Lekshey said, "If we weren't boiling water for tea, we were fighting the Chinese." Shaking his head as we talked about the past and his part in it, Baba Lekshey claimed there was always fighting in Bathang (commonly referred to as Ba), and much of it involved the Chinese in some shape or form. Born in 1917, Baba Lekshey participated in the Bathang revolt against growing Chinese oppression in the 1950s. Along with two of his brothers, Kalsang Tsering and Kalsang Tashi, he was sent from Ba to Lhasa to report on events in Kham and to see if help could be sent. From Lhasa, the three men went to Kalimpong, where they met with Tibetans who were secretly in contact with the U.S. government.

The story of Ba in the 1950s and of the men from Ba in the Tibetan resistance is an important one because of all the territories of Kham, Bathang had some of the closest relations with China during the Kuomintang period. There was a small Chinese population in Ba as well as an American and European Christian missionary community. The Americans and Europeans ran schools there, and as a result the people of Ba had access to educational opportunities not found in most areas of Kham. Politically, this meant a number of things: a disproportionate number of Babas were politically active not just in Kham, but also in China under the Kuomintang; and one of the leading Tibetan communists, Phuntsog Wangyal, was from Ba, as were many prominent Tibetan leaders in the early days of the PRC.[33] Yet if some Bathang Tibetans were closely integrated into Chinese worlds, most people in Bathang were not. In 1949, when communist troops arrived in Ba, they were received not with open arms but with suspicion as "the enemy of the dharma." The story of Ba was written and published in exile by Lobsang Gyaltsen.[34] I draw on his version as well as versions told to me in India and Nepal by Baba Lekshey and Baba Yeshi, a chieftain who would go on to be one of the highest leaders of the Tibetan resistance.[35]

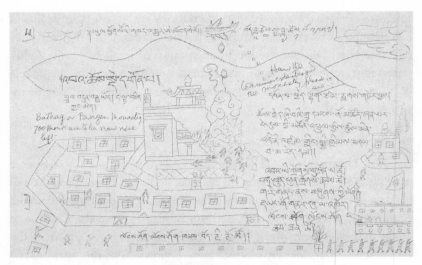

FIGURE 14 The Bombing of Bathang Monastery (*Melong*, July 1, 1957, 5)

According to most Babas, all was well in Bathang before the Chinese Communists came. People were free to conduct business, to be under local leaders, and to practice their religion. The first communist Chinese who went to Ba were civilian officials, and they assured the people that communism was the same as Buddhism. Just like Buddhism, they said, communism makes people equal and produces peace and happiness. The Tibetans would be able to continue to practice their religion, the traditional system of chieftains could continue, and the only reforms that would take place would be voluntary. For six years they deceived the Tibetans in Bathang with their "sweet mouths and sour minds" (*kha 'jam khog rtsub*).[36]

Things soured when the Chinese began collecting weapons from the local people and the monastery. Next, the Chinese paid one thousand lower-class citizens to disrupt life in the Ba community. Finally, they took the chief leaders of Ba, Chiefs Chime Dorje and Yonden, to Dartsendo for a meeting, where they were detained and not allowed to return. In the first Tibetan calendar month of 1956, Chinese civilian and military officials announced that Bathang would be liberated. The people of Ba protested that they did not need to be liberated; besides, their leader was the Dalai Lama, not Mao. In return, the Chinese said that with the signing of the Seventeen-Point Agreement in 1951 it was their constitutional right to liberate Bathang.

In response, the people of Ba gathered to discuss their fate. They held a nine-day religious ceremony, after which they decided to fight against the Chinese. Every ten Tibetans were to fight one hundred Chinese soldiers. Fighting broke out, and many Chinese casualties resulted. In an effort to convince Tibetans there was a lack of widespread support for the fighting, Chinese officials publicly announced that the fighting resulted from the influence of just a few bad Tibetan individuals. They also released the two chiefs being held in Dartsendo. Nine days after fighting broke out in Ba, it began in neighboring Lithang. Messengers were sent from Ba to Lithang, Chatreng, and Gyalthang requesting all Tibetans to unite against the Chinese. The message read as follows:

> Lingkha shi of Ba is already engaged in fighting against the Chinese. No matter what the Chinese Communists say, their aim is to occupy Tibet in the name of Ngabo's Seventeen-Point Agreement. Therefore every Tibetan must unite and fight until even if there are no men left, women will have to take up weapons. If we let China do whatever it wants, Tibetan Buddhism and the Tibetan race will become extinct. Our property will be confiscated. Evil people will be the leaders and good people will be the servants. It is clear that things will happen which have never before happened in this world. Therefore, we must not be deluded by the Chinese deceit, and we must rise up in unison. We must completely forget the personal and collected resentments that exist between our different areas, and confront together the enemy of our religion.[37]

The Chinese tried again to get the Babas to cease fighting, appealing in part to the higher education of the people in Bathang as compared to other areas of Kham. The people of Ba counterargued that the Chinese had broken all of the promises they had made to the Ba people. On the tenth day of the second Tibetan month of 1956, the laymen and the monks of Ba decided to continue the fighting. All men between the ages of eighteen and sixty came, about twenty-five hundred men in total.

The fighting began at night and continued until the Chinese troops were driven into the building that had formerly housed the Tibetan government representatives. The Bathang Tibetans surrounded the building, cutting off their water supply. From inside the building, the Chinese radioed China, and two days later two planes appeared overhead. They bombed Bathang for twelve days straight, dropping a total of seventy-three bombs and destroying many houses as well as the Chude Monastery. The Tibetans had no antiaircraft weapons. During this time, people fled to the mountains. More Chinese soldiers were sent to Ba, and the fighting continued throughout the area for months. Baba Lekshey and his two brothers were sent to Lhasa to see if they could obtain help.

At the end of the year, leaders from Ba met with leaders from Lithang and Gyalthang. Although there were long-standing animosities between these territories—as there were in many neighboring areas of Kham—the leaders signed a twenty-two-point agreement in which they agreed to unite to fight against the Chinese. In 1957, some of the Ba troops joined with troops from Nyarong and Derge and fled west to Markham. But there were too many Chinese troops; the Tibetans were outnumbered. Those who stayed behind continued to fight in Ba through 1958, until finally they too had to flee, burning their houses as they left. From there, some groups from Ba fought throughout southwestern Kham with other Khampa groups and others headed to Lhasa, where they joined in forming the united Tibetan resistance army, Chushi Gangdrug.

Proclamation of the Tibetan Volunteer Army for Defense of Religion

The universe was started in this way:
On a foundation made of webs of wind,
A golden land was formed.
On the golden land,
Rolpa Lake was formed.
In the center of the lake,
Mount Meru arose.
Four supreme worlds emerged
[on the four sides of Mount Meru].
The earth was on the southern side.

Tibet: the land surrounded by a fence of snowy mountains:
The upper side of which contains Mnga' ris skor gsum,
In the center, Dbus gtsang ru bzhi,
And in the lower part, Mdo khams sgang drug,
The soul of Tibet is His Holiness the Dalai Lama,
Whose life is as strong as a diamond,
The rays of which light all of the four directions.

Andrug Gompo Tashi has sown the white rice of merit,
The paddy has grown well,
And a good harvest for happiness in Tibet was reaped.

As the six ranges mark the land,
The enemies of Buddhism, the Communists,

Have been demolished like the sun melting frozen dew on rocks.
As the four rivers run through the valleys,
The sand dunes of communism have been washed away.
The flag of prosperity for Buddhism has been raised atop the six
    ranges!
The banner of long-life spans the four rivers!

The world's white marble stupa
Remains without delusion in the three realms of existence
And lives long without negative effect to body, mind, or speech.

Born from the mind of the dharma king,
The fame of the leader of Chushi Gangdrug is louder than
    thunder.
For the sake of all sentient beings and for Buddhism,
We have pledged to reduce the enemies of Buddhism to mere
    specks of dust.
A new era of the dual system of religion and politics has come—
Rejoice! Rejoice!

From the eastern border of our beloved country of Tibet,
The flames of fires burning point to the east.
From the east, the [Chinese] troops fired down bombs like rain.
Oh, isn't it a miracle?
The rain of bombs has not put out the fire,
Instead, the fire burns even stronger.
It is burning all over Tibet.
It burns with a roaring sound,
And the words from the burning fire say,
"Let Tibet be independent! Let us protect the dharma!"

It is a miracle: the fire gets stronger.
The glory of the burning fire spreads around the world.
There is a reason why the fire gets stronger:
The wind of support for justice blows from all corners of the world.
Now is the time for those with faith in dharma to stoke the fire.
This fire is the very foundation of the dharma's own fire.
It cannot be put out with the rain of bombs.
It cannot be blown out by the winds of deceit.

Now stand up, people of Kham and U-Tsang!

Tibetans, who share the same flesh and blood, now is the time to
stand up!

Stand up for the independence of Tibet and Tibetan Buddhism!

FROM THE INFORMATION OFFICE OF THE VOLUNTEER ARMY

FOR POLITICS AND RELIGION, 20TH DAY OF 2ND MONTH,

EARTH PIG YEAR (1959)

Poetry and war go together. Written in 1959 by Chushi Gangdrug soldiers, this proclamation is a heartfelt plea to the people of Tibet—"Stand up! Stand up!"—to unite in defense of "Tibet and Tibetan Buddhism."[1] Its call to action is situated in foundational, unifying versions of Tibet: cultural appeals to sharing the same "flesh and blood," geographic appeals to Tibetan national identity, and religious appeals to the power and glory of the dharma, including the righteous need to protect it. Copies of this proclamation (and others like it) were airdropped into Tibet from CIA airplanes and also published in Tharchin's *Tibet Mirror* newspaper. The proclamation's passionate language reflects the optimism of the Chushi Gangdrug army in the summer following the Dalai Lama's escape to India. The soldiers believed the world would act on their behalf, that there was a distinct possibility of defeating the Chinese, if not militarily, then diplomatically, and that they and the Dalai Lama would soon return to Tibet. Crucially, the soldiers also had faith in the Tibetan people, in their ability and desire to collectively "stoke the fire" in order to defend religion and country.

Impassioned and eloquent—composed, I surmise, by one of the monks who joined the Chushi Gangdrug army—the proclamation has all the makings of an important historical document. Its call to national unity and its rich Buddhist referents resonate deeply with exile discourses regarding community and culture. It reads like a document that might appear in a school textbook, be recited or referenced in public gatherings, or even be officially memorialized in political ceremonies. Yet, like most things having to do with the armed resistance, it is not. I first encountered it in the yellowed pages of the *Tibet Mirror*. All of the veterans with whom I shared it recognized the genre and could speak in general of such calls to action but knew they had been long forgotten.

Remembering what could have been was a common theme across the narrations of Chushi Gangdrug veterans. In the conversations that ground this chapter, many spoke of the mid-1950s as a time of extreme energy and hope, notwithstanding the devastating fighting in Kham and the increasing heavy-handedness of the Chinese throughout the country. If anything, these challenges spurred some Tibetans not only to envision but to act on new possibilities for Tibet. Ideas of the new were crucial in this period: new ideas of democracy, of political cooperation and participation, and of Tibet as a sovereign nation-state in international terms. In Lhasa, a political group was formed to address just these issues—the Mimang Tsogpa (*mi dmangs tshogs pa*), or People's Party.

In 1951, Prime Minister Nehru of India advised a visiting Tibetan delegation to encourage a people's democratic movement as a legitimate alternative to the Chinese. Taking his advice, the Tibetan government catalyzed the founding of Mimang Tsogpa. It was headed by Alo Chhonzed, a Khampa from Lithang who had grown up in Lhasa, and had sixty-two members representing all three provinces of Tibet.[2] The party's activities were mostly political, such as holding protests against the Chinese and recruiting among Tibetans.[3] One officer of the Mimang Tsogpa, Andrug Gompo Tashi, who was later to be the leader of Chushi Gangdrug, reported distributing leaflets which "exhorted all Tibetans to unite and protect their freedom and country in an active and not—what was until now—passive posture."[4]

During Monlam festivities in early 1956, Mimang Tsogpa leaders protested against the Chinese, delivering a letter directly to the Chinese authorities demanding that the Chinese leave Tibet.[5] In response, the Chinese demanded that the Tibetan government arrest those responsible. In the spring of 1956, the Tibetan government arrested three Mimang Tsogpa leaders: Alo Chhonzed, Lhabchug Dhargpa Tinley, and Bumthang Gyaltsen Lobsang.[6] Party members sought the support of Sera, Drepung, and Ganden monasteries to help secure the release of the three leaders.[7] While in prison, Alo Chhonzed was convinced that the United Nations and the world in general would respond: "It's a good thing they put me in prison. Now everyone will know that the democratic party leader is in prison. It is in all the newspapers so everyone will know. After my release, I will go to the United Nations to tell them how bad the Chinese situation in Tibet is. I will ask them to send military aid to help Tibet get her independence."[8] Lhabchug Dhargpa Tinley died in prison, but the other two leaders were freed in August 1956. After their release, Andrug Gompo Tashi sent Alo Chhonzed to India "to further Tibet's cause," giving him two horses and a loaded 40-caliber pistol for the journey.[9] In India, however, the global audience the Mimang Tsogpa leaders were hoping for did not materialize.

Despite this show of indifference, Mimang Tsogpa's very existence was meaningful to Tibetans. In exile, aspects of the party's organizational goals were incorporated into Chushi Gangdrug. Mimang Tsogpa was influential in representing an opportunity for ordinary Tibetans to be active in national politics and defense. As more and more Tibetans streamed into Lhasa to escape Chinese oppression and violence, Mimang Tsogpa was a source of inspiration for their collective action.

Resistance, 1955–57

In 1955, six traders from Lithang arrived in Lhasa.[10] They had come in hopes the Tibetan government would supply them with arms and ammunition to fight the Chinese. They asked Andrug Gompo Tashi, the most successful Lithang trader in Lhasa, for advice. Together and in consultation with lamas and deities, they decided to halt their regular business for the time being to focus their attention on the worsening problems in Kham. Meanwhile, at the southern end of the Tibet–India trade route in Kalimpong, another group of Khampas, all Lithangbas except for Baba Lekshey, were holding similar discussions.[11] They were convinced they needed military help from foreign governments and were considering approaching Taiwan. They approached Gyalo Thondup, the Dalai Lama's brother, with their idea.[12] He told them Taiwan would not serve their purposes, but that he would establish contact with a more powerful country. Unknown to this group of Khampas, the Americans had already contacted Gyalo Thondup regarding the situation in Tibet.[13] In the summer of 1956, the Far East Division of the CIA decided to support ongoing independent Tibetan efforts to fight the Chinese.

Meanwhile, the Dalai Lama traveled to India in the fall of 1956 for Buddha Jayanti, the 2,500th anniversary of the birth of the Buddha. Many Tibetans attended, and ten Khampa bodyguards served the Dalai Lama while he was in India.[14] In Delhi, one of Andrug Gompo Tashi's nephews,

Gyato Kalsang, met with Gyalo Thondup and the former finance minister Shakabpa, who told him they were petitioning the Tibetan army, which had not engaged the Chinese in battle since 1950, to begin fighting the Chinese.[15] They asked Gyato Kalsang to write a letter to Andrug Gompo Tashi telling him of this plan, and they also wrote their own letter to the Tibetan defense minister, which they put in a bottle sealed on top with petroleum jelly. Gyato Kalsang sent the letters with two Lithangba messengers, Lobsang Palden and Tinley, who traveled day and night and reached Lhasa in record time.[16] In reply, Andrug Gompo Tashi sent a coded telegram to Kalimpong reading, "Your Indian goods reached Lhasa, but I cannot sell them right now as the price is very low."[17] His message meant that the time was not right for the Tibetan army to begin fighting.

The time was, in fact, never again right for the official Tibetan army to fight the PLA. Instead, this task fell to Tibetan citizens, many of whom were already fighting. At the end of 1956, Andrug Gompo Tashi sent a message to leaders throughout Kham calling upon them to unite. The message read as follows:

> For some time you people have been rebelling against the Red Chinese. The time has now arrived to muster all your courage and put your bravery to the test. I know you are prepared to risk your lives and exert all your strength to defend Tibet. I also know that the tremendous task that you have undertaken is a noble cause and that you will have no regrets despite the ghastly atrocities committed by the enemy. In this hour of peril, I appeal to all people, including government servants, who value their freedom and religion, to unite in the common struggle against the Chinese. Messages are being sent to people in other parts of Tibet and the neighboring countries, such as India, to explain that the Tibetans now have no alternative but to take up arms against the Chinese.[18]

Such political and military organizing across Tibet was facilitated by Khampa trade networks. These networks between Kalimpong, Lhasa, and Kham connected individuals in each place—political figures such as Gyalo Thondup, Finance Minister Shakabpa, and the high-ranking monk official Khenchung Lobsang Gyaltsen in Kalimpong (also known as *chen khen tsis gsum*) with Phala Dronyer Chenmo (whose position was that of

Lord Chamberlain) in Lhasa. Phala played an important but discrete role as the Tibetan government official unofficially monitoring and coordinating with the resistance army.[19] Wealthy traders such as Andrugtsang were also invaluable to this pan-Tibetan effort, for they were some of the very few members of Tibetan society who could interact with people at all socioeconomic levels.[20]

Coordinating across community divides required the establishing of trust among groups who were working together for the first time. When Baba Lekshey, for example, arrived in Kalimpong, Tibetan officials were not sure who he was or if he was to be trusted. Thinking back on this, Gyato Kalsang recalled the following: "Baba Lekshey had three brothers and came from a good family. They killed many Communists, spoke no Chinese, and were rich. When he came to India, he went to the Tibetan leaders and offered his services. At that time, they were Gyalo Thondup, Shakabpa, and Lhukhang. They wrote to [my uncle] Gompo Tashi in Lhasa, asking about Baba Lekshey's background and if his story was true. Andrug Gompo Tashi found it was true, very clear: his family was a powerful family in Bathang and wrote back they could trust him. He sent the message with me to them in Kalimpong."[21] Based on this endorsement, Baba Lekshey and his brothers became part of the otherwise Lithang-centric early inner circle of resistance organizers.

Under the leadership of Andrug Gompo Tashi, clandestine military preparations began in Lhasa. Arms, ammunition, and horses were bought to support groups in Kham and elsewhere that were already fighting.[22] Covert activities with the CIA also began. In early 1957, Andrug Gompo Tashi sent a list of individuals recommended for military training abroad to Gyalo Thondup in Kalimpong. In April 1957, a group of six men, five from Lithang and one from Bathang, were taken to the island of Saipan for five months of training, focused on radio operations.[23] After their training was completed, the first team, Athar Norbu and Lotse from Lithang, parachuted into the Samye area on 10 September 1957 with instructions to set up radio operations to provide information on the Tibetan government's plans vis-à-vis the Chinese.[24] At the time, the Tibetan government was not able to openly contact the United States, and thus Athar Norbu's and Lotse's role as radio operators was crucial in transmitting information between the U.S. and Tibetan governments.[25] The second team parachuted into Lithang on 13 September 1957.[26] Led by

Andrug Gompo Tashi's nephew, Gyato Wangdu, the team included Chu Bulu and Tsewang Dorje from Lithang and Changra Tashi from Bathang. After arriving in Lithang, the team sent a radio message to the CIA stating that there were approximately fifty thousand Tibetan volunteer soldiers fighting against the Chinese in the Lithang area "with every weapon they had."[27] Meanwhile, in Lhasa, Andrug Gompo Tashi's group began collaborating with others to officially establish a united resistance army.

The Golden Throne: The Founding of the Chushi Gangdrug Army

In this time of upheaval and destruction, many of the Khampas who fled to Lhasa for refuge turned to the Dalai Lama for religious guidance and protection. Individual communities requested teachings and made offerings on behalf of all those who died in the fighting. The Lithang traders decided to offer a long-life ceremony for the Dalai Lama, then decided to expand it to traders from the Ba-Li-Rgyal-Gsum (Bathang, Lithang, Gyalthang) area, then to all of Kham, and finally joined forces with traders from Amdo as well.[28] Together, the Khampa and Amdowa traders requested the Dalai Lama to perform two very powerful Buddhist teachings, the Kalachakra and the Lamrim Chenmo, that would provide protection, blessings, and strength to the individuals participating in or sponsoring these rituals as well as to Tibet in general. The Dalai Lama agreed to their request for the ceremony and teachings. In turn, the traders began preparations for the corresponding ritual offerings, including a special gift for the Dalai Lama—a gold throne.[29] Preparations for the long-life ceremony and construction of the throne began in earnest,[30] as did planning by Khampa traders, former Mimang Tsogpa members, and newly arrived Khampas and Amdowas to form a united resistance army.[31] The golden throne thus served two purposes: to repay the kindness of the Dalai Lama and to secretly facilitate the formation of the new political and military group by providing cover for their frequent meetings.[32]

The traders presented the throne to the Dalai Lama on 4 July 1957. It was truly spectacular, being made of over eighty pounds of gold and encrusted with diamonds, turquoise, and other precious stones.[33] They collected enough money, gold, and silver to make beautiful lamps, offering bowls, and other religious objects to be donated to monasteries in Lhasa as well as to sponsor the Kalachakra initiation. With the success of these offerings secured, the resistance group approached Trijang

FIGURE 15 Andrug Gompo Tashi (portrait in Dharamsala Chushi Gangdrug office).

Rinpoche, the Dalai Lama's junior tutor, and requested him to name the army.[34] Trijang Rinpoche did a *mo* (divination) and suggested the Kham-focused name Chushi Gangdrug. He advised them to ask Ling Rinpoche, the Dalai Lama's senior tutor, and Rato Rinpoche, a highly accomplished *geshe* (*dge bshes*, or holder of the equivalent of a Buddhist doctoral degree) from Kham, for further approval. They approved the name, and the Chushi Gangdrug army was born.

On 18 February 1958, prominent Khampa and Amdo traders gathered at Andrug Gompo Tashi's home in Lhasa. Joining them were two representatives of the Tibetan government army, Gyapön Kelsang Dradul and Gyapön Wangden Tashi.[35] Andrug Gompo Tashi gave a speech about the formation of Chushi Gangdrug; the two army officers professed the army's support, then left the gathering as the other men went into the Andrug family's *lha khang*, or altar room, to take an oath of loyalty to

Chushi Gangdrug.[36] Ratuk Ngawang recalls that all shared ceremonial tea and 'bras sil rice pudding before Chamdo Dronyik Konchog Dorje read aloud the Chushi Gangdrug resolution.[37] As is true of so many Tibetan documents, the original was left behind in Lhasa. Ratuk Ngawang remembered that it included the following: the Tibetan fight against the invading communist Chinese must be carried out until the end; one's life shall be given up to defend the religious and political rights of Tibetans; the orders of Chushi Gangdrug officials shall be strictly obeyed; men who do not have horses and weapons must acquire them soon; each must be prepared to die one after another in battle; resistance plans are top secret and must not be shared even with one's spouse; and every individual shall not only take the oath, but also write his name and put his fingerprint on the resolution. One by one, the forty-two men gathered in the altar room prostrated three times "under the precious commandments of the Buddha," then those who had seal stamps stamped under their names on the resolution, and those without stamps put their fingerprints under their names.[38] Secret oath taken, the men went out into Lhasa to procure weapons and animals and to share the news with trusted men from their area.

Over the next several months, Chinese authorities tightened their control of Lhasa, and as the Chinese presence and policies grew stronger the Tibetan government had little recourse but to follow the new dictates. In late April 1958, the Chinese announced a new security measure in the form of a census and subsequent identification requirements. All persons from outside of Lhasa would henceforth be required to register with Chinese officials and to obtain an identity card to stay in the Lhasa area. To many Tibetans, this announcement foreshadowed a period of mass arrests, and people began to move away from Lhasa to avoid giving information about themselves to the Chinese. In consultation with the protector deity Dorje Shugden (*rdo rje shugs ldan*), Andrug Gompo Tashi decided the time had come for the resistance to move away from Lhasa: "We decided to approach the Shugden oracle to find out what we should do.[39] He told us that the people of Tibet should no longer remain idle but should unite to defend their country. He also said the headquarters of the voluntary army should be established in Lhoka Trigu Thang. With that decided, there would be no further delay."[40] Following the advice of the deity, Andrug Gompo Tashi moved the troops south of Lhasa to the Lhoka region.

Religion was an important part of Chushi Gangdrug. The protection and guidance of the army as a whole were entrusted to the spiritual world via lamas and deities. When a decision needed to be made about which route to take, which pass to cross, or what direction to go in, deities would be invoked and divinations done. Many Tibetans have personal protectors (*srung ma*), assigned or chosen by virtue of one's native place, family, or sectarian affiliation.[41] Dorje Shugden is one such deity to whom many, though not all, Chushi Gangdrug soldiers turned for guidance.[42] Chushi Gangdrug soldiers had full faith in their protectors, and most of them believe the advice they were given was good.[43] However, while the deities were to be trusted, their mediums were occasionally subject to suspicion, in which case respected lamas were consulted to verify whether or not an individual was a genuine conduit for the deity.[44]

On 16 June 1958, the Chushi Gangdrug army held an inaugural cere-mony in Lhoka marking their transition from an unofficial, unorganized force to a fully functioning army.[45] The ceremony included a cavalry parade, a ritual procession of a photograph of the Dalai Lama, and the unveiling of the Chushi Gangdrug flag. The flag consisted of two deities' swords with a religious thunderbolt and lotus flowers on the handles against a background of yellow, the color of Buddhism.[46] Army head-quarters were established at Triguthang, where about five thousand vol-unteer soldiers were stationed. Posts and positions were also assigned: four men were selected as top commanders and five as liaison officers between the soldiers and the community; another five were assigned to take care of supplies and equipment, a secretariat and finance department were created, eighteen field commanders were named, and a captain was selected for each group of ten soldiers.[47] Leaders made a code of conduct consisting of twenty-seven rules, including prohibitions against stealing, rape, entering houses while on a mission, and harming innocent people, and requirements such as protecting local people from bandits in the area. This last rule was important because veterans contend that Chinese authorities paid bandits, who roamed throughout Tibet posing as Chushi Gangdrug soldiers and terrorizing villages, stealing, raping women and nuns, and killing people along the way.[48] Along with the code of conduct, army officials introduced a merit system; for example, soldiers who captured a Chinese army officer's possessions or documents would receive a cash prize of five hundred Indian rupees.[49] Altogether there were thirty-seven organized units of varying size, grouped by *pha yul* (Lithang, Derge, Nyarong, and so on) and assigned names corresponding to the letters of the Tibetan alphabet—for example, "ka," "kha," "ga," "nga."[50] After the ceremony of 16 June, the Chushi Gangdrug army was not simply a loosely organized (or mostly unorganized) series of village- and region-based uprisings, but a formal and united national resistance army.

The Chushi Gangdrug resistance force was organized in ways that reflected the sociopolitical frameworks of eastern Tibet rather than the aristocratic and monastic hierarchies of central Tibet. On the battlefield, trust, loyalty, and familiarity were crucial, and thus guerrilla units were based on native-place affiliations. Leaders of these units were often the same men who had been leaders in their areas—men from chiefly families or wealthy traders. Khampas dominated the army, although units and troops also included Amdowas, men from U-Tsang, *dob dob* (*rdob rdob*), or Tibetan monk-police, Tibetan government soldiers, former Chinese Nationalist army soldiers, and several Chinese Communist spies.[51] In Lhokha and other areas of U-Tsang, many wealthy families such as the Lha Gyari family supported the soldiers by providing food for the men and fodder and stables for their horses.[52] In addition, other groups fleeing the PLA, such as Xinjiang Uighurs, joined forces with Chushi Gangdrug units from time to time.[53] Nonetheless, the army was and still is popularly associated with Kham and Khampas.[54]

In his autobiography, Andrug Gompo Tashi emphasized the national character of the resistance: "Many Tibetans from the central and other parts of the country, including the [Tibetan government] army, joined our movement as Chinese oppression steadily became unbearable. Their decisions were taken on an individual basis as nationalists who could not see their people butchered. *The Chushi Gangdrug as a result grew from a regional to a pan-Tibetan resistance movement.*"[55] The move from a local to a regional and then national effort is historically and ideologically significant. Historically, the Chushi Gangdrug army signifies a citizen-led national initiative, a military effort inspired by the need to defend community, religion, and the state. Ideologically, the national resistance army signaled a new version of Tibetan nationalism, one in which citizens rallied around the state but did so without sacrificing other identities. Defending Tibet did not mean forgoing one's Khampa or Amdowa or Töpa identity. Instead, counter to the dominant version of Tibetan nationalism that takes form around homogenized central Tibetan identities, this version of nationalism recognized region and nation as complementary rather than competing projects.

Chushi Gangdrug and the Tibetan Government

Among the numerous facts obscured by the arrest of resistance history is the involvement of the Tibetan government in the Chushi Gangdrug army. Given the political situation in the 1950s, this involvement was kept secret and vehemently denied, a policy continued through the early 1970s in exile. Even now the actual involvement of the Tibetan government is widely unknown, as is the degree to which the Dalai Lama knew about the resistance, the Tibetan government's involvement in it, and the support received from the governments of the United States, India, and Nepal. Some members of the Tibetan government covertly supported the resistance army, as did some within the governmental Tibetan army, but this support was not consistent among either group.

As a whole, the upper echelons of the Tibetan nobility who controlled Tibetan sociopolitical worlds did not support the efforts of the Chushi Gangdrug resistance. The central Tibetan aristocracy was of the genteel sort.[56] Aristocratic families, most of whom were centuries old, tended to be conservative, and many found themselves in the position of trying neither to appease nor oppose the Chinese excessively. As a result, men from aristocratic families did not join Chushi Gangdrug on their own, and the volunteer army did not seek to recruit such men.[57] In fact, in the case of recruiting men to be trained by the CIA, the resistance specifically chose to use "ordinary, sincere individuals" rather than the sons and relatives of the nobility.[58] Such class-based tensions further sparked the regional tensions already in place.[59] Part of the excitement of the new possibilities of participation in national events was breaking through the aristocratic stronghold on governmental service. The support of senior government officials such as Phala Dronyer Chenmo was crucial to the resistance in envisioning their contributions as being valuable to those in

power, including the Dalai Lama. As important as this support was, however, it is critical to remember that the Chushi Gangdrug army was an independent, nongovernmental organization.

The Chinese constantly pressured the Tibetan government to force the Chushi Gangdrug army to cease its activities. In response, the government would send emissaries to Chushi Gangdrug headquarters. One fourth-rank official sent from Lhasa was the aristocrat Namseling Paljor Jigme, who writes of the episode in his autobiography, "I had been involved in discussions with Andrug Gompo Tashi ever since he had begun gathering the Khampas together in Lhasa. When the Chinese Military head Tang Chin-u found out about my connection with the Khampa volunteer army, I received death threats several times. To my surprise, therefore, my name was included on the list that the Chinese submitted to the Dalai Lama through the Kashag for delegates to negotiate the end of the volunteer army's guerrilla warfare."[60] The delegation sent to Lhokha included Namseling, Tsekor Thubten Samchog, and representatives from Sera, Drepung, and Ganden monasteries. They carried with them an edict (*bka' rgya*) from the Kashag that had been drafted by the Chinese. Namseling writes that before he even left Lhasa, he decided he was going to join with Chushi Gangdrug, but he could not tell his wife or family about it because of the danger this decision involved.[61] Along with Thubten Samchog, he joined Chushi Gangdrug around the time of the newly organized army's first battle.[62]

Chushi Gangdrug's first battle took place at the end of August 1958 near the village of Nyemo Dukhak Sumdo.[63] The Tibetans were victorious, killing an estimated two hundred Chinese soldiers and wounding an unknown number; their own losses numbered forty dead and sixty-eight wounded.[64] After this battle, the volunteer army realized they needed more arms and ammunition and decided to go to the Tibetan government armory located west of Lhasa.[65] Sonam Gelek, from Gaba in Kham, was part of the eight-hundred-strong force that marched to the government army depot. Spirits were high, he recalls: "We would say that we will fight to kill or to be killed."[66] When the army arrived at the armory, the armory officials refused to turn over the arms and ammunition, as they had no orders from the Kashag to do so.[67] Only after several days of negotiating were the Chushi Gangdrug soldiers able to convince the officials to turn over the arms and ammunition; they staged their actions to look as if they had raided the weapons, so as not to get the officials into trouble.[68] The effort was worth it: from the armory the resistance acquired "two sets of 80mm mortar; eighteen lots of shells, each containing six shells; two sets of 60mm mortar, with sixteen lots of shells, each containing eighteen shells; ten Bren guns with five packets of shells each containing 2,660 shells; eighteen Sten guns; 385 '303' rifles; 378 bayonets; and sixty boxes of shells each containing 1,000 shells."[69]

Following the Nyemo battle and the resistance's raid on the armory, the Chinese authorities accused the Tibetan government of secretly supporting Chushi Gangdrug.[70] The government denied the charges; while they were providing covert assistance to the resistance, they were also still attempting to cooperate with the Chinese. In response, the Chinese replied that the Tibetan army, which was not militarily active at this point, should therefore be sent to attack Chushi Gangdrug.[71] In an effort to comply, the Tibetan government sent delegates to Chushi Gangdrug with orders to arrange a temporary cease-fire and called a meeting of all Tibetan government officials at the Norbulingka, the Dalai Lama's summer palace.[72] At this meeting, cabinet officials stated how the Chinese view of the Kashag had changed since Chushi Gangdrug's operations began and read aloud to the assembly letters that had been sent back and forth between the Tibetan government and Chushi Gangdrug.[73] Opinions were solicited in order of rank, highest to lowest, as to how to placate the Chinese authorities and settle the situation. Thubten Khentsun, who was present at this meeting, reports that whereas the top-ranking officials agreed that it was important to be "thoughtful and prudent," all officials from the fifth rank and below said they thought the Tibetans should protest against the Chinese.[74] One Tibetan army company commander, Gyapön Kelsang Dradhul, who had secretly pledged his loyalty to Chushi Gangdrug at Andrug Gompo Tashi's home, gave an especially impassioned plea: "We, the Tibetan army, have been trained and fed by the Tibetan government for this very purpose. We are ready to give our lives to defend our government and religion whenever the Tibetan government gives their order."[75] No resolution was reached, but the gap between the aristocrats who held the highest-ranking positions and the rest of the government officials, including aristocrats of lower social standing, was clearly growing. Among the nonaristocratic Tibetans who composed the resistance army, the gap was already vast.

The Burning Fire, 1958–1960

While the Chushi Gangdrug army battled the PLA, local uprisings and fighting continued around Tibet. Part of the Chushi Gangdrug–CIA plan was to provide support to these local pockets of resistance, and the first area to be helped was Lithang, Andrug Gompo Tashi's native territory.[76] In July 1958, CIA training was shifted to the United States. Ten men, all except one from Lithang, were sent for training. Lhamo Tsering, Gyalo Thondup's secretary and right-hand man, accompanied them as translator.[77] Over the next three years, eight teams of CIA-trained soldiers parachuted into Tibet, often in remote areas where local troops needed assistance. Not all of these missions were militarily successful, but they were vital in spreading the message that the outside world (although not the CIA or the United States by name) was supporting Tibet. In addition, the CIA made over thirty airdrops of weapons, ammunition, radios, medical supplies, hand-operated printing presses, and other goods to Chushi Gangdrug teams between 1958 and 1961.[78] Statements written by Chushi Gangdrug soldiers for distribution throughout Tibet such as the "Proclamation of the Tibetan Volunteer Army for Defense of Religion" were sometimes included in the airdrops to rally local support.

Fighting continued throughout the fall of 1958. Chushi Gangdrug troops fought in Lhokha and also headed east into Kham for a series of battles. Despite the CIA airdrops and provisions from India carried on foot by soldiers, the resistance army was running low on supplies. Soldiers soon outnumbered the available arms and ammunition. Whenever possible, the troops would claim weapons from government depots or salvage them from battles in which the Chinese had retreated, leaving behind their weapons. The CIA was seen as a sponsor of their efforts, but with the exception of the CIA-trained parachute teams, Chushi Gangdrug operations were very much controlled by Andrug Gompo Tashi and his team of officers. In early 1959, they decided they needed additional help and sent a delegation to India to try to gain further assistance from the outside world and to raise needed funds from Khampa traders in India; the delegation consisted of Jagod Namgyal Dorje of Derge, Sadhu Lobsang Nyandak of Trehor, and Janga Chozak from Lithang.[79] Two months later, things were to change drastically.

In early March of 1959, Chinese officials invited the Dalai Lama to attend a theatrical show alone at a PLA military camp. As told to me by a number of resistance soldiers, the general public immediately feared that the Chinese were planning something sinister. It would be unusual for the Dalai Lama to travel to Chinese grounds and highly unusual to do so without his usual entourage of attendants. Rumors of a kidnap attempt began to fly about Lhasa, and plans were made to prevent any possible harm coming to the Dalai Lama. Crowds of angry people, including armed Chushi Gangdrug soldiers, gathered outside the Norbulingka on the morning of 10 March, the day the Dalai Lama was to attend the show. The Dalai Lama did not leave the Norbulingka, and the crowd kept up their vigil for the next few days. Anti-Chinese sentiment grew, and rumors surfaced that the Chinese were going to attack the demonstrators. Rumors turned to reality on 16 March.

For two days, the Chinese fired on the crowds with guns and cannons. On the evening of the seventeenth, the Dalai Lama secretly left the Norbulingka dressed as a layperson. He and his small entourage were led out of Lhasa by Tibetan army officers to a river crossing, where they met up with a Chushi Gangdrug unit led by Ratuk Ngawang that escorted them on their three-week escape to India. Athar Norbu and Lotse, the two radio operators who had been trained by the CIA in Saipan, joined them along the way. Meanwhile, back in Lhasa, no one knew the Dalai Lama had escaped. The Tibetan public, including many monks, continued to defend the Norbulingka in the belief the Dalai Lama was still inside. Two days after the Dalai Lama's escape, the Chinese began to bomb the city, heavily shelling the Norbulingka, the Potala (the Dalai Lama's primary palace, monastery, and seat of the Tibetan government), and many other buildings across Lhasa. Thousands of people were killed. Just west of Lhasa, at Sera Monastery, the monks could hear the bombing.

Tenchoe, who was then a monk at Sera recalls that day: "Early in the morning, we heard firing. About one thousand monks from Sera went to Lhasa to fight. At about nine o'clock in the morning, I removed my monk's robe and put on a chuba [*phyu pa*], a traditional Tibetan robe with a belt. Then I left. In Lhasa, the Chinese were using cannons indiscriminately, firing at the public. Later that day, they fired cannons at Sera Monastery. For three days we stayed in the main hall of the monastery and then escaped one evening. On the way, we saw many dead bodies. We finally arrived in Lhokha, where we joined Chushi Gangdrug. We fought with them until we could no longer oppose the Chinese; then we went to India."[80] After this turn of events, so many monks from Sera, Drepung, and Ganden monasteries fled Lhasa and joined with Chushi Gangdrug that the resistance army was composed of approximately equal numbers of monks and laymen.

In other parts of Tibet fighting continued. The number of PLA soldiers continued to grow, and Chushi Gangdrug units found themselves repeatedly retreating. The situation was aggravated by the fact that more people than ever were on the move—families with salvaged belongings and livestock were moving in groups large and small toward India. In April, Andrug Gompo Tashi decided that the resistance army should cross over into India to regroup and make plans for continued fighting. On 29 April 1959, he and approximately two thousand Chushi Gangdrug soldiers entered India, turning over their arms and ammunition to the Indian authorities.[81] In recognition of the resistance army's service in escorting him safely to India, the Dalai Lama awarded Andrug Gompo Tashi with the title of *dza sag*, equivalent to an official of the third rank in the Tibetan government.[82] Once in India, the resistance entered a new stage. While CIA-trained teams continued to parachute into Tibet and localized resistance against the Chinese continued, the Chushi Gangdrug volunteer army now became an army in exile.

Retreating into India was not something the soldiers had anticipated. In retrospect, many veterans commented on how they believed they would defeat the Chinese. The following quote from Sonam Gelek is representative of the sentiments of many:

> At that time, I was about thirty-one years old. I was rather young, and was also courageous. We talked about how we must fight against the Chinese. We felt we could handle them, and we thought of returning to our native place after our victory. At that time we did not know the real situation. We did not know the tremendous number of Chinese soldiers that we were to fight. We, the Khampas, were stubborn and had not particularly thought about the consequences of war with the Chinese. My wife and children stayed in Lhasa. They told me not to go fight against the Chinese. They said that we would be no match for

them. My wife cried and asked me not to leave her. She also reminded me that we might not meet again after my departure. However, I said that I must go fight for our country and countrymen. I never felt that I would die during the war.[83]

Sonam Gelek survived the fighting, as did his wife and son, who both managed to escape to India. Many others did not survive. In some cases, entire battalions were killed, and certain territories suffered more casualties than others. The veteran Thubten Thargy estimates that of the five hundred or so men from Kongpo who fought against the Chinese only a handful survived.[84] For the survivors, multiple battles remained, including the battle not to forget those who had died.

To all Tibetans from the three regions:

Our nation, Tibet, has been independent for thousands of years....

[The Chinese Communists] destroyed all the monasteries in Kham
    and started such practices in U-Tsang also. Therefore Khampas
    and Amdowas revolted and settled in the Lhokha region....

All Tibetans living in Tibet should unite themselves, avoid the
    Chinese Communists' deceptions, and cherish our patriotism
    until Tibet regains its independence....

I pray for those who lost their lives for Tibetan freedom and for
    those who are suffering. With the blessing of the Three Jewels
    and inexorable karmic consequences, we can trust that the sun
    of Tibetan independence and happiness shall soon rise.

THE DALAI LAMA, 20TH DAY OF THE 6TH MONTH IN THE
YEAR OF THE EARTH PIG (1959)

Every Chushi Gangdrug soldier carried a photo of the Dalai Lama
with the above message inscribed on it in their *tson-sung* (*mtshon
srung*) protective amulet box. Although the message was one the
Dalai Lama had delivered to all Tibetans, many soldiers interpreted
it as speaking directly to them. For them, it was a clear statement
from the Dalai Lama of the righteousness of their actions, of the
need for Tibetans to defend Tibet on behalf of the Dalai Lama, and
of the need for unity in these efforts. This communiqué from the
Dalai Lama still resonates with Chushi Gangdrug veterans, especially given all that has happened in the past several decades. The

FIGURE 16 Image of His Holiness the fourteenth Dalai Lama carried by resistance soldiers (front)

FIGURE 17 Message from the Dalai Lama carried by resistance soldiers (back)

Dalai Lama's visible agitation with internal politics in the exile community, including resistance politics, is tempered somewhat by veterans' knowledge that privately, if not publicly, he and some members of the Tibetan government supported Chushi Gangdrug from its earliest days onward.

Such private support is referenced through the veterans' consent to the arrest of resistance. Veterans often express concern and empathy for the difficult position the Dalai Lama is in. Their consent to historical arrest is directly linked to its blunt connection to the Dalai Lama. This connection relies on community interpretation of the Dalai Lama's words, actions, and decisions as much as on his direct admonishments to the refugee community regarding proper behavior. Consent is most often explained through ideas of community welfare, particularly of what will benefit the community in its attempt to regain Tibet. In line with Buddhist notions of accumulating merit, the concept of beneficial action (*phan thogs*) is of prime importance to many Tibetans. People frequently use the word "phan thogs" to talk about whether "telling this or that history will not be beneficial" or if so-and-so "has done work that has benefited the community." Veterans see their participation in the resistance, specifically their defense of the Dalai Lama and the nation, as an example of such beneficial action. Although opinions may vary on what actually benefits community, in general what is beneficial is anything that is believed to benefit the Dalai Lama.

Every year on 10 March the Dalai Lama makes a public statement to the Tibetan people commemorating the uprising of 1959 in Lhasa. Of his first such statement in 1960, he explained, "I stressed the need for my people to take a long-term view of the situation in Tibet. For those of us in exile, I said that our priority must be resettlement and the continuity of our cultural traditions. As to the future, I stated my belief that, with Truth, Justice, and Courage as our weapons, we Tibetans would eventually prevail in regaining freedom for Tibet."[1] The "long-term view" suggests a temporal approach compatible with historical arrest: the delay of certain things, actions, and acknowledgments until some future time. Established in his first statement were the still-prevalent goals of maintaining cultural traditions and regaining Tibet through the righteousness of the cause rather than through military defense. The Dalai Lama's public statements are closely analyzed by Tibetans as much for what he does not say as for what he does. Learning how to listen to the Dalai Lama is a cultural skill; throughout the diaspora, parents such as Lobsang Tinley educate their children on just how to interpret and implement the Dalai Lama's wishes.

In terms of Chushi Gangdrug, the Dalai Lama speaks mostly privately, if at all, to Tibetan audiences. Publicly, he acknowledged the resistance in his two autobiographies—*My Land and My People* (1962), and *Freedom in Exile* (1990).[2] In 1962, he expressed his admiration for the Khampa "guerrilla fighters," for their bravery in trying to "save our religion and country in the only remaining way they could see," yet he also shared his fears that their efforts would pale in the face of Chinese atrocities and violence. In 1990, he again tells the story of the fighters, mentions the CIA for the first time, and calls the resistance movement "one of the saddest episodes in the history of the Tibetan diaspora."[3] He explains that he did not know the entire story of the resistance: "On more than one occasion, I tried to discover detailed information about [the resistance], but I have never heard the full story."[4]

In an interview conducted in 1975, a Western journalist asked the Dalai Lama about the Tibetan fighters who had been stationed in Mustang, Nepal. Although the connection to the CIA was still denied at that time, the Dalai Lama spoke about the soldiers as follows: "It's difficult to comment. I have sympathy for the people who formed this group. They sacrificed a good deal. I have met some and exchanged letters with others. . . . It certainly helped to boost the morale of Tibetans in Tibet and to make them feel that the exiles were doing something. It's not a question of whether I approved or not. Events were such that the resistance came into existence in any case. In the overall struggle we have nothing to hide. Put clearly the true situation. That is my request."[5] At that time, the Dalai Lama himself did not know the entirety of the "true situation." As he explained in 1990, much about the resistance was kept secret from him. Thus, although he says there was "nothing to hide," his knowledge of the situation was most likely partial. Even today, putting the true situation forward remains difficult for reasons beyond the involvement of the CIA. Although the history of the resistance is finally starting to be told, it remains a public secret with repercussions both very real and very raw for the individuals and communities involved.

The morning of 16 June 1999 seemed like any other in Dharamsala. People of all ages rose early and headed to the main temple complex to perform kora and make offerings. Walking down the paved ridge roads and forest paths to the temple were families, couples, and groups of older men, each carrying *khatas* (*kha btags*, white silk offering scarves) and bags filled with juniper incense. They all wore the respectful dress Tibetans don for social and religious occasions: a chuba and apron for married women and either a chuba or Western dress for the men, standard attire in Lhasa. Although it was early, the morning was already saturated with the warmth that precedes the monsoon, and the mood was festive as people joked, chatted, and greeted old friends. Although it could have been almost any day, it was not; it was the forty-first anniversary of the founding of the Chushi Gangdrug resistance army on 16 June 1958.

Throughout South Asia, resistance veterans and their families gather on the sixteenth of June. Speeches and offerings are made and prayers are said for the Dalai Lama, for the protection of Tibet and Tibetans, and in honor of the martyrs of the Tibetan resistance movement, especially Andrug Gompo Tashi. In the Dharamsala ceremony I witnessed, veterans made offerings to portraits of the Dalai Lama and Andrug Gompo Tashi and raised the resistance flag next to the flag of Tibet; Chushi Gangdrug leaders gave speeches. A key reference point in the ceremony was the gold throne the resistance gave to the Dalai Lama in 1957. The gift of the throne was designed to express "the people's loyalty and confidence in the Dalai Lama's leadership and [to] confirm his earthly sovereign powers" in light of growing Chinese political oppression.[6] In the minds of resistance veterans, the gift of this throne unequivocally demonstrated their devotion to the Dalai Lama and to a unified Tibet. The anniversary on 16 June, however, is commemorated only by resistance veterans and their families. Other members of the Tibetan community do not mark the day with any special fanfare; indeed, many are not even aware of it. Instead, they celebrate the tenth of March, Tibetan Uprising Day.[7]

Along with the Tibetan New Year and the Dalai Lama's birthday, 10 March is one of the primary Tibetan holidays in exile.[8] It is specifically a political holiday: in all diaspora locations except Nepal, it is marked by

FIGURE 18 Raising the Chushi Gangdrug flag, 16 June 1999, Dharamsala.

FIGURE 19 Chushi Gangdrug (Dharamsala) leader, Tashi Dorjee, with offering table, 16 June 1998.

marches of slogan-shouting Tibetans and Tibetan supporters of all ages, by political posters, awareness programs, newspaper editorials, protests at Chinese embassies and consulates, and by the Dalai Lama's annual statement of 10 March.[9] Yet for some veterans of the resistance, the tenth of March commemoration is an inadequate substitute for a holiday recognizing the organized resistance army. As one veteran told me, "March 10th is not so important. It was not the real fight for Tibet."

Most veterans celebrate both the holidays of the sixteenth of June and the tenth of March. However, the lack of public recognition of the sixteenth of June is a sore spot for many veterans. They realize that community rituals, school holidays, and so forth publicly mark the category of national history. As the sociologist Paul Connerton argues, such commemorative ceremonies and the bodily practices associated with them are crucial for passing on memories across generations.[10] A young Khampa woman in Delhi would agree with him: "The younger generation does not know resistance history. It is not taught in schools. This is because the past is controlled by the same people who control the present." The people "who control the present," she implies, are neither resistance veterans nor individuals sympathetic to them. Despite veterans' efforts to continually demonstrate allegiance to the Dalai Lama and to Tibet, the resistance remains unknown or controversial in exile. The Dalai Lama, for example, does not attend the ceremony of 16 June in Dharamsala; his absence is one means by which historical arrest is communicated. The sixteenth of June is a nonevent for the larger Tibetan community.

If the event is that which can be narrated, as the historian Hayden White contends, then what happens to events that cannot be narrated?[11] Is historical recognition predicated on narratability, and if so, then where do nonevents fit into history? As multiple scholars have argued, events are real not because they happened but because they are told in culturally meaningful ways.[12] Historical arrest works by withdrawing the culturally meaningful frameworks that would validate the national significance of events or histories. Not all experiences require narration, and meaning is not located only in narration. In the context of resistance histories and veterans' desires for recognition, the categorization of the resistance as a historical event matters. However, although cultural meaning is actively divorced from certain events and histories, this does not mean arrested histories solely pass the time of arrest as unnarratable nonevents. Commemorations of the founding of the Chushi Gangdrug resistance demonstrate that such struggles over nation and narration illuminate the importance of the past as a form of present-day politics.

In "The Return of the Event, Again," Marshall Sahlins suggests that historical events consist only of actions that "change the order of things."[13] In Sahlins's synthetic view of event and structure, events alter the structural relations and forces through which they are constituted. Arrested histories challenge the order of things, but events change them. The categorizing of resistance history as nonevent places it in a liminal state between challenge and change such that its transformative potential is defused. At present, the Tibetan national past is constructed as a simplified version of history with room for external, but not internal, conflict. Chushi Gangdrug problematically presents a history of both—of external conflict with China and of internal conflict ranging from Tibetan government debates in the 1950s over whether or not to support the resistance to contemporary debates on the Internet over the place of the resistance in Tibetan history.[14]

Most happenings quietly reproduce already existing cultural formations. Things take place, they happen, and then gently slip away as time passes. Converting happenings to events or nonevents is to work both with and against already existing conditions, and thus requires active, if not necessarily visible labor. Even those "acts that might appear as fruits of absolute contingency" are in fact given life through histories, institutions, and the everyday.[15] As Veena Das explains, "The everyday grows the event."[16]

Everyday life in Dharamsala grows events and nonevents such as the sixteenth of June commemoration. Nonevents rest uneasily in the everyday. They drape themselves in the garb of events—speeches, flags, offerings, gatherings—but are not recognized as such. Yet for some people the epistemological stuff of nonevents such as feelings, memories, knowledge, and dreams is an indispensable part of what makes the everyday habitable. This is the contradiction of hegemonies, that one must live such contradictions rather than be fully anaesthetized to them—live, that is, with memories that have structurally been forgotten. Everyone does this differently; some do it more quietly than others, some more successfully than others. Each, however, acknowledges that happenings such as the sixteenth of June are not events in a national sense. If "events bring about historical changes in part by transforming the very cultural catego-ries that shape and constrain human action," many veterans are only too aware they remain shaped and constrained by the very cultural categories they sought to transform.[17] Forgetting the sixteenth of June into non-event status, however, is itself an active process, one in which renewal pushes up against delayed transformation.

Theorizing Forgetting

Forgetting is not an absence of memory. It is not a neutral or passive state, but an active process, a state of becoming, a goal worked toward rather than an immediate or wholesale elimination of knowledge or expe-rience or thought. Traces always remain. Forgetting is as social as remem-bering; it is composed of similar parts and processes, residing in and indebted to similar social landscapes, political projects, historical times, and cultural frameworks.[18] From Halbwachs to Connerton, theorists of memory contend that remembering is a social process, a collective expe-rience (albeit one often intimately associated with the individual), and a process communally and individually reinforced in multiple arenas: cul-tural, physical, political, emotional, and so on.[19]

Even in collective form—or collected form, as some scholars prefer—memory is perhaps better thought of as memories, as existing in the plural rather than the singular.[20] A social theory of memory always pre-sumes a countermemory, or if not alternative memories, then at least parallel ones, that is, multiple memories existing in the same time–space continuum, drawing on the same political energy and cultural system in an effort to direct not just historical accounts of the past, but historical outcomes in the present and future. Crucial to an understanding of memory is an analysis of its processual aspect, of the various ways in which certain pasts are remembered and codified as history (or as memo-rable in some other way).[21] At the same time, however, in assessing what is remembered and how and why it is remembered, one would do well to consider what is forgotten in the process. In the case of the Tibetan resistance, forgetting matters as much, if not more, than memory and countermemory.

Theories of forgetting tend to center around its productive nature rather than its vanishing one. In a productive mode, forgetting one thing clears a space for the remembering of another thing. As Debbora Battaglia argues, forgetting might very well "give rise to society," enabling "not oblivion but an experience of sociality."[22] Drawing on her fieldwork in Papua New Guinea, Battaglia explores practices of acknowledged and unacknowledged social forgetting. Her concept of unacknowledged forgetting, that to which attention is not drawn and is made to look "not-forgotten," yet has a "persistent non-presence" is especially useful in trying to assess the multiple and complex registers in which forgetting takes place.[23] In the case of the Tibetan resistance, memories of the guerrilla war are never forgotten among certain groups of community, while other groups might never have had knowledge of them in the first place. The persistent nonpresence of this forgotten history is not consistent across the community. Instead it ducks and darts through time and space, wildly present in some locations, peoples, and times and quietly absent in others.

The commemoration of 16 June of Chushi Gangdrug's founding is one example of such forgetting. If not all Tibetans in exile are aware of the sixteenth of June ceremonies, absolutely everyone is familiar with the tenth of March anniversary. As veterans perceive things, this remembering includes related forgettings: "On March 10th, when the people voluntarily rose up, this was all because of Chushi Gangdrug and Andrug Gompo Tashi. They guarded the Potala and the people joined in. This was the first time that Chushi Gangdrug was supported by all the people. In Tibetan history, they don't say this, that Chushi Gangdrug started it. They only say that this was the first time that all the people rose up, but it was Chushi Gangdrug that started it, and the people joined them."[24] Collective forgetting of such origins makes sense in light of the practice of arrested history. Who was going to agitate for 10 March activities to include acknowledgment of Chushi Gangdrug? The precariousness of refugee status does not allow much room for such protests. Living with such restrictions is to pace oneself via the "persistent non-presence" of resistance history, awaiting the time when their historical experiences and knowledge will be collectively validated. Until then, veterans pass the time in unremarkable ways, sitting and reading scripture, as Baba Lekshey does in his small, dimly lit room on the top floor of an old house at the top of a ridge in Kalimpong, where, he says, the air is fresh and the breezes good.[25]

In the rush to study collective memory, anthropologists have been criticized for losing sight of the individual. David Berliner critiques the

"overextension" of the concept of memory, suggesting that current scholarship considers only how memory or forgetting serves the continuity or
reproduction of any given society.[26] As a result, he argues that we miss the
individual memory holder in favor of solely assessing the social place of
memory.[27] My reading of the anthropology of memory literature is less
narrow and more aligned with Jennifer Cole's assessment of the field.[28]
She suggests that current work on social memory does not bypass the
individual but instead provides anthropology with the means to take a
new and recuperated look at the relationship between society and the
individual: "Memory connects the individual and private with the social
and public in complex ways. As such, memory remains a key site at which
one can witness the multiple ways in which individual subjectivity is tied
to larger projects of political struggle and historical transformation."[29]
Contra to Berliner's critique, Cole sees the anthropology of memory as
assessing not just social reproduction, but also "the historical constitution of the remembering subject."[30] This constitutive process is culturally
and historically specific, varying not just across cultures but also across
individuals.[31] That is, there is never a "total fit" between individual and
collective memory.[32] Instead, drawing on the interdisciplinary work of
memory scholars from across the twentieth century, Cole contends that
individuals use and internalize culturally produced memory in different
ways such that even the most universally shared collective memories are
often porous and short-lived.[33]

Tibetan practices of historical production bear this out: individuals
are impacted by collective forgetting but do not necessarily entirely suc-
cumb to it. Veterans of the guerrilla war accept to varying degrees the
arrest of resistance history, but this does not mean they forget the past. In
accepting that resistance history has been arrested, veterans continue to
remember the war privately or in closely delineated public settings. Remembering, however, does not negate forgetting. As veterans made clear
to me, forgetting occupies spaces that might otherwise be filled with
knowledge.

Knowledge, Narration, and Genre

Histories of the resistance do not occupy a singular genre. Individuals are
flexible with their categorizations of them. Of the three primary Tibetan
historical forms, people most commonly used the category *lo rgyus* for

resistance histories. Lo rgyus, literally, the "tiding of the years," tends to "present a narrative of events, historical, quasi-historical, or even ahistorical, in rough chronological sequence."[34] As narrated to me, lo rgyus could be the product of one's personal experience or knowledge learned from others as well as what one would consider event or place history. In practice, lo rgyus was a narrative of experience and most often a historical, nonchronological one. At other times, the same type of narrative histories were described as *sgrung*, a word that translates into English as "story." Sgrung are not assumed a priori to be fictional rather than factual; indeed, Tibetans who described their own or others' historical narratives as sgrung consistently spoke of them as being factual.[35] If the veterans did distinguish between lo rgyus/ historical narration and sgrung/story, it was to imply that story makes weaker claims to historical authority than history.

Veterans narrate their histories onto surfaces primed for different stories than the ones they keep. Dorje Yudon, for example, the woman who led the uprising in Nyarong, told her history with an awareness that the production of history is a process to which people have unequal access. As the anthropologist Michel-Rolph Trouillot explains, the production of history is concrete, not abstract, and as such involves people as differently positioned and privileged agents, actors, and subjects.[36] The making of history, the remembering of events, and the forgetting of the same are all social practices and are habitual in that they are unconsciously folded into everyday social life.[37] Habit is a tactic of hegemonies in making only certain things expected and other things not.

"When I tell my story, it sounds like hearsay," Dorje Yudon said to me as I began the formal part of my interview with her in 1997. As I did with most of my interviewees, we chatted and drank tea before I turned on the tape recorder. I had visited Dorje Yudon's home in New Delhi several times; I knew one of her sons, the Dalai Lama's Special Envoy, Lodi Gyari, and had interviewed her husband several times as well. Our conversation took place in the presence of her daughter-in-law and, part of the time, of her elder sister, Norzin Lhamo. Like so many of the histories shared with me, that of Dorje Yudon is known by few people.

Those who do know her story are usually from her area of Nyarong or have connections to her husband or children. One veteran from another part of Kham told me she was a "real heroine who fought a lot and fought bravely," while others knew only that she had a story to tell (as opposed to knowing what the story was). Awareness that one's past is not yet history does not close down memories or eventual narrations. The notion of beneficial action, of service to the Dalai Lama, always holds promise for potential narrators. When people tell stories that trouble the status quo, their narrations are made in reference—and in deference—to the Dalai Lama. Unease is usually unavoidable. For example, knowing that her story was not known, Dorje Yudon said that voicing it felt like "hearsay" rather than history. She was not the only one to feel this way.

"This is the first time I have told my story," one veteran said to me. "I haven't even told it to my children. I always thought that maybe people wouldn't believe it."[38] Even among intimate acquaintances, these histories are not always shared or, if shared, believed. If known, they are considered to belong personally to oneself or to one's uncle or husband and so on rather than to reside in the category of legitimate national or state history. No one spoke of these histories as *rgyal rabs*, or "royal chronology," which refers to state or official history.[39] Instead, they exist as lo rgyus or as sgrung or as still tentative, unnamed, unnarrated genres. They do not have the well-polished sheen of family stories passed down through the generations or traded over the years between friends. At the end of my interview with Dorje Yudon, her daughter-in-law thanked me, saying she had never heard these stories before and adding that usually they just sat around "gossiping and talking about the weather." Spaces filled with such small talk are not ahistorical (or asocial).[40] They are, instead, part and process of historical production, revealing the cultural intertwining of a delayed temporality and a cautioned sociality.

Gendered Battlefields, Gendered Histories

Gender matters to historical production.[41] Culture orders history through limits on the possible such that history is made, unmade, and made sense of through the normative frameworks of any given culture or society. Gender is as central an axis as any other—class, ethnicity, region, religion, and so forth—in animating this process. Yet in Tibet as a general (and gendered) rule, women's narratives claim and are allotted smaller amounts of historical authority than men's narratives.[42] Janet Gyatso and Hanna Havnevik suggest that women and their histories are simply not a part of Tibetan historical literature from the earliest periods up to the present day.[43] That is, regardless of the time period involved, Tibetan women's histories are mostly unnarrated and unknown even within the Tibetan community. As one Tibetan woman explained to me, the sentiment in exile is that women's issues will be addressed once the political struggle is won. Despite the various cultural forces contriving against the telling of women's histories or Khampa histories or histories of resistance, Dorje Yudon tells her story not just as a personal tale but as part of a bigger history. She says, "In Kham, these may have been only minor revolts, but together they were part of larger events." Like the Chushi Gangdrug veterans who tell their stories as part of Tibetan history—albeit gently and respectfully, given the arrest of resistance history—she tells her story with culturally generated limits of politics and gender in mind.

Bu mo gcig kyang yod ma red ("There was not one woman"). These simple words eliminate women from the Tibetan resistance army. Lobsang Tinley was the first to tell me this, to claim that there "was not even one woman" within the Chushi Gangdrug army. The force of his statement surprised me, and over the course of interviews with other veterans the same sentiment and tone were voiced repeatedly. Baba Lekshey and Lobsang Jampa and many others all claimed the same thing: there were no women in the resistance. Yet Dorje Yudon and other women such as Ama Adhe, Ani Pachen, and Beri Lhaga had fought in Tibet.[44] Women organized villagers' uprisings, fought against Chinese troops, and aided the resistance army in invaluable ways. So why were they not considered a part of the Chushi Gangdrug army? Why were the veterans so adamant about this exclusion? As they explained, it had to do with the particularly dangerous feminine combination of power and pollution.[45] For Tibetans, the female form is inherently impure, but menstruation and the blood associated with childbirth or miscarriage are wildly impure and highly polluting. The ability to reproduce renders women physically and morally dangerous, not just to men but to the cultural and spiritual order.[46] If women are disempowered by their impurity, they nevertheless draw a dangerous power, a latent power, from this very impurity.

Battlefields in Tibet were places of war, survival, and religion. Many soldiers consulted with their lamas before going into battle and prayed throughout the battles they fought in. All Chushi Gangdrug soldiers wore a tson-sung amulet. These vary in shape, size, and form but are commonly stylized metal boxes of several inches in diameter with fancy metalwork on the outside, a glassed window for a photograph of a high lama, and an open space inside for blessing objects, prayers, precious pills, religious photographs and images, and the like, including a copy of the Dalai Lama's message. Once consecrated, a tson-sung will protect one against many things, including pollution, misfortune, and harm by weapons.[47] Veterans claim that Chushi Gangdrug soldiers wore many blessed cords and often several tson-sung during the fighting with the Chinese. As one veteran claimed, "Back then if you shook out someone's chuba, lots of tson-sung would fall out!"

Chushi Gangdrug soldiers filled their protective amulets with a variety of blessing items. Blessed objects from the Dalai Lama were considered especially powerful. A pill called 'jigs byed ma lhe blessed by the Dalai Lama and a precious pill from the Dromo Geshe Rinpoche were renowned for their potency. The Dreru Shabdrung distributed pieces of his shoe straps on the battlefield, Gangkhar Lama gave soldiers "iron pills" from mountains considered to be powerful places in the Tibetan religious landscape (for example, from gter sites), and other lamas distributed centuries-old hairs believed to be those of dakinis, or female deities. Commonly worn under the clothes, on one's skin, soldiers believed the tson-sung made them bulletproof in battle.[48] Such protective blessings required faith along with consecration. Many soldiers could not resist testing their tson-sung. I was told several stories of men putting their amulet onto a yak or sheep and then shooting at the animal from a distance. Although some animals were hit by the bullets, never once, so it is claimed, did an animal die. But even the strongest protective powers and most devout soldiers were not immune to two feared elements. If a bullet had gold in its tip or if it was dipped in women's menstrual blood, then the protective powers of the tson-sung were canceled.[49] A gold-tipped or blood-dipped bullet would kill you.

The highest of lamas, so the veterans claimed, did not have protection against bullets dipped in or filled with women's menstrual blood or gold. According to some veterans, the PLA troops knew this and would collect menstrual blood in which they dipped their bullets.[50] While I have not been able to determine why gold was considered so fatally efficacious on the battlefield,[51] menstrual blood has a long cultural history of pollution in Tibetan society, and soldiers were ordered to keep away from menstruating women in general.[51] Menstrual blood was one of the most

powerful forms of contamination, or *grib*, and had what the soldiers considered to be very real physical repercussions as well as critical
social ones.[52]

The power attributed to menstrual blood by the Chushi Gangdrug
soldiers has societal links in religious prohibitions forbidding menstruating women (and sometimes women in general) from being present in
sacred sites.[53] Such religious and social "anxieties about [women's] un-
controllable sexuality" have real effects on the lives, histories, and bodies
of Tibetan women.[54] Before going into battle, Chushi Gangdrug soldiers
were prohibited from having sexual relations with women. To do so, it
was believed, would render useless one's protective blessings from injury
or death on the battlefield. This fear was communal since an individual's
transgression would affect his entire battalion. As a result, a ban on sexual
intercourse with women was one of the twenty-seven rules of conduct for
the soldiers.[55] Such institutionalized beliefs reinforce a philosophical and
cultural relegation of women to a lower status than men. Women are *skye
dman*, or "lower born."[56] In her ethnography of a nunnery in Ladakh, Kim
Gutschow argues that gender is not just a "significant . . . fault line in
Buddhist discourse," but also a hierarchical project in which male (and
specifically monastic) power is built upon, and at times built by, the
female body.[57] Tibetan history rests on and reproduces this gendered
fault line.

Women reproduced it as well. In addressing women's role in the resistance, Dorje Yudon differentiated between the uprisings in Kham and
the later formation of the Chushi Gangdrug army. She agreed with the
veterans that women fought only in the uprisings, not in the army's
battles. She explained this as owing to the fact that Chushi Gangdrug was
meant to specifically defend and protect the Dalai Lama: "So, since it was
meant for His Holiness the Dalai Lama's personal security, it was composed only of men."[58] The cultural inappropriateness of women protecting the Dalai Lama was self-evident, and for Dorje Yudon that fact did
not need explanation. While normalization may cancel explanation, however, it does not prevent action or narration. Dorje Yudon, of course, is
not the only woman who fought on the battlefield. Adhe Tapontsang, for
example, tells in her memoir of how women in Kanze formed an underground group to coordinate actions against the Chinese, primarily to

support men who had taken to the mountains.[59] Stories such as hers, however, remain separate from that of the Tibetan resistance army.

Women may not have served in the Chushi Gangdrug army, but they did fight in Kham, and they do participate in remembering Chushi Gangdrug histories. Women participate in the ceremony of the sixteenth of June, they debate the past and its politics with their husbands and friends, they share or do not share their stories of war and life. Nonetheless, histories of the Tibetan resistance are gendered male; cultural logics set this process in place long before the first PLA soldier stepped on Tibetan ground. Until the gendered aspects of resistance history and historical production are recognized, the unfinished histories of the Tibetan resistance will remain even more incomplete than they already are.

Starting in April 1959, Chushi Gangdrug battalions crossed the border into India. Four decades later, veterans, still feeling acutely the poignancy of leaving Tibet, told me about this moment as if it had happened the day before. Lobsang Palden explained how they were required to turn over their weapons to the Indian border guards: "Our guns were so beautiful, not like the ones the Indians had, and we just threw them like pieces of wood onto big piles."[1] The Tibetans also had to give up their beloved horses, which they sold for "throw-away prices" according to Lobsang Jampa.[2] These losses incurred at the border were the soldiers' initial impression of India. Unfortunately, things did not improve from there.

Most Tibetans who escaped into India followed the route taken by the Dalai Lama. This was a southeasterly route from Lhasa, not the most direct route, and one that ended in Mon Tawang, a forested area of northeastern India in the state of Arunachal Pradesh, close to the border with Assam. The government of India set up transit camps for the refugees in the towns of Misamari and Bomdila. The climate there could not have been more different from Tibet's dry and arid plateaus or even the deep mountain valleys in Kham. The first groups of refugees, suffering from the humid, hot, malarial climate, did not fare well in India. For them, it was a place of sickness and death, of unfamiliar food and unfamiliar people. It was a different country altogether. Most refugees who arrived in India expected their situation to be temporary. Like the relentless

FIGURE 20 Refugee camps in Misamari. Photo by Tsepon Shakabpa, courtesy of Jigme Deden Shakabpa and the Center for South Asia at the University of Wisconsin.

heat and humidity, however, India seemed to close in around them, and hopes of a quick return to Tibet diminished each day.

Colonies of large bamboo shelters were constructed to accommodate the thousands of Tibetans who fled into India; each housed around one hundred people. Rations that included rice, wheat, flour, oil, vegetables, and weekly portions of meat were provided by the government of India. Those who had money left quickly, heading to Kalimpong and Darjeeling. Monks and lamas were sent to Buxar, West Bengal, and then on to Mussoorie, where they studied English along with Buddhist scriptures. Most Tibetans, however, were in Misamari or Bomdila for many months, some for years. Schools were opened for those between the ages of fifteen and twenty-five, including a Chushi Gangdrug school in which Tibetan and Hindi were taught.[3] Adult men and women worked in road construction in the surrounding areas, for which they were paid up to two rupees per day.[4] Many Tibetans arrived in India in bad condition—the

513-351-6917 Dina

physical and emotional toll of the journey was great, and health problems, in conjunction with the difficulties of the hot climate and physical labor, plagued the burgeoning refugee community. People remember the temporary hospital in Misamari as being always full.[5] During the monsoon, everything and everyone was constantly wet, and many individuals had no change of clothes. Day-to-day survival was as much a priority in the beginning as strategizing a return to Tibet.

The Regrouping of Chushi Gangdrug in Exile

Tibetans' belief that they would return to Tibet were not naïve. Many of the soldiers and certainly the Chushi Gangdrug leadership were aware that Tibet and the world at large were in a time of great change. Formerly colonized countries were now independent, and shifts in the realm of the possible were globally visible. Many Tibetans found themselves with new civic duties in India, including giving testimony to the *Tibet Mirror* and to government officials, or with new roles as community leaders in refugee camps or in relations with local communities. These new responsibilities translated into a new sense of national community. It was against this backdrop of the new with its possibilities and tensions, of the internal tensions and logistical problems of refugee life, and of continuing fighting in Tibet that Chushi Gangdrug operations in exile took shape.

Immediately after arriving in India, a number of Chushi Gangdrug soldiers held a meeting to discuss their future. Most soldiers wanted to return to Tibet to fight. Some, including Gyari Nyima from Nyarong, argued against returning to Tibet: "I said, 'That would be great if we could return to Tibet, but we wouldn't be any match for the Chinese.' Andrug Gompo Tashi appreciated what I said. Others were getting emotionally carried away, but I felt that we needed to be realistic."[6] Realism was the model followed, and the resistance dispersed throughout northeast India rather than return to Tibet. Andrug Gompo Tashi and some of the wealthier members went to Kalimpong and Darjeeling, while the majority of the soldiers remained in the temporary camps in Arunachal Pradesh.

In 1958, with Gyalo Thondup's support, Baba Lekshey and a group of twelve men opened an office in Kalimpong dedicated to working for Tibetan independence.[7] They wrote letters to officials in approximately 150 different countries asking for their support. Following the exodus of

1959, this group expanded to include newly arrived Chushi Gangdrug members and other interested individuals. They decided to write a seven-point letter to Prime Minister Nehru requesting India's help for Tibet. Forty members of this ad hoc group, including Baba Lekshey, Kargyal Thondup from Chatreng, and Alo Chhonzed of Mimang Tsogpa, traveled to New Delhi to deliver the petition in person; the Reverend Tharchin served as their translator.[8] Discussions with Indian and U.S. officials encouraged the men, contributing to their overall belief that Chushi Gangdrug's efforts were a crucial service to the Tibetan government and destined to be effective, especially with foreign support.

Meanwhile, Chushi Gangdrug members in Misamari held a meeting.[9] Considering the large number of deaths the community had suffered in India, they decided to move to a cooler, more hospitable place, Gangtok, the capital of Sikkim, where jobs building roads in the mountains were available. Gangtok's climate was not all that was attractive to the Tibetans: Sikkim was an ethnically Tibetan area, and there were strong relations between the Sikkimese royal family and the Tibetan government. Gangtok was also very close to Kalimpong and Darjeeling, both of which had long been home to Tibetan expatriates and traders alike. But Gangtok was not perfect. Building roads was not fighting the Chinese. As time passed in Gangtok, many soldiers grew dissatisfied with the current situation. They sent word to Chushi Gangdrug leaders in Kalimpong that they had not come to India to build roads and asked them to take action.[10] A meeting attended by over two hundred leaders of Chushi Gangdrug and three thousand members was held in Gangtok. All options were thoroughly discussed and debated, including the popular suggestion to return to Tibet to continue fighting. "In the name of all three regions—U-Tsang, Kham, and Amdo," three decisions were made.[11]

First, it was decided to continue to accept aid from the United States rather than from Taiwan. Darjeeling-based Taiwanese agents were financially supporting some of the resistance leaders (and refugee leaders in general) as well as attempting to recruit Chushi Gangdrug members in India to serve in the Taiwanese army. Although some leaders continued to maintain individual relations with the Taiwanese government, Chushi Gangdrug as an organization did not have relations with them.[12] According to a Khampa politician, these relations were all an open secret. Second, Chushi Gangdrug would set up a military camp in Nepal for

FIGURE 21 Road construction in Sikkim. Photo by Tsepon Shakabpa, courtesy of Jigme Deden Shakabpa and the Center for South Asia at the University of Wisconsin.

operations; the location would be Mustang, an ethnic Tibetan kingdom that jutted up from the border of Nepal into Tibet.[13] And, third, they would nominate Chushi Gangdrug leaders as *mdo stod*/Kham and *mdo smed*/Amdo representatives for election to the Commission of Tibetan People's Deputies; the commission (later the Assembly) was the Tibetan Parliament as reconstituted in exile in 1960. Elections were held; with the exception of the top leaders, Andrug Gompo Tashi, Baba Yeshi from Bathang, Sadhu Lo Nyendak from Markham, and Jagod Namgyal Dorje from Derge, all members were eligible to be nominated.[14] The ten men to receive the most votes included Gungthang Tsultrim from Amdo, Jangdha Chozed from Lithang, Dorje from Chamdo, Drawo Pön from Gaba, and Bachung Pön from Derge.

Resistance leaders elected to the commission were also assigned to different government offices as representatives of their regions rather than of Chushi Gangdrug. This distinction reveals their awareness of the difficulties in crafting new means of participating in national politics. As Baba Lekshey explained to me one day, thinking back to his political efforts at this time, "We were not educated, but we tried to work for the Tibetan government." For some in Dharamsala, the idea of noneducated Khampas serving as deputies was laughable; a government official shared with me his memories of educated aristocrats scoffing at the Khampa deputies and gossiping about what office assignments such illiterate or semiliterate individuals might receive. Working both with and against such sociopolitical beliefs and structures was a conscious part of resistance rebuilding. As most of the veterans recall, the meeting in Gangtok was an important and successful turning point in restarting efforts in exile.

Word that military resistance to the Chinese was starting up again spread like wildfire among Tibetans in northern India. A group of Sera monks who had been sent to Dalhousie to study English traveled to Darjeeling, where they met with Andrug Gompo Tashi. He asked if they would like to join the guerrilla force in Mustang to fight against the Chinese. As Lobsang Tinley recalled, "We said we were ready to do anything against the Chinese."[15] Other monks, former peasants, traders, and many men from the road construction camps shared their sentiments, making their way to Darjeeling and later to Mustang to participate in the resistance. At the same time many were traveling overland through India and Nepal to restart operations, others were en route to the United States.

Chushi Gangdrug in Colorado

From 1958 through 1964, several hundred Tibetans attended CIA training camps in the United States. Training at first was conducted at a secret site in Virginia but was quickly moved from there to a more suitable site, Camp Hale in Leadville, Colorado. During the Second World War, Camp Hale was a U.S. Army training site for winter and mountain warfare and was home to the famed Tenth Mountain Division. Situated in the Rocky Mountains in an area with altitudes ranging from ten thousand to fourteen thousand feet, it was as close to a simulated version of Tibet as there was in the United States. At the time of the Tibetans' stay, Camp Hale was no longer in use by the U.S. Army. Nonetheless, the Tibetan operation was highly secret, and their camp was tucked away in a valley well out of sight of any passersby. At Camp Hale, named Dumra, *ldum ra*, or "garden," by the soldiers, CIA officials trained the Tibetans in a range of guerrilla warfare techniques, including paramilitary operations, bomb building, map making, photography, radio operation techniques, courses in world history and politics, and intelligence collecting.

Twenty-six men were trained in the United States to be the leaders of the Mustang force. Ratuk Ngawang from Lithang was slated to be trained as the head commander but could not make the trip to the United States for health reasons. Another man from Lithang, Lobsang Jampa, took his place as commander-in-training. Baba Yeshi from Bathang was named as the first general of the Mustang force. Rather than traveling to the United States, he remained with Andrug Gompo Tashi in Darjeeling, where U.S. agents held private training sessions for the two men. The rest of the Chushi Gangdrug soldiers received training in India from both Tibetan soldiers and American agents and later from Indian soldiers as well. From India, soldiers trained in photography were sent into Tibet armed with cameras to document the fighting.[16] Those recruits sent to Mustang received a year of guerrilla training by graduates of the CIA training camp in Colorado.

All of these training missions were top secret, whether in India, Nepal, or the United States. Soldiers were told repeatedly by both Chushi Gang-drug leaders and the CIA that their activities were secret and not to be disclosed at all. This prohibition, elongated by the arrest of resistance history and combined with Tibetan preferences for firsthand truths (rather than secondhand information), resulted in a privatizing of resistance history in which American parts of the Chushi Gangdrug narrative were known only by some. Rather than being accessible to all narrators, for example, the story of Colorado is limited to certain tellers. These narrators often adorn references to training in America with personal memories before retreating to a broader, more inclusive resistance history. While situated experience drove resistance history in many ways, a privileging of time spent training in the United States lent that portion of resistance history a special place in resistance history to which veterans had differential access. For those who trained in the United States, their collected memories of Colorado cover disparate territory, from comments on daily life and specific details of training received to fond reflection on the American instructors with whom many of the Tibetans developed close bonds despite the fact they could communicate only through interpreters.

One of the first things assigned to the Tibetans upon their arrival in the United States was an American name. Clay, Roger, David, Conrad, Frank, Lee, Eddie, and Saul all trained in Colorado. The Tibetans had no contact with any Americans other than those involved in the training, although some recall seeing shepherds on nearby mountainsides. Life under the training regime was tough: it was cold in Colorado and there was lots of work to do, films to watch, and lessons to learn. Mealtimes are remembered fondly, primarily for the variety and quality of food available: Tibetan tea, black tea, coffee, milk, hot water, fruit, meat, butter, and sometimes even *momo*, Tibetan dumplings filled with meat, and *thukpa*, Tibetan noodle and meat soup.[17] Other aspects of life stood out for their peculiarity: changing into a set of clean clothes everyday, standing in line with a plate in one's hands waiting for food, and the unavailability of snuff, which was widely snorted in Tibet. The snuff dilemma was resolved by unwrapping cigarettes, grinding the loose tobacco, and then moistening it with some water, resulting in homemade snuff.[18] In all their recollections of Colorado, Tibetan veterans refer with respect to their American teachers, presenting this relationship as one of cooperative assistance given rather than one of subordination or exploitation in any form.

Indeed, relationships between the Tibetan soldiers trained in Colorado and their American teachers confound expectations: Two groups of men from highly divergent backgrounds and unable to communicate without translation were quartered together in a military camp in the Rocky Mountains that did not officially exist. The two sides shared a mutual admiration that continues to this day. As one retired CIA officer recalls, "[The Tibetans] all treated me with a great deal of respect. They were polite and attentive and were by far the best students I ever worked with. It was a hell of a lot of work and the living conditions were much too military for my taste but it was satisfying and I felt that it was an honor to work with them."[19] The Tibetans were appreciative of the assistance they were given, the skills they were taught, and the hope for their cause fostered by U.S. support. In turn, the U.S. agents were in awe of the Tibetans' field abilities, and they admired their character. According to several of the retired CIA officers I interviewed, they connected with the Tibetan men in ways not matched in CIA operations in other parts of the world. Forty years and several states removed from his time in Colorado, the officer known to Tibetans as Mr. Ray told me about the day another CIA officer attempted to teach the Tibetans how to set up tents. Halfway through his demonstration, he turned around and the Tibetans already had all the tents set up. Laughing at the memory, Mr. Ray said, "Class was canceled," adding, "I didn't believe we could teach the Tibetans anything about how to live in the field."[20]

The Tibetans went on to conduct military and intelligence missions against the Chinese from their camps in Mustang through 1974. The U.S. agents, following CIA protocol, would work on the Tibetan operation for a few years before being transferred to another case, whether Vietnam, the Philippines, or Eastern Europe. Although U.S. support might look paltry and self-interested today, Chushi Gangdrug veterans remain convinced it was an important part of their personal and collective experience of struggle. This is not to say that Tibetans did not question the nature, timing, and volume of assistance granted by the Americans, for they did then, and still do, albeit respectfully and quietly.

Years of Hope: Resistance Operations in Nepal

While Lobsang Jampa and the other men chosen as leaders were training in Colorado, Baba Yeshi and resistance soldiers began to make their way to Mustang from India. According to Baba Yeshi, the Americans agreed to support twenty-one hundred troops.[21] The first wave of soldiers to arrive in Mustang numbered around four hundred and included teachers sent to continue the schools begun in the camps. Although the initial plan had been to build the Mustang force slowly, both to avoid drawing attention and because of a lack of resources, large groups of men began to surge into Mustang from India, traveling on foot to Kathmandu, then to Pokhara and on to Mustang, as at the time—and still to this day—there were no roads to Mustang, only Himalayan footpaths. Others came from Tibet en route to Nepal or India, and some of them joined the resistance soldiers.[22]

Within a short span of time, the initial group of four hundred grew to twenty-three hundred, more than the Americans wanted and too many mouths to feed. The situation in the beginning was dire. According to Baba Yeshi, "So many people came to Mustang out of sheer nationalism or patriotism. There was a big rush. Everyone wanted to fight for freedom. When so many people came, the Americans refused to give us aid. They said that the secret had been leaked out because there were so many Tibetans in Mustang. The Americans stopped helping us. We had no food. We had to face great difficulties. Some of our soldiers fled."[23] Food was not the only scarcity. The men had few, if any, possessions, save their protective amulets and the clothes on their backs. Many had lost their families in Tibet. Some had bags of *tsampa* to eat on the journey to Mustang, and others ate wild grasses along the way. To men arriving in Mustang, the boiled hides of yaks sometimes qualified as food. Even tea was scarce; the men would drink one of the lowest grades of Indian tea, with the brand name "ja-ri," but only when they were able to stoke a fire hot enough to boil water.[24]

Finally, the Americans relented and began to assist the Tibetans. They made three airdrops, two in 1961 and one in 1965, containing arms, ammunition, food, and other supplies.[25] From Delhi, Gyalo Thondup and Lhamo Tsering managed things, especially relations with the Americans and Indians. As time passed, the Mustang force, called the Lo army, took shape.[26] The men were divided into battalions of one hundred men each, performed military exercises (albeit sometimes with long sticks standing in for guns, which were always in short supply), and continued weaponry and warfare training. The army's headquarters were in Kesangbuk. Military parades were held here, and there were always between three hundred and five hundred men in residence. In addition to training grounds, there was a library, storage areas for grain and other supplies, and areas where the men would play basketball. Reaching Kesangbuk required passing through three checkposts for both Nepalis and Tibetans. As the guerrilla force grew and became more organized, the soldiers addressed their food shortages by creating a trade business. Several soldiers were instructed to set up a small business in Pokhara from which they would purchase supplies and send them up to Mustang.[27] Five men who could speak some Hindi and Nepali were chosen (including Lobsang Tinley), and, disguised as Nepali traders, they traveled from Mustang to Pokhara and back. Once they were established in Pokhara, money was sent to them from Darjeeling, and they would buy rice, wheat, sugar, salt, clothes, and other necessities to send to Mustang. Later these men began to travel further afield, to Calcutta and Delhi to buy supplies in bulk.

Rudimentary uniforms were fashioned out of earth-colored cloth in shades of tan, rust, and clay. Guerrilla units rotated in and out of Tibet. They would travel at night and during the day sleep in the forest or in boulder fields. Their activities in Tibet were a combination of guerrilla

FIGURE 22 Kali Gandaki riverbed, looking north into Mustang.

maneuvers and intelligence gathering. Lobsang Jampa describes their Mustang-based efforts as a series of periodic strikes rather than ongoing battles: "We fought against the Chinese from time to time [using] guerrilla warfare tactics. They were hit-and-run operations. We killed many Chinese and destroyed their vehicles. . . . We fought for almost fifteen years with American weapons."[28] Soldiers made raids into Tibet in the summer, when the mountain passes were still covered with snow but the danger of frostbite was less.

None of the Mustang soldiers had any identity papers. Locally, they were referred to as the Pine Tree Khampas because of their practice of lining their bunkers with conifer boughs in attempts to combat the brutal cold of Mustang, where the average altitude is well above eleven thousand feet. Unlike the smoky scent one acquired from the interior of Mustang homes, the soldiers all smelled like pine trees.[29] Relations with the local people varied. The resistance built bridges and airstrips and maintained trails, which were welcomed services. On the other hand, they were a serious drain on local resources, and local people were often compelled to sell foodstuffs and animals to the soldiers at low prices. The king of Mustang, the Lo Gyalpo (*lo rgyal po*), supported the resistance and was aware of why the Tibetans were there. The local people, however, did not really know exactly what was taking place, according to former soldiers. Some soldiers had relations with Lo women. As it was explained to me, men who were attracted to local women would develop a relationship with the woman and her family; they would visit their families, share meals with them, and even spend the night.[30] Some of these couples married and had children during the Mustang effort; families became a part of the Mustang force. The women did not participate in military activities, and none of them served in this army. Resistance life was not romantic; it was plagued by the uncertainties of external support, by internal squabbles, and by changing relations with the local Mustang population. Key to their presence in Mustang was the support of two kings: the local support of the king of Mustang and the silent consent of the king of Nepal.

The Tibetans' use of Mustang as their resistance base was approved by the Nepali government, which was encouraged to do so by the United States, and monitored by King Mahendra through January 1972 and after that by his son, King Birendra. Veterans recall that there were always at least two and sometimes as many as five Nepali intelligence officers stationed at Dzong Sarpa who traveled by horseback to collect information. King Mahendra also visited Mustang by helicopter to hold discussions with General Baba Yeshi.[31] Although the government of Nepal made resistance activities in Mustang possible by allowing them to use the territory, Nepali armed forces did not participate in Tibetan resistance activities, and the presence of the Tibetan resistance army was kept top secret.

Secret Operations in India

The Mustang guerrilla force was not the only military endeavor in exile. Tibetan guerrilla units also entered Tibet on foot from India to conduct intelligence-gathering missions.[32] Unlike the situation in Nepal, however, in India the Tibetan units were not independent of local militia or government but incorporated into them. Connections with the government of India were coordinated with the CIA and began almost immediately after the Tibetans came into exile in 1959. While things were getting started in Mustang, another group of men was sent to Rajasthan for training by the Indian Central Intelligence Bureau (CIB; then called the IB). Training in Rajasthan focused on technical subjects: Morse code, map reading, guerrilla tactics, judo, and intelligence-gathering techniques.[33] Some of these men continued to work for the CIB in a variety of capacities, including Chinese language instruction.[34] Following the Sino–Indian War of 1962, the government of India created two new armed forces: on 24 October 1962, the Indo–Tibetan Border Police Force (ITBF) under the auspices of the Ministry of Home Affairs, and on 24 November, one month later, they inaugurated an all-Tibetan force in the Indian army popularly called Establishment 22 (Est. 22), later known as the Special Frontier Force (SFF).[35]

Establishment 22/SFF was considered by many of the Mustang soldiers as the Chushi Gangdrug sister organization in India. As understood by the Tibetans, while the ITBF included Tibetans in its ranks, Est. 22/SFF was specifically created "to restore independence to Tibet."[36] Unlike Mustang, which was solely a Tibetan operation, Est. 22/SFF in Dehra Dun was a joint Tibetan–Indian operation. Soldiers were initially trained by both American and Indian officers but were led by four Tibetan officers: Ratuk Ngawang and Gyatso Dhondup, both from Lithang; Jampa Kalden, from Chamdo; and Jampa Wangdu, from Lhasa.[37] The force was jointly trained by the United States and India until U.S.–India bilateral relations soured; at that point, the Americans stopped their participation, and the Russian KGB began supplying trainers and equipment.[38] These Tibetan forces have fought in numerous military initiatives, including India's war with East Pakistan (now Bangladesh) in 1971. Fifty-six Tibetan Est. 22/SFF soldiers died in that war, and the government of India decorated 580 Tibetan soldiers with medals for bravery.[39] The Dalai Lama attended the award ceremony at Est. 22/SFF headquarters in Chakrata, outside of Dehra Dun.

Est. 22/SFF differed from the Mustang force in several ways: first, it was directly incorporated into the Indian army with links to Indian intelligence; second, it accepted only those under the age of forty; and, third, it accepted women as well as men. Female presence signified a major departure from the protocols of Chushi Gangdrug. Women in these forces received full battle training, although they primarily held medical and office positions. Among Tibetans connected to SFF or ITBF, stories circulate about the bravest and strongest of these women, for example, about a female trainee in the 1970s who parachuted even though she was eight months pregnant. One former official in the SFF explained the female presence to me in ways that contrast bluntly with the Chushi Gangdrug exclusion of women: "In India, the number of female Tibetans is slightly larger than the males. When Establishment 22 was started, we requested that the government of India allow Tibetan girls there. This was done to provide them with job opportunities. In the army, the women can be employed as nurses, office secretaries, and so on. It is compulsory for both men and women to jump from planes. Everybody must do it. All are paratroopers." The emphasis is not on power and pollution, but on "job opportunities" and female bravery in parachuting. As one veteran reminisced, the women would just jump, but the men would often share a nip of whiskey with the American instructors before jumping.

As in all Tibetan endeavors in exile, religion is involved in SFF. Monks from the Dalai Lama's personal monastery in Dharamsala, Namgyal Monastery, are posted to Est. 22/SFF to serve as RT Lamas, or religious-teacher lamas. They have one-star deputy leader rank and serve at headquarters as well as at border posts. One former RT Lama told me, "It was a really tough job; the toughest I've had. We had to do all the jobs of monks and lamas: divinations, healings, exorcisms, rain-making, weather controlling, teachings and rituals on special occasions such as the Buddha's birthday, and also private teachings to individuals who requested them. We would do prayers for the soldiers when they were jumping, going to the border, and so on. We gave them protection cords from His Holiness [the Dalai Lama]." Palden Lhamo, the female chief guardian of the Tibetan Buddhist pantheon, of the Gelugpa sect, and of Tibet itself, is taken by the Tibetan soldiers as the protector deity of Est. 22/SFF.[40]

Relations between Est. 22/SFF and the Mustang force were complicated. There was a handful of Est. 22/SFF soldiers stationed in Mustang who did communications work independent of that done by the Mustang troops.[41] Mustang force wireless operators sent their messages to the United States via a Tibetan office in Delhi, where the information would be relayed to Washington. The wireless operator Norbu Dorje recalls that those in Mustang did not even know the name of the Delhi office. All information was kept confidential, although they knew the office was connected in some way with the government of India.[42]

According to the former CIA officer Ken Knaus, this secret office was the Combined Operations Center (COC), established in Delhi in late 1963 and a joint effort of the Tibetans, Americans, and Indians. As Knaus explains, "The United States underwrote the costs of the operations, trained the agents, provided the radios and other gear, and contributed operational guidance and its presumed expertise. The Tibetans provided the manpower for the missions. But the Indians controlled the territory and thereby the operations."[43] Knaus's reference to Tibetans means the Tibetan government-in-exile. As veterans consistently pointed out to me, Chushi Gangdrug leaders and the Tibetan government intermediaries working directly with the Americans at the COC were not one and the same. General Baba Yeshi contends that the difference between the Mustang force and the Est. 22/SFF force was that whereas Est. 22/SFF was controlled by the government of India, Mustang was purely a Tibetan operation.[44] As he and many veterans saw it, Mustang was a Chushi Gangdrug operation, led by the people of Tibet, but Est. 22/SFF was a multigovernmental operation with motives other than the regaining of Tibet.[45] These differences in interpretation reflected problems within the exile community not necessarily visible to the CIA.

Involved, directly and indirectly, in many of the problems faced by the resistance was the Dalai Lama's brother, Gyalo Thondup. The years following the Chinese takeover of Tibet and the early years of exile, roughly 1951 through the early 1970s, involved a series of political conflicts among Tibetan expatriates and, later, among refugees in India. Much of the controversy revolved around Gyalo Thondup's rise to power in the 1950s as the unofficial ambassador of Tibet to the outside world, primarily the West and Taiwan (and later the PRC). Factions formed in the exile community, loosely around region but also with political interests crosscutting regional affiliations.[46] Internal controversies are found in any community, but in a refugee community struggling to regain its country under the leadership of an individual such as the Dalai Lama and sensitive to external attempts to divide the community, these controversies (and subsequent ones) hit particularly hard.

No history can be written without mixing in politics. Without
politics, then we wouldn't be able to do justice to military power.
[Most veterans] don't know about politics. They know their own
life stories. They don't know about the political history of Tibet.
And they are not to be blamed. . . . [So-and-so, for example,]
knows all about guerrilla warfare. I don't know anything about
it. But he does not know what I know.

HIGH-RANKING KHAMPA OFFICIAL, DHARAMSALA

History, politics, and military power: making sense of a war involves
understanding the politics behind both the war and the histories
made of it. Writing a history thus requires "mixing in politics," but
not just of governments and elections, factions and disputes. In the
mix must also be a *politics of knowledge*, that is, of the particularities
of and conditions for knowledge that compose any past. A history
of Chushi Gangdrug as a history of Tibet, therefore, must include—
to use the Khampa official's words—life stories, the political history
of Tibet, guerrilla warfare, and what he, the official, knows. Such a
history cannot stay with the perspectives and experiences of just the
high official or just the foot soldier but must traverse the ground
between them, including those aspects of politics that are painful
and problematic to recount. In the case of the resistance army and
of the exile community more generally, one such period that needs
to be addressed is the first two decades of exile.

The early years of exile were marked by growing pains well

beyond the logistical dilemmas associated with the unexpected creation of a refugee community. A series of controversies and internal problems plagued the Tibetan community in exile. Power, money, regional difference, and more were involved. Clouded in rumor and suspicion, histories of this period are subject to arrest on two grounds: first, through community consent to their categorization as detrimental to the exile cause; and second, through fears of repercussive personal injury in either a legal or physical sense. Tibetans speak of their histories as reflections in a mirror, thereby emphasizing their clarity and truth. However, the telling of histories of this period involves looking into a mirror far more clouded than clear, that is, into a *gya'a ma dag pa'i me long*. With the exception of one detailed book in German written by a Tibetan, very little scholarship exists on the tensions found in Tibetan exile experiences and politics.[1] One must look into that most clouded of historical mirrors—internal political problems in the early exile community—to understand the making and unmaking of histories during this period.

Gyalo Thondup's Rise to Power

While Kalimpong and Darjeeling had long been home to Tibetan expatriates, the community grew newly politicized with the advent of Chinese rule in Tibet in the 1950s. The turning point was the Dalai Lama's political retreat to the Indian border in the winter of 1951. The parties involved in determining what his next plan of action should be—either to seek refuge in India; travel to the United States, Thailand, or another Asian country; or return to Lhasa—were numerous, including members of the Dalai Lama's family, government officials such as Pangda Yamphel and Yuthok Tashi Dondrup (commonly referred to by their family names: Pangdatsang and Yuthok), and a variety of foreign parties and governments. On internal advice from his government officials, the Dalai Lama decided to return to Tibet to try to make things work with the Chinese. It was from this moment that exile political factions began to take shape.

In terms of the Tibetan community, Kalimpong was the domain of the Khampa trader Pangda Yamphel, the trade agent of the government of Tibet and the richest man in Tibet.[2] He enjoyed good relations with the Dalai Lama's family, the royal families of Sikkim and Bhutan, and local political and business powerhouses, almost everyone, in fact, except for the former British colonial officers who ruled India and had tried to control trade in and out of Tibet. Pangda's invincible status was challenged with Gyalo Thondup's arrival in Kalimpong. Gyalo Thondup had been in Taiwan and then the United States during the emergency of 1950–51, returning to Tibet in 1952.[3] On his return he was more worldly and more politically savvy than he had been as a young man trying to warn the Tibetan government of the plans the PRC had for Tibet.[4] His Chinese education now supplemented with time spent in discussions with Taiwanese and American government officials, Gyalo Thondup converted his privileged status as the Dalai Lama's brother into a position as envoy of the Tibetan government to foreign governments. This ascent to power, beginning roughly in the mid-1950s and consolidated in the 1960s, came at the expense of other individuals in the Tibetan community and involved a particular view of what was best for Tibet.

It is difficult to trace the exact trajectory of Gyalo Thondup's rise to power.[5] Lhasan aristocratic families, some of which had pedigrees reaching back centuries, did not always respect the *yabshi* (*yab gzhis*), or Dalai Lama's family.[6] Nonetheless, aristocrats were bound by certain cultural obligations to the yabshi family. For example, yabshi family members were financially provided for by the state and also economically supported by a range of patrons with either sociocultural obligations to the Dalai Lama, such as Pangdatsang, or with political interests in Tibet, such as the governments of China and the United States. This system resulted in an irregular source of income for the family and a reliance on the benevolence of others. According to some Tibetans, as Gyalo Thondup's financial requirements rose in line with his increased political activities, the aristocrats of the Tibetan government declined to provide him with sufficient funds (as would have been long-standing tradition). In addition, although Pangda Yamphel had been one of Gyalo Thondup's earlier financial supporters, Pangda did not support his new political agenda. Disagreements between the two men—Pangda Yamphel elder than Gyalo Thondup by a full generation—were to set the stage for the exile power struggles that followed.

Tibetan hierarchies of social and political power worked differently in India than they had in Tibet, whether in Lhasa or in Kham. The Kalimpong status quo was more of a mix of central and eastern Tibetans, of systems of ascribed and achieved merit, of misfit Tibetan individuals and families living alongside those solidly stationed at the center of ruling hierarchies. Other than Pangda Yamphel, the Tibetan government had no official representatives in India. Although, for example, the British (and later the Indians) had stationed a representative in Lhasa for many years, the British government of India did not grant reciprocal facilities of representation to the Tibetans. Although he was governor of Dromo, a territory bordering India, as well as Tibetan trade agent, Pangda Yamphel had not carved a political component into his posts. He was a businessman rather than a politician and lent his personal and financial support to his aristocratic friends, specifically, the Tibetan government ministers Surkhang Wangchen Gelek and Yuthok, and to groups of Khampa men engaged in politics. Over time, as Gyalo Thondup's power was consolidated, each of these groups came into conflict with him. The repercussions were often severe.[7]

Following his dispute with Gyalo Thondup, Pangda Yamphel was eventually driven out of India, as were Surkhang and Yuthok, who went to Taiwan. Members of the Pangdatsang family were also "struggled" against in exile; there was an assassination attempt on his brother Rapga while he was shopping in Kalimpong. According to one veteran, CIA trainers in Colorado would say to the Tibetan trainees, "Pangdatsang no good."[8] Many of these events remain uninvestigated. Social protocol in the community prevents most inquiries of mishaps involving individuals of high status, and it is difficult to track with certainty the origins of many of these arrests, deportations, and attempted and actual murders.[9] Privately, many of the Khampas with whom I spoke traced these events to either Gyalo Thondup, the people who surrounded him, or people acting in ways they thought would please him. A clouded politics of knowledge still surrounds the history of the Pangdatsang family today.

Gyalo Thondup's attempts to create sociopolitical reforms were publicly manifest in his directing of a new political party. The reform United Party (*gcig sgril tshogs pa*) was a Dharamsala-generated idea turned over to Gyalo Thondup in Darjeeling to lead. At the time, Dharamsala was the symbolic capital of the refugee community, but Darjeeling was the political center.[10] United Party leaders drafted a constitution based on that of the Indian National Congress, and the party immediately became prominent within the refugee community. Just as immediately, it generated conflict. The United Party represented an effort to bring together Tibetans from across regional and sectarian divides. But, in the perception of at least some Tibetans, it still represented the Lhasa/Dharamsala status quo.

As one Khampa government official explains, this rubbed some people the wrong way: "Things had worked differently in Lhasa than they had in Kham. Khampa traders had more influence in Lhasa than in Kham. In Kham, it was the chieftains who were in charge."[11] These regional power structures traveled with refugees to India, where many refugees looked to their local chieftains for day-to-day leadership rather than to the Tibetan government-in-exile. Such differential relationships to power holders took on new meanings in exile as groups that were once distant now inhabited the same geographic and political spaces. Tensions were inevitable and allegiances were never clear-cut or singular. The resentment that existed between Khampa chieftains and traders such as Andrug Gompo Tashi or aristocrats such as Gyalo Thondup was mitigated for most by cooperation in Chushi Gangdrug efforts. As a result, participation in the United Party became "almost compulsory" for politically active Tibetans.[12] Others, however, took a stance against the United Party. A group of thirteen settlement and monastery leaders created an oppositional political party to distance themselves not only from the United Party, but also from Gyalo Thondup's reforms and the Tibetan government-in-exile. They called themselves the Thirteen Group (*tsho khag bcu gsum*).[13] Many of the settlements involved were Khampa camps, and overall the Thirteen Group was headed by the Karmapa, head of the Kagyu sect.[14]

The split between the Thirteen Group and the Tibetan government-in-exile had immediate repercussions in the exile community, including in Chushi Gangdrug, members of which were now on opposing sides of the political fence.[15] The unity of the Mustang force was irreparably damaged by the split. The parallel split created in Chushi Gangdrug continues to plague the organization today, individuals commonly identifying others as being aligned either with or against Gyalo Thondup. Misunderstandings run throughout the politics of this period. Gyalo Thondup's vision for the exile community included reform but not dissent; and by virtue of his yabshi pedigree, his vision of community triumphed over those who sought other varieties of reform. Relations between the Thirteen Group and the Tibetan government-in-exile were eventually mended, yet scars remain in the community, especially in the form of disputes between

FIGURE 23 Gyalo Thondup and the author.

those who consider themselves beyond and those who consider themselves bound by regional and sectarian affiliations.[16]

Events such as the controversy between the United Party and the
Thirteen Group served to further mark Khampas as troublemakers in the
exile community. This label fit their traditional stereotype as congenital
warriors and their contemporary image as admired yet feared soldiers
engaged in battle with the Chinese.[17] Yet Khampa Tibetans were not a
singular group. Among various points of difference, they held divergent
views on how to convert their local loyalties to national participation.
Some strove to highlight Tibet in their political work and identities, and
others to highlight Kham. As a government official explained to me,
"Some Chushi Gangdrug leaders were so possessive of their own identity
and legacy. Sharing it or making it national would dilute it."[18]

Gyalo Thondup's accession to political power complicated matters further. His status as the Dalai Lama's brother, his growing political power, and his critical position as contact between the resistance and the CIA made it very difficult to challenge him. While his political power was at times unchecked, Gyalo Thondup was acting for Tibet in arenas well beyond the ability of most of the exile Tibetan populace. His contributions to the Tibetan exile cause, especially in regard to the negotiations with the United States and at the United Nations, are substantial and important. While he is a controversial figure within the exile community, his historical contributions remain to be fully explored, analyzed, and appreciated.[19]

The Value of Things

In November 1961 Allen Dulles, then-director of the CIA, appeared at a meeting of the National Security Council's Special Group carrying an unusual item, a Chinese army commander's pouch, bloodstained and perforated by bullets.[20] No less graphic than the blue leather pouch was what it contained, over sixteen hundred classified Chinese documents described as not merely an "intelligence goldmine," but "the best intelligence coup since the Korean War."[21] The pouch and documents were well traveled, having been carried on foot by Tibetan guerrilla soldiers out of Tibet, through Nepal, and into India. In Darjeeling, Lhamo Tsering translated them from the Chinese and, on realizing their importance, carried them himself in a large burlap bag to his CIA contact, Clay Cathey, in Calcutta. Cathey personally flew the documents back to the United States on a PanAm flight: one seat for himself, one seat for the documents.[22] The Tibetan soldiers who captured the documents were part of the Chushi Gangdrug Mustang force.

The Tibetans did not have uniform support in Washington.[23] In the early 1960s, with the transition from the Eisenhower to the Kennedy administration, the Tibetan operations were brought up for debate—should they or should they not be continued was the question on the table.[24] Dulles's dramatic introduction of the bloody bag, literally "shot through with explanation," could not have been better timed from the Tibetans' viewpoint.[25] The documents the pouch contained were of priceless value to the U.S. government, for, at the time, very little intelligence information existed about the PRC. China itself painted a picture of a seamlessly functioning state, one that was militarily secure and flourishing in every way. What the documents revealed was just the opposite: the Great Leap Forward was in fact a great failure. There was widespread famine in China, serious internal problems in the military and the party, and more.[26] The importance of the documents to the United States was unparalleled, and the scholarly community exploded when they were released several years later, as no one had had access to such documents and information.[27] Nowhere, however, was it revealed how the U.S. government obtained the documents. President John F. Kennedy approved the continuation of the Tibetan project, but the story of the men who captured the documents remained a secret.[28]

Like Washington, the Tibetan government was interested in the documents, but for a different reason. In the aftermath of their escape from Lhasa, the only evidence the Tibetan government-in-exile had of the atrocities committed by the Chinese was the oral testimony of refugees.[29] These testimonies were valuable, but not as valuable as hard evidence would be, and the set of documents captured by the guerrilla unit contained crucial and tragic confirmation of the sheer volume of violence inflicted upon Tibet and Tibetans. This information was the only documentary proof the Tibetan government had of the Chinese atrocities and therefore invaluable. At the time, as was the case with the CIA, the substance of the documents, not tales of how and by whom they had been obtained, was what mattered to the Tibetan government-in-exile. It was not until 1990 and the beginning of the period of release of resistance histories that the Dalai Lama acknowledged in his autobiography that the documents were "captured by Tibetan freedom fighters during the 1960s."[30]

Five decades after their capture, the documents remain the defining feature of the Tibet operation (codenamed ST Circus) for the CIA. On 26 October 2009, the first piece of artwork commemorating the Tibet mission was dedicated at the CIA Art Museum in a ceremony that included the remaining surviving members of the CIA Tibet team, their families, and myself.[31] Following remarks and reminiscences by retired officers, the artwork was dramatically unveiled revealing a massive painting by British military artist Keith Woodcock. Titled *The Secret PLA Pouch Heads to K Building*, the painting depicts Tibetan resistance soldiers capturing the PLA commander's pouch in full battlefield detail: the army truck on fire, its driver and passengers shot dead, blood on the snow, rifles in the arms of the retreating Tibetan soldiers, and the blue leather pouch

FIGURE 24 Unveiling ceremony of *The Secret PLA Pouch Heads to K Building*, with the donor Bruce Walker (left) and the artist Keith Woodcock (right). Photo courtesy of the CIA Museum.

being safely carried away. Now hanging in the CIA's Intelligence Art Gallery, this painting further cements the capturing of these documents as the most significant part of the CIA Tibet operation. Considering the longstanding importance accorded to the documents by the U.S. and Tibetan governments, one might expect resistance veterans to highlight this in their narrations of resistance history. As I found out, this was not the case at all. The histories that the soldiers told me neither began nor ended with the documents, and they usually did not include them at all. Why is it that this particular achievement, so valued by the U.S. and Tibetan governments, is not remotely as memorable for the soldiers?

In Mustang, the Chushi Gangdrug soldiers established camps from which they would periodically sneak across the border into Tibet, raiding army camps, dynamiting roads, stealing animals, collecting information and transmitting it by radio to the United States. One of their goals was to stop Chinese PLA convoys, to kill the soldiers, and to confiscate their weapons, supplies, and materials. On one especially successful raid they captured a large pouch stuffed with documents. The documents were all in Chinese, which none of the Tibetans in Mustang could read. Lobsang Jampa was one of the few veterans who mentioned the documents to me. He said, "There was a man called Gen Rakra. He was very popular among us. He led an attack on the Chinese and secured some very important documents from a Chinese official. This proved very useful to us. . . . We sent those documents on. But I don't know what they were about."[32]

Other veterans who discussed the documents were similarly unimpressed by them. In Pokhara, Palden Wangyal explained, "Our soldiers attacked Chinese trucks and seized some documents of the Chinese government. After that the Americans increased our pay scale. Nobody knew what the contents of those documents were. At that time, questions weren't asked. If you asked many questions, then others would be suspicious of you."[33] Baba Yeshi clarified, "A group of thirty Tibetans on horse traveled into Tibet. . . . Nine days later the group returned with uniforms, hats, diaries, Chinese government documents, and a lot of ammunition. . . . All that was captured resulted from the ambush of two Chinese convoys in western Tibet. [I] sent the diaries and government documents to Darjeeling. . . . [Later] four CIA officials congratulated me on overcoming such difficult initial conditions and praised me for our success in attacking the Chinese. As a reward the CIA gave me an Omega chronograph."[34]

The Americans appear not to have known that the Tibetans had discriminating taste. As former transnational traders, many of the Khampa soldiers had sophisticated knowledge of the market value (and not just the use value) of international commodities such as timepieces. On this topic, Lobsang Jampa adds that at an earlier time "we were also given Omega wristwatches by the American instructors. They also gave us one trunk of other watches. These watches were of cheap quality, and some of our soldiers did not want them."[35] What the soldiers did want was the restoration of Tibet to the rule of the Dalai Lama, and the ability to return to their homes and families. Captured documents whose contents were unknown were but a small victory and earned what seemed to be trivial rewards to the Tibetans. At that particular moment the capture of the documents was difficult for the soldiers to interpret as a concrete accomplishment in their effort to reach their goal.

The clear marginality of the Tibetans to broader U.S. Cold War goals vis-à-vis China and beyond was produced by a larger set of discourses, institutions, and experiences. Yet, as Anna Tsing has shown in the case of the Meratus in Indonesia, people find ways to engage and challenge their marginality.[36] One way Tibetan soldiers dealt with marginality was by denying it, by placing the resistance, unlike the watches, squarely within the realm of the valuable. Many of them were convinced they would defeat China, diplomatically if not militarily, and return to Tibet soon or at the very least in their lifetimes. If their hope was encouraged while in residence in Mustang, however, their marginality was amplified following the dramatic and destructive end of resistance operations there.

Mustang: The Beginning and End of the End

The controversial tragedy that brought the Mustang era to an end is often blamed on one man: Baba Yeshi, who headed the Mustang force for almost the entire duration of its existence. While Baba Yeshi was certainly a participant in internal power struggles within the resistance, the popular caricature of him as being solely responsible for the downfall of the resistance is problematic.[37] Casting one individual as culprit deflects attention away from larger issues of transparency, accountability, dissension, and power in governmental and organizational decision making.

Charges against Baba Yeshi center on two issues: the question of the misuse of funds and his relationship with Gyato Wangdu, who was sent by Gyalo Thondup and the COC to be the deputy commander in Mustang in the late 1960s. Baba Yeshi explained to me that he initially resisted his appointment as leader of the guerrilla force in Mustang, accepting it only after several days of protest. His term as leader was to be for three years, but no one was sent to replace him when the three years were up. As a result, he continued to serve.[38] As explained by other Chushi Gangdrug veterans, however, someone was sent to share command with Baba Yeshi, if not to relieve him entirely of command, and that person was Lobsang Jampa from Lithang, who had been trained at Camp Hale in Colorado.

Some contend that the Colorado-trained leaders were not welcomed by Baba Yeshi. Disputes began over the chain of command and between the organizational styles of Baba Yeshi and the American-trained soldiers. Baba Yeshi refused to turn over or share power with Lobsang Jampa, whom Andrug Gompo Tashi had earmarked for (at least) joint leadership.[39] Lobsang Jampa did not challenge Baba Yeshi but instead accepted leadership of a one-hundred-man battalion. A number of soldiers broke off from the main force in protest and established themselves in other valleys. Some of these groups were tolerated, while others were not. Gaba Tsewang Dorje's breakaway group, for example, was reportedly killed by other members of the Mustang force.[40] These controversies within the resistance force were directly related to controversies in the refugee community more broadly as well as to the death of Andrug Gompo Tashi.

In 1963, Andrug Gompo Tashi traveled to England for medical treatment.[41] Gyalo Thondup and Chushi Gangdrug representatives saw him off at the Calcutta airport.[42] He recovered successfully from surgery and treatment and returned to India. Once back in India, his health took a turn for the worse, and on 27 September 1964 he died at the age of fifty-nine. His funeral in Kalimpong was attended by a large, diverse crowd who witnessed for the first time the covering of a deceased body with a Tibetan flag as well as with a resistance flag at the request of some Chushi Gangdrug members.[43] The funeral was covered in the *Tibet Mirror* newspaper of October 9. The Dalai Lama's representative in Darjeeling, a Chushi Gangdrug representative, and Reverend Tharchin all gave speeches. The Chushi Gangdrug representative, Bachung Pön Thutob Gompo, called Andrug Gompo Tashi "the hero of heroes," saying that "remembering the deeds of such a hero is important for both the politics and customs of Tibet."[44] He relayed Andrug Gompo Tashi's last message to the crowd: "I have done everything I could sincerely do for the reestablishment of the nation and the dharma. Now it is unavoidable that I must leave this world. None of you can do anything to prevent this. Therefore, you must always obey and do everything according to the guidance of our leader, His Holiness the Dalai Lama, in this life and the next without disloyalty. And you must not forget the pledge for independence for our nation of Tibet."[45] Obey. Be loyal. Do not forget. Andrug Gompo Tashi's message to the Chushi Gangdrug soldiers reinforced the central goals of the refugee community—follow the Dalai Lama and regain Tibet—and located the resistance solidly within this shared and hegemonic project.

In his speech, Tharchin Babu exhorted those gathered to set aside their personal differences and to "drown" the Chinese out of Tibet by working as one united community: "To follow after Andrug Jindak [*sbyin bdag*, "sponsor"], his family, friends, and all the people of the three regions must not only share one name ("Tibetans"), but also be one—get rid of personal issues—under the leadership of His Holiness the Dalai Lama in order to achieve Tibetan independence."[46] Andrug Gompo Tashi, he claimed, should be remembered in Tibetan history as "the second Ling Gesar."[47] Tharchin's calling for cooperation across regions presents regional affiliations as problems that only pan-Tibetan unity can defeat. In referring to Andrug Gompo Tashi as the second Ling Gesar, the infamous Khampa warrior who defended Buddhism and is memorialized in epic, Tharchin suggests that he and the Chushi Gangdrug army carry Gesar's mantle in defeating enemies of Buddhism and Tibet.

Prior to his death, Andrug Gompo Tashi named Baba Yeshi his successor as the head of Chushi Gangdrug.[48] Baba Yeshi's relations with Tibetan forces in India were already tense, and his new status served only to further strain overall relations between Chushi Gangdrug and the resistance activities under Gyalo Thondup and Lhamo Tsering, Gyalo Thondup's secretary and right-hand man. These strains reflected the troubles taking place in civilian life between the United Party, the Thirteen Group, and the government-in-exile. The Delhi office sent more Est. 22 soldiers to Mustang, thus increasing the number of "internal squabbles" among the troops.[49] In the summer of 1964, tensions were further compounded when unannounced visitors arrived in one of the valleys several days east of Mustang, where a resistance battalion was stationed. The visitors were a British film crew led by the Scots missionary George Patterson, a longtime Tibet supporter (and friend of the Pangdatsang family) who was frustrated with the lack of international support for Tibet.[50] Patterson was convinced that if he could document the unknown Tibetan resistance to the Chinese, the world would support them. Patterson's group met up with a battalion led by a soldier named Tendar and followed them on a raid into Tibet. Patterson had discussed his plan with Tibetans in India, but Chushi Gangdrug officials were not aware of his activities until after the fact. Although Patterson's film did not air in England until two years later, the Americans were livid that the secret nature of the Mustang operation was compromised. They wanted Baba Yeshi to be replaced as the leader.[51]

From this point on, the story becomes blurred through a series of successive controversies. Although Gyalo Thondup did not initially support the replacing of Baba Yeshi, who, after all, was Andrug Gompo Tashi's handpicked successor, in time things changed. Money became an issue. Whereas there were accusations that Gyalo Thondup had squandered both Tibetan government and Chushi Gangdrug money, similar accusations were also leveled at Baba Yeshi, specifically that he was misappropriating funds sent to Mustang in order to increase his personal wealth. Some say the dispute was really between Baba Yeshi and Lhamo Tsering. At any rate, Lhamo Tsering or Gyalo Thondup or both decided to make a change, sending a nephew of Andrug Gompo Tashi—a man named Gyato Wangdu—to Mustang to serve as Baba Yeshi's assistant.

Gyato Wangdu was a graduate of CIA training at Camp Hale. He had parachuted into Tibet and was a veteran of numerous battles there.[52] According to everyone with whom I spoke, Wangdu was a good man, "brave, enthusiastic, fearless, and a man of action."[53] He is also remembered as someone who had a temper and stood his ground in disagreements, even with social superiors such as Gyalo Thondup, a character trait that surely placed him in good standing with the Americans. In Mustang, Gyato Wangdu's style was markedly different from Baba Yeshi's. According to Sonam Tsering, both men had about twenty bodyguards, but Baba Yeshi always traveled on horseback, kept seven or eight Alsatian dogs, and was feared by the local people. They referred to him as the Big General and would close their doors when he came through town. Gyato Wangdu, on the other hand, always walked and didn't wear the military cap and small round glasses the other leaders wore. His philosophy was that all men are equal and that you should therefore fear no one.[54]

Disagreements between Gyato Wangdu and Baba Yeshi turned tense and gave rise to unrest between their supporters. The Tibetan government-in-exile sent three officials—Taklha Phuntsok Tashi, Dronyik Lhamo Tsering, and Chatreng Kalsang Choezin—to Mustang in an unsuccessful attempt to resolve the dispute. After some time, Baba Yeshi was summoned to Dharamsala. With several aides, he made the long journey and on arrival was offered the post of deputy minister of the Tibetan government-in-exile's Security Office. In exchange, he was to resign his position as general in Mustang without returning to Nepal. From Dharamsala he traveled to Delhi, where he took Lodi Gyari, then a young assistant cabinet secretary in the exile government, into his confidence. "Baba Yeshi was very honored to have received an audience with His Holiness," Gyari recalls, "and especially to have been offered a government position as a regular person" rather than as an aristocrat, chieftain, or royalty. "But, he told me, he must return to Mustang on time. His men expected him to return, and he wanted to hand over command with dignity. He wanted to do it in person, so had to go back. He was gone the next day."[55] Gyari was the only government official Baba Yeshi told before he quietly left Delhi and returned to Mustang. Upon arrival he discovered that Gyato Wangdu had unilaterally taken control of the Mustang force rather than waiting for Baba Yeshi to officially hand over command to him. The situation disintegrated. Neither Baba Yeshi nor Gyato Wangdu would abdicate power to the other; both had important connections to Andrug Gompo Tashi, and both had the following of some of the resistance soldiers.

Along with the soldiers loyal to him, Baba Yeshi moved to the south and east to the valley of Manang. He was based there for several years while Wangdu controlled the main army in Mustang. Eventually, Baba Yeshi surrendered his arms and ammunition to the Nepali government. By 1972, he had relocated to Kathmandu and was living in the Gyaneswor neighborhood. Meanwhile, the Americans had decided to stop funding the Tibetan guerrillas. In the face of discontinued U.S. support, Gyalo Thondup and others in the Delhi office felt the Mustang operations could not be successful and wanted to shut down the army and resettle the soldiers. Roughly two hundred soldiers were settled in Pokhara, while others were supposed to go to India to join the SFF. Many senior Khampa leaders, including Jama Ngatruk, were against this plan and wanted to keep on fighting, as did Gyato Wangdu. As Baba Yeshi had earlier, Wangdu traveled to Delhi, where he asked Lodi Gyari for help.

Desperate to keep the Mustang operations going, Wangdu asked Gyari if the Russians or perhaps the Kuomintang would be willing to help the Tibetans.[56] According to Gyari, despite his training in Colorado and close relations with CIA officers, for Wangdu the Tibetan resistance was not about the CIA or connections to the United States or defeating communism. It was about regaining Tibet by whatever means necessary and with help from whomever might offer it. Although dealings with the Taiwanese were "politically forbidden at the time, Wangdu was willing to do anything" at that point.[57] Gyari arranged a meeting for Wangdu at the Janpath Hotel with Surkhang Wangchen Gelek, a former Tibetan government official and Pangdatsang associate who had fallen out of favor with the exile government and was living in a twice-removed exile in Taiwan. Ever the cautious Lhasa aristocrat, Surkhang exhibited a style vastly different from Wangdu's short-tempered Khampa approach. As Gyari recalls, Wangdu asked Surkhang point blank for help in contacting the Taiwanese government, and Surkhang offered only to speak with Gyalo Thondup. Wangdu felt insulted; furious and frustrated, he returned to Mustang.

In 1973, the Nepali government ended their policy of turning a blind eye to covert operations against China from within its borders. Lhamo Tsering, who was helping resettle soldiers and establish income-generating businesses for them in Pokhara, was arrested and imprisoned by the Nepali government as the political situation grew more tense.[58] Pressured by China, the government of Nepal tried to get the guerrillas to shut things down, publicly calling them bandits and claiming they had never known the guerrillas were there in the first place. The Royal Nepal Army was sent to Mustang to stop Tibetan operations. None of the soldiers would turn their weapons over to the Nepalis. Finally, the Dalai Lama's brother-in-law, Taklha Phuntsok Tashi, hand-carried a taped message from the Dalai Lama to the soldiers in Mustang. In his message, the Dalai Lama told the soldiers to surrender, saying it would not be good for them to fight with the Nepali army. Many of the soldiers were in despair, and some committed suicide rather than surrender to Nepal. Eventually Gyato Wangdu decided to surrender.

Following the complete surrender of Tibetan army weapons, the Nepali Home Ministry agreed it would settle the soldiers in the Pokhara area; the exile government sent the high-level officials Wangdu Dorje, Taring Jigme Namgyal (George Taring), and Alak Jigme Rinpoche to help with this process. Meanwhile, in Mustang, Wangdu traveled from army camp to army camp surrendering arms. When he was almost done, he sensed the Nepali army was behaving more aggressively, which seemed a sign something was wrong.[59] In response, he took about four dozen soldiers with him and made a valiant effort to flee to India.[60] His party was ambushed by the Nepali army at the Indian border. Four people, including Gyato Wangdu, were killed.

The death of Gyato Wangdu cast a pall upon an already sober situation. Along with Lhamo Tsering, the Nepali government imprisoned five of the Mustang leaders—Gen Rakra, Chatreng Gyurme, Jama Ngatruk, Gen Pega, and Gen Tashi—in Kathmandu.[61] Despite the dedicated efforts of the Dalai Lama's representatives in Nepal, the men spent seven years in prison. They were not released until 28 December 1981, when King Birendra symbolically ordered their release on his birthday in response to a request from the Dalai Lama.[62]

Initially, veterans contend, the Nepali authorities conveyed to the Tibetan soldiers the message that they would be able to stay in Mustang. According to Amdho Choedak, however, after the soldiers handed over their weapons, the authorities changed the story:

> They told us that we had to go down [to the lowlands] where we should be put in jail for breaking the laws of the country. As the Dalai Lama had told us to do as we were told to do, we went to the prison without complaining. Some of us lived in prison for three months, while others lived there for four to six months. All the Tibetan soldiers were imprisoned [in military barracks] along with their wives and children, about fifteen hundred people. We were imprisoned in Nuwakot district. There wasn't enough space to hold all of the soldiers. Upon release, we were only allowed to travel between Pokhara and Kathmandu. The authorities said that if they gave us the freedom to go anywhere in Nepal, then we would commit more crimes.[63]

The dissolution of the Mustang force in 1974 left the Tibetan soldiers in dire straits. Most could not speak Nepali and had no obvious means of livelihood. Upon being released from detention camps, they were resettled in refugee camps in Pokhara and the surrounding area. Many soldiers were settled in the Jampaling camp and a smaller number in the Paljorling camp; some headed to Kathmandu to try their luck in the Nepali capital. Other soldiers chose to follow one of two men: Baba Yeshi or Amdo Kesang.

Amdo Kesang's camp in Pokhara was called the Amdo Camp.[64] Amdo Kesang was a shrewd businessman who was known as a troublemaker but who was very good with languages, politically savvy, and funded by the Taiwanese government.[65] He welcomed soldiers to his camp but was not otherwise connected to the Mustang force. While it was mostly soldiers from Amdo who joined his camp, those joining Baba Yeshi in Kathmandu were mostly Khampa who disagreed with the label of traitor some pinned on Baba Yeshi.[66] Upon his surrender to the Nepali authorities, Baba Yeshi had been rewarded with land in several places in Nepal, and he and his followers were granted Nepali citizenship. With assistance from the

Nepali government, he established a camp at Jorpati, slightly east of the Boudha chorten in Kathmandu. He sent a man to the Nuwakot jail to invite people to come to Kathmandu, offering not only housing but also food, which the jail did not provide for the Tibetan prisoners. Unlike the refugee camps at Jampaling and Paljorling, those associated with Amdo Kesang and Baba Yeshi were initially not affiliated with the Tibetan government-in-exile. Instead, they were excommunicated from the Tibetan government-in-exile; that is, residents of the camps were not eligible for government refugee citizenship status and such services as education. This adversely affected their status in the community in many ways; these men and their families were still Tibetan but were now distanced from the refugee community in ways that pierced the heart of what mattered: as Andrug Gompo Tashi had requested of them, to follow and be loyal to the Dalai Lama. The pain in this split was felt by those on all sides.

With the Mustang operation disbanded and the soldiers scattered, Chushi Gangdrug continued to operate. The head office in Darjeeling, and later in Delhi and Dharamsala, maintained a political and social (and at times antagonistic) presence in the refugee community that continues to the present day. In Nepal, the Mustang veterans formed an organization called Lothik (*lo sgrig 'dzugs*) to address issues of economic and social welfare. Veterans did not receive pensions in the 1970s (nor do they now) from either the Tibetan government-in-exile or the U.S. government, so the Lothik provides them one based on their years of service. Pension funds are generated through various Chushi Gangdrug business ventures in Nepal and India. The Lothik bought the land for the Paljorling camp in Pokhara and over the years has run a number of businesses, including the Hotel Mount Annapurna in Pokhara (established in 1972); carpet factories in Pokhara, Kathmandu, and Dolmaling (near Mugling); and hotels in Darjeeling and Butwaling.[67] Many of the veterans, of whom there are perhaps two hundred or fewer left in Nepal, stay in an elders' home at the Jampaling camp, to which the Tibetan government-in-exile sometimes allocates funds. Most of their stories—"their names and what they did for Tibet," according to one woman—are not known within the exile community. As the veterans and their families see it, to know their names and what they did for Tibet would be to grant them the collective recognition they desire so intensely.

The end of the Mustang operations marked the close of a specific chapter in the history of the Tibetan resistance. As Chushi Gangdrug, a social and political organization with a military past, and as a component of the Indian armed forces, the resistance continues. Yet the dissolution of the Mustang force signaled the end of an autonomous Tibetan military force. Although the United States viewed the Mustang operation primarily as an intelligence-gathering force, the Tibetans themselves viewed their activities as within the continuum of a military battle, not just as the gathering of information. For many of the veterans, the loss of American support and the order from the Dalai Lama to quit Mustang left them with little hope as to what the future might hold. Nonetheless, the support the United States provided and the close bonds formed between Tibetan trainees and CIA teachers combined to sustain the belief that the United States would help the Tibetan cause in the future. In terms of the Tibetan mirror of history, however, the connection to the CIA undoubtedly contributed to its clouded state.

Colorado's mountain roads can be treacherous in the winter, and in December 1961 a bus crashed on an icy road in the middle of the night.[1] The accident delayed the journey, and it was morning by the time the bus pulled into its destination, Peterson Airfield in Colorado Springs. The coffee was just beginning to brew when airfield workers discovered that army soldiers with rifles had surrounded them. The soldiers ordered them into two hangars whose doors were then shut and locked. Peeking out the windows of the hangar, the workers saw the delayed bus, its windows blackened, pull up to a waiting Air Force plane; fifteen men in green fatigues got out and boarded the plane. After the plane took off, an army officer informed the airfield employees it was a federal offense to talk about what they had just witnessed. He swore them to the highest secrecy, but it was already too late: the hangars in which the scared civilians had been locked had phones in them, and they had made several calls to local newspapers. The next day the Colorado Springs *Gazette Telegraph* ran a brief story quoting a student pilot, who said that "several Oriental soldiers in combat uniforms" were involved. The story caught the attention of a *New York Times* reporter in Washington, D.C., and he called the Pentagon for more information. His call was returned by the secretary of defense, Robert McNamara, himself. McNamara killed the story not only by uttering the words "top secret national security," but also by confiding to the reporter that the men were in fact Tibetans.

The Social Life of Secrets

A Tibetan proverb states that "an unspoken word has freedom, a spoken word has none." The freedom of things unspoken or unnarrated, however, is not without end. Secrets, for example, while supposedly not to be told, derive their value in part not by being kept but by being shared. Sharing secrets—revealing the unspoken, reining in freedom—often involves cultural systems of regulation regarding who can be told, whom one can in turn tell, and what degree of disclosure is allowed. As a form of control over knowledge, secrecy is recognized in many societies as a means through which power is gained and maintained.[2] Secretary McNamara didn't just tell the *New York Times* reporter that the story was secret but secured his confidence by sharing part of the secret, by telling him the men involved were Tibetans. Together, Tibet and the CIA present an irresistible combination of two twentieth-century icons of forbidden mystery and intrigue—Tibet, Shangri-La, the supposed land of mystical and ancient wisdom; and the CIA, home of covert activities, where even the secrets have secrets. The Tibet–CIA connection was almost too good a secret to keep.

Yet stories of this guerrilla war were kept secret for many years. The war involved multiple governments and the covert moving of men, money, and munitions across international borders, so it is perhaps no surprise that information about the resistance, and more specifically about U.S.–Tibet relations, was suppressed until recently and even now is only slowly being released. The secrets of the Tibetan resistance, however, are not always as they appear. They are not, for example, only political but also ethnographic, built upon cultural systems of meaning and action. Secrets are social: they find their energy in their keeping and their breaking and their value in the ways they are used, displayed, hidden, referenced, and exchanged. As the historian Luise White argues, "Keeping a secret requires negotiating a social world at least as much as lying does. Keeping a secret isn't something a self does, it's something that continually has to be reconstituted and renegotiated through changing political and discursive practices."[3]

Historical arrest is just such a process in that secrets are reconstituted and renegotiated through it. Arresting something places it in the category of the forbidden, the secret, the unspoken. The secrets involved in the

Tibetan resistance are plural; some are public, some official, and some private, kept by veterans. Some hide in plain sight, like the veterans themselves and the sixteenth of June ceremony, as public embodiments and enactments of resistance history. As White suggests, secrets "reveal a shifting terrain of ideas about danger, about risk, about importance, and about the public meaning of those conditions."[4] Danger, importance, and their public meanings lie solidly at the core of Tibetan resistance histories.

Tibet and the United States

"*Gsang ba* [secret]." Time and again, Chushi Gangdrug veterans would tell me that everything they did with the CIA was secret: travel in the dark of night; the windows of cars and buses blacked out; unmarked planes; code names; cyanide capsules and pledges not to tell a word if captured. Secrets then and arrested histories now, however, were not necessarily one and the same for the veterans. Soldiers understood secrets then to be a requirement of Cold War politics and guerrilla warfare. Veterans understand arrested histories now to be a component of community politics in exile. For veterans, relations with the CIA were only a part of the resistance army's operations. They were an important part but not a defining, founding, or continuing feature of Chushi Gangdrug's existence. Situating Chushi Gangdrug history within a broader Cold War history was a different sort of exercise than telling it as Tibetan history. Reverend Tharchin's efforts to place Tibetan history in world history in his editorials and exhortations in the *Tibet Mirror* were continued by CIA officers who included world history classes in their training of Tibetans in Colorado. Lessons on the global spread of and struggle against communism served to further convince the Tibetans not just of the righteousness of their struggle, but of its place among other such battles around the world. They did not necessarily want their struggle to be secret. The Americans, on the other hand, not only promoted secrecy, but also aided the Tibetan struggle with their own interests in mind and with a glaring lack of knowledge about the region.

The United States and Tibet do not have a long history of relations. Contact was first made under President Franklin Roosevelt in 1942, during the Second World War, when the United States wanted to transit wartime supplies over and through Tibet to troops in China. Roosevelt sent two undercover envoys of the Office of Strategic Services to Lhasa, thus beginning U.S.–Tibet relations. The mission was successful, and the next interaction between the two countries came in 1947–48, when the Tibetan Trade Mission, traveling on Tibetan passports, came to the United States as part of their global mission to strengthen Tibetan international economic and political relations in light of growing political danger from China. With the advent of Communist control in China, U.S. interest in Tibet grew exponentially as part of their broader Cold War policies. Tibet had an important role in U.S. Cold War strategy in Asia as both counter to Communist China and facilitator of U.S. relations with India and Pakistan.[5] Although many Americans politically involved with Tibet at this time developed strong personal support for the Tibetans, Tibet remained, in the view of the United States, what it had been in that of the British, a "pawn on the imperial chessboard,"[6] and the Tibetans themselves were, to use the words of a former CIA agent, "orphans of the Cold War."[7]

Asia is not usually recognized as a key site in the evolution of the Cold War. A growing body of literature seeks to challenge this categorization through discussions of Cold War politics in China, Korea, and Vietnam as well as in the less familiar political landscapes of South and Central Asia.[8] Tibet figured prominently in Cold War disputes between India and China.[9] Throughout the 1950s and 1960s, India proclaimed a nonaligned status, all the while secretly courting and being courted by Washington, Moscow, and Beijing. The top secret, constantly changing, and often contradictory allegiances between these governments resulted in several armed conflicts, including the Sino–Indian War of 1962, the Indo–Pakistan War of 1965, the ongoing battle in Kashmir, and the Tibetan conflict with China.

U.S. government intervention legitimated the threat China posed to Tibetan national security. The covert nature of American military assistance to the Tibetans, however, meant that this external validation was not presented to the world, and much of the Western world was unaware of the Tibetan resistance to the Chinese. If U.S. action on Tibet was fueled by anticommunism and the evangelization of democracy, Tibetans' reasons for working with the Americans fit a decolonization-era pattern of seeking external assistance for internal political goals. For Tibetans, U.S. assistance was not a denial of their own agency and autonomy but an acknowledgment of it. At this time in history, as well as in

Tibet–U.S. relations, the CIA was not quite the internationally notorious organization it is in the present. Thus Tibetan sentiment offers not just naïveté regarding international or imperial politics, but a window onto a historicized Tibetan view of the United States, empire, and personal experience as foreign policy.

At the ground level, the Americans and the Tibetans saw each other as mutually providing the assistance needed to accomplish their goals, be they securing rare intelligence on the PRC or securing one's country. Notions of working together on these goals involved acknowledged differential access to information and resources (as evidenced by the differences in responses to the captured documents in Mustang). At higher levels, U.S. interest in Tibet never extended as far as the Tibetans wanted, as revealed in a memorandum of 9 January 1964: "The CIA Tibetan Activity consists of political action, propaganda, and paramilitary activity. The purpose of the program at this stage is to keep the political concept of an autonomous Tibet alive within Tibet and among foreign nations, principally India, and to build a capability for resistance against possible political developments inside Communist China."[10] The degree to which Tibetan exile political projects have been influenced and shaped by U.S. interests remains widely unknown and hence underappreciated by both Tibetans and their foreign supporters.[11] However, U.S. interests were not impersonal. Just as important to the soldiers was the face-to-face support they received from the Americans with whom they worked closely—the CIA officers in Colorado and Asia. Cooperation between the men on the ground enabled a sense of imperialism as opportunity, as a chance for agency, action, national participation, and independence.[12]

Imperialism as Opportunity

One of the soldiers' self-initiated projects in Colorado was the writing of short books for distribution in Tibet. Written in colloquial Tibetan with accompanying narrative illustrations, the books spoke directly to communist propaganda and beautifully demonstrate the convergence of Tibetan political projects and American imperial guidance. One example is *A Pleasure Garden for Blossoming the Tibetan People's Wisdom to Reestablish an Independent Republic of Tibet*.[13] Written in 1960 "by the people of Camp Dumra," this twenty-six-page book is a combination of handwritten text and line drawings that together compose a primer on Tibetan history and world politics. The book has five textual sections: reasons for the rebellion, regaining independence, today's world, global independence struggles, and friends of Tibet, and a sixth history section composed solely of illustrations.

A Pleasure Garden lays out the reasons for the Tibetan rebellion, contending that the Chinese not only invaded an independent Tibet but also intend to destroy the Tibetan people and their culture. The book's authors next explain the need for an organized and united rebellion force that complements an accompanying nonviolent aspect of the political struggle. Part of their explanation compares Chinese rule in Tibet to examples of European colonialism: "A country called Algeria was occupied by France one hundred years ago. Algeria was very much like today's Tibet. For example, because they did not have good leadership, the people of the country were not unified, and therefore the country was defeated by the French. After six years of French occupation, an educated Algerian man living in a neighboring country started the Algerian Freedom Movement. He planned for five years how best to unify the people and revolt. Through the dual violent/nonviolent method, the country regained its independence. Today, Algeria is a developed and democratic nation."[14] The narrative structure of this minihistory parallels that presented for Tibet, thereby legitimating the Tibetan rebellion against the Chinese. Paired with a discussion of Tibet's "friend countries" around the world, some of which were formerly colonized and all of which are now democracies that "love world peace and freedom," the Tibetan revolt is effectively globalized as an anticolonial, anticommunist struggle.[15] This narrative places Tibet squarely within an imperial circuit of knowledge production emanating from the United States over the course of the twentieth century.[16]

In a telling example of U.S. imperial invisibility, the United States is not mentioned in *A Pleasure Garden*. Empire recedes on behalf of a national liberation struggle. While the United States could be included among the "sixty countries" which support Tibet, the specific nature of U.S. assistance was not acknowledged. U.S. support for the resistance was a public, but not a printable, secret among Tibetans. That the presence of American influence goes unacknowledged in *A Pleasure Garden* is attributable to the covert nature of U.S. support as well as to Tibetan soldiers' notions of partnership with their American counterparts. These partnerships were not transparent on any side of the equation—the Tibetan veterans were not the Dalai Lama's exile government, nor were the CIA officers simply carrying through dictates they received from Washington or from headquarters at Langley. As a retired CIA officer explained to me, "We had a significant aspiration in helping Tibetans represent themselves in the world as something other than resistance fighters."[17] Multiple interests and multiple strategies were at work to achieve parallel goals: the expansion of U.S. influence and the regaining of Tibet. For the majority of Tibetans with whom I worked, discomfort with American empire building on the back of the Tibetan struggle pales in comparison to the gratitude for the support. Secret or not, U.S. intervention provided (and continues to provide) external legitimization of the threat China posed to Tibet.

Chushi Gangdrug and the CIA

"The [Tibetans] were the best men I worked with," claimed Tony Poe, a retired CIA officer who trained the Tibetan soldiers and later worked in Laos. Journalists have long speculated Poe was the real-life model for the character of Colonel Walter E. Kurtz in *Apocalypse Now*.[18] In turn, Tibetans remember Poe and the other American instructors fondly: "They were good people" (*khong tsho mi yag po red*) was a common refrain I heard during my research. Despite the mutual admiration, a series of misunderstandings marred the relationship between the Tibetans and the Americans.[19] While the U.S. interest in preventing the spread of communism rather than providing serious and committed aid to Tibet was one key misunderstanding, a second one remains unexplored in most discussions of the resistance: the importance of regional allegiances and political status within the Tibetan community.[20]

Tibetan social and political divisions were far more complex than the CIA realized. The Chushi Gangdrug army was organized on the basis of native place affiliations and favored a Khampa sociopolitical system over a central Tibetan one. The CIA does not appear to have considered these facts. Two reasons might explain this: first, U.S. intelligence analysts had little information about Tibet, and what they did know was based on British sources which downplayed the importance of regional difference in favor of a focus on Lhasa; and, second, the Tibetans upon whom the Americans relied for updated information were not from Kham. The primary contact between the Tibetan government, the resistance, and the U.S. government was Gyalo Thondup. Additionally, only one CIA officer could speak some Tibetan; communication was otherwise through Tibetan interpreters, some of whom had only a rudimentary knowledge of English.[21]

The American oversight of the importance of regional identity to the Tibetans was ironically at odds with the CIA officers' personal admiration for the soldiers they trained. This resulted in disaster on several occasions. For example, the CIA vetoed soldiers' suggestions to organize operations around native place allegiances. On one occasion, this had particularly devastating results when a guerrilla unit was sent against its wishes into an area of Tibet where they did not have local support. Unit soldiers were not from this area and culturally unable to forge the needed relationships and trust with the local community within a short time frame. Information about the soldiers' location leaked out, the Chinese ambushed them, and all died except one.[22]

On a broader level, the overall administration of the resistance—and the varying interpretations and suppressions of its history—was affected because of the American misinterpretation of relations between the different leaders of the resistance, and between the leaders and the soldiers. The CIA's military-style ranking of the men was based on an achieved status, whereas among the Tibetan soldiers, achievement and military prowess did not outrank ascribed statuses. For the most part, resistance leaders were men whose social power was long established and legitimized through the same sort of personal and place connections operative in Tibet prior to the Chinese invasion. Such ascribed statuses were important to the two primary figures in the resistance—Andrug Gompo Tashi's status as an important Khampa trader, and Gyalo Thondup's status as the Dalai Lama's brother.

In the eyes of the U.S. government, Gyalo Thondup was the chief architect of the Tibetan resistance.[23] Among resistance soldiers, however, Andrug Gompo Tashi was the recognized leader of the united Chushi Gangdrug force. Gyalo Thondup's position among the Chushi Gangdrug soldiers was different. To them, Gyalo was more a patron than a leader of the resistance, a very high-status intermediary responsible for managing U.S. aid to the resistance. The status of patron is a recognized and esteemed one within Tibetan society: the contributions of a patron are acknowledged and praised, and a patron's efforts enhance, rather than detract from, the authority of the group being sponsored. For the soldiers, Gyalo Thondup's contributions to the resistance did not outweigh those of Andrug Gompo Tashi but were assessed differently and accorded different historical weight.

Gyalo Thondup was someone who operated in vastly distinct worlds from even the leaders of Chushi Gangdrug. As Baba Yeshi explained, "We thought that Gyalo Thondup knew the ways of the world. He had experience."[24] Gyalo Thondup was further distinguished by being Amdowa, that is, a Tibetan from the Amdo region, as well as a cosmopolitan individual educated in China. He spoke Mandarin and English, had many foreign friends, and was married to a Chinese woman. His social and political status and experience were elite and influential. As a result, serious gaps existed between Gyalo Thondup and the mostly Khampa resistance force, gaps that were partially filled in with rumors and misunderstandings.[25]

Not all misunderstandings or hard feelings revolved around Gyalo Thondup. Other problems had to do with *pha yul* loyalties and cross-territory resentment. For example, the majority of the men Andrug Gompo Tashi chose for initial training by the CIA and for leadership positions were ones he knew, men and relatives from his area of Lithang. Men from Lithang came to dominate Chushi Gangdrug, which was not always appreciated by other Khampa leaders and battalions. As one Khampa explained, "The current split in Chushi Gangdrug is in part because it has always been dominated by Lithangbas and Babas. Others have deep resentment of this—from Trehor, Derge, and so on. There is also deep anti–Gyalo Thondup sentiment. He patronized Lithangbas, and he didn't know anything about Khampa politics. Men from Trehor and Derge all wanted to be close to Gyalo Thondup but realized that the Lithang mafia was the closest."[26] Lithang favoritism within Chushi Gangdrug both replicated and troubled the Khampa spirit of independence. As some veterans might ask, if Kham was a region of equal leaders, then why privilege Lithang?

In line with these trends in leadership and organization, the resistance saw itself as a mostly autonomous entity. In exile, veterans present the resistance organization as an equal partner to, rather than a subordinate of, the U.S. and Tibetan governments. The inability of the Tibetan government army to fight against the PLA, along with the necessarily secret relationship between Chushi Gangdrug and the Tibetan government, granted the resistance a large measure of autonomy vis-à-vis the government, and that independence carried over into exile. The resistance movement was not a creation of the CIA, of Gyalo Thondup, of the government, or even of Andrug Gompo Tashi: it was a citizens' organization formed in response to Chinese oppression. As narrated to me time and again by both former leaders and soldiers, resistance decisions about policy and actions were internal affairs; this was a group that was assisted, but not directed, by outsiders.

The Soldiers' Art of Critique

Lobsang Jampa was one of the unsung heroes of the resistance. When he was a young boy, his parents enrolled him in the local monastery in their town of Lithang. At the age of twenty-one, he left the monastery to become a trader, and when communist Chinese reforms became too oppressive in the mid-1950s he joined the resistance, leading and financially supporting a group of ten horsemen. His group fought throughout Tibet, and in 1959 he and his men followed the Dalai Lama to India. There, he was chosen to go to the United States for military training in Colorado, after which he joined the resistance in Nepal. He married a woman from Mustang and spent his remaining years in Kathmandu in pursuit of his three passions: Tibetan language media, visiting with friends, and religious practice and prayer, including sixty kora (circumambulations) of the Boudha stupa each day. This same devotion characterizes his relationship to the Dalai Lama and Tibetan government-in-exile.

Everyone described Lobsang Jampa as honest and humble. I had known him for some time before I found out he had been in the resistance; even after that, it was only from others that I learned he was the man the CIA trained to be the commander in charge in Mustang, a position he did not take up out of respect for Baba Yeshi, whom he was sent to replace. Friends of his tell me he was an excellent shot, and amidst the posters of deities and horses that adorned the walls of his apartment in Kathmandu there hung a plastic rifle with white prayer scarves wrapped around it.

For Lobsang Jampa, the story of Chushi Gangdrug began well before

FIGURE 25 Lobsang Tinley and Lobsang Jampa.

the socialist reforms of the 1950s.[27] In the histories he told me, he inter-
wove his own experiences with broader historical events. He presented
this history as not merely a local or personal story but as a history of
Tibet, ignoring or perhaps defying the fact that resistance histories were
ignored in narratives of national history. In particular and like many of
the veterans, he narrated an agency for the resistance army independent
of both U.S. and Tibetan histories.

Against the appreciation veterans have for CIA support and the loyalty
and devotion they have to the Dalai Lama, the importance of autonomy
evidenced in stories such as Lobsang Jampa's is all the more evident. As
he told it, resistance leaders contacted the U.S. government on their own
initiative through a request to Gyalo Thondup to ask the United States
for military help. Such decisions, he said, were made by consensus: decisions about battle strategies in Tibet before they fled to India, the deci-

sion to set up headquarters in Nepal, decisions about who would go to the United States for training, and decisions about the relations the resistance would have with the Tibetan government. Decisions affecting the resistance were made by resistance leaders. "In those days," according to Lobsang Jampa, "Chushi Gangdrug was very powerful [and] His Holiness the Dalai Lama also had a very good opinion of our organization." While soldiers deferred to the Dalai Lama, deferential politics were not an inherent aspect of resistance relations with either the Tibetan or the U.S. government. In Lobsang Jampa's narrations, these relations were described as having been built on notions of equality and respect.

In talking about his time in Colorado, Lobsang Jampa described the type of training the Tibetans were given (for example, how to jump from a plane and land safely on the ground) and the code names assigned to Tibetans by the Americans (his was Saul).[28] In one training session, the U.S. instructors ambushed them, pretending to be Chinese soldiers. On other occasions, the Tibetans answered hundreds of questions the U.S. instructors asked them about how the Chinese fought and what kind of weapons they used. After finishing their training and preparing to return to Asia, Lobsang Jampa recalled with a smile that both the U.S. teachers and the Tibetan soldiers shed tears when they separated. The gravity of the situation was evident to all: "Eight of us [were to] parachute into Tibet. We had excellent weapons. Each of us carried three different types of guns. We were also provided with a cyanide capsule that we wore around our neck. In times of need, we were simply to put it into our mouth. The most important point was that we must not allow ourselves to be captured alive by the Chinese." The histories Lobsang Jampa told me had an independent form which posited the resistance as an equal partner with the U.S. and Tibetan governments. This view was not one shared by the two governments. In both Washington and Dharamsala, the resistance army was seen as a project to be managed rather than a partnership to be maintained. The agency Lobsang Jampa claims for the resistance is not part of governmental versions of the story. Although this agency and the autonomous histories it inspires are themselves generated out of Tibetan senses of obligation for service and sacrifice to the nation and to the Dalai Lama, to claim this agency is nonetheless to launch a critique.

Tibetan exile society does not allot much space for public critique, and therefore critiques are more often privately aired in people's homes and among friends.[29] Lobsang Jampa's critiques are subtle, taking the form of departures from how resistance history has and has not been told, and informing both what he says and how he says it: "[After the end of the Mustang operation], the Tibetan government-in-exile in Dharamsala . . . told all the soldiers to join the Indian army. Tibetan settlements [established for Chushi Gangdrug members and other Tibetans] should be shifted to India. But nobody wanted these things. Instead we bought land and built houses in Nepal. We opened carpet industries, shops, and hotels." Lobsang Jampa makes declarative statements rather than defensive ones; he describes the resistance not just as a guerrilla army but as a political entity in the community at large; he tells not just a history of resistance but also a history of Tibet viewed through the lens of resistance.

Lobsang Jampa's critiques are an example of Foucault's definition of critique as "the art of not being governed quite so much."[30] As a response to authority, critique draws energy from the relationships of power, truth, and the subject. That is, "critique is the movement by which the subject gives himself the right to question truth on its effects of power and question power on its discourses of truth."[31] Lobsang Jampa's narrations enact just such a questioning. In telling Tibetan history as one of struggle, including armed struggle, he questions other truths claimed for the past. He does so, however, in a parallel register, rather than in a reactive one. His is critique as the "art of involuntary insubordination, that of reflected intractability."[32]

Reflected in the sense of mindful and respectful, intractable in the sense of stubbornly holding tight to unrecognized pasts as histories, Lobsang Jampa continues the Khampa practice of criticizing the Tibetan government while at the same time building direct positive links to it. He makes these subtle critiques from the position of solidly supporting the exile government, of being grateful to the CIA for all they did to help, and of being proud of his part within the resistance. These matter-of-fact elements reveal that the tensions between arrested and national histories are about much more than just the secret story of a guerrilla war. They are instead about the politics of truth as played out in and across communities of belonging.

Secrets Told and Untold

Everything is over now. Now we can tell the secrets.

CHUSHI GANGDRUG VETERAN, DARJEELING, NOVEMBER 1997

The time for telling the secrets has come. Thirty-five years after the end of the Mustang operation, the period of release has begun, and resistance veterans are beginning to tell their stories with greater frequency and in louder voices. In the Tibetan exile community, there is no open, transparent access to information; there is, for example, no equivalent to the freedom of information act in the United States. Knowledge in Tibetan society has long been the exclusive domain of elite communities—monastic, aristocratic, royal, and chiefly. In exile, shifts in knowledge production like the valuing of eyewitness testimony work to break down elites' control of knowledge. Turning secrets into stories, however, is not a matter of securing singular truths. As Tsering Wangmo Dhompa writes in "As remembered," her poem on refugee memory, "It is not the accuracy of the story that concerns us. But who gets to tell it."[33]

The story of the Colorado Tibetans that opened this chapter is an example of how Cold War ideas of government secrets dominate the literature on the CIA–Tibet connection. As words not quite unspoken but spoken only to a select few, secrets have the freedom and the license to travel, circulating not just as acknowledged silences, but also as truths to be pursued and revealed. Outside the Tibetan community, the constraints that control the internal circulation of secrets are not necessarily operative.[34] For outsiders, revealing secrets does not require understanding why something was originally categorized as secret. Given this, it should come as no surprise that most early writings on the resistance were by outsiders rather than by Tibetan authors. Outsider or insider, however, history does not simply stop in the time of arrest. There are always ways to relate secret or arrested pasts, especially in a community in which lay knowledge and history are not primarily textual. Despite the arrest of resistance history, a number of written histories mention the resistance either in passing or in various degrees of detail. But who exactly writes what? And when, and why?

Chushi Gangdrug soldiers have been writing their history since the early 1960s. Political tensions disrupt the work, the great physical distances between refugee settlements interfere, and, as the decades go on, time intervenes with stories not only growing distant, but with people passing away before being able to tell them. Additionally, in a society in which history has long been an exercise in demonstrating continuity, veterans write in a time marked by a lack of continuity.[35] They realize that not much has been written about the resistance and that some Tibetans would rather not discuss Chushi Gangdrug at all in light of the internal politics involved. Nonetheless, since the initial days in exile, Chushi Gangdrug soldiers recognized the need to tell their story, specifically, to document the names and place affiliations of people who struggled to defend Tibet. Given all that has happened in the years since 1956, they write their history from a particularly situated location: that of being largely unknown, unappreciated, and positioned in an antagonistic relationship to the Tibetan government-in-exile. Their struggle to tell their history as one of opposing the Chinese, supporting the Tibetan government, and defending Tibet is thus a complicated endeavor. Like any history-making project, it is processual, ongoing, and contextual.

As a group of veterans in Delhi explained to me, their history project was to be comprehensive: "Our work was rather difficult. It was divided into two. The first part dealt with what had happened in the various regions of Kham. What was the condition of the place before the advent of the Chinese? How did the people oppose the Chinese arrival? Secondly, we had to prepare a history of Chushi Gangdrug in general."[36] Thus far, Chushi Gangdrug has published several Tibetan-language political critiques over the years and, more recently, short histories of the resistance— an English language pamphlet,[37] and a Tibetan language book,[38] in addition to maintaining websites and circulating DVDs of resistance activities then and now. Most resistance publications have been censored by the exile Tibetan government.[39]

The bulk of resistance history writing remains in progress. Pha yul information collected in the 1960s is still waiting to be published. In the mid-1970s, resistance leaders returned again to the project, and then again in the early 1980s following the mending in 1977 of United Party and Thirteen Group political relations within the group. Work on the texts in Dharamsala in the 1980s cut across earlier splits, bringing together individuals who held differing political stances to work on the project—"yabshi supporters, anti-yabshi, everyone."[40] At present, these manuscripts are with the Chushi Gangdrug group in Delhi, and plans are still underway to publish them.

In general, literature about the Tibetan resistance is loosely classifiable by period (pre- or post-1959), author's national origin (Tibetan or Western), and focus (resistance or the CIA). In the late 1960s and early 1970s, despite the best efforts of the U.S. and Tibetan governments to keep matters hidden, bits and pieces of what was going on began to slip out. The first to write openly about the resistance were Westerners concerned with the lack of global support Tibet was receiving,[41] or who were committed to uncovering and exposing CIA operations around the world,[42] or, in the case of the French anthropologist Michel Peissel, who had stumbled across the resistance in the pursuit of other projects.[43]

Unlike their Western counterparts, the much smaller group of early Tibetan writings on the resistance focused on the pre-1959 period and did not mention U.S. and CIA support. The most important of these is Andrug Gompo Tashi's posthumous brief history of the resistance, *Four Rivers, Six Ranges*, which the Tibetan government-in-exile published in 1973.[44] The book was ghost edited by young Tibetans, including Dhondup Tsering and Lodi Gyari, who describes himself at the time as a politically active and "restless civil servant."[45] The Tibetan government-in-exile had given Andrug Gompo Tashi the honorary rank of Dzasa, and Gyari and his colleagues convinced the government to publish his book. "We wanted to show him as a national hero, a national leader, not just a regional or provincial one," Gyari recalled, "but some Chushi Gangdrug leaders were not keen on having Dharamsala publish it. They were intensely loyal to Andrug Gompo Tashi and saw him as their leader, as a Khampa leader, not a national leader."[46] Given the politics at the time, it is remarkable the book was published at all. It does not discuss operations in exile or the CIA connection but is an excellent source on Chushi Gangdrug's ideology and operations in Tibet.

Earlier in Darjeeling, Chushi Gangdrug published a newspaper for a short while in the 1960s, called *Rang dbang srung skyob* (Defend Tibet's freedom).[47] This later became the popular independent newspaper *Bod mi'i rang dbang* (Freedom).[48] Other Tibetan publications include Jamyang Norbu's biography of Aten Dogyaltshang, also published by the Tibetan government-in-exile and focused solely on operations in Tibet.[49] Dawa Norbu's editorials and articles from the 1970s in issues of *Tibetan*

FIGURE 26 Phupa Pön.

Review and *China Quarterly* also fit this model of focus on the pre-1959 period.[50] The Dalai Lama's autobiographies of 1962 and 1990 discuss the resistance; in both, he comments on the bravery of the soldiers in defending their families, religion, and country and the difficulty he faced advising nonviolence given the depth of the Chinese atrocities.[51] The Tibetan historian Tsepon W. D. Shakabpa mentions the resistance only briefly in his Tibetan-language history of Tibet[52] and not at all in the English-language translation, *Tibet: A Political History.*[53] Other English-language histories of twentieth-century Tibet do include brief political discussions of the resistance.[54]

In line with the arrest of resistance history, Tibetan government publications of resistance narratives are exclusively in the realm of personal or secondary history rather than that of national history.[55] In contrast, external publications mostly remain in the vein of history as government secret. In general, as time passes and this particular instance of arrest is gradually released, accounts of the resistance are on the rise,[56] especially in terms of publications by retired CIA officers and Tibetan veterans.[57] Individuals are also self-publishing resistance histories as part of personal and place histories.[58] Kargyal Thondup's book about Chatreng is one example, as is a book about Markham by pha yul Phupa Pön. Phupa Pön's

FIGURE 27 Ratuk Ngawang.

book lays out the political, social, and religious organization of Markham and tells the history of the 1949–59 period, with specific attention to resistance to the Chinese.[59] The most important nontextual history of the resistance is the film *Shadow Circus* made by the filmmaking team of Tenzing Sonam and Ritu Sarin, Lhamo Tsering's son and daughter-in-law, which includes oral interviews with both Tibetan veterans and retired CIA officers.[60]

Especially notable are two recent Tibetan-language multivolume publications: Tsongkha Lhamo Tsering's combination autobiography and resistance history and Ratuk Ngawang's work on resistance in Lithang and exile.[61] Published by the independent Amnye Machen Institute in Dharamsala, the two works call attention to the importance of Tibetan historians in incorporating the resistance into the annals of contemporary Tibetan history. More specifically, the volumes highlight the specific importance Tashi Tsering continues to play in documenting resistance history. One of the leading historians and intellectuals in the exile community, former research scholar of the exile government's Library of Tibetan Works and Archives, and current director of the Amnye Machen Institute in Dharamsala, Tashi Tsering's commitment to documenting the Tibetan past in oral and written form is evident in his efforts over the decades to collect, edit, and publish resistance histories. At present, the literature in both English and Tibetan on the resistance is growing, but not quite in conversation with each other, and in both cases giving away some secrets while still keeping others.

Beyond Government Secrets

Admittedly, by their very nature, guerrilla resistance war and government intelligence work are secretive enterprises. Much—most, perhaps—still remains unwritten, untold, or denied. The U.S. government has released only heavily edited information about its involvement with the Tibetan resistance; at the same time, only some State Department files and no CIA files have been declassified. While historical arrest may be as much or more about the sociopolitics of community as about the secrets of governments, the government secrets of resistance history are by no means entirely clear yet.[62] Camp Hale, where the Tibetan soldiers were trained in Colorado, is currently a Historic Interpretive Site administered by the U.S. Forest Service. Unlike the Second World War facilities at Camp Hale, the remnants of which are still visible, the CIA Tibetan training compound there was disassembled after operation ended so that no evidence would remain. In July 2002, I traveled to Camp Hale in the hopes of finding some sign of the Tibetans' stay there. Located northwest of Leadville, Colorado, the Camp Hale historic site consists only of the ruins and a series of interpretive tablets. To my disappointment but not surprise, the text and accompanying timeline for the "Post World War II" period included no mention of the Tibetans' use of the camp from 1958 through 1964.[63] The tablet simply reads, "The Mountain and Cold Weather Training Command used Camp Hale for operations, training, and maneuvers from 1951 to 1957. In 1965 the flag at Camp Hale was lowered for the last time." In a textbook case of elision and erasure, simply no information at all is recorded for the period during which the Tibetans were resident. Marked by an absence, it is as if they were never present.

In Asia, even less official information is available. The Nepali government denied all knowledge of, not to mention complicity with, the Tibetans' use of Nepali territory for their resistance operations. Privately, however, the king of Nepal had first told the U.S. government he was willing to aid the Tibetans in 1950.[64] In India today, very little is known by the Indian public about their government's collaboration with the United

FIGURE 28 Camp Hale.

States regarding Tibet.[65] Tibetan service in the Indian armed forces, for example, is almost entirely unknown by the Indian public.[66] During the Kargil War in Kashmir in 1998–99, Indian newspapers ran stories almost daily about martyred Indian soldiers and the families they left behind. Deaths of Tibetan soldiers in Kargil were not included. There was no public paper trail of Tibetan war deaths and no public presentation of grieving children, mothers, and spouses in newspapers or on the nightly television news. What is a public secret among Tibetans is simply unknown among Indians.

Other secrets are only beginning to come to light, such as the revelation that the Tibetan resistance provided key intelligence information to the U.S. government, including information about PLA military capacity, internal dissent during the Great Leap Forward, and information about the first Chinese nuclear tests at Lop Nor in northern Tibet.[67] Secrets between governments persist and compose a key part of the history of the resistance, yet what for India, Pakistan, Nepal, and the United States was an official secret was for the Tibetans much more. For the Tibetan community, the story of the resistance is not just one of clandestine politics and government secrets but is multiple stories, such as personal tales of serving the nation and the Dalai Lama, accounts of the armed struggle for their country, and continuing debates over facets of communal identity and politics in the exile community. Nonetheless, the tensions and substance of these stories remain internal. As a result, when outsiders consider why the resistance is not historically recognized, it is usually in relation to external reasons, either the connection to the CIA or the Dalai Lama's decision that the Tibetan struggle would be nonviolent.

The CIA's link to the Tibetan resistance reveals the political immaturity of the Tibetan state in this era. In the 1950s and through the 1960s, most Tibetans were not familiar with the CIA. As Tibetans associated with the exile government came to realize the global reputation the CIA held and the nature of some of its actions in the world, they began to distance the exile government and the Dalai Lama from this relationship. As a former official explains, "To acknowledge Chushi Gangdrug would be to acknowledge the CIA and so efforts were made to not highlight it so much."[68] At the same time, the Dalai Lama and the Tibetan government-in-exile were developing a formal political policy of nonviolence. Their philosophy and practice of nonviolence are strict and are both built upon and generative of secrets of the Tibetan resistance. For resistance veterans, there are karmic, narrative, physical, and political components all involved in grappling with past violence and present nonviolence. It is anything but simple. Veterans' commitments to nonviolence overlap with those to war in that each are rooted in Buddhist principles and devotion to the Dalai Lama but also diverge in important and often deeply personal ways. As the next chapter reveals, a nonviolent history of war is not without casualties.

On 27 April 1998, Thubten Ngodup set himself on fire to protest the government of India's forceful ending of a Tibetan hunger strike in New Delhi. Two days later he died from his burns. Ngodup was sixty years old, a former monk at Tashilhunpo Monastery in Tibet and a former soldier in the Est. 22/SFF Tibetan force of the Indian army. Since 1988, he had worked as a cowherd and cook at a monastery in Dharamsala, living quietly in a small hut and participating whenever possible in Tibetan independence protests and marches.[1] During the Unto Death Hunger Strike of 1998 demanding UN action on Tibet, Ngodup volunteered as an assistant, tending to the needs of the hunger strikers. On the morning of the forty-ninth day of the hunger strike, as Indian police forcibly dragged away the hunger strikers (in line with Indian laws prohibiting suicide) and beat volunteers who protested the police actions, Ngodup doused himself with a flammable liquid, and, shouting pro-Tibet, pro–Dalai Lama slogans, lit a match and set himself on fire. His self-immolation drew the attention of the world's media, immediate martyrdom status within the Tibetan community, and the "deeply saddened" criticism of the Dalai Lama, who had spoken against the proclaimed nonviolent hunger strike as a form of violence.

How has a history of nonviolence replaced that of war? Nonviolence has always been a component of the Tibetan struggle. Officially, the Tibetan government never advocated violence, but they did covertly support the Tibetan resistance in its armed defense of Tibet. Since laying down arms in 1974, Tibetans in exile have waged a solely nonviolent political campaign in accordance with the Dalai Lama's wishes. In 1987, the Dalai Lama clearly—and globally—articulated nonviolence as the sole Tibetan political strategy in his Five Point Peace Plan presented to the U.S. Congress.[2] Grassroots Tibetan nonviolence consists of a series of protests, media publications and coverage, global community building, hunger strikes, and, in the case of Thubten Ngodup, immolation. Hunger strikes and immolations do not fit the Dalai Lama's platform of non-violence in that they are a form of violence against one's body. As advocated by the Dalai Lama in line with his Middle-Way approach, Tibetan nonviolence both builds on and departs from Gandhian principles of nonviolence in that it focuses on compromise more than confrontation, on compassion more than challenge, and specifically marks what some consider nonviolent physical self-sacrifice as violent.[3] While histories of the Tibetan resistance army conflict with present-day nonviolent Tibetan political strategies, so too do nonsanctioned, nonviolent actions such as hunger strikes (or in Gandhi's term, "fasts") and immolations.

Reconciling Tibetan beliefs about the need to defend country and religion with the Dalai Lama's version of nonviolence is not a simple task. One reason why is that Buddhism does allow violence in defense of religion. Given this disjuncture, veterans and activists experience contradiction in moving between deference and action. Persistent global images of Tibet as a pacifist Shangri-La also have impact, resulting in the increasingly frequent view of Tibetans as not only conducting a nonviolent struggle, but also being a nonviolent people. Absent in such a view is an understanding of nonviolence not as abstract or general, but as practiced and prescribed in specific historical, political, and cultural contexts.

Nonviolence is not a Tibetan genetic trait. It is instead a philosophical component of Buddhism and a political component of state struggle, one the Dalai Lama himself notes is the only practical recourse to dealing with the infinitely more populous PRC. Tibet has not historically been a nonviolent society.[4] Tibetan history is full of wars and battles, of local skirmishes and major disputes with neighboring countries. The Tibetan government had an official army, and monasteries kept arms and engaged in armed disputes. A policy of nonviolence in the present makes it difficult to narrate violence in the past. But narrating past violence does not—

and should not—cancel out a contemporary policy of nonviolence. Current Tibetan nonviolence provides a legitimate, inspiring alternative to violent conflict around the world. Yet it is important to understand the historical contours of this political strategy in order to acknowledge the realities and complexities of the Tibetan experience and thus best speak to peoples engaged in similar political struggles.

The Dalai Lama's decision to conduct the Tibetan struggle by nonviolent means meets with a range of responses from Tibetan refugees, responses that include pride, acceptance, frustration, tension, and more. When you are not the Dalai Lama, that is, not an incarnation of a bodhisattva (or even a simple monk, as he prefers), living nonviolence is not always easy. Given the stringent form of nonviolence the Dalai Lama advocates, expressing oneself in a nonviolent idiom can be difficult. As hunger strikes (and self-immolations) replace guerrilla warfare, a new sort of awkwardness, a new realm of controversy, and a new need for secrets all pervade the community.[5] The tension between violence and nonviolence is one that Tibetan veterans, activists, and refugees navigate with care. It is not a coincidence that Thubten Ngodup was not just a former monk but also a former soldier. What veterans like Ngodup are encouraged to forget—a history of war—is directly correlated to what the world is encouraged to remember—a nonviolent Tibet.

Forgetting Tibet, Forgetting War

I dream and I hope and I won't forget
Some day I'm going to visit on a free Tibet
BEASTIE BOYS, "IT'S ABOUT TIME"

The year 1991 marked a global campaign to ensure that Tibet was not forgotten. Performances were conducted, protests held, speeches given, prayers offered, film projects launched, governmental resolutions passed, promises made, and "Free Tibet" bumper stickers put on vehicles.[6] This 1991 International Year of Tibet was a watershed year. It succeeded in putting Tibet on the global map in a new way. In countries around the world, from the United States to India, Germany to Brazil, South Africa to Japan, the Tibetan story was broadcast widely and loudly. Individuals and communities around the world who were not previously familiar with the Tibetan plight became newly aware of it. Central to this broadcasting was the adherence to a singular narrative. The Free Tibet story that circulates globally is a sanitized one in which the two-decade Tibetan armed struggle against the PRC is almost entirely erased. Multiple external factors join internal ones to ensure that the Tibetan history of war is perceived as nonviolent. However, while the Chushi Gangdrug resistance army was many things—a public undertaking as well as a public secret—one thing it was not is nonviolent.

The crafting of a nonviolent history in the face of a violent past is a complicated project. It requires active forgetting of certain pasts at the same time that other ones are remembered or created. Forgetting the Tibetan resistance thus means not just remembering a different past but emphasizing a different past, narrating it into existence, and then repeating it until it becomes truth. In *Remembering Partition*, Gyanendra Pandey argues that "even when history is written as a history of struggle, it tends to exclude dimensions of force, uncertainty, domination and disdain, loss and confusion, by normalizing the struggle, evacuating it of its messiness and making it part of a narrative of assured advance towards specified (or specifiable) resolutions."[7] Just such a normalizing process is at work in the Tibetan resistance. The claim that the Tibetan struggle is and has been nonviolent is as much a direct product of forgetting violence as it is a claim staked to a certain view of Buddhism. Historical arrest is only one means of forgetting; beyond the Tibetan community, what does forgetting look like across multiple ways of organizing culture, politics, and experience?

Historical narratives organize experience in specific and collective ways. Such narratives are rarely neutral or disinterested; they are instead but one way to represent a past, an event, or a person that is represented differently by other narrators. As Hayden White instructs, history exists only when there are two (or more) competing narratives.[8] Whether collected, collective, privileged, subaltern, or occupying another category altogether, all historical narratives claim not just representative but transformative powers. The ability to name history is to produce or reproduce certain visions of the past, present, and future. Naming history always involves refusing other pasts: for every named historical narrative, there is one refused; for every remembered past, there is one forgotten. Histories centered on the forgetting of war organize experience around the removal of certain violences and struggles.[9] Forgetting war means something else must be remembered in its place. Forgetting war means that individual and collective experiences of war must now find other spaces and times to haunt; they do not so much disappear from memory as find other shadows and recesses in which to reside.

Buddhism, Nonviolence, and War

Is Buddhism a nonviolent religion? A better question might be the following: Are Buddhist societies necessarily nonviolent? At the moment in the West, Buddhism is often romanticized as nonviolent. Buddhist societies, however, do not necessarily follow nonviolent paths in their political, social, and other struggles. In the course of the twentieth century alone, one finds a devastating religious war in Sri Lanka, militant monks in Japan and China, monasteries in Tibet that were as much forts as they were monasteries, and throughout Buddhist lands ordinary people who rose up in the name of defending religion.[10] Buddhism advocates nonviolence, but it is not a nonviolent religion any more than it is a violent religion. Buddhism is also not just a religion or a philosophy but a lived, cultural practice. Its interpretation by religious scholars and teachers is reinterpreted and lived by lay practitioners in cultural ways. As lived practices, such interpretations are rarely, if ever, neutral reproductions of orthodox texts and scriptures.[11]

Chushi Gangdrug soldiers, for example, saw their army service as both a sin, in that it potentially involved killing, and as service, in that they were defending their religion, religious institutions, and religious leaders, including the Dalai Lama. Monks disrobed to join the army, and some veterans became monks to more effectively atone for their wartime sins and to commit themselves to religious service in a different way. In the 1950s and 1960s, the discourse of nonviolence among the soldiers was not equivalent to that which circulates today. Soldiers understood they were taking on violence on behalf of others, specifically, the Dalai Lama. Their strategy was a joint violent and nonviolent one in which the armed struggle was paired with a political, diplomatic one. Soldiers discussed among themselves how to effectively fight to defend religion, including constantly seeking religious protection and guidance. They dedicated themselves to the Dalai Lama, had specific deities to whom they prayed, and called on the assistance of numerous lamas and rinpoches throughout Tibet for special blessings, protective relics, and predictions. Religion permeated the army at the same time that fighting violated a fundamental principle of Buddhism, namely, not to create suffering for any sentient being. The allowance of violence in the case of war, as explained to me by many soldiers, was owing to the threat to Buddhism from an opponent determined to destroy it.

In his autobiography *My Land and My People* (1962), the Dalai Lama directly addressed his personal and political dilemmas regarding violence and the resistance. He explains that he spoke frankly with some of the Khampa leaders during his escape from Tibet: "In spite of my beliefs, I very much admired their courage and their determination to carry on the grim battle they had started for our freedom, culture, and religion. I thanked them for their strength and bravery, and also, more personally, for the protection they had given me. . . . By then, I could not in honesty advise them to avoid violence. In order to fight, they had sacrificed their homes and all the comforts and benefits of a peaceful life. Now they could see no alternative but to go on fighting, and I had none to offer. I only asked them not to use violence except in defending their position in the mountains."[12] As soldiers then and as veterans now, Chushi Gangdrug members consistently confirm his request: their actions were in *defense* of Tibet in the face of Chinese aggression.

In *The Tibetan Independence Movement: Political, Religious, and Gandhian Perspectives*, Jane Ardley explores the place of violence in the Tibetan struggle.[13] Specifically, she asks whether or not Gandhian strategies of nonviolence are suitable given Tibetan circumstances. Focusing primarily on exile activists but also briefly considering the resistance army, Ardley concludes that contemporary Tibet has a legacy of using violence as a last resort to defend religion.[14] For the soldiers and activists, she argues, "if violence is motivated by compassion for others—and the desire to save Buddhism—then it can be rationalized in a Buddhist context."[15] The dilemma of such violence in the Buddhist context is not only philosophical, but also historical and cultural. Specific violent histories in the past are arrested in service to specific nonviolent policies in the present; however, not all Tibetans agree that avoiding discussions of past violence best serves present-day politics. The Tibetan writer Jamyang Norbu has long argued that the promotion of the Tibetan struggle as wholly nonviolent "ignores the sacrifice and courage of the many thousands of Tibetan freedom fighters, monks and lamas included, who took up arms for the freedom of their country."[16]

What are the implications of a nonviolent state policy? Norbu contends that "truth has, unfortunately, become the first of casualties."[17] In the international realm, Ardley argues that a focus on nonviolence has turned the Tibetan struggle from a political one to a cultural one focused on cultural preservation and human rights such that multiple global actors position Tibetans as occupying the "moral high ground" while not taking them seriously as political actors.[18] This transformation began early in the twentieth century with British imperial efforts to map Tibet, with Chinese imperial claims to Tibet, and later, with U.S. Cold War politics of interference and intervention.

If the International Year of Tibet accomplished anything beyond raising general awareness of Tibet, it is to have branded the Tibetan struggle as a nonviolent cause. In 1989, two years prior to the International Year of Tibet, the Dalai Lama was awarded the Nobel Peace Prize. A man of peace whose message extends well beyond Buddhist and Tibetan concerns, the Dalai Lama's personal religious and political stances represent and even personify the Tibetan cause. Within the Tibetan community, living with a policy of nonviolence has meant many things—the arresting of resistance history, the recruitment of Western Buddhists to the cause, and the development of hunger strikes as a primary form of protest and self-immolation as a secondary form.[19] Given the Dalai Lama's disapproval of these globally recognized forms of nonviolence, it is telling that hunger strikes are nonetheless valued within the Tibetan community as having a high probability of success in terms of attracting attention, as meeting nonviolent criteria, and as providing service in defending, in the manner of the Tibetan resistance soldiers, both nation and religion. These protests are another example of how Tibetans try to follow the Dalai Lama while simultaneously pushing past hegemonic constraints on political action.

The Unto Death Hunger Strike

The Unto Death Hunger Strike began in New Delhi on 10 March 1998, Tibetan National Uprising Day. It was organized by the Tibetan Youth Congress (TYC), the largest Tibetan nongovernmental organization,

founded in 1970 for the "struggle for the restoration of complete independence for the whole of Tibet."[20] A TYC press release regarding the hunger
strike specifically called it a nonviolent struggle: "Considering the very
nature of [the] nonviolent struggle of the people of Tibet, Mahatma
Gandhiji's nonviolent method of hunger strike is the only option [in
which] Tibetan people could participate."[21] Honoring the Dalai Lama's
request that the Tibetan protests be nonviolent, the TYC organizers point-
edly align themselves with Gandhi and thereby offer a coded critique of
the Dalai Lama in choosing to launch a hunger strike.

Six volunteer hunger strikers represented the "six million Tibetans
inside Tibet and their sufferings under the brutal Chinese rule."[22] The
hunger strike also included demands made of the United Nations based
on the recommendations of the International Commission of Jurists
issued in 1997:

1. To resume its debate on the question of Tibet based on its resolutions of 1959, 1961, and 1965;
2. To appoint [a] Special Rapporteur to investigate the situation of
   human rights in Chinese-occupied Tibet;
3. To appoint a Special Envoy to promote a peaceful settlement of the
   question of Tibet and initiate a United Nations supervised plebiscite to ascertain the wishes of the Tibetan people.[23]

The Unto Death Hunger Strike received fairly broad press coverage in
India and some international press coverage, and it generated responses
from Kofi Annan, then secretary-general of the United Nations, as well as
from leaders and parliamentary bodies around the world. Within the
Tibetan community, it generated immediate attention and action as well
as fear and hope.

"Nga dro-gi-yin." "Nga dro-gi-yin." "Nga dro-gi-yin" (I will go. I will go.
I will go). For forty-nine days, these simple words rang throughout the
Tibetan refugee community. Drowned out at times by the sound of
communal prayer, Tibetans in South Asia pledged their allegiance to the
cause by offering to participate in the hunger strike. By popular accounts,
the list of potential participants numbered over one hundred people, all
fully committed to die for the cause in successive groups of six until
someone, somewhere, at the United Nations or beyond, decided to act for
Tibet. As the hunger strike progressed, Tibetans carried out numerous

FIGURE 29 Hunger striker Karma Sichoe receiving offerings at the Unto Death Hunger Strike, 1998. Photo courtesy of Eugene Louie, *San Jose Mercury News*. http://www.eugenelouie.com.

acts of solidarity and support. Candlelight processions, fasts, communal prayer sessions, special religious rituals, cash donations for the families of the hunger strikers, volunteer trips to Delhi to assist the hunger strikers, and constant monitoring of the print and televised media's coverage (or lack thereof) of the hunger strike. During the period of the hunger strike I happened to be traveling between five of my six field sites—Kalimpong, Darjeeling, Delhi, Pokhara, and Kathmandu. In each place, the hunger strike was part of almost every conversation and was present through various communal acts; it lent the community an air of both gravity and optimism.

Throughout India and Nepal, Tibetans knew the first names of each of the hunger strikers as well as intimate details about their lives.[24] If they personally did not know one of the hunger strikers, then they knew someone who did. In this way, the struggle was personalized in ways that cut across the community. Volunteers came from everywhere—the young, the old, men, women, former monks, former soldiers, current monks, current soldiers, and individuals from all regions of Tibet. Conversations about who was going to participate were quiet and serious.

FIGURE 30 Lighting butter lamps at Boudha. *chorten*

They were tinged with awe in recognition of the sacrifice being made and the belief that if you died as a hunger striker you would accumulate a significant amount of merit. People were also sad and scared, especially for those participants who would be leaving behind families.

As time went on, the situation grew more and more grave. On day thirty-seven there was a candlelight procession at the Boudha chorten in Kathmandu. Over one thousand people participated. The procession started from the top of the chorten, with people circumambulating on top of it and then descending to the kora path below. As I wrote in my field notes the next day,

> It was unlike anything else that I have ever experienced at the chorten. It was phenomenally moving and also frightening and beautiful. . . . [Everyone] did three or four kora and then some went to a gonpa [monastery] and some went home. People were chanting the one chant that has been used at all three candlelight marches I've been to now, and then stopped after the three kora. I was in a large group of people and we all had our candles raised high and everyone sang the Tibetan National Anthem. Candles had been placed into all the niches in the side of the chorten and as people left they grouped their candles

on tables, and on the little chorten in front of Boudha, and these candles were stunning and together so tightly touching and bright and it all felt very Catholic—the candles together, the fear, there was an element of witness and testimony to it that I cannot quite find the right words for. . . . The feeling in the air was one of solidarity—no pushing, a lane kept open for people to walk through, but still a fervent kind of urgency.[25]

Somewhere around day forty-five people began talking as if the hunger strikers might die. They were existing on water and lemon juice, and no one was quite sure how long one could survive on those two liquids. Hope began to turn to resignation that death was imminent. All-day prayer sessions continued, and Tibetans everywhere sought information about what was going on in Delhi and whether or not the world had responded.

Listening a few minutes to Radio Free Asia's Tibetan broadcast, watching the news on Zee TV or CNN, checking the *International Herald Tribune* or *Times of India* to see if the hunger strike was covered. In these ways, but primarily through word of mouth and TYC phone networks, information about the hunger strike spread. I was in Pokhara on day forty-nine when the news came that the hunger strikers had been taken to the hospital and that someone had set himself on fire. Until now, people had talked quietly about the Dalai Lama's opposition to the hunger strike, commenting on how the TYC had asked him not to intervene and on why the Dalai Lama considered the hunger strike a form of violence. After Thubten Ngodup's self-immolation, discussions of nonviolence turned bolder. Thubten Ngodup did a great thing, many of my Tibetan friends contended. As one young man in Pokhara explained, "He killed himself, he didn't harm anyone else. Unlike a suicide bomber, he didn't kill anyone else when he set himself on fire."

Following Thubten Ngodup's self-immolation, the next batch of hunger strikers began their fast. This time there were five strikers, the sixth spot being left empty in honor of Ngodup. Throughout the Tibetan community things began to feel sadder, more serious. At Boudha, prayer sessions continued as before, except more frequently, with more participants, and with more stringent rules. Earlier, participants refrained only from eating lunch, but now the prayer sessions included all-day fasting:

FIGURE 31 Thubten Ngodup, right, assists one of the hunger strikers. Photo courtesy of Eugene Louie, *San Jose Mercury News*. http://www.eugenelouie.com

no food, no tea, no water. One night, as we lay awake in our beds talking, my host and friend Kesang Tsering said to me, "I think a lot of Tibetans are going to die. The first six are in the hospital, the next five are doing the hunger strike, and Thubten Ngodup has died. After these five will come six more, and then it will be twelve, and so many people will die." We pondered this for a while, both saying entirely insufficient things such as, "It's difficult" and "I don't understand at all," and we discussed the Dalai Lama's opposition to the hunger strike. There is no real Tibetan response to his opposition; Kesang Tsering's response that night was perhaps the one I heard most often: "What else is there to do? Nothing."

Volunteers continued to travel to Delhi to support the hunger strikers. One friend who returned from Delhi reported that people there had begun talking more earnestly about violence. About destroying Chinese things, about setting off bombs, about other models for action like the Irish Republican Army or the Palestine Liberation Organization. These were not new topics of conversation for Tibetans in exile. While the Tibetan struggle has primarily been a nonviolent one since the end of the guerrilla war in 1974, violence as an option has never been fully abandoned by some in the refugee community. In teahouses and private homes, in TYC meetings, school dormitories, and Internet chat rooms, Tibetans discuss political strategy, including military and guerrilla tactics. In south India in the late 1970s and early 1980s, co-ed military training took place, albeit independent of Dharamsala.[26] Tibetans, including the Dalai Lama's younger brother Tendzin Choegyal, or Ngari Rinpoche,[27] served and continue to serve in the Indian militia[28] as well as in the militias of other countries, including that of the United States.[29] While taking a life even in defense of religion is considered a sin, one for which many Chushi Gangdrug veterans are still atoning, all Tibetans do not renounce violence in general. As Kesang Tsering said, "What else is there to do?"

Bodily Burdens

On day thirty-four of the hunger strike, I emailed a friend in Berkeley to get a sense of people's knowledge of and reactions to the hunger strike around the world. My friend, a fellow academic, had deep connections to India and was sympathetic to the Tibetan cause, and he lived in one of the Tibetan hubs in the United States. I thought for sure he would be able to give me a good reading of the global or at least the U.S. response. To my surprise, he wrote back that he was not aware of the hunger strike at all. My email was the first he had heard about it. The Unto Death Hunger Strike concluded on 15 May 1998. The European Union and the U.S. government as well as numerous other governments and the United Nations each conveyed to the TYC the message that they would raise the issue of Tibet in meetings with China. The hunger strike was over, but the language the TYC officially used was that it was temporarily halted.

Nine years later, as I double-checked the names of the hunger strike participants on the TYC website, I was surprised to learn of a TYC-sponsored hunger strike in New Delhi that was in its seventh day. Fourteen Tibetans—twelve men and two women ranging in age from twenty-six to seventy-five—had begun what was called an Indefinite Hunger Strike on 8 July 2007 directly across from the location of the strike in 1998 and of Thubten Ngodup's self-immolation. Instead of making demands of the United Nations, the hunger strikers made demands of the PRC.[30] If their demands were not met by 7 August, the TYC announced, it would orchestrate a nonviolent People's Mass Movement to mobilize "hundreds of thousands of Tibetans" to seek the truth from China about conditions in Tibet. The seventh of August came and went. The next day over twenty thousand Tibetans gathered in Delhi for the mass movement, including twenty-four-year-old Yangchen Choephel, who attempted to immolate himself. On 9 August the hunger strike ended following a request from the Dalai Lama. The Chinese did not respond, and much of the world was unaware that the hunger strike had taken place.

One year later, concurrent with the Olympic Games in Beijing in the summer of 2008, the TYC launched another, more drastic hunger strike in Delhi—this time, without any food or water at all. The first six hunger strikers, five monks and one layman all under the age of forty, were forcibly taken to the hospital by Indian police on day nine. Six more Tibetan volunteers took their place, again five monks and one layman, all under forty (they were joined in solidarity by an Indian woman who fasted with them for four days). After deceiving the Indian police on day eight by having decoy hunger strikers in place for an anticipated police raid, the Indian police forcibly took the actual hunger strikers to the hospital for treatment on day nine. The day eight entry on the daily TYC hunger strike journal included the following:

> The eighth day of the fast reveals drastic signs of breakdown in their health, most of them are carcasses, their bodies shriveled up. The textures of their skins have turned pale due to dehydration. Numerous symptoms which in the long run can be life threatening are visible in them, this self infliction of pain by them is truly the epitome of sacrifice for a cause which is more precious than their physical self. It is for the six million Tibetans whose lives in Tibet are always a question of survival. It is for Freedom, a feeling cherished by humanity and which is a privilege enjoyed by the world but not by the Tibetans. The sacrifices which these brave men and women give will be remembered by generations to come as it is on these that the golden glories of Tibet will be restored.[31]

Drama, frustration, commitment, sacrifice. Once again, Tibetans in exile seek to be heard, to effect change, to serve their country. Receiving little news coverage outside India despite its newly severe format, this hunger strike gave body—literally—to the depths of Tibetan political sentiment.

Forgetting is an active process. At the same time some Tibetans re-member the war fought against the Chinese, they also actively incorpo-rate their actions in the present within an idiom of nonviolence. Tibetans currently do so in a number of ways: by protesting at Chinese embassies and consular offices around the world, conducting letter-writing cam-paigns, recruiting international support, and, since the 1970s, going on hunger strikes.[32] Yet nonviolence was not always the grounding force for the Tibetan struggle. During the period of the Tibetan resistance in the 1950s and 1960s, neither the Dalai Lama nor the Tibetan government explicitly articulated a nonviolent stance. Tibetan guerrilla soldiers were not caught between violence and nonviolence as a political platform, but between violence and nonviolence as a tenet of their religion, one with particular repercussions for them in this life and in future lives. Their understanding at the time, however, was that they had the tacit approval of the Dalai Lama in their efforts to defend Tibet.[33] The individual and collective repercussions of forgetting their war are burdens borne with both patience and pain.

Thubten Ngodup had four images of the Dalai Lama on his altar and a Free Tibet cap hanging on his wall.[34] Five days before he immolated himself, he gave an interview to the Norwegian Voice of Tibet radio. In the interview he stated,

> I joined the Hunger-Strike because I am a Tibetan and I have a duty to perform. . . . No, there is no fear in my heart at all. When I met the six hunger strikers I felt very happy. It is now nearly forty years since we lost our country and much of our culture and religion has been de-stroyed. Inside Tibet and all over the world much has been done for the struggle. The Dalai Lama has tried so hard to implement his Peaceful Middle Path program, and has attempted to communicate with the Chinese. But this work has achieved no results. Therefore the situation has become desperate. . . . When my turn comes to go on hunger-strike I have decided to make it more effective. In my own case I have decided not to accept any kind of massage treatment or drink any water. The Tibetan situation has become desperate. . . . I am giv-ing up my life to bring about peace and fulfillment to my unhappy

people. . . . I have one hundred percent confidence that the people inside Tibet will not only continue the struggle but will intensify it. They will never sit back and not struggle.[35]

The Dalai Lama visited Thubten Ngodup in the hospital, and later that night, just after midnight on 29 April, he died. The TYC proclaimed 29 April Martyr's Day to commemorate the "Death Anniversary of Pawo Thubten Ngodup." The day is marked by prayer vigils as well as by memorial soccer and basketball tournaments in Tibetan communities in exile. His "duty to perform" fulfilled, Thubten Ngodup lives on in memory as an example of action, contradiction, and faith. His story is now part of the clouded annals of Tibetan history. In showing devotion to the Dalai Lama at the same time that he deviated from prescribed actions, Ngodup is an example of lived impermanence brought to an embodied conclusion. Thubten Ngodup's struggles against forgetting were not in the service of memory, but, as in the case of other veterans, in the hope of encouraging recognition and action.

CONCLUSION
TRUTH, FEAR, AND LIES

"History is truth and fear. And some lies." Kesang Tsering said this to me one day as we sat in her altar room enjoying the late afternoon sun. She laughed after adding "lies" and so did I, saying, "You're right." Both of us were amused at her saying out loud what was usually left unsaid. We continued talking about claims individuals made to specific Tibetan histories until it was time to put on our nice clothes and go for kora and gossip at the Boudha stupa. As we debated whether so-and-so, who had not actually fought against the Chinese, could be considered a member of the Tibetan resistance, I was thinking through the implications of this latest fieldwork revelation. Kesang Tsering's equating of history to truth, fear, and lies was compelling because it challenged what scholars think we know about history. We know about struggles over truth, lies disguised as truth, and the fear that induces secrets and silences. Yet it was not just truth and lies but truth and fear that she linked together, suggesting a different approach to history.

Kesang Tsering's view of history resonates with Benjamin's famous statement that to "articulate the past historically . . . means to seize hold of a memory as it flashes up at a moment of danger."[1] Challenges to the Tibetan status quo in exile are an example of such danger. Danger implies a depth to things, but as Renato Rosaldo observes, depth does not always mean substance or elaboration.[2] That is, culturally deep or significant things—people, happenings, ideas—are not always historicized. Nonetheless, they often possess a force of "affective intensity and significant consequences that [will] unfold over a long period of time."[3] Tibetan resistance veterans taught me much about force and depth in relation to history and danger, specifically, that their histories of the resistance are still unfolding and are indeed dangerous, but not always for the expected reasons.

The Tibetan scholar Tsering Shakya argues that the political struggle between Tibet and China generates a "denial of history."[4] As a result, both Dharamsala and Beijing produce simple and stubborn histories with room for neither complexity nor responsibility, and when they do so history is, in effect, denied.[5] Two young women in Majnu-ka-Tilla echoed this sentiment one day, asserting that "everyone talks about how the Chinese government changes Tibetan history, but the Tibetan government changes it too. No one—Tibetans or Westerners—wants to hear about this." Histories denied necessarily involve secrets as well as government action and surveillance.[6] Following Foucault, Luise White argues, "If the modern era . . . sought a way for subjects to speak as a way to govern them, secrecy became a site in which governance was made intense. Those with secrets had to be policed more than others, and the content of that policing itself became a secret."[7] Policing resistance history through arrest is a public secret in the Tibetan community. More public than secret for some, more secret than public for others, Chushi Gangdrug histories are now in a period of release. Narrations have begun, but—as this book evidences—they remain in process and under close watch.

In his essay "Nietzsche, Genealogy, History," Foucault states that "truth is undoubtedly the sort of error that cannot be refuted because it was hardened into an unalterable form in the long baking process of history."[8] Challenging truths baked long and hard is not easy work. At issue is all the "truth" represents, claims, and orders in the name of the normal or natural. To refute truth as error is to historicize. It is to ask how something came to be and with what effects; it is to unravel relationships of power and to distill what matters from what happened. In so doing, I follow the veterans' contingent understanding of truth. They understood truth to be discursive, to be put into practice through discourse, especially through the regulatory discourses of community. In interpreting Foucault's insights on silence and secrecy, Wendy Brown argues that both are shelters for and shelters from power.[9] As a result, truths buried in subjugated knowledges do not emerge from periods of silence or secrecy without complications. As Brown explains, "The work of breaking silence can metamorphize into new techniques of domination, . . . truths can become our rulers rather than our emancipators, . . . our confessions [can] become the norms by which we are regulated."[10]

Veterans have long lived with such dilemmas. Although some of the veterans hold that the story of the resistance is the true history of Tibet, not all hold this view or even the view that everything will be resolved once the period of arrest is over. They recognize that there is not simply one but different and even ranked versions of the history that has been arrested. Many of the veterans with whom I spoke, some more consciously than others, realized that just as secrets may have their own secrets, so too do excluded pasts have their own exclusions. A Khampa Tibetan government official explains: "Even before the CIA was involved, there was resistance throughout Kham. There was lots of fighting. This has been excluded from history in general but also from the history of Chushi Gangdrug. Chushi Gangdrug history now begins in Andrugtsang's living room in Lhasa. But by this time lots of men and women were already dead. Tens of thousands of people were already fighting." The focus on Chushi Gangdrug founder Andrug Gompo Tashi overwhelms the histories of other Tibetans who fought, providing an example of how hegemonic interpretations of the past hold the possibility to "metamorphize into new techniques of domination." Even within the resistance, certain histories and hierarchies are codified through stories, persons, and events that become iconic. The irony is that even icons such as Andrug Gompo Tashi remain marginalized and unknown beyond the resistance community. If truth as error is irrefutable, truth as irony is biting.

The Social Being of Truth

Making sense of where truth intersects with fear, which intersects with lies, is undoubtedly a cultural operation. It cannot solely be about "what happened" in the past. In *Shamanism, Colonialism, and the Wild Man*, Michael Taussig explores the murkiness that exists in relationships involving truth. As he explains, "My subject is not the truth of being but the social being of truth, not whether facts are real but what the politics of their interpretation and representation are."[11] The social being of truth is exactly what is at play in arrested histories. How facts are interpreted and represented, how power is recognized, and who determines the hierarchical rankings of given interpretations, representations, and recognitions are all involved. Combined with the time-delay factor, the exile parameters of hegemony and the sociality of truth lead almost all individuals involved to consent to arrested histories. As a result, while some histories are told during the time of arrest, they are not heard as loudly as collective silence. Silence is not just repression or passive acceptance but can also be active engagement in historical processes.

Silences such as those I associate with historical arrest are, as White argues, "a kind of socially constituted understanding of memory, loyalty, and accountability."[12] Recall the freedom of the unspoken word: "Silence carries hints, allusions, references, and opinions that are not contained in the other information, but it remains silence, powerful because it is not spoken, and cannot be pulled—or decoded—into speech. . . . Silences are not sites of repression but eloquent assumptions about local knowledge. They are not spoken of, not because they are unspeakable, but because they isolate fragments of powerful stories."[13] Silence as local knowledge explains in some ways how historical arrest works. Participating in a cultural system—even or perhaps especially if one is interested in changing it—requires just that: participation *in* the system. Local knowledge in the Geertzian sense is both the cultural lay of the land, an understanding of the order of things, as well as a familiarity with the stories groups tell themselves to explain, justify, and re-create their communities.[14] Together with Benjamin's idea of stories expending power over time that information loses, the silences generated by historical arrest contain stories with the power to trouble the ground of local knowledge.[15] For this reason, they absolutely involve fear.

Fear cuts across Tibetan historical projects in exile. It is linked to struggles about what really happened in the past, about who determines which version of the past is true, and about the consequences for challenging or changing history. But the link between fear and history is not entirely clear. Fear is not just a response to certain histories and their implications. It is a condition of their production and a part of the process through which certain political projects are made true. The assignment of truth to certain histories and certain forms of history is a process that requires constant renewal and defense. Fear is found in attempts to both maintain and challenge the status quo through the creation and assertion of particular historical truths. What are the risks involved in certain versions of the past, for example, in the differences between what people can say and what they can write? In the case of exile, where unity is considered to be of paramount importance, historical variation is at times a precarious project. Under such circumstances, the possibility and power of alternative pasts to challenge present and future is both empowering and disabling. In some ways, as Nicholas Dirks writes (and as Kesang Tsering would agree), "danger is what history is all about."[16]

The Social Politics of Historical Production

The woman behind the truth, fear, and lies formulation is important to this discussion of history. At the time of our conversation about history, Kesang Tsering was thirty-eight, a Tibetan refugee who escaped from Tibet into Nepal in 1982. Kesang Tsering is the mother of one child and the wife of the veteran and ex-monk Lobsang Tinley. Her life both is and is not typical of women her age in exile. She is competent, strong, and smart, and is self-taught in Nepali. She drives a hard bargain at the market and brews a mean batch of 'bras chang, or Tibetan rice beer. She is significantly younger than her husband, and in this respect the couple's relationship is not unusual. A number of veterans, after serving for almost two decades in the resistance—and in some cases, such as that of Lobsang Tinley, being monks prior to joining the army—found themselves in the post-Mustang years to be single and relatively old by local marriage standards. As a new refugee in Nepal without any immediate family for support, Kesang Tsering found Lobsang Tinley to be a suitable marriage partner: good, kind, employed, dedicated to the Dalai Lama, a member of Chushi Gangdrug, and a fellow Khampa. Theirs was a pairing, she believed, her parents would have approved of.

Like most Tibetan refugees in South Asia, Kesang Tsering and her family have a very modest lifestyle, what might be called comfortably poor. She is well aware of the worlds closed to her by virtue of her refugee status, her lack of education, and her illiteracy. While Kesang Tsering's comments on history may be transferable to other places and times, they are nonetheless grounded in the reality of her life. This girl from Tibet learned her history as a woman in Nepal. She grew up in the period just

FIGURE 32 Kesang Tsering.

before and during the Cultural Revolution, a time when histories were rarely discussed, even in hushed tones. Kesang Tsering did not personally experience the histories of the period I focus on (1950–74) but learned them from others only after leaving Tibet. In this regard her story is common in a community in which most histories circulate orally and are associated with specific individuals or groups. Historical knowledge in exile reflects the diaspora, stories scattered like the people but joined by a solid center (in this case, the cause and the Dalai Lama).

For many Tibetans, clear and true histories are recognizable through the trust that comes from personal knowledge. One sees this in battalions in the Tibetan resistance movement, which were organized by pha yul because the people of your territory were known to you, you could trust them, you knew their genealogies. In contrast, the Tibetan community in

South Asia is widely dispersed throughout India and Nepal. People from the same village may be scattered throughout the subcontinent, seeing each other only once in a great while, if ever. In lieu of daily interaction, people and their stories are connected by native place networks that stretch from remote corners of Nepal to camps in Arunachal Pradesh, Mysore, and Orissa, among other Indian locales. These networks supplement the trust from personal knowledge with trust produced out of a shared heritage and generations of connection in Tibet. Supplements are not substitutes, however, and earlier continuities of native place-based systems (for example, the importance of *pha yul chig pa'i mi*) grow weaker with each successive generation in exile. Creative verification processes for history are required in light of the wide dispersion of the Tibetan diaspora community. In this community, truth follows from familiarity and trust, and if these are lacking, suspicion and uncertainty reign. To legitimate histories, a series of questions are asked. Who is the narrator? What does one know about them, their family, and where they are from? How many degrees of separation are there between their social, geographic, and political worlds and yours? As these distances increase, the verification process becomes more difficult.

The legitimization of a certain version of history is a social and political process. Kesang Tsering, for example, is from the same territory as Phupa Pön, who has written two books about Markham.[17] Although she has never met him, his family was known and important. The histories he wrote in his books as well as those he told me are histories she considers her own, even though she cannot read them. Dorje Yudon's histories are further from Kesang Tsering. The two women have never met, are of different generations, and are from different places in Kham. Dorje Yudon comes from a prominent family, one publicly known to everyone; Kesang Tsering accepts her story, but with some hesitation because Dorje Yudon is not personally known to her. If Kesang Tsering wanted to decide whether or not to trust her story, she would turn to people from Dorje Yudon's native place. Do they validate and treasure this history? Do they recognize it as true? For Kesang Tsering, written histories are held to the same verification process as oral ones—what counts is who told them, not the medium in which they are told. These intimacies and uncertainties of history are found throughout the shared exile project of regaining Tibet.

Commitment to this project, however, does not rule out alternative ways of viewing the past or of conceptualizing futures that differ from official plans.

These struggles between alternative and official histories are in some ways particular to a refugee community and in other ways specific to Tibetan stylistics of mediating community. But they also reveal that alternatives to official history may be more complicated than one usually acknowledges. The stakes involved in historical arrest and in telling arrested histories as they are released are part of a broader slate of fears that saturate everyday life in the refugee community. The histories that are now beginning to be told engage these fears by making claims on the past, present, and future of Tibet. More often than not, these are claims to a united, but inclusive Tibet—claims to inclusion through historical recognition. These are efforts not to separate from the community, but to strengthen it in line with new ideas about participation and persistent ideas about identity. In every step of this process, attention is focused squarely on the Dalai Lama.

History over Breakfast I

"The Tibetan government did not help Chushi Gangdrug, not one bit." One winter morning in Delhi in 1997, two older men lectured a younger man over a breakfast of fried eggs, Tibetan bread, and endless cups of buttery tea. Their lesson to this young man recently arrived from Kham was a shorthand version of resistance history not available in Tibet itself. The young man's father, he said, had taught him about the history of Tibet, but all he had known was that Tibetans organized a military resistance to the Chinese. People in his area did not know the details or the full story of the resistance.[18] That morning he heard a version of Chushi Gangdrug history, as full and as partial as any, skimming over or avoiding certain aspects while emphasizing others. Chushi Gangdrug, his elders instructed him that morning, was a Khampa group responsible for helping the Dalai Lama to escape Tibet safely, but, although it took the Dalai Lama as their religious leader, it disagreed with some of his political positions. Absent from this history lesson was much of what one of the men, Athar Norbu, the CIA-trained radio operator commonly known as Lithang Athar, had discussed with me earlier—the splits within the resistance generated as much by ego and greed as by political factions and regional allegiances that predated exile, splits in which Athar had taken different sides over the years.

The day before, Athar had handed me a copy of a new book he had just received in the mail. It was by Roger McCarthy, the head of the CIA Tibet operation.[19] As I looked through it, he said, "All the stories are there. He was the leader, the key leader. He knows all between the CIA and the Khampa guerrillas. You can find everything in this book. He wrote all [about] my life and the lives of my friends, the Khampa guerrillas." A moment passed, and he rethought this glowing endorsement: "However, not everything [in the book] is correct." The next day, after the young man had left, the two older men spoke directly to me: "So much is still unknown," said Athar. "The good and the bad, it will all come out in the future." His friend added, "You should know the details, and then you can be truthful. Otherwise it will spoil your book."

How can one know the details and be truthful in the time of arrest? Although many resistance veterans were sharply aware that there were different truths in circulation, they recognized that history was to be found in the aggregate of dissenting, rather than consenting, truths. Almost to a fault, veterans I met with encouraged me to talk with a range of people, from colleagues who wanted a more prominent place for Chushi Gangdrug in exile society to those who were content to defer to the Dalai Lama, if not to Dharamsala. In the early 1990s, a new governmental focus on democracy was accompanied by an overture toward acknowledging resistance history. However, the release of resistance histories remains tenuous and gradual. For the veterans, the most important signs of release come from the Dalai Lama.

In the spring of 1994, a group of resistance leaders led by Lithang Athar signed a political agreement with the Tibetan and Mongolian Affairs Office of the Taiwanese government. As Athar explained to me, the agreement stated that Tibet would be independent on Taiwan's reclamation of mainland China, and the Dalai Lama would be recognized as the sole legitimate head of Tibet.[20] Although there was some precedent for a nongovernmental group engaging in governmental affairs, this was a bold move, but one the resistance leaders thought the Dalai Lama would support.[21] The Dalai Lama and the Tibetan government-in-exile were unaware that the resistance was making this arrangement, and by all popular accounts they were furious when it was presented to them.

Relations with Taiwan were very delicate at the time (as they are today), and unauthorized negotiations with Taiwanese representatives were seen as insolent, naïve, and disrespectful. The government excommunicated the leaders who signed the agreement and the veterans who supported them; those who did not support the Taiwan agreement were installed in Dharamsala as the true representatives of the resistance.[22]

This new split within the resistance and between the resistance and the government was especially difficult and remains so today. As the years go on and the men involved grow older (into their sixties, seventies, and eighties), such splits take on a new poignancy. For men in the twilight years of their lives, these divisions separate families, friends, and neighbors in an already fragmented community. In October 2000, six years and several months after the agreement was signed, the split was finally mended, albeit somewhat fragilely. The Dalai Lama (and the Karmapa) met with the renegade resistance group, and relations were restored to some degree not only between the two resistance groups, but also, more importantly, between the Dalai Lama and the renegade group. The Dalai Lama's meeting with the veterans was crucial to them at this time. Even though two competing branches of Chushi Gangdrug exist at present (the new, *gsar pa* group in Dharamsala and the old, *rnying pa* group in Delhi and New York), veterans in general feel that the air has been cleared. As a result, although representatives of the government like Prime Minister Samdhong Rinpoche may speak out against Chushi Gangdrug, veterans consider such statements to be less important than those of the Dalai Lama.[23] As a veteran's son explains, "It doesn't matter what Samdhong Rinpoche says; all that matters is what the Dalai Lama says and does."

Three years after the meeting in 2000, Lobsang Tinley recalled that the Dalai Lama asked the veterans to let him know if things were hard for them, and if so, that he would help them. With a smile Lobsang Tinley said that all the veterans immediately said, "No, no, things aren't hard [*dka' las khag po mi 'dug*]." "But," he said to me, laughing, "we're all poor! We have no money!" Admitting this to the Dalai Lama or asking for his help at a time of reconciliation and recognition was out of the question. The Dalai Lama's actions at this meeting were a clear sign to the veterans and to the Tibetan community generally that the release of arrested histories was now in progress. This does not mean, however, that all veterans are rushing to tell their stories.

Breakfast is not an occasion immune to attempts to fix one version of the past as the real one. Despite her proclamation that history is truth and fear and (some) lies, Kesang Tsering is as guilty of inciting historical controversy as anyone. One day over breakfast she told me the story of what had happened to Tibetans in Bhutan in the 1970s. The story was vivid, frightening, and very damning of the Bhutanese government. The king of Bhutan, she said, rounded up all the Tibetan government officials and threw them in a dungeon. Many were killed, and some were tortured with hot irons![24] As she spoke, her voice grew animated, and her husband began to interject: "Who told you that? You don't even know what you're talking about. You don't even know why the troubles began." Lobsang Tinley often felt compelled to correct his wife's explanations. She had escaped from Tibet in 1982. The histories she learned in Nepal were ones he had lived through. In a reasoned voice, Lobsang Tinley began to tell his version of the story: some bad elements in the Tibetan government caused some troubles with the Bhutanese government. Yes, it was unfortunate that many people were arrested and killed, but that was all in the past, and we do not need to talk about these things now. He stopped with a look that implied the discussion was over; it was, of course, just beginning.

Kesang Tsering and I objected, she arguing the truth of her version, I arguing some sort of middle road between the sensational and the censored. Our debate continued without real resolution but with a mutual acceptance that we did not know what had really happened. The story of Tibetan refugees in Bhutan is an example of an arrested history the release of which has not yet been authorized. Kesang Tsering's transgression of this arrest provoked her husband to defend what is not to be told, to patrol those boundaries her story threatened to cross. For Lobsang Tinley, the dilemma was not just in the historical disobedience of crossing unreleased boundaries, but also in risking a weakened power and position for the Tibetan government-in-exile by telling an arrested history. Why was Kesang Tsering willing to discuss Bhutan when her husband was not?

Like the histories of the Chushi Gangdrug army, those of the time in Bhutan are not just about facts but also about relations. Relations between individuals, communities, and governments; between pasts, presents, and futures; and relations also to histories themselves. Lobsang Tinley, for example, was in Nepal at the time of the disturbances in Bhutan. He knew people who had been in Bhutan and had heard their stories. He remembers the subsequent difficulties the Tibetan government and refugee community encountered as a result. In 1998, when Kesang Tsering told this story, it was easy to forget that in the early 1970s the Tibetan government-in-exile did not have the international support or even the degree of regional security it has now. For Kesang Tsering, telling this story is a way of connecting pasts she did not experience with the continuing difficulties of being *so so'i lung pa med pa*, or without one's country. For both wife and husband, the story of Bhutan shows the importance of grounding oneself within current sociopolitical realities. For Kesang Tsering, this involved determining how her version of exile came to be; for Lobsang Tinley, it required withholding certain stories so that blemishes of the exile community are covered; and yet for both it included persistent, mostly unvoiced questions of why the story of Tibet has come to be told in the ways it has.

Release

Nietzsche pleads in vain for historians who can write histories equal to the events they relate. We need to do the same with our dead. Benjamin says something similar where he cautions that truth is not a matter of exposure that destroys the secret but a revelation that does justice to it.

MICHAEL TAUSSIG, *WALTER BENJAMIN'S GRAVE*

Arrested histories of the Tibetan resistance are now in their period of release. Release as a "revelation that does justice" to secrets captures the sentiments of many veterans. Telling these histories might enable the secrets to be appreciated, recognized, and given their proper place in Tibetan national history. Yet some Tibetans hold on to the idea of release as the "exposure that destroys," that is, of thinking of resistance histories as collective dirty laundry that should not be aired. Released they have been, however, in an ongoing, gradual, and government-associated process. One noteworthy example was a section devoted to the resistance in Demton Khang, the exile government's Museum of Tibet in Dharamsala, which opened in the spring of 2000. Publicity literature for the museum gave a prominent location to an image of the resistance founder Andrug

Gompo Tashi. Although Andrugtsang's image often hangs in the homes of veterans, this is the first nonresistance, non-Khampa public display of his image of which I am aware.[25] The significance of this is evident in one veteran's bitter comment: "When Andrug Gompo Tashi died, the Taiwanese government declared a national holiday. But here he is a national enemy."[26] In Nietzschean terms, histories for Tibet's war dead are still not close to approximating the events they might relate.

Veterans are now writing and telling their individual stories to Tibetans and outsiders, but doing so is not easy in either genre or for either audience. Beyond the problem of low literacy rates, the specific cultural difficulty of writing is something several veterans often commented on; as one government official explained, "Tibetan people do not have the practice of writing about events. My generation and the previous generation did not realize the importance of writing about past events. Even if we did write, it was not a vivid account, but a haphazard one." Other veterans chose not to write, instead deciding to spend their time in religious activities, atoning for sins committed. Baba Lekshey chose this route, explaining, "[Resistance leaders] told me to write my life story. But I did not write anything. War is futile. I saw a film on the dropping of atom bombs on Japan. If modern weapons are used, the consequences are disastrous. Instead, I spend my time practicing religion and saying prayers for the well-being of others."

Another veteran who also spent most of his time in prayer was Baba Yeshi, the former leader of the Mustang force. Speaking with him in his altar room in his old home in Kathmandu felt like being in a monastery; the bright Nepali day outside would give way to the dark monastic-like room filled with butter lamps, deity statues, and *thangkas* in which he sat almost all day, every day in prayer. "I am a sinner," he told me. "I committed a lot of sins. Out of twenty-four hours each day, I sleep for six hours. I recite prayers most of the time."[27] If he was not unusual in this respect, given that most veterans recited prayers to atone for their war sins, Baba Yeshi also had his controversial position within the community to reckon with as well. The "black" name he was given when excommunicated by the Tibetan government-in-exile struck the Nepal community of Mustang veterans particularly hard. The majority of the veterans lived in refugee camps associated with the Tibetan government, and the political strife between the government and their Mustang leader was difficult for

FIGURE 33 Baba Yeshi.

many of the men to reconcile. In 1990, Baba Yeshi met with the Dalai Lama to "explain everything to him."[28] The Dalai Lama personally pardoned him. The pardon not only removed the black mark from his reputation, but also allowed (in theory) for residents of Baba Yeshi's camps to be associated with the Tibetan government-in-exile. For many Mustang veterans, the reunion of Baba Yeshi with the Dalai Lama was of great importance. His history can now safely be told, according to a group of veterans in Delhi who had long-standing animosities with Baba Yeshi stemming from Mustang: "Baba Yeshi has done a lot of work. We must make the effort to write the deeds of those people who have died for the cause of Tibet. We cannot forget what they have done for our country. It will be difficult to find people as brave in the times to come. What they have done must be put clearly in black and white. Also, from the point of view of politics, the work of these people forms the basis of our thought.

Our government itself was not stable, and we lost our country to the Chinese. If the government had been stable, then there would have been less trouble and controversy." Baba Yeshi's story, which still remains mired in trouble and controversy for some, is both a collective and an individual fear realized, a strong example of the connections between historical arrest, the Dalai Lama, and the status quo. Explaining his story and "putting things clearly in black and white" requires ongoing exploration of the gray zones of history and community.

The internal and external amnesia that accompanies historical arrest fosters bitterness for some. On a Chushi Gangdrug website that ran from the mid-1990s through 2001 veterans expressed their frustration with perceived underappreciation by their government and community, claiming "those who find Chushi Gangdrug embarrassing are ignorant."[29] Within Chushi Gangdrug, internal tensions persist. These mostly reflect the existence of two separate resistance groups exist, one based in Dharamsala and one in Delhi.[30] Despite this division, I do not want to give the impression that cynicism predominates among the veterans; it does not. The cynicism that exists does not outweigh other sentiments toward the community, the government, and the Dalai Lama. Overall, veterans consider themselves contributing members of the community. As a central Tibetan former government official commented, "The thing that is important is that despite all these differences, political troubles and the like, all of these people still identify as Tibetans. There are no separatist movements. Athar and his friends aren't running around trying to bring down the Tibetan government or even to say that they are not Tibetans. We need to remember that this community-wide identification as 'Tibetans' is new. It is not something that Goloks, for example, would have agreed with before."[31] His comments underscore two main points of this book: first, veterans walk a fine line between hegemonic consent and resistance, and, second, ideas and practices of Tibetan identity are strategic, shifting, and newly politicized in exile.

The politics of history is not just a Khampa issue. Non-Khampa family members and supporters of veterans often speak frankly about the community shame involved in "not knowing" about resistance contributions. In Kathmandu, one woman encouraged me to speak with "ordinary" men in the refugee camps in Pokhara: "It is so sad. These soldiers are now all old men living in the camps. They fought in Chushi Gangdrug for Tibet and His Holiness [the Dalai Lama] and now their lives are wasted. They couldn't fight any longer because His Holiness chose nonviolence as a political strategy. They now just sit and spin wool all day. They never would have done that in Tibet." Telling the stories of these men would be valuable for her children, she continued. The fact that resistance history is not known by the younger generation in exile (often even by those whose family members—fathers, uncles, and grandfathers—were involved) is considered a problem to be remedied. The idea of history as inheritance runs throughout the histories I have collected. The great majority of veterans believe that the story of the resistance is a key part of national Tibetan history. They have thus abided by arrest by withholding their histories and yet protested its most difficult aspects by publicly defending themselves in times of political strife. Lacking a heroic nationalism into which to fit, arrested histories of the Tibetan resistance do not represent attempts to return to an idealized past but instead to construct the future as a return to a different past.

Histories of Fear, Politics of Hope

History is truth and fear. And some lies. Yet if truth and lies seem familiar to the process of history making, what characterizes histories built of fear? A negative politics is one component, the avoidance of perceived evils rather than the pursuit of perceived goods. Fear is part of the production of arrested histories and a response to it, processes through which certain political projects are made true. It is not always possible to "seize hold of a memory," even when its danger is well concealed.[32] As a result, telling resistance histories quietly is the most radical step many veterans take toward challenging historical arrest, and I emphasize that even decisions to tell history are done with respect for the Dalai Lama, with the notion of beneficial action in mind and with the hope, if not the belief, that telling will benefit the Tibetan cause.

As arrested histories move through different stages of their arrest, the gap between meaning and event contracts and expands, moving through periods when some individuals tell parts of the story and then returning to long spells of silence until another narrative opening is either seized or created. Alongside temporal ebbs and flows are sociopolitical ones: the resistance was a unified effort composed of individuals who did not always agree. In addition to institutional arrest, therefore, histories of the resistance move through other stages in step with the internal rhythms of the organization such that the content and temperament of resistance histories are not static. Although arrest holds the promise of national recognition, those who sought national acknowledgment in this lifetime considered the deferral of this recognition problematic. Other veterans dissented from this urgency, content in the faith that the authorities would choose the right time for release. Although dependent on ethnographic and political context, historical arrest is perhaps a tool not so much for denying history as for producing certain types of community.

On Lobsang Jampa's wall in his apartment in Kathmandu, along with his toy rifle, pictures of running horses, and deity images, he hung a poster, a still life of fruits and vegetables, on which was imprinted the slogan, in English, "All for one, and one for all." The Tibetan refugee community is a relatively small one. Yet despite five decades of being dispersed throughout the world, it is remarkably coherent and united in its goal of restoring Tibet to some form of Tibetan rule. As Tibetan refugees try to simultaneously forge a modern democratic government and preserve their cultural traditions, they increasingly feel the limits of exile. Although the political stakes involved in remembering and forgetting certain histories and the identities and relations they index are undoubtedly high, they are not, as historical arrest demonstrates, irreversible. Working with the exile government rather than against it, resistance veterans and other refugee Tibetans abide mostly by an "all for one" motto in the forging of community and the telling of history, such that life in exile is defined as much by a politics of hope as by a politics of fear.

On a crisp day in February 2003, Samten and I sat at the Himalayan
Restaurant overlooking the Boudha kora path. We had met in this
same restaurant and sat at the same window table on the second
floor numerous times over the years, watching the people below do
kora as we talked. That day, I had just returned to Kathmandu after
a three-and-a-half-year absence. Follow-up research was part of my
agenda, but much of my visit was social. My goals were simple: to
sit at Lobsang Tinley's and Kesang Tsering's table, to visit with
people in their homes, to do kora at Boudha, and to meet and
discuss life and research with Samten.

Of the many people who helped me with my research, Samten
was invaluable. Skilled in English and literary Tibetan, he helped
me translate and transcribe my interview tapes. During my research, we regularly met at the Himalayan Restaurant to discuss the
interviews and talk about history and politics and Tibet. Samten
spent hours listening to the voices of the veterans as they poured
out from the tapes. Through their words he came to know resistance history, and in his quiet way he explained to me the col-
loquialisms so many veterans used, directing us to, as Benjamin
so poetically put it, the ruins of stories upon which proverbs
are built. Samten's immersion in this project left me unprepared
and surprised by what he asked upon my return to Nepal: he
wanted to meet some of the veterans whose stories he had tran-
scribed and now carried with him. As much as he now knew about
Chushi Gangdrug history, it was still distant from him in ways that

FIGURE 34 Dadhag at Boudha, 2003.

mattered. Lived impermanence and the exile politics of knowledge con-
verged in his desire to meet these unknown men who lived in his city and
whom he had likely walked past on the street without realizing it. He
knew the timbre of their voices but not the contours of their faces. He
wanted to meet in person those men passing below us as we talked, men
known to me but anonymous kora-goers to him.

Looking out the window, I showed him several of the veterans as they
came around on one of their circumambulations of the stupa. Lobsang
Tinley, walking first with his friend Dadhag, a Khampa veteran of the Est.
22/SFF force in India and then later walking with Pala Wangyal from
Chatreng, who was one of the Dalai Lama's resistance bodyguards during
his escape in 1959. Lobsang Tinley liked to walk in what I thought of as
the fast lane of the kora path, passing people in quick but mindful motion,
in kora as in life: calm, focused, his *sems*, which best translates as "heart-
mind," devotedly at work. Lobsang Jampa took a different though no less
devoted approach: slowly but steadily he made his way around the stupa,
his eyes lighting up upon crossing paths with any friends also doing kora
and always, always suggesting they stop and share some tea together
before continuing round and round in prayer. Looking out at them as

they passed, Samten told me how much he appreciated their interviews, how much he had learned, and how important this history was.

Veterans repeatedly stated the importance of publicly naming those who had fought for Tibet. In a variation on their request, Samten asked me to include in this book photos of the people I had interviewed so as to make these people real to the readers beyond just putting their words to paper. Not a Khampa and not previously having any connection to Chushi Gangdrug, Samten confessed that most Tibetans knew little about Chushi Gangdrug, and if they did know anything it tended to be only that Gyalo Thondup and Lhamo Tsering did good work for Chushi Gangdrug. Beyond that, little to nothing was known. "This needs to be corrected," he said. I agreed that the lack of knowledge was problematic. We left the restaurant: I went to the kora path to meet with Lobsang Tinley and Kesang Tsering, and he got on his motorcycle to return home.

Fifty Years of Forgetting

In much of the Tibetan world, 16 June 2008 came and went without any notice. The fiftieth anniversary of the founding of the Chushi Gangdrug army was commemorated in a small ceremony in Dharamsala and at a large function in New York City. The Dharamsala Dhotoe Cholkha Welfare Society (Central Committee of Chushi Gangdruk) issued two public statements, the first presenting a history of the founding of Chushi Gangdrug and directly addressing the need to make this history known, and the second praising the Dalai Lama and detailing the offerings they made to him in commemoration of the anniversary:

1. a gold and bronze statue of the Buddha of Longevity,
2. a copy of the Kangyur (*bka' 'gyur*) scripture,
3. a statue of Thugs rTen Byang Chub,
4. a set of robes for the Dalai Lama, and
5. "a promise" not to worship Dorje Shugden (*dol rgyal*), which, they note, is a promise they have made before and remake now, including that they will not associate with any groups who worship Dorje Shugden.

They conclude with more praise for the Dalai Lama. Their donations reference those made in 1958—the golden throne and prayers for the

Dalai Lama's long life—while also situating themselves in the present as the Chushi Gangdrug group most closely adhering to the religious preferences of the Dalai Lama as well as supporting his political views.

In New York, the Dokham Chushi Gangdruk organization hosted a conference honoring several founding members of the resistance army. This group is affiliated with the late Lithang Athar and those who signed the covert agreement with Taiwan in 1994 and, in a reversal of former policy, is currently recognized by the Tibetan government-in-exile. It consists of veterans and their adult children, who have begun to move into administrative roles within the organization. In a striking departure from earlier gender politics within the resistance, in 2008 it was headed by a woman, Doma Norbu, the daughter of Lithang Athar. During the conference, Dokham Chushi Gangdruk passed the following resolution:

1. His Holiness the Dalai Lama is inseparable from the organization, and as our founding fathers and veterans risked their lives for His Holiness, so will we continue with their work of ensuring that the institution of the Dalai Lama is respected and preserved.

2. The Tibetan Government-in-Exile (TGIE) is the Government of the Tibetan people and it is the duty of all our members to work towards ensuring that our government is given due recognition and respect in the world political arena. Recognition of the TGIE is vital for Tibet's political future.

3. To work towards the goal of independence for Tibet with all like-minded organizations, lending our support in every capacity.

4. To be involved in activities that will bring more awareness about the Tibetan situation worldwide.

5. To initiate support from international organizations towards the Tibetan cause.

Consistent with the history of Chushi Gangdrug, the organization starts by reaffirming its homage to the Dalai Lama, expressing not just their "inseparable" connection to him, but also the contributions Chushi Gangdrug made on his behalf.[1] Consistent also with the tensions in their relationship (and with refugee sentiment in general), the organization asserts their goal to be the independence of Tibet, not the Dalai Lama's preferred genuine autonomy for Tibet. They call for global respect and recognition to the Tibetan government-in-exile and articulate their commitment to the Tibetan cause. Absent is any sense of resentment.

In Dharamsala, the Dalai Lama and the Tibetan government-in-exile did not honor the anniversary in 2008 in any public way. Neither did they mark the fiftieth anniversary of the initial uprisings in Kham in 2006. In taking note of this, the Tibetan intellectual Jamyang Norbu asserts that there would be no Tibetan government-in-exile if not for the publicly marked uprising of 1959 and the forgotten uprising of 1956.[2] "Why," he asks, is "Dharamsala not observing this important national anniversary?"[3] Norbu, himself a veteran of the Mustang force, frames his questioning of this "bizarre neglect" in terms of the lack of recognition of the depth of the resistance's contributions.

As he argues, the exile community would not exist were it not for the resistance:

> In the aftermath of the Lhasa uprising nearly everyone who managed to escape from central Tibet did so largely because the major Chinese garrison at Tsetang, south of Lhasa, was under siege by the resistance, which allowed a safe corridor for refugees to flee to India. Refugees from . . . western Tibet had a relatively easier time escaping because Chinese troops were tied down by the fighting in central Tibet and Kham. Later, when the Mustang base became operational, Chinese military movement in western Tibet became greatly curtailed. . . . This allowed more refugees from western Tibet to escape. . . . All the Tibetans from Kongpo and Pemako area who escaped to India in 1962 managed to do so because of the leadership and guidance of the ten-man guerrilla team that had earlier been inserted into that area. . . . From the mid-sixties onwards after the resistance was completely crushed and the Tibetan border sealed, the flow of refugees to India and Nepal virtually dried up to nothing.[4]

Reorienting history to include the resistance makes visible the very conditions of possibility for escaping from Tibet during this period. Making visible the conditions of possibility for escape reveals that resistance history remains forgotten. And revealing that resistance history remains forgotten begs the question of why and thus troubles the truths that ground the Tibetan struggle.

Laughter and the Sociality of Sadness

During my trip to Nepal in 2003 Lobsang Jampa invited Kesang Tsering and me over for lunch. As we walked up the stairs to his humble apartment we could smell food cooking, and, walking into his kitchen, we could see that he and his nephew Pemba had been busy all morning. Together, we sat down to a feast that included momos, maksha mushrooms Pemba had brought from Lithang, a potato-morel dish, homemade hot sauce, Coca-Cola, jasmine tea, changkol, and two bottles of Tuborg beer. Happy to be reunited, we ate and talked and laughed the afternoon away. Lobsang Jampa told long stories about Mustang and Baba Yeshi and about his friend Chatreng Gyaltsen, who was one of the best shots in Chushi Gangdrug. He joked about the plastic rifle hanging on his wall, about how he kept it for when the Maoists came to get him.[5] Kesang Tsering and Pemba traded present-tense questions about their homes in Kham: "What is it like in your place? Do you slaughter your own animals for meat or buy it at a market? How many Chinese are there? What is your *gon pa* like?" Kesang Tsering reminisced about her girlhood in Markham. She spoke about riding in a saddlebag on the side of a slow-moving yak, about bickering with her younger sister, who was in a saddlebag on the other side of the yak, and about saying "mani" with children in her village during the Cultural Revolution, using puffed rice for counting rather than prayer beads, which were outlawed.[6] Laughter punctuated the afternoon, as did a wistfulness and, later that evening, a sadness.

Returning home, Kesang Tsering and I found Lobsang Tinley and two friends talking and getting ready to go for kora. But first they wanted to hear the details of our visit to Lobsang Jampa's. As we related the stories Lobsang Jampa told about Mustang, about riding horses from Lithang to Lhasa and his joke about his gun and the Maoists, Lobsang Tinley and his friend Dadhag provided running commentary. "As a little boy, Lobsang Jampa loved guns, and he still does now as an old man," said Lobsang Tinley. Dadhag offered that Lobsang Jampa was one of the bravest of them all: "He killed so many Chinese. He'd be riding his horse, shooting his gun. Me? I fell off my horse, I was so scared!" Like earlier in the day, the laughter that followed had a melancholy feel to it. A widower, Lobsang Jampa lived quietly in his small apartment near Boudha and would

FIGURE 35 Lobsang Jampa.

sometimes confide in Kesang Tsering how sad he was to be old and alone. Early every morning, she told me, he would feed the birds at the chorten before he did kora.

On this return trip to Nepal, I felt the sadness of community more than ever. As I wrote in my field notes: "The very sadness in not being in one's country, in not having been there since 1959, and in believing—reluctantly accepting—that you will die in a foreign country. The sadness in family and friends being so spread apart, no longer just Tibet and South Asia, but now the US and Canada, Australia and Taiwan, and so on. . . . The sadness is balanced by hope but weakened by the knowledge that life was, or could be, better in Tibet."[7] Hope for this group of Tibetans and indeed for Tibetan refugees in general lies with the Dalai Lama. Sadness is not dwelled upon; Tibetans surround themselves with laughter rather than pity.[8] As much as they relish friendship, family, and human connections, I find that they thrive on hope, religious practice, the promise of future lives, and the deeply held spiritual leadership of the Dalai Lama.

The Boudha kora path is a busy place in the early morning and late afternoon. One afternoon as scores of people did kora, someone rigged up a television above the kora path to play a video disk of the Dalai Lama's recent Kalachakra initiation teachings in Bodhgaya. Everyone stopped to watch, placing their hands together over their head in prayer pose as a sign of respect, and listening for a while before doing another round of kora and then stopping again at the television set on their next circuit, hands above head, lips in motion praying, and head and heart grateful for this taped glimpse of the Dalai Lama. It was next to impossible to pass through the crowds of people, and as the afternoon turned to evening people began to head home for dinner, the television was taken down, and a shop along the kora path began to play a cassette of one of the Dalai Lama's teachings. His distinctive voice spoke loudly to those remaining, who gathered around to hear and be touched by his words. Although the Dalai Lama's image could be found in all the Tibetan homes and shops ringing the chorten, and tapes and disks could be purchased and played at any time, the Dalai Lama's "presence" at the chorten that afternoon was unusual, auspiciously providing kora-goers with the blessings of his taped words alongside the prayers they made and the merit they gained through doing kora. If kora at Boudha is beneficial for one's religious practices and rebirths, then kora at Boudha while technologically accompanied by the Dalai Lama is doubly beneficial. As I wrote in my field notes that night, "To live near the chorten is good." Lobsang Jampa told me once when I asked if he had thought about moving to Pokhara, where there was a special home for Chushi Gangdrug veterans, "No. There is nowhere to do kora there." What would one do without kora?

In Memoriam

Lobsang Tinley died in Kathmandu in April 2004. He was seventy-one years old. He was the only one from his family to escape Tibet. Like most of the refugees, he left behind parents, siblings, relatives, and friends. One year in exile turned into two. One decade turned into two, then three, then four. His dream was to return to Lithang, to be reunited with his elder sister, and to die in Tibet. His wishes did not come true, at least not in this lifetime. His beloved daughter inherited his dreams, inherited family prayers of reunion, inherited the memory and love of a man whose faith in the Dalai Lama ran deep.

Several years later, *Kesang Tsering* immigrated to Canada, where she applied for and received political asylum. She is now studying English, working the night shift in a factory, and, with characteristic bravery and good humor, making her way in a brand-new society for the second time in her life.

Dorje Yudon and her elder sister *Norzin Lhamo* still live in New Delhi, where they are blessed by frequent visits from their children and grand-children and now great-grandchildren. Their husband, *Gyari Nyima*, died on 30 August 1999.

Gyalo Thondup has still not published his eagerly awaited memoirs. He divides his time between several locations in India, but I think of him at home in Kalimpong. His home there is one he designed himself and, with its attached noodle factory, grounds him in work of the hands rather than the politics that so define his life elsewhere.

Baba Yeshi died in Kathmandu in 1999. Services for him were attended by veterans and others paying their respects. The politics surrounding him and the end of the Mustang operations were never able to quite diminish his power in the community. He was a physically imposing man and, toward the end of his life, would come to Boudha from time to time to do kora. On the days he was present, you could sense a hushed respect (or, if not respect, an awareness) over the crowd. Baba Yeshi is here, people would murmur. And round and round he would go, doing his kora.

In 2006, *Lobsang Jampa* died. For years, I had feared the phone call that would announce his death. And finally it came. I cried and lit incense and thought about how whenever I came upon him on the kora path, he would take my hand in his and hold it tightly and ask me how my day had been. He would tell me about his and about what was happening in the world and who was at kora (and if he hadn't yet seen Lobsang Tinley, would ask where he was and if he was coming). He would make lists of the things he wanted to tell me about the past and then exceed these lists as other stories and other thoughts came to him. Forty years after the war, he once mused to me, "Sometimes I wondered why I was killing these Chinese."

Representing one's life to an interlocutor such as me, distilling into fragments and narratives what was not necessarily experienced as either, was not always easy. At times, Lobsang Jampa and other veterans would simply shake their heads at the paths their lives had taken. How had things ended up like this? Living as a refugee. Four decades removed from family members left behind in Tibet. Memories of their homes, memories of the taste of tea made with butter from their own yaks, memories of seeing the Potala for the first time, memories of carrying a gun and of using it on the battlefield. Memories they treasured, and memories they wished they could forget.

And *Baba Lekshey*? Of Baba Lekshey, I do not know. Is he reading scripture in his room in Kalimpong? Or has he entered the cycle of rebirth on his way to a new life? Either way, I wish for his continued well-being and grace on this earth.

The End

The first time I met Baba Lekshey, he sang to me and said it would take a month to tell me everything. The second time he told me about his family, his now-adult sons and daughters back in Tibet. The third time he spoke about war and knowledge. What he said was this: "Without knowledge, one can only fight for small things." For Tibetans of Baba Lekshey's generation, men such as Baba Yeshi, Lobsang Jampa, and Lobsang Tinley, and women such as Dorje Yudon, the 1950s were a period when clarity arose out of confusion. Clarity on China's plans for Tibet. Clarity on Kham's status within the Tibetan nation. Clarity on Tibet's status within the international system of states. The things these Tibetans fought for were not small. They fought for their families, their communities, their religion, their country, their stories. And, at the time of my research, they continued to fight by quietly and patiently finding ways to tell pasts not yet codified as official history.

The time has come for these histories to be told. The complications of region, the national dominance of the aristocracy, the desire to contribute to community, the accepted imprecision of the premodern Tibetan state, the connection to the CIA, the tensions surrounding nonviolence: each of these continues to factor into histories of the resistance. Truths of the resistance are actively searching for a historical place in the present. Resistance pasts persist, waiting if not actively voiced, embodied if not overtly written, and reflected back in clouded mirrors. Veterans pay close attention to the Dalai Lama for guidance through this period, to his words and actions, even and especially if they are not entirely clear. While the current conditions of exile and empire show no clear signs of abatement, a Tibetan Buddhist worldview presumes impermanence, if not change. Believing this, the veterans anticipate changes in the world and in their community that will signal new possibilities for telling—and living—Tibetan history.

In his final testament, the thirteenth Dalai Lama prophesied a period of destruction for Tibet that, if prepared for, could be survived with effort. Survival would not be easy, but it would be possible and require the efforts of all. In conclusion, he advised the Tibetan people "to overcome what needs to be overcome, and to accomplish what needs to be accomplished. Do not," he wrote, "confuse the two."

APPENDIX

Who's Who

Alo Chhonzed: Mimang Tsogpa leader from Lithang

Andrug Gompo Tashi: Chushi Gangdrug founder from Lithang; Mimang Tsogpa officer

Athar Norbu: Chushi Gangdrug soldier from Lithang; member of the first group of six trained by the CIA; served as radio operator during the Dalai Lama's escape in 1959; head of Chushi Gangdrug group who signed an agreement with Taiwan in 1994; also known as "Lithang Athar"

Baba Lekshey: Chushi Gangdrug soldier from Bathang; trained in Colorado; personal name is Kalsang Lekshey

Baba Yeshi: Chushi Gangdrug soldier from Bathang; general of the Mustang force

Bachung Pön: chieftain and Chushi Gangdrug leader from Derge; personal name is Thutub Gompo

Dadhag: Est. 22/SFF soldier from Sok; friend of Lobsang Tinley

Dorje Yudon: leader of resistance to the Chinese in Nyarong, ca. 1956; sister of Norzin Lhamo, wife of Gyari Nyima, mother of Lodi Gyari Rinpoche

Gungthang Tsultrim: Chushi Gangdrug leader from Amdo, general secretary of the Thirteen Group, murdered in 1977

Gyalo Thondup: elder brother of the fourteenth Dalai Lama; ambassador to the outside world; coordinated CIA–Tibet relations

Gyari Nyima: chieftain in Nyarong; member of Chushi Gangdrug; husband of Dorje Yudon and Norzin Lhamo; father of Lodi Gyari Rinpoche

Gyato Kalsang: Chushi Gangdrug soldier from Lithang; nephew of Andrug Gompo Tashi; brother of Gyato Wangdu

Gyato Wangdu: Chushi Gangdrug soldier from Lithang; parachuted into Tibet in 1957; trained in Colorado; sent to Mustang to replace Baba Yeshi; killed in ambush by Nepali army; nephew of Andrug Gompo Tashi; brother of Gyato Kelsang

Jama Ngatruk: Chushi Gangdrug leader from TreHor Kham; a leader of the Mustang force; imprisoned in Nepal for seven years, 1974–81

Jamyang Norbu: intellectual, writer, and public critic; member of the Mustang force

Kargyal Thondup: resistance fighter from Chatreng; witness to monastery bombings; author of book about history of Chatreng

Kesang Tsering: Tibetan woman from Markham; wife of Lobsang Tinley

Lhamo Tsering: senior exile government official, assistant to Gyalo Thondup; imprisoned in Nepal for eight years; known as Dronyik/Secretary Lhamo Tsering; family name, Tsongkha

Lobsang Jampa: Chushi Gangdrug soldier from Lithang; trained in Colorado, served in Mustang, where he was supposed to replace Baba Yeshi as general

Lobsang Palden: Chushi Gangdrug soldier from Lithang; carried important message from India to Lhasa

Lobsang Tinley: Chushi Gangdrug soldier from Lithang; former Sera Monastery monk; served on supply team in Mustang; husband of Kesang Tsering

Lodi Gyari Rinpoche: Dalai Lama's Special Envoy; Dharamsala–Beijing negotiation team leader; co-founder of Tibetan Youth Congress; son of Dorje Yudon, Gyari Nyima, and Norzin Lhamo

Lotse: Chushi Gangdrug soldier from Lithang; member of the first group of six trained by the CIA; served as radio operator during the Dalai Lama's escape in 1959

Norbu Dorje: Chushi Gangdrug soldier from TreHor Kham; wireless operator in Mustang

Norzin Lhamo: member of Nyarong chiefly family; sister of Dorje Yudon, wife of Gyari Nyima, mother of Lodi Gyari Rinpoche

Pangda Yamphel: Tibetan government trade agent, governor of Dromo, originally from Markham; had dispute with Gyalo Thondup in Kalimpong

Pega: Leader in Mustang; imprisoned in Nepal for seven years, 1974–81

Phala Dronyer Chenmo: lord chamberlain of the Tibetan government; key government official involved in relations with Chushi Gangdrug

Phuntsog Wangyal: Tibetan communist from Bathang

Phupa Pön: chieftain from Markham; resistance fighter; author of books about Markham and Chushi Gangdrug; personal name is Tsering Tobgye

Rakra: Mustang force leader from Lithang; imprisoned in Nepal for seven years, 1974–81; referred to as "Gen" Rakra

Ratuk Ngawang: Chushi Gangdrug soldier from Lithang; leader of the Est. 22/SFF in India

Sonam Gelek: Chushi Gangdrug soldier from Gaba

Surkhang Wangchen Gelek: Tibetan government official and Lhasa aristocrat; had dispute with Gyalo Thondup, left India for Taiwan

Taklha Phuntsok Tashi: brother-in-law of the Dalai Lama; carried Dalai Lama's message to end operations to Mustang force

Tashi Tsering: director of the Amnye Machen Institute; former research officer at the Library of Tibetan Works and Archives, Dharamsala; editor, publisher, historian

Tharchin: Christian Tibetan in Kalimpong who ran the Tibetan language newspaper *Yulchog Sosoi Sarguyr Melong (Tibet Mirror)*; known as Reverend Tharchin or Tharchin Babu

Thubten Ngodup: Est. 22 soldier; immolated himself in 1998 during the Unto Death Hunger Strike in New Delhi

Trijang Rinpoche: the Dalai Lama's junior tutor, originally from Lithang

Yonru Pön: chieftain from Lithang who shot a Chinese official during a public meeting and was then shot dead by Chinese forces

Introduction

1. On the production of history, see Trouillot 1995.
2. Das 1995.
3. DuBois 1969 in Pandey 1995.
4. For example, the literatures on the Holocaust (e.g., Friedlander 1992, Young 1993), colonialism (e.g., Amin 1995, Gold 2002, Pandey 2001, Stoler 2008), and communism/socialism (e.g., Mueggler 2001, B. Wang 2004, Watson 1994).
5. On "dominance without hegemony" as a key aspect of colonial rule and elite national rule in India, see Guha 1997.
6. Gramsci 1971, 1988, Laclau and Mouffe 2001, Williams 1977. See also Comaroff and Comaroff 1992:28: hegemonies are "that order of signs and material practices, drawn from a specific cultural field, that come to be taken as the natural, universal, and true shape of social being—although its infusion into local worlds, always liable to challenge by the logic of cultural forms, is never automatic."
7. On imperial formations as polities of dislocation, processes of deferral, and states of becoming, see Stoler and McGranahan 2007.
8. This version is from G. Mullin 1998:109–13. On violence, nonviolence, and the Dalai Lama lineage from the fifth Dalai Lama (1617–82) to the present, fourteenth Dalai Lama (1935–), see Sperling 2001.
9. On this period in Tibetan history, see Goldstein 1989, Shakabpa 1967, 1976.
10. On this question, see Robert Barnett's essay in Blondeau and Buffetrille 2008:88–90.
11. Taussig 1993, 1999.
12. Taussig 1993:xvii–xviii.
13. Brown 1995.
14. Ibid., 74–75.
15. On the politics of recognition, see Fraser 2000. In a similar vein, Nicholas Dirks

(1992:25) argues that history as a form of recognition is not only "the outcome of political representation, but also its necessary condition."

16. In contrast, the Tibetan population of China in the 1990 census was 4.6 million.

17. Brown 1995.

18. Although the Dalai Lama held vast power within pre-1950 Tibet, it was not as concentrated as it is now in exile. Specifically, the three monasteries of Sera, Drepung, and Ganden considered their collective power (at least) equal to that of the Dalai Lama. On power struggles between the Dalai Lama and these monasteries, see Goldstein 1990.

19. See the Dalai Lama's two autobiographies (T. Gyatso 1962, 1990) and Iyer 2008.

20. Nowak 1984, Klieger 1992. For the thirteenth Dalai Lama, see Bell 1987 [1946] and G. Mullin 1988.

21. Said 1984, Kaplan 1996.

22. On the Tibetan government-in-exile, see French 1991, McConnell 2009, Roemer 2008, and on governments-in-exile around the world, see Shain 1991.

23. Hansen and Stepputat, 10, emphasis added.

24. Arrangements for the Tibetan refugees were particular to each country. In India, especially in the Darjeeling and Kalimpong area, Tibetans resident prior to 1959 are citizens not legally categorized as "foreigners" or refugees. On Tibetan politics of citizenship, see DeVoe 1987, Hess 2006, 2009, and Falcone and Wangchuk 2008. On refugee politics in South Asia more generally, see Bose and Manchanda 1997, Oberoi 2006.

25. On Maoist revolution in Nepal, see the collected essays in Hutt 2004.

26. Malkki 1995a, 1995b. See also the collected essays in Daniel and Knudsen 1995.

27. The forty-six representatives are divided as follows: ten members each from Amdo, Kham, and U-Tsang; two members each from the four major sects of Tibetan Buddhism and the Bon religion; two representatives from Europe and one from North America.

28. While the government's high officials were primarily Lhasan aristocrats in the early decades of exile, things started to change in the 1980s. Appointed and elected officials—cabinet secretaries, the chief justice, and the chairman of the Assembly, for example—began to include Tibetans from Kham and Amdo as well as from all of the major sects and the Bon religion (and increasingly including women as well as men). The fourteenth Dalai Lama and his family are originally from the northern province of Amdo, although they became part of the Lhasan aristocracy by becoming a part of the Dalai Lama lineage.

29. Kapstein 1998:145. On the cultural and academic politics of Tibetan identifications within and beyond the Tibetan state, see Shneiderman 2006.

30. Taussig 1993:xvii–xviii.

31. Williams 1977:110.

32. Ibid.

33. Ibid., 112.

34. Ibid.

35. Diehl 2002, McGranahan 1996.

36. Jackson 2002:40.

37. Derrida 1982.

38. Foucault 1972, 1973.

39. On memory "work," see Cole 2001, Fujitani et al. 2000, Litzinger 1998, Stoler and Strassler 2000, and Yoneyama 1999.

40. Halbwachs 1992 [1941/1952].

41. The literature on history and memory is vast; some important starting points are Boyarin et al. 1994, Cole 2001, 2005, Connerton 1989, Gillis et al. 1994, Halbwachs 1992 [1941/1952], Le Goff 1992, Nora 1989, Watson 1994.

42. Grossberg 2000:158.

43. Das 2007:87. See also Collins 2008 on history as relations in real time, i.e., as a "working out of a positioning in the world."

44. Hall 1996:4, cited in Ang 2000:1. See also Hall 2000a, 2000b.

45. Ang 2000:9.

46. Interview, April 1998.

47. Foucault 1977 [1971]:217.

48. Foucault 1972, 1973.

49. Foucault 1973:xx.

50. Ibid., xx–xxi.

51. Bourdieu 1977:157.

52. Foucault 1973:xxi.

53. Studies of the Tibetan nation and nationalism include Dreyfus 1994, 1997, Karmay 1994, Klieger 1992, D. Norbu 1995, Stoddard 1994, W. Smith 1996.

54. Dirks 1990:25; see also Chatterjee 1986, 1993, Duara 1995.

55. Renan 1996 [1882], Anderson 1983 [1983]:204, Bhabha 1990, 1994.

56. Stoler 1995:8. On the politics of internal difference, exclusions, and cultural categories, also see Stoler 1989, 1992a, 1992b, 2002.

57. Foucault 1977 [1971]. For a discussion of the politics of order and identification in the cognate context of Ladakh, see van Beek 2001b.

58. Goldstein 1989, 2007, Grunfeld 1996, Laird 2006, Shakabpa 1967, 1976, Shakya 1999, W. Smith 1996, 2008. For an astute critique of contemporary Tibetan historiography, see P. Hansen 2003.

59. Foucault in Stoler 1995.

60. On the polemics of Chinese and Tibetan state histories, see Powers 2004 and the 2002 exchange in *New Left Review* between the Chinese dissident Wang Lixiong and the Tibetan scholar Tsering Shakya.

61. Prakash 1994:1481. See also Chakrabarty 1992, 1996, 2000.

62. For an introduction to the subaltern studies literature, see the *Subaltern Studies* vols. 1–10 (Delhi: Oxford University Press), vol. 11 (New York: Columbia Uni-

versity Press), as well as Guha and Spivak 1988 and collected essays by Chaturvedi 2000 and Ludden 2002.

63. Butler and Spivak 2007:32.

64. P. Hansen 2003. On contemporary scholarship on Tibet, see Shakya 1994,
Barnett 2008. Similarly, Rey Chow (1997) contends that Chinese cultural studies has yet to critically address "the contradictions of Chineseness as a constructed identity" in relation to Tibet (or Hong Kong or Taiwan).

65. On the singular truths of Indian national history, see Partha Chatterjee
(1993:115), who argues for the confederal unity of alternative regional histories
of India: "We do not yet have the wherewithal to write these other histories.
Until such time that we accept that it is the very singularity of the idea of a
national history of India which divides Indians from one another, we will not
create the conditions for writing these national histories."

66. Pandey 1995:296.

67. On the anthropological importance of the ways cultural groups explain themselves to themselves, see Geertz 1973.

68. J. Gyatso 1998.

69. On the politics of Tibet–Taiwan relations, see Rabgey and Wangchuk 2004.

70. Interview, Kathmandu, 8 November 1997.

71. Dirks 1996:32; see also Cohen 1994, Comaroff and Comaroff 1992.

72. Foucault 1980:81–82.

73. On treasure teachings, see Doctor 2006, Gardner 2006, J. Gyatso 1986, 1996,
1998, Thondup 1986. For accounts of specific treasure finders, see Aris 1988,
Germano 1998, Hanna 1994, Terrone 2002.

74. J. Gyatso 1996. See also Dreyfus 1994 on the role of the *gter ma* tradition in
fostering a unified historical identity among Tibetans, and Makley 2007 on
Tibetans hiding religious and political material during the Cultural Revolution.

75. Bhabha 1994:191–98.

76. Koselleck 1985 [1979]:xxiv; see also Feldman 1991.

77. Spiegel 2002:158. In the context of the Holocaust, Gabrielle Spiegel suggests
that durational time orders Holocaust testimonies such that they are "structurally unavailable as history." The content of durational time "has always been
there, suspended atemporally, not to be 'recovered' but only uncovered and
then covered once more, buried again beneath the fruitless struggle to expose
'the way it was'" (Spiegel 2002:158). Her understanding of durational time as
resisting closure ("the putting an end to the past") is resonant of the temporal
work of historical arrest and suggestive of the value of further inquiry into the
cultural particularities and similarities of notions of historical time other than
chronological and linear forms. See also Chakrabarty 2000, Gupta 1994, Hughes
and Trautmann 1995, and in the Tibetan context, March 2002, Mumford 1989,
and Ramble 2002.

78. Young 1993. On this point, see also Herzfeld 1997.

79. Taussig 1991:48.

80. Comaroff and Comaroff 1992:31.

81. On the critical merger of anthropology and history, see ibid., Axel et al. 2002, Ballinger 2003, Chatterjee 2001, Cohen 1994, Cohn 1987, Daniel 1996, Davis 1987, Dirks 1993 [1987], 2001, Evans-Pritchard 1962, Papailias 2005, Price 2008, and Stoler 1995, 2002.

82. In present-day Tibet, the treasure tradition is being revitalized as part of the reformation of Tibetan identity under socialist Chinese rule (see Germano 1998). In a time of religious and cultural persecution, this revitalized practice serves to connect the present to both recent and distant pasts, to "artwork and texts buried just a few decades ago in response to Chinese-initiated repression of Buddhism," and also to material and scriptural treasures of Tibet's own imperial age, a time when Tibet ruled portions of China (Germano, 55). In general, the treasure tradition remains slightly outside the mainstream of Buddhist practice. Issues of legitimacy and authenticity haunt the practitioners and their discovered treasures, much the same as with Chushi Gangdrug and their histories. That the treasure tradition and the Chushi Gangdrug resistance are both associated with the region of Kham may not be entirely a coincidence.

83. Benjamin 1969:262.

84. In an academic context, his words are echoed by Renato Rosaldo (1980), who asks, "Does all narrative meander, now bending for another perspective, then for an overview, and again to tell what was happening in the meantime? Narrative in fact does not move in a straight line. And those who restrict narrative to linear chronology . . . have both misread history and underestimated the variegated potentialities of story-telling."

85. Haraway 1991 [1988]:191–92; see also Foucault 1972, 1980.

86. Bourdieu 1994 [1977], Coronil 1996, Foucault 1973, 1980.

87. Fortun 2006:301.

88. Ibid., 312.

89. Marcus 1998 [1995].

90. On kora as cultural and political practice in contemporary Tibet (under the PRC), see Schwartz 1994 and Makley 2007.

91. Field notes, Kalimpong, 17 November 1997.

92. Bourdieu 1977, 1990, de Certeau 1984, 1988, Ortner 1984, 1996, 2006.

93. On these protests, see Tsering Shakya's interview of 2008 in New Left Review, as well as Makley nd, McGranahan et al. in press, Smith 2010, and Yeh 2009.

94. See, for example, Makley 2003, 2005b, 2007, Tuttle 2005, Yeh 2007b, 2008, and the collected essays in Hartley and Shiaffini-Vedani 2008.

95. Guha 1997.

96. On Tibetans as "prisoners" of Shangri-La, see Lopez 1998. For critical discussions of Lopez's arguments, see Dreyfus 2005, Germano 2001, Lopez 2001, Shakya 2001, and Thurman 2001. For histories and analysis of the "myth of

Shangri-La," see Anand 2007, Bishop 1989, Dodin and Rather 2001, Hovell 2001, J. Norbu 1998b, Richards 1992, 1993, and Shakya 1991, 1993. On the contemporary global spread of Tibetan Buddhism, see Moran 2004 and Zablocki 2005.

97. See John Beverley's argument on the rights of Rigoberta Menchu and the Mayan people of Guatemala; Beverley 2004:93.

98. On the need for radical critique as engagement with the hegemonic practices of existing institutions, see Laclau and Mouffe 2001, Mouffe 2008. On possibilities for anthropology as engaged critique, see Hoffman 2004.

99. I refer here to such authors as Israel Epstein and Anna Louise Strong in an earlier era, and Michael Parenti, Barry Sautman, and Slavoj Žižek in the present. On the reductionist tendencies of leftist critique regarding Tibet, see Yeh 2009.

1. Empire and the State of Tibet

1. 790–2/393 U.S. Undersecretary to Department of State, 8 October 1959, in *Foreign Relations of the United States, 1958–60*, vol. 19, *China*.

2. 790–2/393 U.S. Undersecretary to Department of State, 8 October 1959, ibid.

3. At this time, the PRC was not a member of the United Nations, although the Republic of China (Taiwan) was. On the global politics of human rights discourse, see Mamdani 2009.

4. On this point, see Barnett 1998, 2001.

5. On U.S. and Chinese imperialism in Tibet in the era of decolonization, see McGranahan 2007.

6. For studies of colonial state making, see Dirks 2001, 2008, Leach 1960, Prescott 1987, Rudolph and Rudolph 1984, Strang 1996.

7. Thongchai 1994.

8. Ibid., 17–18.

9. On this aspect of state sovereignty, see the collected essays in Biersteker and Weber 1996 and Wilson and Donnan 1998.

10. On the global spread of the European nation-state, see Anderson 1991 [1983], Chatterjee 1986, 1993, Dirks 1990, and Hobsbawm 1993.

11. Samuel 1993:3, 586n1. See also Samuel 1982.

12. Ibid., 39, 140–41.

13. Dreyfus 1997:136.

14. For a brief review of social, religious, and political organization by *pha yul*/ territory, see Samuel 1993:64–86.

15. In exile, one's pha yul has come to mean one's native place (or, if born in exile, that of one's father) at the territory level. For example, someone from the village of Mola in Lithang, would identify their pha yul as Lithang, not as Mola.

16. On religion and landscape in Tibet, see Blondeau et al. 1997, Blondeau and Steinkellner et al. 1996, Buffetrille and Diemberger 2002, J. Gyatso 1989, Huber 1994, 1999a, 1999c, and Karmay 1994, 2005.

17. Samuel 1993.

18. Interview, Dadhag, Darjeeling, November 1997.

19. Curzon 1907:7.

20. For studies of British policy toward and relations with Tibet, see Addy 1984, Goldstein 1989, Hansen 1996, Lamb 1986 [1960], McKay 1997, and Mehra 1974. On Qing and Nationalist Chinese claims to Kham territories, see Sperling 1976 and Lin 2006.

21. Lord Curzon describes this "expedition," which included the Anglo–Tibetan War in Gyantse, to be a retaliatory mission: "Had the Tibetans respected our Frontiers, we should never have marched three years ago to Lhasa" (1907:6).

22. See Curzon's outlining of the "forward" policy in his *Frontiers* (Oxford, Romanes lectures, 1907). For a history of this British policy in the Tibetan context, see McKay 1997.

23. I use the term "British" to refer to both Great Britain and British India in accordance with their joint administration of Tibetan policy.

24. McGranahan 2003a, 2003b.

25. In Kham, Bell included the territories of Derge, Chamdo, Dragyab, and Markham in "political" Tibet; Golok, Nyarong, Bathang, and Lithang were placed in the "in-between" zone; all other territories were considered "ethnographic" Tibet. Bell 1992 [1924]:6.

26. On contemporary conflicts along the Sino–Indian border (from the war in 1962 to the present day), see Ganguly 1989, Garver 2001, Mehra 2007, and Sperling 2008.

27. Dirks 1992.

28. The situation in Amdo regarding political relations with Lhasa and boundaries with China is different from that of Kham but unfortunately beyond the scope of this book. On contemporary Amdo, see the collected essays in Huber 2002.

29. For a discussion of the simultaneity of these events, see Shakya 1999:43. On Mao, Tibet, and the Korean War, see Sheng 2006; on Beijing's approach to Tibet over the decades, see Carlson 2004 and Chen 2006.

30. The Chinese government, however, vociferously claimed this was a legally binding document. For a discussion of these competing claims, see Blondeau and Buffetrille 2008, Shakya 1999.

31. For the most comprehensive presentations of U.S. and CIA relations with Tibet, see Knaus 1999 in English and Tsongkha 1992, 1998, 2002, 2003 in Tibetan.

32. On U.S.–Tibet Cold War relations, see Ali 1999, Conboy and Morrison 2002, Knaus 1999, Laird 2002, McCarthy 1997, and the essays in Kramer 2006.

33. The United States did not start a global campaign to win Tibetan hearts and minds until relatively late. The two countries first had diplomatic contact in 1942, when President Franklin Roosevelt dispatched two Office of Strategic Services (oss) officers on a covert mission to Tibet (see Starks and Murcutt 2004). Strong U.S. relations with China (i.e., Chiang Kai-shek's Republican China) meant an acknowledgment of Chinese proprietary sentiment toward

Tibet but also an awareness that (1) Chinese officials held multiple opinions on Tibet; and (2) Tibet was an independently functioning government at the time. As President Y. P. Mei of Yengching University (and also Tibetology Professor Li An-che) explained to U.S. consular officials in Chengdu, "Any attempt to extend Chinese control over Tibet by force would be bitterly resented by the Tibetans" (The Charge in China [Atcheson] to the Secretary of State, 20 September 1943, in *Foreign Relations of the United States, Diplomatic Papers, 1943: China* [Washington: U.S. Government Printing Office, 1957], 639). Thus, while Roosevelt addressed the Dalai Lama as a religious rather than a secular leader, the OSS officers, Ilya Tolstoy and Brooke Dolan, traveled to Lhasa via India with no mediation by or discussion with the Chinese. This first contact set the tone for all future U.S.–Tibet relations as secretive and cautious.

34. Under various titles, offices exist in Australia, Belgium, France, Hungary, India, Japan, Nepal, Russia, South Africa, Switzerland, Taiwan, the United Kingdom, and the United States.

35. In 2001, President George W. Bush signed into law the Tibet Policy Act of 2001 (H.R. 1779 and S. 852), which contended that the PRC had not upheld the terms of the Seventeen-Point Agreement, established programs and protocols for U.S.–Tibet relations and actions, and required the United States to encourage China to negotiate with the Dalai Lama and the Tibetan government-in-exile.

36. Goldstein 1991:9.

37. T. Tsering 1997.

38. For example, consider the following Tibetan critique of Goldstein's position by Phintso Thonden, former New York representative of the Tibetan government-in-exile. In the pages of *Tibetan Review*, Thonden took issue with Goldstein on four counts: (1) for misrepresenting the British model; (2) for implying that Chinese-stated Tibetan borders were more legitimate than Tibetan-claimed ones; (3) for suggesting that the *chol kha gsum* view of Tibet was merely an exile creation; and (4) for claiming "that the 1930s and 1940s somehow constitute a watershed mark from which all subsequent events of history must be judged" (Thonden 1991:13). Thonden instead advocated a version of Tibet including Kham and Amdo as well as central Tibet based on the *Bod chol kha gsum*, or "Tibet is three regions," formula. On this debate, see also J. Norbu 2004.

39. Thongchai 1994:130.

40. The chol kha gsum formation is also used in contemporary political protest in Tibet; see Schwartz 1994 and Sperling 1994. Other ways of organizing Tibet include the saying used in the Proclamation in the beginning of chapter 4: *mnga' ris skor gsum dbus gtsang ru bzhi mdo khams sgang drug*, or "the (1) 'three circuits' of Ngari in the west, (2) the 'four horns' of Ü (the 'Center') and Tsang, and (3) the 'six ranges' or 'three realms' constituting the eastern provinces of Amdo and Kham" (Kapstein 2006:4).

41. Sir Charles Bell had another unique idea for settling the boundary issue. In-

trigued by a suggestion from one of his Tibetan staff members, in 1924 Bell proposed a plebiscite for the eastern Tibetan territories under dispute. Noting a democratic tradition in Tibet, he suggested putting the boundary dispute to a vote by the local people, with the ballots to be counted by a trio of British, Tibetan, and Chinese officials. Each territory would vote for an affiliation with either Tibet or China. Bell's proposal was the only suggestion for a boundary settlement that involved the participation of the peoples of the frontier. As far as I can tell, British officials never considered the plan. See Bell 1992 [1924]:249–50.

42. International Commission of Jurists 1997:349–54.

43. "Memorandum on Genuine Autonomy for the Tibetan People," 7.

2. The Pains of Belonging

1. Das 1995. On the complexities of national belonging, see also Litzinger 2000 and Rutherford 2003.

2. As Pierre Bourdieu (1990:73) observes, "What is 'learned by the body' is not something one has, like knowledge that can be brandished, but something one is." Cited in Gutschow 2004:187.

3. On this point, see the collected essays in Das and Poole 2004.

4. On Tibetan relations with Indian communities, see Goldstein 1978, Lau 2009.

5. On identity and mobility, see Gupta and Ferguson 1997, Ong 1999.

6. Stoler 1989, 1992b, 1995, 2002.

7. For an astute analysis of place and identity in the context of Palestinian refugees, see Peteet 2005.

8. On the social impropriety of being one who stands out—i.e., the nail that sticks up—see the discussions in Diehl 2002.

9. On the Middle Way in Tibetan Buddhism, specifically the works of Nagarjuna, see Garfield 1995, Jinpa 2002, Samten and Garfield 2006. For an alternative Tibetan interpretation of Nagarjuna's thought, see Lopez 2005.

10. The Dalai Lama held his position on independence for Tibet through 1979. In 1988, in his "Strasbourg Proposal" address to members of the European Parliament, he formally outlined the Middle-Way Approach, which advocates autonomy for Tibet within China.

11. "The Middle-Way Approach: A Framework for Resolving the Issue of Tibet," www.tibet.net.

12. Keila Diehl's (1997, 2002) work on a Tibetan rock-and-roll band in Dharamsala makes these points particularly well, especially in relation to cross-generational conflicts and strategies for both merging and separating traditional and modern aspects of Tibetan culture. See also Calkowski 1991 and Harris 1999.

13. On the construction and privileging of the traditional, see Hobsbawm and Ranger 1992 [1983]. On contemporary Tibetan modernities, see the collected essays in Barnett and Schwartz 2008.

14. On Tibetan efforts to democratize their government and society, see Frechette

2002, 2007, Sangay 2003; on Tibetan society and politics over time, see Aziz 1978, Lichter and Epstein 1983, Goldstein 1971, 1990, D. Norbu 1974c, French 1995.

15. For contemporary studies of Kham, see the collected essays in Epstein 2002.

16. The literature on Ling Gesar is voluminous. Some starting points are Kornman 1997 and Samuel 1989, 1993, 1994.

17. Personal communication, Dawa Norbu, Delhi, 8 April 1998.

18. Ibid.

19. Ibid.

20. Not all types of difference are labeled as dangerous. For example, issues of class are left mostly unaddressed in the exile Tibetan community. In a related discussion of identity politics in Ladakh, Martijn van Beek reports a similar evasion of discussions of class and new local demands to address "skudragism," or aristocratic dominance (2001a, 545).

21. On the nation as imagined community, see Anderson 1991 [1983].

22. Barth 1969.

23. The first kiduk in exile is believed to have been started by Khampas in Kalimpong in the 1950s. On kiduk, see Miller 1956.

24. On the complexities of identification between Tibetans from the PRC and those from exile, see Yeh 2007a.

25. Especially from Tibetans in the United States following the Immigration Act of 1990, which enabled one thousand Tibetans—and later their spouses and children—to legally immigrate to the United States.

3. 1956: Year of the Fire Monkey

1. K. Thondup 1992.

2. Interview, Tenchoe, Kalimpong, 22 March 1998. This saying was common in many areas at the time, and during the course of my research numerous Khampa Tibetans quoted it to me. In contemporary Lhasa, the kind parents/ silver coins refrain still circulates (Emily Yeh, personal communication, August 2008).

3. *Yul chog so so'i gsar gyur me long*, 1 November 1957, vol. 24, no. 7.

4. This transliteration and English translation are the ones that Tharchin himself used. In Tibetan, the full title of the newspaper was *yul chog so so'i gsar gyur me long*. I refer to the newspaper as either *Melong* or *Tibet Mirror*. In spring 2009, Columbia University Libraries launched "The Tharchin Collection" online, including ninety-seven issues of the *Tibet Mirror* newspaper available at http://www.columbia.edu.

5. On the Reverend Tharchin, see Fader 2002 and D. Norbu 1975.

6. Interview, Baba Lekshey, Kathmandu, 15 December 1997.

7. *Melong*, vol. 24, no. 3, July 1, 1957, 4.

8. Ibid., 5.

9. Ibid., 6.

10. Ibid., 3.

11. Ibid., 3–6; *Melong*, vol. 24, no. 6, October 1, 1957, 5. Tharchin was most likely drawn to the range of Tito's political ideologies—antifascist, Yugoslav nationalist, and socialist but willing to work with Allied forces during the Second World War and also stand up to Stalin following the war. In 1961, Tito would join with four other world leaders (including India's Jawaharlal Nehru) to form the Non-Aligned Movement.

12. *Melong* 23, no. 10 (5 October 1956), 2.

13. Anderson 1991 [1983]. Although I call attention to the *Melong* newspaper here, I would argue that it is the loss of country, not print media, that grounds contemporary Tibetan nationalism.

14. Anderson 1991 [1983]:63.

15. Beverley 2004:30–31.

16. Ibid., 61.

17. Ibid., xvi.

18. Agamben 1999.

19. Ibid. On testimony, see also Das 1990, 2003, Ricouer 2004.

20. The story of Lithang is included in the following histories and memoirs: Andrugtsang 1973, Dewatshang 1997, *Gyon ru dpon* 1997, Ratuk 2006, Shakya 1999, W. Smith 1996, and has also been performed as a play in Dharamsala and Toronto.

21. Interviews: Athar Norbu, Delhi, 6 December 1997, 8–9 April 1998; Chodak, Darjeeling, 1 April 1998; Dadhag, Darjeeling, 19 November 1997; Lobsang Jampa, Kathmandu, 19–25 October 1997, 23–24 April 1998; Lobsang Tinley, Kathmandu, 29 October 1997, 5 May 1998.

22. "Pön" (*dpon*) is a Tibetan title meaning "chief."

23. Compiled from interviews with ten Lithangbas in Kathmandu, Pokhara, Kalimpong, Darjeeling, Delhi, and New York.

24. I draw the term "tense and tender" from Ann Stoler's work on the paradoxes of colonial memory (see her essay "Tense and Tender Ties" in Stoler 2006).

25. Interview, Chodak, Darjeeling, 1 April 1998.

26. Interview, Dadhag, Darjeeling, 19 November 1997.

27. Kargyal Thondup 1992.

28. Interview, Kargyal Thondup, Kathmandu, 11, 14, 15 July 1994.

29. Kargyal Thondup, 1992:162–73.

30. Interview, Dorje Yudon, Delhi, 7 December 1997; interviews, Gyari Nyima, Delhi, 5 April 1998, 20 March 1999. Parts of Dorje Yudon's story are also told by Elwood 1989 and J. Norbu 1986. I am grateful to Hubert Decleer for providing me with a copy of the Elwood interview.

31. This group of twenty-three included Dhargye Gonpa and Drago Monastery as well as many areas of Kham.

32. Dorje Yudon implied that all the "model citizens" agreed to these terms and were thus released; Jamyang Norbu contends that one of her soldiers told him that those who did not comply were thrown into the river. Personal communication, 29 June 2006. Issues of class and loyalty are clearly at work on several levels here; Nyarong society was highly hierarchical from the Gyari family on down to the lowest-class families. Across classes as well as within them subjectivities were not the same, with the result that some model citizens would have honored without issue their bonds of loyalty to the Gyari family, while others might have resented their place in society and appreciated the opportunities offered to them as model citizens.

33. Wanggyal 2002. See also Goldstein, Sherap, and Siebenschuh 2004.

34. Lobsang Gyaltsen 1971.

35. Interviews with Baba Lekshey, Kalimpong, 16 July 1995, Kathmandu, 15 December 1997, 2 February 1998; Baba Yeshi, Kathmandu, 16 December 1997, July 1999.

36. Lobsang Gyaltsen 1971:125.

37. Lobsang Gyaltsen 1971:134.

4. The Golden Throne

1. Reprinted in *Yulchog Sosoi Sargyur Melong*, vol. 26, nos. 2–3, July/August 1959. I thank Tenzin Bhagen for translation assistance with this text.

2. Interview, New York, 12 April 2000 See also Alo Chhonzed 1983 and Shakya 1999:144–47.

3. Mimang Tsogpa protested the Dalai Lama's trip to China in 1954, urging him not to go, and organization members met him in Kham on his return to Lhasa in 1955.

4. Andrugtsang 1973:40.

5. Interviews, Gyato Kalsang, ibid.; Ratuk Ngawang, Delhi, 5 December1997; Lobsang Jampa, Kathmandu, 19–25 October 1997. See also Andrugtsang 1973.

6. At the time of their arrest, Andrug Gompo Tashi was in Lhokha on a business trip with one of his nephews, Gyato Kalsang. After hearing about the arrests and subsequent imprisonments, they went to Samye Monastery to have a divination performed to see if it was safe for them to return to Lhasa. The result was favorable, and they returned to Lhasa, where Andrug Gompo Tashi met with Phala Dronyer Chenmo and other government officials to arrange for the release of the Mimang leaders. It was decided that the men would be released if Andrug Gompo Tashi could obtain the support of Sera, Drepung, and Ganden monasteries. Interview, Gyato Kalsang, ibid. See also Andrugtsang 1973.

7. The monasteries were deemed a better source of potential aid than the aristocrats, many of whose positions were compromised in that they encouraged the Tibetan people to revolt against socialism at the same time they were accepting money from the Chinese. Interview Lobsang Jampa, ibid.

8. As recalled by Gyato Kalsang forty years later, Andrug Gompo Tashi ar-

ranged with the military commander of the prison for him to covertly visit Alo Chhonzed. Gyato Kalsang arrived on a warm summer night and found Alo Chhonzed outside reading on a porch. He gave him the good news that his release had been arranged via support from the monasteries and assurances to the government that the imprisoned men would not engage in further political activities. Andrug Gompo Tashi had been concerned that Alo Chhonzed might be worried, but Gyato Kalsang found him exuberant with the expectations that their imprisonment would have a positive impact on global response to the situation in Tibet. Interview, Gyato Kalsang, ibid.

9. Andrugtsang 1973:42.
10. Interview, Ratuk Ngawang, Delhi, 5 December 1997.
11. Included in this group were Athar, Lotse, and Tsewang Dorje of Lithang and Baba Lekshey from Batang. Ratuk Ngawang joined them after arriving from Lhasa. Interview, Ratuk Ngawang, ibid.
12. Gyalo Thondup confirmed this in an interview with me in Kalimpong on 2 July 1999: "The resistance sent emissaries to ask me to approach [foreign countries] on their behalf, for arms, training, and the like."
13. See the discussion in Tsongkha 1998:25–31.
14. Athar Norbu and Lotse were among these bodyguards. Interviews, Gyato Kalsang, ibid; Ngawang Dadhag, Darjeeling, 19 November 1997.
15. Interview, Gyato Kalsang, ibid.
16. Interview, Gyato Kalsang, ibid. Confirmed by Lobsang Palden, Kalimpong, 26 March 1998.
17. Interview, Gyato Kalsang, ibid. Different codes and signals were used by the Tibetan traders-turned-military-strategists between Lhasa and Kalimpong and Lhasa and Kham. The codes had been developed by the Mimang leader Alo Chhonzed in 1955 when he went to receive the Dalai Lama on his return from China. At that time, Alo Chhonzed had met with several Lithang leaders, Yonru Pon, Gyato Bhugan, and Tenyu Aten, arranging signals that used the price of tea for communications between Kham and Lhasa. If the price was low, then the communists had the upper hand; if the price was high, then the Tibetans were in a strong position.
18. Andrugtsang 1973:42–43.
19. See Phala 1996 for an abridged version of Phala Dronyer Chenmo's autobiography.
20. Andrugtsang writes of receiving a letter from the "Tibetan Trade Mission" in Kalimpong praising his efforts during this time. The head of this mission was Pangda Yamphel, who appears to have supported Chushi Gangdrug in theory if not through direct financing of resistance activities. Gendun Phintso, a former mule herder of Pangda's, tells of Pangda Yamphel providing his muleteers with horses and guns and sending them to join with Chushi Gangdrug. Interview, Gendun Phintso, Kathmandu, 4 July 1995.

21. Interview, Gyato Kalsang, New York, 24 June 1998. He also added, "So, because of this, Baba Lekshey likes me. We're friends."
22. Interviews, Ratuk Ngawang, ibid; Lobsang Jampa, Kathmandu, ibid.
23. Tsongkha 1998:25–26.
24. Ibid., 31.
25. Interviews, Ngawang Dadhag, Darjeeling, 19 November 1997; Ratuk Ngawang, Delhi, 5 December 1997.
26. Tsongkha 1998:82.
27. Ibid.
28. Interview, Ratuk Ngwang, ibid.
29. Money and gold were needed in great quantities, and the Tibetan people complied, donating cash as well as personal belongings such as jewelry. According to individuals involved in soliciting donations, under the existing situation money seemed futile, so people gave generously; the success of their donation collecting was also due in part to the wealth of the Khampa traders. Interviews, Ratuk Ngawang, ibid.; Tachen, Kathmandu, 23 April 1998.
30. Only Tibetan government goldsmiths employed by the Tibetan aristocracy, not Nepali (Newari) goldsmiths, were allowed to work on the throne (see the story of one of these goldsmiths in *Bod gyi lo rgyus*, book 17, 239–46). Approximately fifty goldsmiths from the Namseling family received official permission to construct the throne. They were joined by five silversmiths, nineteen engravers, six painters, eight tailors, six carpenters, three blacksmiths, three welders, and thirty general assistants. Interview, Ratuk Ngawang, ibid; Andrugtsang 1973:52.
31. Andrugtsang 1973:51.
32. Interviews, Lobsang Jampa, ibid; Sonam Gelek, Kalimpong, 28 June 1999.
33. Andrugstang 1973:53.
34. Interview, Ratuk Ngawang, ibid.
35. Gyapön/ *brgya dpon* is an army rank for a leader of one hundred soldiers.
36. Interview, Ratuk Ngawang, ibid. Details of this meeting are in Ratuk 2008a, 234–38.
37. *'Bras sil* is a ceremonial rice pudding—each family has its own recipe, but common ingredients include butter, sugar, raisins, and *gro ma*, a small, sweet tuber that grows wild throughout Tibet.
38. Signatories to the Resolution were Andrug Gompo Tashi, Chatreng San Gelong, Chatreng Choephel, Chatreng Dawa, Chatreng Kelsang Choezin, Amdo Ngawang, Amdo Tselo, Amdo Trangmo, Julpa Samdong Chakzod Lobsang Phuntsok, Lithang Gyato Dhondup, Lithang Ratuk Ngawang, Lithang Kunga Samten, Nyarong Yeshi, Nyarong Abong, Tsawa Rongpa Awang, Tsawa Rongpa Dhampa Lodoe, Gyalthang Karchen Chakzod Thubten Geleg, Gyalthang Amban Tsultrim, Kanze Lamdrag Chakzod Pema Yeshi, Kanze Kyabgon Chakzod Tsultrim, Dhargye Gonpa Jama Ngatruk, Dhargye Gonpa Pema Dorje, Tau Norbu, Tau Khendrup, Gojo Dhondrup Phuntsok, Tehur Beri Shiser Wang-ga,

Drago Lobsang Tashi, Chamdo Dortse, Chamdo Konchok Dorje, Chamdo Tsega, Derge Jagod Namgyal Dorje, Derge Phurpa Trilen, Dragyab Atrug Lama, Gyalrong Yarphel, Gaba Drau Pon Rinchen Tsering, Gaba Wangchen Lhagon, Markham Lobsang Rabgye, Markham Lotse, Minyak Yonten Gyatso, Sadu Tenzin Phuntsok, Serge Shi-nyen Tsering Dhondrup, Amdo Ongkyo, and Andrug Dronyik Dragyab Loten. Ratuk 2008a, 234–38.

39. Dorje Shugden has the ability to possess mediums. De Nebesky-Wojkowitz (1993:144) reports that "the best known of the prophetic seers who act as the mouthpiece of *rdo rje shugs ldan* lives at a shrine in Lhasa called *spro bde khang gsar* (*rgyal khang*) or *spro khang bde chen lcog*. This is one of the few Tibetan oracle-priests who is not allowed to marry." I suspect this is the oracle Andrug Gompo Tashi consulted.

40. McCarthy 1997:141–42. See also Andrugtsang 1973:59. This story is common knowledge among Chushi Gangdrug soldiers.

41. On Tibetan protective deities, see de Nebesky-Wojkowitz 1993. In his autobiography, the resistance veteran Kunga Samten Dewatshang tells of a mission to Lhasa in which his protector provided him guidance. He and his colleagues were en route to Lhasa when an old man appeared from nowhere, suggesting they take another route as there were Chinese soldiers ahead. Unsure of whether the old man was telling the truth or not, they went ahead cautiously until they could just see the Chinese soldiers, confirming the old man's warning. Kunga Samten states that the old man's mysterious appearance, for it was an odd hour of the day, could only be a manifestation of his personal protector: "I can only attribute his appearance to my *sungma*, my protector, who must have come in the guise of this old man to warn us of the imminent danger" (Dewatshang 1997:121).

42. Dorje Shugden is a guardian deity of the Gelugpa sect, associated with a pure form of Gelugpa doctrine, in which mixing with other sectarian beliefs and practices is prohibited. According to Georges Dreyfus (1998:252–54), Dorje Shugden was a minor Gelug protector until aggressive promotion to a higher status by Phabongka Rinpoche in the 1930s. While there is currently a religious and political controversy (indeed, what some might consider a public secret, if not an arrested history) surrounding the worship of Dorje Shugden, based on the Dalai Lama's belief that Shugden worship is dangerous because Shugden is a worldly rather than transcendent deity with the power to harm the Dalai Lama and cause internal turmoil in the Tibetan community, there was no prohibition on Shugden worship in the 1950s. Many areas of Kham had mixed sectarian representation, in line with the *ris-med*, or nonsectarian movement of the nineteenth century. Certain areas, however, including the Ba-Li-Gyal area (including Chatreng as well as Bathang, Lithang, and Gyalthang), were heavily Gelugpa. As such, many people from these places took Shugden as a protector, and many Chushi Gangdrug soldiers were from these areas, including Andrug Gompo

Tashi. For an introduction to the contemporary Shugden controversy, see Dreyfus 1998, 2005 and the coverage in the spring 1998 issue of *Tricycle* magazine, including brief articles by Stephen Batchelor and Donald Lopez and interviews with Geshe Kelsang Gyatso and Lobsang Tinley Norbu by Lopez. On the success inside Tibet of the Dalai Lama's request for Tibetans to abandon Shugden as protector, see "Shugden in Kham."

43. Shugden appears one additional time in Chushi Gangdrug history: Dorje Shugden was given shelter by Sakya Rinpoche in Sakya Monastery. Sakya practitioners, therefore, while they do not (usually) worship Shugden, will often include his image on their personal altars. The king of Mustang, a Sakya patron and practitioner, was known to keep a mask of Dorje Shugden on his shrine. Mustang was the site where Chushi Gangdrug military operations into Tibet were based from 1960 through 1974.

44. In an interview in 1997, Lobsang Jampa recalled such an incident during battles in Kham. The incident, "still fresh in his mind," concerned a grave moment when the troops had to decide whether to return to Chamdo or not. Andrug Gompo Tashi consulted an oracle, and the deity said it was safe to return to Chamdo. Taso Choeze, the leader of the Dhargye Gonpa battalion, grabbed the neck of the oracle and accused him of being an evil spirit determined to mislead the group. After much heated discussion, the soldiers decided to proceed toward Chamdo. The Dhargye Gonpa battalion left and set out on its own. Following this, Andrug Gompo Tashi consulted with a learned geshe in Tateng, who confirmed the genuineness of the oracle's ability to transmit the deity's advice.

45. Andrugtsang 1973:62.

46. Ibid.

47. Ibid.

48. Interview, Lobsang Jampa, Kathmandu, October 1997. See also Andrugtsang 1973, Reting 2001, and Thubten Khentsun 1998:36. Lobsang Jampa also states that the Chinese would put Khampa clothing on dead Chinese soldiers and take photographs for propaganda purposes.

49. Interviews, Lobsang Jampa, Kathmandu, ibid.; Tachen, Kathmandu, ibid. According to several former soldiers, these rewards existed in theory only.

50. "Brief Introduction," 1998:3. Also, interviews, Tachen, Kathmandu, 23 April 1998; Jagod Se Dhonyod, Bir, 12 March 1999.

51. In 1997, Lobsang Jampa told me the story of Lobsang Tashi: "In 1958, there was a Chinese military camp in Dip Tsechogling outside of Lhasa. Gya (Chinese) Lobsang Tashi was a commander in that camp. He was Chinese. Due to infighting in the camp, he fled on horseback and was chased by Chinese soldiers. He abandoned his horse near the Potala Palace and surrendered to the Tibetan army in Drapchi. The Chinese could not find him. Later we were asked to receive someone from the Drapchi army camp. The person was disguised as a

woman. We didn't know who it was. It turned out to be Gya Lobsang Tashi, who joined us in Chushi Gangdrug." Andrugtsang (1973:60–61) also tells the story of Lobsang Tashi (Chang Ho-ther), adding that the Tibetan army wanted to turn him over to the Chinese, but Andrug Gompo Tashi requested that he be sent to join Chushi Gangdrug. Gya Lobsang Tashi fought with Chushi Gangdrug in Lhoka, fled to India with the Tibetans, and lived in a Tibetan refugee camp in Bylakuppe, Mysore, south India until his death. See also the chapter on Gya Lobsang Tashi in Phupa 2008.

52. Personal communication, Rinchen Dharlo, 26 May 2009. On some occasions, local Tibetans gave freely to the resistance troops, and on others they were forced to provide food and fodder. Reting Tenpa Tsering, a nomad who joined with the resistance in Lhoka, relates stories about the demands the resistance made on local communities, including the taking of barley—intended for human consumption—from storehouses to feed army horses, such that local people would joke that resistance horses shat only barley. Reting 2001:81.

53. Interview, Tachen, Kathmandu, ibid.

54. On this last point, see Dawa Norbu (1974a:3–4), who argues that to refer to all resistance soldiers as Khampas is not accurate: "Nothing can be more off the margin than the current notion that the recently disarmed Tibetan guerillas are all Khampas. It is true that the Khampas have a long martial tradition and are certainly the fiercest warriors among the Tibetans. It is also equally true that the Khampas were the first to rise in revolt against the Chinese occupation of Tibet. . . . [But] the notion that only Khampas are carrying on the fight for Tibet's freedom is a myth, born out of tradition, romanticized by Western writers and sustained by Chinese propaganda for obvious reasons."

55. Andrugtsang 1973:58.

56. The Tibetan aristocracy is solely a central Tibetan institution. Chiefs and kings from other parts of Tibet are not considered part of the aristocracy.

57. Interview, Gyalo Thondup, Kalimpong, 2 July 1999.

58. Ibid.

59. One aristocrat, Lhalu, is remembered by a veteran as stating that the Khampas, that is, resistance soldiers, were stubborn and foolish and that their efforts were in vain as neither the United States nor India was really helping the resistance effort. Interview, Jama Ngatruk, Darjeeling, 12 April 1998.

60. Namling 1988:95.

61. Ibid., 95–96.

62. Andrugtsang 1973:69.

63. Ibid., 72.

64. Ibid., 73.

65. The Chushi Gangdrug army faced not just a much larger opponent but a better equipped one. Chushi Gangdrug soldiers had to supply their own weapons, and

in Lhasa the local people would make fun of them, saying the volunteer army could not beat the Chinese by just buying guns in the public market. Interview, Jama Ngatruk, Darjeeling, 2 April 1998.

66. Interview, Sonam Gelek, Kalimpong, 28 June 1999.
67. Andrugtsang 1973:74.
68. Interview, Lobsang Jampa, Kathmandu, ibid.
69. Andrugtsang 1973:74–75.
70. Thubten Khentsun 1998:34.
71. Ibid.
72. Ibid., 35.
73. Ibid.
74. Ibid.
75. Ibid., 36. But not all Tibetan army officers felt this way, especially those of higher rank. See *Bod dmag gcig gi mi tshe* (Life of a Tibetan army soldier) by Sonam Tashi 1997.
76. Tsongkha 1998:24–25.
77. On this mission, Lhamo Tsering writes, "Gyalo Thondup took the eleven of us in his car from Darjeeling through the tea fields of Siliguri to the border of East Pakistan [Bangladesh]. From the border we walked through rice paddies for about an hour until we reached the banks of the Maharanda River, which was at the border of India and East Pakistan. We then saw a red light, which was the signal for where we were to go. The next morning we were taken by train to Dhaka, where an American met us. We then got in an airplane with no markings or color on it. The plane landed in the Philippines, Taiwan, and then in Okinawa, where we all had medical exams. We were next given U.S. military uniforms and got back on the plane. Our next stop was Washington D.C., and after that Richmond, Virginia. Waiting for us there was Amdo Dhondup Gyaltsen [the Tibetan interpreter on Saipan], who was to be cook and an interpreter for the group. Our training area was in a forest, surrounded by a wire fence. The American trainees all spoke Korean and Chinese. We trained there until March 1959. After that, I was sent to Washington for special training in establishing secret organizations in Tibet. In April, the Tibetan trainees were sent to Camp Hale in Colorado. This was the first time that Tibetans received real guerrilla warfare training in the United States." See ibid., 82.
78. Knaus 1999:154–55.
79. "Brief Introduction," 1998:9.
80. Interview, Tenchoe, Kalimpong, 22 March 1998.
81. Andrugtsang 1973:105–6.
82. *Melong*, 9 October 1964.
83. Interview, Sonam Gelek, Kalimpong, 28 June 1999.
84. Interview, Thubten Thargy, Delhi, 13 February 1999.

5. History and Memory as Social Practice

1. T. Gyatso 1990:159.
2. T. Gyatso 1962, 1990.
3. T. Gyatso 1990:193.
4. Ibid., 191.
5. C. Mullin 1975:33.
6. Andrugtsang 1973:51.
7. The tenth of March is, of course, only publicly celebrated in exile. In 2009, on the fiftieth anniversary of the uprising of 1959, the PRC government proclaimed 28 March "Serf Emancipation Day." For an incisive critique of the historical politics involved, see Sperling 2009.
8. McLagan 1996, 2002.
9. While Tibetans do not have guaranteed rights in either India or Nepal, their ability to express themselves and to gather publicly are severely restricted in Nepal. As a result of Nepal's weak position vis-à-vis China, the various governments of Nepal have progressively hardened their stance toward Tibetans in Nepal as part of an effort of prohibiting "anti-China activities."
10. Connerton 1989. See also Gillis 1994 and Sider and Smith 1997 on the politics of commemoration and silence, and Aggarwal 2004 on performance and political identity in Ladakh.
11. H. White 1987.
12. Das 1995, Halbwachs 1992 [1941/1952], Ricoeur 1984, Sahlins 1981, H. White 1987.
13. Sahlins 1991:46. See also Sahlins 1985, 2004.
14. See, e.g., Sonam Tashi 1997 and contemporary debates on www.phayul.com.
15. Das 2007:136.
16. Ibid.
17. Sewell 2005:101.
18. For an effort to categorize types of forgetting, see Connerton 2008.
19. Connerton 1989, Halbwachs 1992 [1941/1952]. For a differently oriented discussion of forgetting in relation to forgiveness, see Ricouer 2004.
20. On collected memories rather than collective memory, see Schwarcz 1994 and Young 1993.
21. On the role of memory in Tibetan nationalism, see Dreyfus 1994.
22. Battaglia 1993:430.
23. Ibid., 438.
24. Interview, 14 January 1999.
25. Field notes, 5 July 1999.
26. Berliner 2005.
27. Ibid.

28. Cole 2005; see also Cole 2001, 2006. On memory in the discipline of history, see Confino 1997.
29. Cole 2005:104.
30. Ibid.
31. Ibid., 112–13.
32. Ibid.
33. Ibid., 113.
34. Van der Kuijp 1996:42–43. On Tibetan historiography, see Martin 1997 and Vostrikov 1970.
35. Larry Epstein (personal communication) suggests that this notion of *sgrung* as factual history (and not just fictional story) might be specific to eastern Tibet as opposed to central Tibet, where sgrung are more explicitly associated with fantasy and fiction.
36. Trouillot 1995.
37. Bourdieu 1994 [1977]; de Certeau 1984, 1988.
38. Interview, Chodak, Darjeeling, 1 April 1998.
39. Van der Kuijp 1996.
40. On gossip and rumor as social and historical category, see Gluckman 1963, Merry 1984, Stoler 1992a, and White 1994.
41. On the gendered politics of history, see Scott 1988. On gender politics in Tibetan history, see McGranahan 2010.
42. The one exception to the elision of women's history in exile Tibet is the marking of Women's Uprising Day on 12 March. In many ways, this one day (and its supporting organization, the Tibetan Women's Association) stands in for the spectrum of women's history from 1950 to the present.
43. On the subject of Tibetan women in written history, Gyatso and Havnevik argue that there are very few "women's autobiographies in the entire history of traditional Tibetan literature. Indeed women are rarely discussed in historical writing at all, except for the briefest mention of someone's mother, or consort, who not infrequently is nameless or referred to only elliptically" (2005b, 8).
44. See Pachen and Donnelly 2000 and Tapontsang 1997.
45. Then again, veterans did not always explain the absence of women in the Chushi Gangdrug force as due to female polluting dangers. Lobsang Tinley once opined that the reason women were not in Chushi Gangdrug was because it was "too hard, too cold, and fighting was for the men." His wife immediately challenged him, saying that in Kham it is women who do hard work throughout the year and who could certainly fight alongside men if needed. He laughed, immediately backed down, agreed with her, and the conversation turned to something else.
46. Gutschow 2004, J. Gyatso 1989.
47. See de Nebesky-Wojkowitz 1956:503–37, chapter 26, "Protection against Evil."

According to de Nebesky-Wojkowitz, among the specific things a consecrated amulet may protect one against are "accidents, misfortune, illness, bad dreams, evil omens, dog bite, injury from wild animals, pollution, poison, theft, harm by weapons, harm to the harvest, against injury by lightning, and failure in business."

48. Tibetan veterans claim Chinese troops were often astonished at the protective powers of the Tibetans. One veteran told me that "Chinese soldiers would say that even machine gun fire turned to ash on Tibetans because all the butter and meat that the Khampas ate made them bulletproof." Certain Tibetan soldiers came to be known as invincible, forces whom even "dirty" bullets could not kill. Some were believed to be born with this power and could be killed only by being smashed with rocks. One Chushi Gangdrug soldier from Amdo was believed to be such an individual. He fought with the Chinese many times and was shot at hundreds, if not thousands, of times, yet was never killed. When the Chinese finally killed him, so it is claimed, they took his clothes and shared them, using them as their own protective amulets. Chinese troops would also collect small clay offerings (*tsha tsha*) that the Chushi Gangdrug soldiers would leave in sacred spots for the long life of the Dalai Lama; they would wear these inside their shirts for protection in battle. Although PLA communist troops ironically turned to Buddhist sources of protection, they also had their own means of protection, primarily red strips of cloth they tied to their guns. Tibetan veterans summarily dismissed these efforts, claiming they "didn't do anything for them."

49. Bullets from Russia that had a small amount of gold in the tip were thought to be especially dangerous. Interview, Jagod Se Dhonyod, Bir, India, 13 March 1999. Not all veterans were familiar with the danger gold presented, but they unanimously agreed that menstrual blood would cancel an amulet's protective power.

50. Interview, Chodak, Darjeeling, 1 April 1998.

51. Why is it that gold might cancel protective powers? Gold is treasured within Tibetan culture but also involves elements of danger and pollution. According to Heidi Fjeld, who conducts research with Tibetan artisans, including goldsmiths, work with fire is considered to be polluting (and thus blacksmiths, goldsmiths, and other metal workers are considered to have very low social status). Goldsmiths in Shigatse told Fjeld that gold is considered to be poisonous; when they blow gold, they keep a piece of meat in their mouths to avoid the poisonous gasses emitted, but nonetheless working with gold in this way leads to illnesses, especially of the lungs, one does not encounter when working with silver, iron, or other metals. Personal communication, Heidi Fjeld, October 2006.

52. Other types of blood were also considered *grib* and thus hazardous to the soldiers. According to veterans, Chushi Gangdrug soldiers who got Chinese officer's blood on their uniform were required to throw it away. Wounded

Tibetan soldiers posed similar dilemmas to battalion members, as contact with their blood would weaken the protective amulets of those helping them. For a discussion of grib in social and religious context, see Huber 1999a.

53. See Huber 1994, 1999a, 1999b and Makley 1994, 2003.

54. J. Gyatso 2003:111. Charlene Makley's work on the sexualization of nuns in Labrang is consonant with this: she argues that there is a social perception of the sexualized "dilemma and danger of nuns" despite nuns' claims to a "monastic androgyny" via a visual asexuality of body and dress (2005a:270). See also Havnevik 1989.

55. Veterans I interviewed stated that the penalty for violating this rule was one hundred lashes and, at times, death. According to one Khampa veteran, "Bad things happened, especially with the men from Amdo." Another told me the story of a Khampa soldier from Dhargye Gonpa who was renowned for fighting bravely against the Chinese but also notorious for acting just as rough in Tibetan communities: "He robbed the local people, raped local women. He did whatever he liked, so he was killed in Chushi Gangdrug." That is, he was killed by his fellow soldiers for these violations.

56. For example, in terms of reincarnation, the male bodily form is understood to be farther along the path to enlightenment than the female bodily form.

57. Gutschow 2004:200. See also Makley 2003, 2007.

58. Gutschow 2004:200.

59. Tapontsang 1997. Interview, Adhe Tapontsang, Dharamsala, June 1995. See also the story of Ani Pachen in Pachen and Donnelley 2000.

6. War in Exile

1. Interview, Lobsang Palden, Kalimpong, 26 March 1998.
2. Interview, Lobsang Jampa, Kathmandu, 19–25 October 1997.
3. Interview, Baba Yeshi, Kathmandu, 14 July 1999.
4. Interview, J. Paljor, Kalimpong, 27 March 1998.
5. Interview, Lobsang Jampa, Kathmandu, 19–25 October 1997.
6. Interview, Gyari Nyima, New Delhi, 20 March 1999.
7. Interview, Baba Lekshey, Kathmandu, 2 February 1998.
8. Interview, Kargyal Thondup, Kathmandu, 11, 14–15 July 1995; also K. Thondup 1992:206.
9. Lobsang Jampa, ibid.
10. Interview, Wangyal Lama, Pokhara, 27 March 1998.
11. Interview, Baba Yeshi, Kathmandu, 14 July 1999.
12. For a preliminary sketch of Tibetans in Taiwan, including former Chushi Gangdrug soldiers, see Okawa 2007.
13. On Mustang, see S. Craig 2008, Ramble 2002, 2007.
14. Other important leaders of Chushi Gangdrug at this time were Dhampa Lodö,

Karchem Chagzö, Kyabgon Chagzö from Kanze, Pe Dudzom from Dhargye Gonpa, Atuk from Dhargye Gonpa, Derge Phurpu Tinley, Namgyal Dorje from Derge, Bachung Thutop Gonpo, Gaba Gelek Phuntsok, Gaba Wangchen, Amdo Jinpa Gyatso, Jerung Jampa, Chatreng Wangdu Tsultrim, Chatreng Kelsang Chophel, Chatreng Se Kelsang, Gyatso Dhondup from Lithang, Shalkham Chonzed, Kelsang Tobgyal from Nyarong, Tau Khedup, Tau Norbu, Chamdo Kelsang Dorje, Chamdo Dortse, Trayab Lama Atuk, Trayab Ngawang Yonten, Gojo Gyau, and Gojo Atsang among others. Interview, Ratuk Ngawang, Delhi, 5 December 1997.

15. Interview, Kathmandu, 29 October 1997.

16. According to Gyato Kalsang, "a man called Kelsang was sent into Tibet and took many photographs of Chushi Gangdrug. But he came back only with the camera. He had put all his film on a mule and during a fight with the Chinese lost the mule and all the film! We also sent a man named Thubten to Lithang with a camera and a videocamera. He traveled with Baba Lekshey's brother but was captured by the Chinese and died in jail. One other guy brought back some photos of His Holiness [the Dalai Lama's] escape from Tibet." Interview, Gyato Kalsang, New York, 24 June 1998.

17. Interviews with Norbu Dorje, Pokhara, 28–29 April 1998; Tenzin Tsultrim, Darjeeling, 19 November 1997; Baba Lekshey, Kathmandu, 2 February 1998.

18. Interview, Jama Ngatruk, Darjeeling, 2 April 1998.

19. Unpublished MS shared with author, July 2002.

20. Another story Mr. Ray told me was about how the CIA officers were always trying to swat the flies that the Tibetans would catch and release outside. As Mr. Ray told me, "I'd tell them that those same flies were just going to come back inside and I'd try to get them then and they would just laugh and laugh." Interview, "Mr. Ray," June 2002.

21. Interview, Baba Yeshi, Kathmandu, 14 July 1999.

22. One group that came through Mustang was led by Lithang Gana. Although born in Lithang, Lithang Gana was a powerful nomad leader from Ligtse in southern Tibet. His family was one of the wealthiest nomad families, and he was an old friend of Andrug Gompo Tashi. In the initial days of establishing the guerrilla force in Mustang, Lithang Gana and his family arrived in Mustang. Andrug Gompo Tashi sent him a letter asking him to become a leader of the guerrilla army. At this time, the CIA had not yet sent supplies or money to the troops in Mustang, and so Lithang Gana shared his wealth with the Mustang force. Over time, Lithang Gana and Baba Yeshi had a falling out, and Lithang Gana and his family moved south into Nepal. Interview, Gyato Kalsang, New York, 24 June 1998.

23. Interview, Baba Yeshi, Kathmandu, 14 July 1999.

24. Interview, Lobsang Tinley, Kathmandu, 5 May 1998.

25. Included was a type of Tibetan *tsampa*, or ground barley, with extra vitamins in it that had been specially developed for the Mustang soldiers by Kellogg's cereal company; Knaus 1999:280.
26. Tibetans commonly refer to Mustang as "Lo" after the name of the kingdom's capital, Lo Monthang.
27. Interviews, Lobsang Tinley, Kathmandu, 25 September 1997; Norbu Dorje, Pokhara, 28–29 April 1998.
28. Interview, Lobsang Jampa, Kathmandu, 19–25 October 1997.
29. Ibid.
30. For a different view of relations between soldiers and local women, see the narrations in S. Craig 2008.
31. Interview, Baba Yeshi, Kathmandu, 16 December 1997.
32. For example, in addition to operations directly under the government of India, Chushi Gangdrug and the Tibetan government-in-exile also maintained other intelligence activities in India. Some men who had trained in Colorado were sent neither to Mustang nor to Est. 22/SFF but on different, often independent missions. Kundaling Thubten Gyaltsen, a Camp Hale graduate and former secretary to Gyalo Thondup, was one such agent. Upon his return from the United States, Thubten Gyaltsen was sent via Simla to try to enter Tibet to collect information. While in Simla, he posed as a fruit vendor but was detained by the police for appearing suspicious and left Simla for Kulu Manali. In Manali he befriended a Ladakhi doctor whose students traveled to the Indo–Tibetan border to collect medicinal plants. The students collected information for Thubten Gyaltsen that he sent on to headquarters in Darjeeling, until he was reassigned to Dharamsala. He and his sister opened a restaurant in Lower Dharamsala, and he would collect information at night, which he would pass on to the Dalai Lama's elder sister, the late Tsering Dolma. After half a year or so in Dharamsala, Thubten Gyaltsen was given a Tibetan government-in-exile post and sent back to the Darjeeling-Kalimpong area to recruit people for government service. Later, after recovering from a bout with tuberculosis, he was sent to Assam to recruit soldiers for Est. 22/SFF and from there to Nainital, Uttar Pradesh, to oversee Tibetan soldiers just returned from training in the United States. Interview, Thubten Gyaltsen, Darjeeling, 2 April 1998.
33. Interview, Tachen, Kathmandu, 8 July 1995.
34. Interview, J. Paljor, Kalimpong, 27 March 1998.
35. The most detailed history of the Special Frontier Force is found in Conboy and Morrison 2002.
36. Interview, Ratuk Ngawang, Delhi, 5 December 1997.
37. Interview, Jampa Kalden, Dharamsala, 22 June 1999.
38. Interview, Tachen, Kathmandu, July 8, 1995.
39. "Brief Introduction" 1998:21.
40. On Palden Lhamo (*dpal ldan lha mo*), see de Nebesky-Wojkowitz 1993:22–37.

41. Interview, Norbu Dorje, Pokhara, 28–29 April 1998.

42. Ibid.

43. Knaus 1999:276.

44. Interview, Baba Yeshi, Kathmandu, 14 July 1999.

45. The four-decades-old SFF is composed partially of Tibetan troops. According to Calcutta's *The Telegraph,* the top secret SFF force was placed under internal surveillance in April 2008 when the Olympic torch came to India accompanied by Chinese commando troops. According to a newspaper source, "SFF personnel are under watch at their center in Chakrata (near Dehra Dun) just like Sikh officers were after Operation Blue Star" (Dholabhai 2008).

46. See B. Miller 1990 on the difficulties of doing anthropological fieldwork among Tibetan communities in Darjeeling in the early-mid 1950s.

7. In a Clouded Mirror

1. Tethong 2000. *In Exile from the Land of Snows,* an important book by the journalist John Avedon (1986 [1979]), is one of the very few works that explores issues of internal tension within the Tibetan refugee community. Additionally, a brief account of the difficulties of this period is found in the autobiography of a Tibetan man who currently resides in Lhasa (Goldstein, Siebenschuh and Tsering 1997).

2. On the Pangdatsang family, see McGranahan 2001, 2002.

3. Interview, Gyalo Thondup, Kalimpong, 2 July 1999.

4. For more on Gyalo Thondup during this period, see Tsongkha 1992.

5. Tethong (2000: chap. 5) dates Gyalo Thondup's rise to a meeting of Tibetan government officials in Mussoorie on 21 April 1959. Specifically, he argues that during this meeting it was evident to participants that Gyalo Thondup's knowledge of the political situation, linguistic abilities, contacts with the Indian and U.S. governments, and relationship with the Dalai Lama ensured him a leadership role in the exile community.

6. For a sense of some of the aristocratic sentiment towards the fourteenth Dalai Lama's family, see the autobiography of the Gyalyum Chenmo, the Dalai Lama's mother (D. Tsering 2000). For a history of the fourteenth Dalai Lama's family, see M. Craig 1998.

7. In Kalimpong, one group of Khampa men used the Lhasa Mimang Tsogpa (People's Party) as a model for their fledgling political efforts. Their goals were to realign the Tibetan social and political system with regard to regional representation and participation in the national government. Individuals involved in this group included Markham Thoesam, Tseta Lobsang, Gara Lama, Lhasang Gyaltsen, and Manang Abo (a relative of the Pangdatsang family). This group did not acknowledge Gyalo Thondup as representative of the Tibetan community in India, and they accused him of not distributing U.S. money throughout the Tibetan community. Members of this group were all eventually arrested by

the Indian government and sent to prisons throughout India (in Rajasthan, Calcutta, etc.). Alo Chhonzed was also affiliated with this group and was later subject to the grotesquely ironic exile practice of *thamzing*, or political struggle, imported from Chinese-ruled Tibet. His book on the history of Tibet (1983) remains banned by the Tibetan government-in-exile.

8. Gyato Wangdu relayed this information to his close friend Jagod Se Dhonyod in India. Interview, Jagod Se Dhonyod, Bir, 12–13 March 1999.

9. See also McGranahan 2002 for the story of the murder of Pangda Yamphel's father, Pangda Nyigyal, in Lhasa in the 1920s.

10. Interview, November 2001.

11. Ibid.

12. Ibid.

13. The thirteen settlements were: (1) Gungthang Tsultrim's settlement in Clementown, near Dehra Dun; (2) Zongnor Rinpoche's settlement in Clementown; (3) the Lingtsang settlement in Manduwalla near Dehra Dun; (4) the Karthok settlement in Himachal Pradesh; (5) the Kamro or Drawo Pon's settlement in Himachal Pradesh; (6) the Tibetan Bon Foundation in Himachal Pradesh; (7) Chokling Rinpoche's Nangchen settlement; (8) Dorzong Rinpoche's Tashijong settlement; (9) the Derge division of the Bir settlement; (10) Gyelrong Thonche Pon's settlement; (11) Penor Rinpoche's settlement in Bylakuppe; (12) Rumtek Monastery in Sikkim; and (13) Namkha Dorje's settlement in Manipat, Madhya Pradesh.

14. Many Kagyu and Nyingma lamas were associated with the Thirteen Group, as was Baba Yeshi's refugee settlement in Nepal.

15. Gungthang Tsultrim, the general secretary of the Thirteen Group, who was murdered in 1977, was a former elected official of the Chushi Gangdrug army. His murder was never solved, although rumors proliferated (then and now) in the refugee community that Amdo Tenzin confessed to the murder. Although he proclaimed his innocence, Amdo Tenzin was arrested and imprisoned in Nepal and extradited to India, where he was imprisoned in Lucknow. He was later acquitted of all charges by an Indian court and returned to civilian life as a sweater seller in India (personal communication, Rinchen Dharlo, 29 May 2009). Critics of the Thirteen Group and Gungthang Tsultrim allege that both received funding from Taiwan; at the time to accuse someone of taking money from Taiwan was to accuse them of being pro-Chinese anti-Dalai Lama, both serious allegations within the refugee community.

16. Other controversies took place during this period as well. One I do not discuss here but that also had (and continues to have) reverberations through the community is the scandal involving Taiwan and the Tibet Office in Japan in the 1980s. As one veteran explained to me, "All these stupid things happened for money."

17. See, for example, the discussion in D. Norbu 1974c of Khampas in the Sakya area.

18. Interview, January 1999.

19. Gyalo Thondup is in the process of writing his memoirs. Interview, Kalimpong, 2 July 1999.

20. The "5412 Special Group" was a secret group focused on covert activities under the National Security Council Directive 5412. Its members were Gordon Gray, national security affairs advisor to the president; the deputy secretaries of state and defense; and one staff member, an assistant to Allen Dulles. Unlike the National Security Council, the Special Group "was usually able to decide and coordinate the government's covert programs on the spot without its members having to check with their principals." Knaus 1999:351n46.

21. Knaus 1999:249; McCarthy 1997:236. The documents included twenty-nine issues of the *Bulletin of Activities of the General Political Department of the People's Liberation Army*.

22. Personal communication, Clay Cathey, October 26, 2009.

23. Tibet policy was, of course, linked to China policy. On U.S.–China policy during the Cold War, albeit without reference to Tibet, see the collected essays in Ross and Jiang 2001.

24. One of the most vocal opponents of the Tibet operation was John Kenneth Galbraith, ambassador to India under Kennedy. For a discussion of Tibetan policy under Eisenhower, see Willner 1995.

25. Walter Benjamin 1968 [1955]:89.

26. Knaus 1999:249–50; McCarthy 1997:231–36.

27. According to Knaus 1999:366n24, the documents were released to the Library of Congress on 4 August 1963, were announced on the front page of the *New York Times* the very next day, and were published in Cheng 1966.

28. One CIA officer says, "I've sort of trained myself to forget about the operational detail. You don't talk very much about specific operational details, or even specific operations for anyone who's alive" (Roberts 1997b:34).

29. For example, the International Commission of Jurists report for 1960.

30. T. Gyatso 1990:148.

31. My thanks to retired CIA officer Bruce Walker for inviting me to attend this event.

32. Lobsang Jampa, T. Gyatso 1990:148.

33. Interview with Palden Wangyal, Pokhara, April 1998.

34. This quote is taken from R. Smith 1998. I thank Gen Baba Yeshi, his nephew Lobsang Palden, and niece-in-law Dolma for sharing this manuscript with me. As it is a direct translation of Baba Yeshi's autobiography, I have changed the pronouns from "he" to "I."

35. Lobsang Jampa, ibid.

36. Tsing 1993.
37. See, for example, how Baba Yeshi is portrayed in Dunham 2004.
38. Interview, Baba Yeshi, Kathmandu, 16 December 1997.
39. Interviews, Ratuk Ngawang, Delhi, 14 February 1999; and Gyato Kalsang, New York, 12 April 2000.
40. Interview, Gyato Kalsang, New York, 24 June 1998.
41. *Melong*, February 1963:2. See also Andrugtsang 1973.
42. *Melong*, February 1963:2.
43. Interview, Lodi Gyari, January 2009. This was noteworthy, as Tibetans considered the national flag to be sacred and dead bodies to be polluting, so there was controversy over covering any dead body—not just Andrugtsang's—with the flag.
44. *Melong*, 9 October 1964.
45. Ibid.
46. Ibid.
47. Ibid.
48. Group interview, Majnu-ka-Tilla branch of Chushi Gangdrug, 26 June 1999.
49. Interview, Baba Yeshi, Kathmandu, 14 July 1999.
50. Patterson 1970, 1974. Interview, George Patterson, San Diego, March 1999.
51. Knaus 1999:276–79.
52. Interview, Jagod Se Dhonyod, Bir, 12–13 March 1999; Gyato Kalsang, Delhi, 15 February 1999; Wangyal Lama, Pokhara, 27 April 1998.
53. Interview, Wangyal Lama, Pokhara, 27 April 1998.
54. Ibid.
55. Interview, Lodi Gyari, Denver, 8 May 2009.
56. Ibid.
57. Ibid.
58. For an accounting of Lhamo Tsering's contributions to the resistance force, including the general respect the soldiers had for him, as well as details about this imprisonment in Nepal, see J. Norbu 2001. The title "Drongyik" (*drung yig*) means "secretary," a respected and important position in Tibetan society.
59. Personal communication, Rinchen Dharlo, 17 May 2009.
60. Lobsang Jampa explains that Gyato Wangdu gave the Nepalis five conditions under which he would surrender: (1) Lhamo Tsering must be immediately released from prison; (2) the resistance will have no means of supporting itself after surrendering, so the Nepali government should provide them with a sum of twenty lakh (or two million) rupees per month; (3) resistance soldiers should be allowed to stay in Nepal; (4) the Nepali government should provide them with land for settlements; and (5) the weapons would be handed over in three stages. After a week or so of negotiations, the Nepali government accepted all of the conditions except for the last one. Wangdu was not satisfied, and as time

went on and Lhamo Tsering was not released from prison, Gyato Wangdu decided to flee to India through Tibet. Interview, Lobsang Jampa, February 2003.

61. Two wireless operators—Norbu Dorje and Samdup—were also arrested and imprisoned.

62. Personal communication, Rinchen Dharlo, 19 May 2009. Rinchen Dharlo served as the representative of His Holiness the Dalai Lama in Nepal from 1978 through 1986.

63. Interview, Amdho Choedak, Pokhara, 28 April 1998.

64. Interview, Lobsang Tinley, Kathmandu, 5 May 1998.

65. Amdo Kesang ran a restaurant in Pokhara and would invite all the visiting officials from Dharamsala for dinner. He was in contact with all the leaders even though he was a controversial member of the community right from the beginning. Personal communication, Rinchen Dharlo, 17 May 2009.

66. Amdo Kesang mysteriously disappeared around 1993; following his disappearance the camp leaders petitioned the Tibetan government-in-exile for aid and reconciliation.

67. The land for the Jampaling camp—unwanted by locals because it was believed to be haunted—was donated by the Nepali government.

8. Secrets, the CIA, and the Politics of Truth

1. Wise 1973:239–62, 557–59.

2. Simmel 1950, Taussig 1999, Tefft 1980, L. White 2000b.

3. L. White 2000b:22.

4. Ibid.

5. Ali 1999.

6. Addy 1984.

7. Knaus 1999.

8. On the Cold War in Asia, see Ali 1999, McMahon 1994, Nagai and Iriye 1977, and Willner 1995.

9. Ali 1999 provides the most comprehensive view of the Cold War in South Asia with relation to Tibet.

10. *Questions Pertaining to Tibet*, 337. Memorandum for the Special Group (9 January 1964), 731 (from Department of State, INR Historical Files, Special Group Files, S.G. 112, 20 February 1964. Secret; Eyes Only).

11. One scholar who has repeatedly directed attention to this connection is A. Tom Grunfeld (for example, Grunfeld 1996). Grunfeld's argument, however, is not congruent with mine: whereas he contends that the U.S.–Tibet connection reveals the compromised position of the Tibetan exile government, my argument is that one must understand this relationship as part of broader U.S. geopolitical imperial policies that complicate and influence, but do not neces-

sarily compromise, Tibetan governmental decision making. See also McLagan 2002 for a discussion of how Tibetan use of Western aid and discourses does not imply an "automatic co-optation of Tibetans or the Tibet issue."

12. Many of the veterans with whom I worked believed that the United States would help them in some way, some day. In 2006, this belief almost came true. In the summer of 2005, President George W. Bush proposed including five thousand Tibetans from Nepal in the U.S. Refugee Admission Program of 2006. Although official details on how individuals would be chosen for resettlement in the United States were not released, unofficially word spread that Tibetan veterans of Mustang, i.e., Lothik members, would have priority. Under presumed pressure from China but also perhaps in response to withheld U.S. military aid, His Majesty's government of Nepal refused to cooperate with the United States to facilitate the resettlement process. As a result, the plan stalled, and whether or not the new democratic government of Nepal will approve such a program remains to be seen.

13. I am unaware if any of these texts are extant (or, perhaps more accurately, remain hidden) in Tibet or in the veterans' community in India and Nepal. At present, none of the texts are in the public domain. For access to these texts, I am grateful to a retired CIA officer.

14. *A Pleasure Garden*, 9–11.

15. Ibid., 13–14.

16. On the United States and "circuits of knowledge production" in its imperial domains, see the collected essays in Stoler 2006. For ethnographies of twentieth-century American empire, see Lutz 2001, 2006, and Vine 2009.

17. Part of this larger vision included enrolling two groups of Tibetans at Cornell University, one in 1964 and one in 1965, a total of approximately fourteen students, thirteen males and one female. Each group studied at Cornell for one academic year, focusing on world history and politics. Interview, Bruce Walker, San Francisco, 7 January 2000.

18. Interview, Tony Poe, San Francisco, 17 December 1999. Tony Poe's given name was Anthony Poshepny.

19. Forbes 1989 discusses similar cultural misunderstandings between Swiss sponsors and Tibetans in Nepal in the 1960s and 1970s.

20. For example, Gen Yeshi, the chief leader in Mustang through the early 1970s, says, "In the beginning, I thought that the Americans were helping us, really helping us, to regain our country and our freedom. But, later, after many things, seeing what they gave, what they asked for, I realized they were only looking for their own benefit." Interview with Gen Yeshi by Thomas Laird, Kathmandu, December 1993.

21. This was Bruce Walker, who studied Tibetan at the University of Washington in Seattle in the early 1960s. Walker attended classes as a supposed member of

the U.S. Air Force. His classmates included two now-prominent Tibetologists, E. Gene Smith and Melvyn Goldstein. Interview, Bruce Walker, San Francisco, 7 January 2000.

22. This story has been told to me orally several times; a written version is available in Tsongkha 1998.

23. Knaus 1999.

24. Interview, Baba Yeshi, Kathmandu, 14 July 1999.

25. On conflicts between Gyalo Thondup and Chushi Gangdrug, see also Tethong 2000.

26. Interview, January 1999.

27. My formal interviews with Lobsang Jampa began in October 1997. Along with informal conversations, they continued through August 1999 and then again in February 2003.

28. In McGranahan 2005, I wrote that Lobsang Jampa's training name was Solo. In conversation with three former CIA officials, I determined that it could not have been Solo (nor was it Sally, as Conboy and Morrison 2002 state), but instead was Saul. Confirmed by Bruce Walker, 1 May 2009.

29. Social and political critique was also highly policed in pre-1950s Lhasa. See Goldstein 1982 for a discussion of the ways in which people, especially those of high rank, got around this prohibition through street songs.

30. Foucault 2007 [1997]:45.

31. Ibid., 47.

32. Ibid.

33. Dhompa 2002:11.

34. Simmel 1950:402–8.

35. Aris 1997; Klieger 1989.

36. Group interview with Dokham Chushi Gangdrug members, Majnu-ka-Tilla, 26 June 1999.

37. "A Brief Introduction," 1999.

38. Phupa 2008.

39. See, for example, the three *"Drang bden"* volumes from the 1970s, the book *Ma rung ba'i bya spyod spel bar lan 'dbas ngo sprod dgag bzhag gtam gyi thog mda'i* (*Discursive Thunderbolt: An Introductory Response to Immoral Conduct*) (1999), or the pamphlet "Brief Introduction of Chushi Gangdrug Defend Tibet Volunteer Force and Welfare Society of Central Dokham Chushi Gangdrug of Tibet" (1998), which is available online in modified format at www.chushigangdruk .org. On governmental (and public) censorship within the Tibetan community, see J. Norbu 1989:13.

40. "Yabshi" refers to members of the Dalai Lama's family, and in this context refers primarily to Gyalo Thondup. Personal communication, Tashi Tsering, June 1999; Group interview, Majnu-ka-Tilla, 26 June 1999.

41. See Avedon 1986 [1979], Cowell 1967, and Patterson 1968, 1970. Adrian Cowell was the filmmaker who traveled with George Patterson to film the Chushi Gangdrug troops' raid into Tibet in 1964.

42. For example, Marchetti and Marks 1974, C. Mullin 1975, Robbins 1979, Wise 1973. After a lull in the 1980s (Deane 1987, Long 1986), journalists rediscovered the CIA–Tibet connection in the 1990s (Lane 1994, Leary 1997/1998, Liu 1999, Roberts 1997a, 1997b, Salopek 1997). The majority of these articles focus on retelling the CIA-Tibet connection, and much to the concern of the Tibetan government-in-exile have at times overestimated the role of the CIA in the resistance. For example, the political magazine *George* for October 1997 was dedicated to the subject of spies. Included was an article about Tibet charging that the Dalai Lama's escape from Tibet was entirely planned and carried out by the CIA and basically contending that the Tibetans were nothing but American stooges of the Cold War (Roberts 1997a). The Tibetan government responded swiftly and sharply, immediately issuing a press release through the International Campaign for Tibet in Washington, D.C., stating, "It is an insult to the Tibetan freedom movement to imply that we were inspired and led by the CIA. On the contrary, the Dalai Lama's flight was planned and executed by Tibetans."

43. Peissel 1972.

44. Andrugtsang 1973

45. Interview, Lodi Gyari, January 2009.

46. Ibid.

47. Ibid. The Library of Tibetan Works and Archives in Dharamsala does not have any copies of this paper, but the British Library lists this paper in its online catalogue as *rang dbang srung skyob gsar sog*.

48. *Rang dbang* is the Tibetan word for "freedom." Upon the debut of the *Rang dbang* newspaper, Tharchin Babu printed this verse in the *Tibet Mirror* newspaper: *Rang dbang yod 'dug / rang dbang med / rang dbang med 'dug / Rang dbang yod*, or "When there was freedom, / there was no *Freedom*; / when there is no freedom, / there is *Freedom*."

49. J. Norbu 1986 [1979].

50. See, for example, D. Norbu 1974a, 1974b, 1979.

51. T. Gyatso 1962, 1990.

52. Shakabpa 1976.

53. Shakabpa 1967.

54. Grunfeld 1996, Shakya 1999, W. Smith 1996. In addition, the resistance was also fictionalized in an obscure Indian novel entitled *The Crusaders of Tibet*. Written by an Indian schoolteacher of Tibetan refugee children and published by Khampa Pocket Books, the book is advertised as a "blood-hot story of LOVE and WAR of the Tibetan guerrillas; their stirring and breathtaking exploits against the Red Chinese occupying forces in TIBET" (Bambi n.d.).

55. In this category, I would include recent Tibetan-language publications by former government officials such as Namling Paljor Jigme (1988), Thubten Khentsun (1998), Dronyer Chenmo Phala (1996, as orally recorded in 1976), and Taklha Phuntsok Tashi's three-volume autobiography (1995). See also Reting 2001.

56. Conboy and Morrison 2002; Dunham 2004; McGranahan 2005, 2006; and the collected essays in Kramer 2006.

57. In English: Dewatshang 1997, Knaus 1999, McCarthy 1997, J. Norbu 1994. Jamyang Norbu is also currently completing a book about Mustang.

58. Some veterans' history writings remain unpublished. Following his death, Lotse's handwritten autobiography was found. According to his brother Dadhag, Lotse wrote, "What he had done since childhood; how he fought against the Chinese; how we reached Lhasa, and how he went to Kalimpong for business. He also wrote about how he and his companions provided security to His Holiness the Dalai Lama." Interview, Darjeeling, 19 November 1997.

59. Phupa 1998.

60. Sonam and Sarin 1998. The U.S. equivalent of their film is underway: Lisa Cathey, daughter of the retired CIA officer Clay Cathey, is currently making a documentary about CIA–Tibet relations; see her website: www.ciaintibet.com.

61. Tsongkha 1992, 1998, 2002, 2003; Ratuk 2006, 2008a, 2008b.

62. For example, Thomas Laird (2002) suggests that what was really at stake in U.S.–Tibet relations was not Cold War covert military and intelligence operations against China, but U.S. atomic secrets.

63. It is believed that at least one other group of Asians trained at Camp Hale for a short time during this period. No Tibetan veteran has mentioned other trainees to me, and to my knowledge this group and the Tibetans were not in Colorado at the same time.

64. NARA 30 March 1950, New Delhi to Department of State, No. 683, "Mis. Dev. Relating to Tibet."

65. Nothing at all was known within India until April 1978, when rumors that the Ganges, the most sacred river in India, had been polluted by the government began to publicly circulate. Much to everyone's surprise, the government of India confessed that the rumors might be true. In 1965, India participated with the United States in a series of secret operations against China, including the installation of plutonium-239 devices for monitoring Chinese missile launches and nuclear explosions on the high reaches of the Himalayan peak of Nanda Devi. Later, when intelligence teams went to retrieve the sensors, a thirty-three-pound pack containing two to three pounds of plutonium could not be found. It was assumed it was swept away by an avalanche and had perhaps ended up in the Ganges River, which runs past Nanda Devi. See Ali 1999, Kohli and Conboy 2002, Takeda 2006.

66. For example, an article on the Indian website rediff.com on 8 January 2003

about Tibetan soldiers serving in the Indian armed services generated publicly posted comments of gratitude and surprise from Indian citizens.

67. Knaus 1999, Laird 2002, Liu 1999.
68. Interview, January 1999.

9. A Nonviolent History of War

1. On "the life and sacrifice of Thubten Ngodup," see J. Norbu 1998a.
2. Nineteen eighty-seven is also the first year the Dalai Lama explicitly mentions nonviolence in his annual statement of 10 March. In 1987, he said, "I have always expressed my firm conviction in the wisdom of following a nonviolent path." Prior to this time, however, it was clear to all Tibetans, including the Chushi Gangdrug soldiers, that nonviolence was an important component of the Tibetan struggle. A component of the struggle, however, is different from the entirety of the struggle. The Dalai Lama's statements of 10 March from 1961 to the present are archived at www.dalailama.com.
3. For example, the Tibetan intellectual and Mustang veteran Jamyang Norbu, one of the few public voices of critique in the exile community, argues that contemporary Tibetan nonviolence is not of the Gandhian kind but is a stricter, less active, and thus less successful version. J. Norbu 1997, 2007. On the Dalai Lama and Gandhi, see the Dalai Lama's two autobiographies, T. Gyatso 1962, 1990, and for an analysis of the Dalai Lama's views on Gandhi and nonviolence as a component of Buddhist modernism, see Dreyfus 2005.
4. On this point, see Maher 2008, 2009, Sperling 2001.
5. At least one hunger strike took place by a resistance soldier: "In 1966, just before the Cultural Revolution, in Drapchi prison in Lhasa, a CIA-trained Tibetan agent, Tede Tashi Gyaltsen, a native of Gyangtse, went on hunger strike. The first time around he was not successful. The Chinese guards force-fed him and injected him with some unknown medication. But a month later he tried again and this time, in spite of every effort by the prison administration, he starved himself to death. A comrade of his, who was with him in prison assured me that Tashi's decision was not actuated by despair, but that it was a deliberate political act of defiance against the Chinese." In J. Norbu 1998a.
6. On the International Year of Tibet, see McLagan 1996, 1997, 2002.
7. Pandey 2001:4–5. See also Pandey 1990, 1992, 1996, 2006. For an analysis of the social life of conflict narratives, see Drexler 2007.
8. H. White 1973.
9. On this point in relation to the Korean War, see Cho 2008.
10. See, for example, Bartholomeusz 2002, A. Hansen 2007, Yu 2005, and the collected essays in Juergensmeyer and Jerryson 2009. On self-immolation in Chinese Buddhism, see Benn 2007.
11. On Buddhism as lived practice, see Childs 2004.
12. T. Gyatso 1962:209–10.

13. Ardley 2003a.

14. Ibid.

15. Ardley 2000:25. See also Ardley 2003a, 2003b.

16. J. Norbu 2004.

17. Ibid.

18. Ardley 2003a:171.

19. The first Tibetan Youth Congress hunger strike was held in 1977, and the second in 1988. Immolations appear to have begun with Thubten Ngodup in 1998. Two have taken place since. On 23 November 2006, the Tibetan activist Lhakpa Tsering, president of the TYC branch in Bangalore, India, set himself on fire in Mumbai to protest Hu Jintao's visit to India and China's continuing occupation of Tibet. On 27 February 2009, a monk at Kriti Monastery in Ngaba, Tibet, was shot by police while immolating himself.

20. See the TYC website: www.tibetanyouthcongress.org.

21. "Unto Death Hunger Strike" update, 16 March 1998, TYC website: www.tibet anyouthcongress.org

22. Ibid.

23. Ibid.

24. The six participants in the first group of hunger strikers were Dawa Gyalpo, Dawa Tsering, Karma Sichoe, Palzom, Yundung Tsering, and Kunsang. Five were male, one was female; their ages ranged from twenty-five to seventy.

25. Field notes, 16 April 1998.

26. In 1980, during a trip to the Bylakuppe settlement, members of the Tibetan Youth Congress told the journalist John Avedon (1981:106) about their training in "guerrilla warfare, weapons use, karate. We practice in the jungle outside the settlement." Avedon's article is accompanied by a photograph of young men and women in field exercises, some of them with wooden replicas of M-16 rifles.

27. For two interesting interviews with Ngari Rinpoche, who served in the SFF as a paratrooper for several years but eventually grew disillusioned and quit military service, see Iyer 2008 and Katayama 2008.

28. According to Jamyang Norbu (2009), in the 1970s and 1980s the Tibetan government-in-exile required a year of mandatory service in Est. 22 for all Tibetans who completed twelfth grade.

29. On 2 April 2005, Marine Lance Corporal Tenzin Choeku Dengkhim was killed by "hostile action" while serving in the U.S. Marine Corps in Iraq. Tibetans have also served in the U.S. Army, Navy, and Army Reserves.

30. For information on specific details of the demands and hunger strike, see www.tibetanyouthcongress.org.

31. Http://www.tibetanyouthcongress.org/2-day08, accessed 15 August 2008.

32. In addition to the TYC hunger strikes of 1998 and 2007, there have been numerous other recent ones of which I am aware. In 1999, three Tibetans held a hunger strike at UN headquarters in Geneva. In 2004, three Tibetans held a

hunger strike at UN headquarters in New York. In 2006, a hunger strike was held at the site of the Winter Olympics in Italy. In each of these cases, the hunger strike was called off as a result of some portion of the strikers' demands being met. In 2008, the number of hunger strikes grew exponentially in conjunction with Tibetans in exile showing solidarity with protesters inside Tibet.

33. In his 1990 autobiography, the Dalai Lama says the following in discussing the events of 1958: "[The freedom fighters] tried to secure my approval for what they were doing. Alas I could not give it, even though as a young man and a patriot I had some thought now to do so." T. Gyatso 1990:128.

34. J. Norbu 1998a.

35. As quoted ibid.

Conclusion

1. Benjamin 1968 [1955]:255.

2. Rosaldo 1989:20.

3. Ibid.

4. One example Shakya gives involves the governmental Library of Tibetan Works and Archives in Dharamsala. Decades ago, the library collected a vast number of oral histories from former government officials and other individuals in exile with particularly interesting histories to tell. Later, however, the government canceled the library's plans to publish the oral histories because some of the accounts "compromised the official versions of history and as a result they remain unpublished." Shakya 1999:xxvii. At present, the collection remains closed to the public, and only a small percentage of the oral histories have been published.

5. Shakya 1999:xxii, Powers 2004. In a related argument, Christiaan Klieger (1989) suggests that versions of history produced by the Tibetan government-in-exile reflect Buddhist historiographic techniques as well as the conversion of foreign relations into religious patronage systems. While elements of earlier historiographical and diplomatic practices remain in the political strategy of the Tibetan government-in-exile, I suggest that they are subject to recalibration in line with Tibetan interpretations of modern global politics. See also McLagan 1996 on the Tibetan government-in-exile and the global Free Tibet movement. The Shangri-La myth is also partially to blame in that it sets Tibetans apart from time and thus out of history.

6. Histories denied might also involve conscious lying. As Jacques Derrida explains, "By definition, the liar knows the truth, if not the whole truth at least the truth of what he thinks; he knows what he means to say; he knows the difference between what he thinks and what he says; he knows that he is lying." Derrida 2001:72.

7. L. White 2000b:22.

8. Foucault 1977 [1971]:144.

9. Brown 2005:83–97.

10. Ibid., 91.

11. Taussig 1986.

12. White 2000a:76–77.

13. Ibid., 77.

14. Geertz 1973, 1985.

15. To recall Benjamin's assertion, "The value of information does not survive the moment in which it was new. It lives only at that moment; it has to surrender to it completely and explain itself to it without losing any time. A story is different. It does not expend itself. It preserves and concentrates its strength and is capable of releasing it even after a long time." 1968 [1955]:90.

16. Dirks 1990.

17. Phupa 1998, 2008.

18. Just as Tibetans inside Tibet do not know the full story of the Chushi Gangdrug resistance in exile, so too Tibetans outside do not know entirely the story of those who stayed behind in Tibet, many of whom continued to fight under the name Chushi Gangdrug, or *bstan srung dang blangs dmag*.

19. McCarthy 1997.

20. Others contend that the contents of the agreement were not as favorable. See *A ri'i mdo khams chu bzhi sgang drug tshogs gtso a thar nor bu'i bden gtam zer b'i 'od sder nang gi 'chal gtam la dgag lan bden gtam mun pa sel b'i sgron me bzhugs so*, published by the Dharamsala Chushi Gangdrug branch in 2008.

21. See, for example, the agreement that Tibetan Youth Congress leaders made with India's ruling Janata Party in 1977. When presented to the exile government, officials were enraged and demanded the resignation of all the TYC leaders. See Avedon 1986 [1979]:112–13.

22. The Tibetan government-in-exile also ran a controversial referendum vote among the Khampa community regarding the scandal. The highly contested results—including accusations of government intimidation in certain communities and voting improprieties in others—was 99.6 percent in favor of the government and 0.4 percent in favor of the signed document with Taiwan. Excellent coverage of the scandal and ensuing politics was provided by the now-defunct Mangtso (*Dmangs gtso*) newspaper.

23. See, for example, his comments regarding Lithang Athar in "*A ri'i*" 2008.

24. Kesang Tsering insists that Tibetans were "ironed," that is, hot irons were used to torture them. I am not aware of any studies of this incident and present this information as social commentary rather than as empirically confirmed historical fact.

25. In December 2005, the now-defunct website for *The Times of Tibet* (www.time softibet.com) featured an image of Andrug Gompo Tashi with the caption, "When are we going to celebrate his birthday?"

26. I have been unable to confirm if the Taiwanese government did in fact publicly recognize the death of Andrug Gompo Tashi.

27. Interview, Baba Yeshi, Kathmandu, 16 December 1997.

28. Ibid.

29. The Chushi Gangdrug in India website, www.chushigangdrug.org, is no longer operative.

30. The Delhi-based group has an active website (www.chushigangdruk.org) and chapters located around the world in Belgium, Bhutan, Canada, Japan, Nepal, Taiwan, and the United States.

31. Golok is a region of Tibet straddling Kham and Amdo. Goloks are notorious for being staunchly independent and insular.

32. Benjamin 1968 [1955]:255.

Epilogue

1. One year earlier, in the summer of 2007, Dokham Chushi Gangdrug presented a long-life offering ceremony to the Dalai Lama. Many Dharamsala dignitaries attended the ceremony, signaling a shift in this group's public political categorization.

2. J. Norbu 2006.

3. Ibid.

4. Ibid.

5. From 1996 to 2006, the Communist Party Nepal (Maoist) waged a civil war against the Nepali government. While Tibetans were not directly targeted, many are wary of the Maoists and the violence they have inflicted upon Nepal. As of 2007, over thirteen thousand people were killed in the civil war and in the continuing violence in Nepal. In 2008, the Maoists were elected to govern Nepal. Their tenure as ruling party lasted one year, through early May 2009, and the country remains in a politically unsettled state as of spring 2010.

6. To say "mani" is to say the common Tibetan Buddhist mantra, "Om mani padme hum," or "O Jewel-Lotus." When turning prayer beads, Tibetans say this or another mantra.

7. Field notes, 13 February 2003.

8. Even in jail, some resistance veterans found ways to pass the time with laughter. In an interview with Jamyang Norbu, Lhamo Tsering told of how the seven imprisoned resistance veterans passed their time: "I told the others it would be difficult to survive if we didn't organize ourselves. I suggested that we kept strictly to an active and productive routine every day without fail. The others agreed. I wrote down the routine and pinned it up on our cell wall. It went like this: We got up at six and then held a prayer service. After that we did exercises till eight when we had our breakfast. From nine we had classes in English, Hindi, and Nepali. Teachers were no problem. The jail was crowded with lawyers and teachers from the banned Congress party and other dissident political groups. In our jail there were more than one hundred such people. The previous prime minister of Nepal was in our jail for some time.

"After lunch we played volleyball till teatime at three, after which you could do as you pleased. Little Tashi used to fly kites. He was from Lhasa and had a passion and the skill for the game. Ngagtruk and Pega were great chess players, and also very religious. They meditated a lot and both managed to recite the 'Praises to Tara' over 100,000 times. The rest of us weren't that spiritual. Our specialty was humor. Rakra was enormously funny and had an inexhaustible fund of hilarious stories and jokes. But Chatreng Gyurme was even better at making up strange tales. He made them all up in [his] head, and they were weird. Our jailers and the Nepalese prisoners were puzzled by the constant laughter that would come from our cell" (J. Norbu 2001).

BIBLIOGRAPHY

Tibetan Language Sources

A ri'i mdo khams chu bzhi sgang drug tshogs gtso a thar nor bu'i bden gtam zer b'i 'od sder nang gi 'chal gtam la dgag lan bden gtam mun pa sel b'i sgron me bzhugs so (Lamp illuminating the darkness: Rebuttal to the fabricated rumors circulated by U.S. Dokham Chu bZhi sGang drug leader Athar Norbu). 2008. Dharamsala: Dharamsala mdo stod chu sgang Central Office.

Alo Chonzed. 1983. *Bod kyi gnas lugs bden 'dzin sgo phye ba'i lde mig zhes bya ba a lo chos mdzad kyi gdamz, spyi lo 1920 nas 1982 bar* (The key that opens the door of truth to the Tibetan situation: Materials on modern Tibetan history). Australia: Self-published.

Kargyal Thondup. 1992. *Mdo khams cha phreng kyi lo rgyus gser gyi snye ma* (The golden grain of Dokham Chatreng's history). Dharamsala: Library of Tibetan Works and Archives.

Lobsang Gyaltsen. 1971. *'Ba' kyi lo rgyus (History of Kham Ba-pa)*. Dehra Dun: Nyingmapa Lamah Press.

Ma rung ba'i bya spyod spel bar lan 'dbas ngo sprod dgag bzhag gtam gyi thog mda'i (Discursive thunderbolt: An introductory response to immoral conduct). 1999. Delhi: Welfare Society of Central Dokham Chushi Gangdrug.

Naga, Acharya Sangye T., and Tsepak Rigzin. 1994. *Bod dbyin shan sbyar gyi tshig tshogs dang gtam dpe* (Tibetan quadrisyllabics, phrases, and idioms). Dharamsala: Library of Tibetan Works and Archives.

Namling, Paljor Jigme. 1988. *Mi tshe'i lo rgyus dang 'bril yod sna tshogs* (My life history and other stories). Dharamsala: Library of Tibetan Works and Archives.

Nangchen Drongpa Kelsang. 1998. *Bod nang tang bstan byol du wong sgabs kyi lo rgyus hrag bsdus* (Abridged histories of Tibet and of coming into exile). Oral History Series No. 6. Dharamsala: Library of Tibetan Works and Archives.

Phala, Dronyer Chenmo Thubten Ongden. 1996. *Sku tshe'i lo rgyus hrag bsdus* (An abridged life history of Phala). Dharamsala: Library of Tibetan Works and Archives.

Phupa, Tsering Tobgye. 1998. *Gangs can bstan srung dang blangs dmag: sMar khams sgang gi rgyal srung dmag 'thab lo rgyus* (The Tibetan volunteer army to defend Buddhism: The history of Markham's battles to defend Tibet). Dharamsala: Narthang Press.

———. 2008. *Mdo khams chu bzhi sgang bsten srung dang blangs dmag gi lo rgyus* (The history of Dokham Chushi Gangdruk soldiers for the protection of Buddhism). Dharamsala: Dharamsala mdo stod sgang Central Office.

Ratuk, Ngawang. 2006. *Mdo khams spon 'bor sgang gi sa'i char 'khod p'i Li thang dgon yul gnyis kyis btsan 'dzul pa la zhum med ngo rgol gyis rang sa srung skyob byas p'i skor: Li thang lo rgyus yig tshang phyogs sgrig, deb gnyis pa.* (Lithang historical records. Volume 2: A brief account of the defense of Lithang by monasteries and tribes during China's invasion, 1936–1959). Edited by Tashi Tsering. Dharamsala: Amnye Machen Institute.

———. 2008a. *Mi tshe'i lo rgyus zol med srong po'i gtam gyi rol mo; Stod cha: Li thang lo rgyus yig tshang phyogs sgrig, deb gsum pa' dang po.* (Lithang historical records. Volume 3, part 1: The autobiography of Dasur Ratuk Ngawang of Lithang). Edited by Tashi Tsering. Dharamsala: Amnye Machen Institute.

———. 2008b. *Mi tshe'i lo rgyus zol med srong po'i gtam gyi rol mo; Stod cha: Li thang lo rgyus yig tshang phyogs sgrig, deb gsum pa' gnyis pa.* (Lithang historical records. Volume 3, part 2: The autobiography of Dasur Ratuk Ngawang of Lithang). Edited by Tashi Tsering. Dharamsala: Amnye Machen Institute.

Reting, Tenpa Tsering. 2001. *Life Experiences of Reting Tenpa Tsering.* Dharamsala: GuChuSum.

Shakabpa, Tsepon W. D. 1976. *Bod kyi srid don rgyal rabs* (A political history of Tibet). 2 vols. Kalimpong: Shakabpa House.

Sonam Tashi. 1997. *Bod dmag gcig gi mi tshe* (A Tibetan soldier's life story). Dharamsala: Sherig Pharkhang.

Taklha, Phuntsok Tashi. 1995. *Mi tshe'i byung ba brjod pa* (Telling the story of my life). 3 vols. Oral History Series No. 2. Dharamsala: Library of Tibetan Works and Archives.

Thubden Tharchin, ed. 1998. *Rong khul gyi rang srung bstan 'gog gi rlabs* (A wave of fire in defending from invaders in the Rongpo area). India [no publication information given].

Thubten Khentsun. 1998. *Dka'a sdug 'og gi byung pa brjod pa* (A tale of sorrow and hardship). Dharamsala: Sherig Pharkhang.

Tsongkha, Lhamo Tsering. 1992. *Bstan rgol rgyal skyob, Deb tang po, Sku'i gcen po llha sras rgya lo don grub mchog gi thog ma'i mdsad phyogs dang gus gnyis dbar chab srid 'brel ba byung stang skor* (Resistance. Volume 1: The early political activities of Gyalo Thondup, older brother of H.H. the Dalai Lama, and the beginnings of my political involvement [1945–1959]). Edited by Tashi Tsering. Dharamsala: Amnye Machen Institute.

———. 1998. *Bstan rgol rgyal skyob, Deb gnyis pa, Bod nang du drag po'i 'thab rstod byas skor, 1957 nas 1962 bar* (Resistance. Volume 2: The secret operations into Tibet [1957–1962]). Edited by Tashi Tsering. Dharamsala: Amnye Machen Institute.

———. 2002. *Btsan rgol rgyal skyob, Deb gsum pa, Glo smon thang du bstan srung dang blangs dmag sgar chags tshul dang Bod nang rgya dmar la phar rgol 'thab 'dzings ji byas dngos rjen lo rgyus deb phreng dang po bzhugs* (Resistance. Volume 3: An account of the establishment of the Tibetan national volunteer defense force in Mustang and operations against the Communist Chinese inside Tibet: part 1). Edited by Tashi Tsering. Dharamsala: Amnye Machen Institute.

———. 2003. *Btsan rgol rgyal skyob, Deb bzhi pa, Glo smon thang du bstan srung dang blangs dmag sgar chags tshul dang Bod nang rgya dmar la phar rgol 'thab 'dzings ji byas dngos rjen lo rgyus deb phreng gnyis pa bzhugs* (Resistance. Volume 4: An account of the establishment of the Tibetan national volunteer defense force in Mustang and operations against the Communist Chinese inside Tibet: part 3). Edited by Tashi Tsering. Dharamsala: Amnye Machen Institute.

———. 1997. *Gyon ru dpon (Yuru Pon)*. Dharamsala: Tibetan Institute of Performing Arts.

European Language Sources

Addy, Premen. 1984. *Tibet on the Imperial Chessboard: The Making of British Policy Towards Lhasa, 1899–1925*. New Delhi: Academic Publishers.

Agamben, Giorgio. 1999. *Remnants of Auschwitz: The Witness and the Archive*. Translated by D. Heller-Roazen. New York: Zone Books.

Aggarwal, Ravina. 2004. *Beyond Lines of Control: Performance and Politics on the Disputed Borders of Ladakh, India*. Durham: Duke University Press.

Ali, S. Mahmud. 1999. *Cold War in the High Himalaya: The US, China, and South Asia in the 1950s*. New York: St. Martin's Press.

Amin, Shahid. 1995. *Event, Metaphor, Memory: Chauri Chaura, 1922–1992*. Berkeley: University of California Press.

Anand, Dibyesh. 2007. *Geopolitical Exotica: Tibet in Western Imagination*. Minneapolis: University of Minnesota Press.

Anderson, Benedict. 1991 [1983]. *Imagined Communities: Reflections on the Origins and Spread of Nationalism*. London: Verso.

Andrugtsang, Gompo Tashi. 1973. *Four Rivers, Six Ranges: A True Account of Khampa Resistance to Chinese in Tibet*. Dharamsala: Information and Publicity Office.

Ang, Ien. 2000. "Identity Blues." *Without Guarantees: In Honour of Stuart Hall*, ed. P. Gilroy, L. Grossberg, and A. McRobbie, 1–13. London: Verso.

Ankersmit, F. R. 1986. "The Dilemma of Contemporary Anglo-Saxon Philosophy of History." *History and Theory* 25, 1–27.

Ardley, Jane. 2000. "Violent Compassion: Buddhism and Resistance in Tibet." Paper presented at the Political Studies Association–UK Conference.

———. 2003a. *The Tibetan Independence Movement: Political, Religious, and Gandhian Perspectives*. London: RoutledgeCurzon.

——. 2003b. "*Satyagraha* in Tibet: Toward a Gandhian Solution?" *Tibet Journal* 28, 23–38.

Aris, Michael. 1988. *Hidden Treasures and Secret Lives: A Study of Pemalingpa (1450–1521) and the Sixth Dalai Lama (1683–1706)*. Shimla: Indian Institute of Advanced Study.

——. 1997. "Foreword." *Tibetan Histories: A Bibliography of Tibetan-Language Historical Works*, ed. D. Martin, 9–12. London: Serinidia Publications.

Avedon, John. 1981. "Tibet-in-Exile: Looking Homeward." GEO: *The Earth Diary* 3 (May): 100–110.

——. 1986 [1979]. *In Exile from the Land of Snows*. New York: Vintage.

Axel, Brian Keith, ed. 2002. *From the Margins: Historical Anthropology and Its Futures*. Durham: Duke University Press.

Aziz, Barbara. 1978. *Tibetan Frontier Families: Reflections of Three Generations from D'ing-ri*. Durham: Carolina Academic Press.

Ballinger, Pamela. 2003. *History in Exile: Memory and Identity at the Borders of the Balkans*. Princeton: Princeton University Press.

Bambi, R. P. n.d. *The Crusaders of Tibet*. Dalhausie: Khampa Pocket Books.

Barnett, Robert. 1998. Untitled essay. *The Tibetans: A Struggle to Survive*, ed. S. Lehman, 178–96. New York: Umbrage Editions.

——. 2001. " 'Violated Specialness': Western Political Representations of Tibet." *Imagining Tibet: Perceptions, Projections and Fantasies*, ed. T. Dodin and H. Räther, 269–316. Boston: Wisdom Publications.

——. 2008. "Preface." *Tibetan Modernities: Notes from the Field on Cultural and Social Change*, ed. R. Barnett and R. Schwartz, xi–xxiii. Leiden: Brill.

Barnett, Robert, and Shirin Akiner, eds. 1994. *Resistance and Reform in Tibet*. London: Hurst.

Barnett, Robert, and Ronald Schwartz, eds. 2008. *Tibetan Modernities: Notes from the Field on Cultural and Social Change*. Leiden: Brill.

Barth, Fredrik. 1969. *Ethnic Groups and Boundaries*. Long Grove, Ill.: Waveland Press.

Bartholomeusz, Tessa. 2002. *In Defense of Dharma: Just-War Ideology in Buddhist Sri Lanka*. London: RoutledgeCurzon.

Battaglia, Debbora. 1993. "At Play in the Fields (and Borders) of the Imaginary: Melanesian Transformations of Forgetting." *Cultural Anthropology* 8(4), 430–42.

Bell, Sir Charles. 1987 [1946]. *Portrait of a Dalai Lama: The Life and Times of the Great Thirteenth*. London: Wisdom Publications.

——. 1992 [1924]. *Tibet Past and Present*. Delhi: Motilal Banarsidass Publications.

Benjamin, Walter. 1968 [1955]. *Illuminations: Essays and Reflections*. Edited by H. Arendt. New York: Schocken Books.

Benn, James A. 2007. *Burning for the Buddha: Self-Immolation in Chinese Buddhism*. Honolulu: University of Hawai'i Press.

Berliner, David. 2005. "The Abuses of Memory: Reflections on the Memory Boom in Anthropology." *Anthropological Quarterly* 78(1), 197–211.

Besuchet, Christophe, ed. 1993. *The Institution of the Dalai Lamas. Lungta 7.* Dharamsala: Amnye Machen Institute.

Beverley, John. 1999. *Subalternity and Representation: Arguments in Cultural Theory.* Durham: Duke University Press.

——. 2004. *Testimonio: On the Politics of Truth.* Minneapolis: University of Minnesota Press.

Bhabha, Homi K, ed. 1990. *Nation and Narration.* London: Routledge.

——. 1994. *The Location of Culture.* London: Routledge.

Biersteker, Thomas J., and Cynthia Weber, eds. 1996. *State Sovereignty as Social Construct.* Cambridge: Cambridge University Press.

Bishop, Peter. 1989. *The Myth of Shangri-La: Tibet, Travel Writing, and the Western Creation of a Sacred Landscape.* Berkeley: University of California Press.

Blondeau, Anne-Marie, ed. 1997. *Tibetan Mountain Deities, Their Cults and Representations.* Wien: Verlag Osterreichischen Akademie der Wissenschaften.

Blondeau, Anne-Marie, and Katia Buffetrille, eds. 2008. *Authenticating Tibet: Answers to China's 100 Questions.* Berkeley: University of California Press.

Blondeau, Anne-Marie, and Ernst Steinkellner, eds. 1996. *Reflections of the Mountain: Essays on the History and Social Meaning of the Mountain Cult in Tibet and the Himalaya.* Wien: Verlag Osterreichischen Akademie der Wissenschaften.

Bose, Tapan K., and Rita Manchanda, eds. 1997. *States, Citizens, and Outsiders: The Uprooted Peoples of South Asia.* Kathmandu: SAFHR.

Bourdieu, Pierre. 1977. *Outline of a Theory of Practice.* Cambridge: Cambridge University Press.

——. 1990. *The Logic of Practice.* Cambridge: Polity Press.

Boyarin, Jonathan, ed. 1994. *Remapping Memory: The Politics of TimeSpace.* Minneapolis: University of Minnesota Press.

Brief Introduction of Chushi Gangdrug Defend Tibet Volunteer Force and Welfare Society of Central Dokham Chushi Gangdrug of Tibet. 1998. Delhi: Welfare Society of Central Dokham Chushi Gangdrug.

Brown, Wendy. 1995. *States of Injury: Power and Freedom in Late Modernity.* Princeton: Princeton University Press.

——. 2005. *Edgework: Critical Essays on Knowledge and Politics.* Princeton: Princeton University Press.

Buffetrille, Katia, and Hildegard Diemberger, eds. 2002. *Territory and Identity in Tibet and the Himalayas.* Leiden: Brill.

Butler, Judith, and Gayatri Chakravorty Spivak. 2007. *Who Sings the Nation-State?: Language, Politics, Belonging.* London: Seagull Books.

Calkowski, Marcia. 1991. "A Day at the Tibetan Opera: Actualized Performance and Spectacular Discourse." *American Ethnologist* 18(4), 643–57.

Carlson, Allen. 2004. *Beijing's Tibet Policy: Securing Sovereignty and Legitimacy.* Washington, D.C.: East–West Center.

Chakrabarty, Dipesh. 1992. "Postcoloniality and the Artifice of History: Who Speaks for Indian Pasts?" *Representations* 37, 1–26.

———. 1996. "Marx after Marxism: History, Subalternity, and Difference." *Marxism Beyond Marxism*, ed. S. Makdisi et al., 55–70. London: Routledge.

———. 2000. *Provincializing Europe: Postcolonial Thought and Historical Difference.* Princeton: Princeton University Press.

Chatterjee, Partha. 1986. *Nationalist Thought and the Colonial World: A Derivative Discourse.* Minneapolis: University of Minnesota Press.

———. 1993. *The Nation and Its Fragments: Colonial and Postcolonial Histories.* Princeton: Princeton University Press.

Chatterjee, Piya. 2001. *A Time for Tea: Women, Labor, and Post/Colonial Politics on an Indian Plantation.* Durham: Duke University Press.

Chaturvedi, Vinayak, ed. 2000. *Mapping Subaltern Studies and the Postcolonial.* London: Verso.

Chen, Jian. 2006. "The Tibetan Rebellion of 1959 and China's Changing Relations with India and the Soviet Union." *Journal of Cold War Studies* 8(3), 54–101.

Cheng, J. Chester, ed. 1966. *The Politics of the Chinese Red Army: A Translation of the Bulletin of Activities of the People's Liberation Army.* Stanford: Hoover Institution on War, Revolution, and Peace, Stanford University.

Childs, Geoff. 2004. *Tibetan Diary: From Birth to Death and Beyond in a Himalayan Valley of Nepal.* Berkeley: University of California Press.

Cho, Grace. 2008. *Haunting the Korean Diaspora: Shame, Secrecy, and the Forgotten War.* Minneapolis: University of Minnesota Press.

Chow, Rey. 1997. "Can One Say No to China?" *New Literary History.* 28(1), 147–51.

Cohen, David William. 1994. *The Combing of History.* Chicago: University of Chicago Press.

Cohn, Bernard. 1987 [1980]. "History and Anthropology: The State of Play." *An Anthropologist among the Historians and Other Essays*, 18–49. Delhi: Oxford University Press.

———. 1996. *Colonialism and Its Forms of Knowledge: The British in India.* Princeton: Princeton University Press.

Cole, Jennifer. 2001. *Forget Colonialism? Sacrifice and the Art of Memory in Madagascar.* Berkeley: University of California Press.

———. 2005. "Memory and Modernity." *A Companion to Psychological Anthropology: Modernity and Psychocultural Change*, ed. C. Casy and R. B. Edgerton, 103–20. Malden, Mass.: Blackwell.

———. 2006. "Malagasy and Western Conceptions of Memory: Implications for Postcolonial Politics and the Study of Memory." *Ethos* 34(2), 211–43.

Coleman, William M., IV. 2002. "The Uprising at Batang: Khams and Its Significance in Chinese and Tibetan History." *Khams pa Histories: Visions of People, Place, and Authority*, ed. L. Epstein, 31–56. Leiden: Brill.

Collins, John. 2008. "'But What If I Should Need to Defecate in Your Neighborhood, Madame?': Empire, Redemption, and the 'Tradition of the Oppressed' in a Brazilian World Heritage Site." *Cultural Anthropology* 23(2), 279–328.

Comaroff, Jean, and John Comaroff. 1992. *Ethnography and the Historical Imagination*. Boulder: Westview Press.

———. 1999. "Occult Economies and the Violence of Abstraction: Notes from the South African Postcolony." *American Ethnologist* 26(2), 279–303.

Combe, G. A. 1989 [1926]. *A Tibetan on Tibet: Being the Travels and Observations of Mr. Paul Sherap (Dorje Zodpa) of Tachienlu*. Berkeley: Snow Lion.

Conboy, Kenneth, and James Morrison. 2002. *The CIA's Secret War in Tibet*. Lawrence: University Press of Kansas.

Confino, Alon. 1997. "Collective Memory and Cultural History: Problems of Method." *American Historical Review* 102(5), 1386–1403.

Connerton, Paul. 1989. *How Societies Remember*. Cambridge: Cambridge University Press.

———. 2008. "Seven Types of Forgetting." *Memory Studies* 1(1), 59–71.

Coronil, Fernando. 1996. "Beyond Occidentalism: Towards Post-Imperial Geohistorical Categories." *Cultural Anthropology* 11(1), 51–87.

Cowell, Adrian. 1967. "I Saw the Secret Shooting War with China." *Argosy* 364(5), 29–33, 96–97.

Craig, Mary. 1998. *Kundun: A Biography of the Family of the Dalai Lama*. Berkeley: Counterpoint Press.

Craig, Sienna. 2008. *Horses Like Lightning: A Story of Passage Through the Himalayas*. Ithaca: Snow Lion.

Curzon, Right Honorable Lord, of Kedleston. 1907. *Frontiers*. Romanes Lecture. Oxford: Clarendon Press.

Daniel, E. Valentine. 1996. *Charred Lullabies: Chapters in an Anthropography of Violence*. Princeton: Princeton University Press.

Daniel, E. Valentine, and John Chr. Knudsen, eds. 1995. *Mistrusting Refugees*. Berkeley: University of California Press.

Das, Veena. 1990. *Mirrors of Violence: Communities, Riots, and Survivors in South Asia*. New Delhi: Oxford University Press.

———. 1995. *Critical Events: An Anthropological Perspective on Contemporary India*. New Delhi: Oxford University Press.

———. 2003. "Trauma and Testimony: Implications for Political Community." *Anthropological Theory* 3(3), 293–307.

———. 2007. *Life and Words: Violence and the Descent into the Ordinary*. Berkeley: University of California Press.

Das, Veena, and Deborah Poole, eds. 2004. *Anthropology in the Margins of the State*. Santa Fe: SAR Press.

Davis, Natalie Zemon. 1987. *Fiction in the Archives: Pardon Tales and Their Tellers in Sixteenth-Century France.* Stanford: Stanford University Press.

Deane, Hugh. 1987. "History Repeats Itself: The Cold War in Tibet." *Covert Action* 29, 48–50.

de Certeau, Michel. 1984. *The Practice of Everyday Life.* Berkeley: University of California Press.

———. 1988. *The Writing of History.* New York: Columbia University Press.

de Nebesky-Wojkowitz, Rene. 1956. *Oracles and Demons of Tibet: The Cult and Iconography of Tibetan Protector Deities.* The Hague: Mouton.

Derrida, Jacques. 1982. *Différance.* Translated by A. Bass. *Margins of Philosophy*, 1–27. Chicago: University of Chicago Press.

———. 2001. "History of the Lie: Prolegomena." *Futures: Of Jacques Derrida*, ed. R. Rand, 65–98. Stanford: Stanford University Press.

Des Chene, Mary. 1991. "Relics of Empire: A Cultural History of the Gurkhas, 1815–1987." Ph.D. diss., Stanford University.

De Voe, Dorsh Marie. 1987. "Keeping Refugee Status: A Tibetan Perspective." *People in Upheaval*, ed. S. Morgan and E. Colson, 54–65. New York: Center for Migration Studies.

Dewatshang, Kunga Samten. 1997. *Flight at the Cuckoo's Behest: The Life and Times of a Tibetan Freedom Fighter (as told to his son Dorjee Wangdi Dewatshang).* New Delhi: Paljor Publications.

Dholabhai, Nishit. 2008. "Olympic Torch Commandos under Watch." *The Telegraph* (Calcutta). April 15, 2008. Accessed online: http://www.telegraphindia.com/1080415/jsp/nation/story_9139537.jsp#.

Dhompa, Tsering Wangmo. 2002. *Rules of the House.* Berkeley: Apogee Press.

Diehl, Keila. 1997. "When Tibetan Refugees Rock, Paradigms Roll: Echoes from Dharamsala's Musical Soundscape." *Constructing Tibetan Culture: Contemporary Perspectives*, ed. F. J. Korom, 122–59. Quebec: World Heritage Press.

———. 2002. *Echoes from Dharamsala: Music in the Life of a Tibetan Refugee Community.* Berkeley: University of California Press.

Dirks, Nicholas B. 1990. "History as a Sign of the Modern." *Public Culture* 2(2), 25–32.

———. 1992. "Introduction: Colonialism and Culture." *Colonialism and Culture*, 1–25. Ann Arbor: University of Michigan Press.

———. 1993 [1987]. *The Hollow Crown: Ethnohistory of an Indian Kingdom.* Ann Arbor: University of Michigan Press.

———. 1996. "Is Vice Versa?: Historical Anthropologies and Anthropological Histories." *The Historic Turn in the Human Sciences*, ed. T. J. MacDonald, 17–51. Ann Arbor: University of Michigan Press.

———. 2001. *Castes of Mind: Colonialism and the Making of Modern India.* Princeton: Princeton University Press.

———. 2008. *The Scandal of Empire: India and the Creation of Colonial Britain*. Cambridge: Harvard University Press.

Doctor, Andreas. 2006. *The Tibetan Treasure Literature: Revelation, Tradition, and Accomplishment in Visionary Buddhism*. Ithaca: Snow Lion.

Dodin, Thierry, and Heinz Rather, eds. 2001. *Imagining Tibet: Perceptions, Projections, and Fantasies*. Boston: Wisdom Publications.

Drexler, Elizabeth F. 2007. "The Social Life of Conflict Narratives: Violent Antagonists, Imagined Histories, and Foreclosed Futures in Aceh, Indonesia." *Anthropological Quarterly* 80(4), 961–95.

Dreyfus, Georges. 1994. "Proto-Nationalism in Tibet." *Tibetan Studies*, ed. P. Kvaerne, 205–18. Oslo: Institute for Comparative Research in Human Culture.

———. 1997. "Law, State, and Political Ideology in Tibet." *Journal of the International Association of Buddhist Studies* 18(1), 117–38.

———. 1998. "The Shuk-den Affair: The History and Nature of a Quarrel." *Journal of the International Association of Buddhist Studies* 21(2), 227–70.

———. 2005. "Are We Prisoners of Shangrila? Orientalism, Nationalism, and the Study of Tibet." *Journal of the International Association for Tibetan Studies* 1, 1–21.

Duara, Prasenjit. 1995. *Rescuing History from the Nation: Questioning Narratives of Modern China*. Chicago: University of Chicago Press.

Du Bois, W. E. B. 1969. *The Souls of Black Folk*. New York: Signet.

Dunham, Mikel. 2004. *Buddha's Warriors: The Story of the CIA-Backed Tibetan Freedom Fighters, the Chinese Invasion, and the Ultimate Fall of Tibet*. New York: Tarcher/Penguin.

Edney, Matthew H. 1990. *Mapping an Empire: The Geographical Construction of British India, 1765–1843*. Chicago: University of Chicago Press.

Elwood, Holly. 1989. "Dorje Yudon: The Leader of the Rebels." Manuscript, Tibetan Studies Program, School for International Training.

Epstein, Lawrence, ed. 2002. *Khams pa Histories: Visions of People, Place, and Authority*. Leiden: Brill.

Evans-Pritchard, E. E. 1962. "Social Anthropology: Past and Present." *Social Anthropology and Other Essays*, 139–54. New York: Free Press of Glencoe.

Fader, H. Louis. 2002. *Called from Obscurity: The Life and Times of a True Son of Tibet, Gergan Dorje Tharchin*. Volume 1. Kalimpong: Tibet Mirror Press.

Falcone, Jessica, and Tsering Wangchuk. 2008. " 'We're Not Home': Tibetan Refugees in India in the 21st Century." *India Review* 7(3), 164–99.

Feldman, Allen. 1991. *Formations of Violence: The Narrative of the Body and Political Terror in Northern Ireland*. Chicago: University of Chicago Press.

Forbes, Ann Armbrecht. 1989. *Settlements of Hope: An Account of Tibetan Refugees in Nepal*. Cambridge: Cultural Survival.

Fortun, Kim. 2006. "Poststructuralism, Technoscience, and the Promise of Public Anthropology." *India Review* 5(3–4), 294–317.

Foucault, Michel. 1972. *The Archaeology of Knowledge*. New York: Pantheon Books.

———. 1973. *The Order of Things: An Archaeology of the Human Sciences*. New York: Vintage Books.

———. 1977 [1971]. "Nietzsche, Genealogy, History." *Language, Counter-Memory, Practice: Selected Essays and Interviews*, ed. D. Boucher, 139–64. Ithaca: Cornell University Press.

———. 1980. "Two Lectures." *Power/Knowledge*, ed. C. Gordon, 109–33. New York: Pantheon.

———. 2007 [1997]. *The Politics of Truth*. London: Semiotext(e).

Fraser, Nancy. 2000. "Rethinking Recognition." *New Left Review* 3 (May/June), 107–20.

Frechette, Ann. 2002. *Tibetans in Nepal: The Dynamics of International Assistance among a Community in Exile*. New York: Bergahn Books.

———. 2007. "Democracy and Democratization among Tibetans in Exile." *Journal of Asian Studies* 66(1), 97–127.

French, Rebecca. 1991. "The New Snow Lion: The Tibetan Government in Exile in India." *Governments-in-Exile in Contemporary World Politics*, ed. Yossi Shain, 188–201. New York: Routledge

———. 1995. *The Golden Yoke: The Legal Cosmology of Tibet*. Ithaca: Cornell University Press.

Friedlander, Saul, ed. 1992. *Probing the Limits of Representation: Nazism and the "Final Solution."* Cambridge: Harvard University Press.

Fujitani, T., Geoffrey White, and Lisa Yoneyama, eds. 2000. *Perilous Memories: The Asia-Pacific War(s)*. Durham: Duke University Press.

Ganguly, Sumit. 1989. "The Sino–Indian Border Talks, 1981–1989: A View from New Delhi." *Asian Survey* 29(12), 1129–31.

Gardner, Alexander Patten. 2006. "The Twenty-Five Great Sites of Khams: Religious Geography, Revelation, and Nonsectarianism in Nineteenth-Century Eastern Tibet." Ph.D. diss., University of Michigan.

Garfield, Jay. 1995. *The Fundamental Wisdom of the Middle Way: Nagarjuna's Mulamadhyamikakarika*. New York: Oxford University Press.

Garver, John. 2001. *Protracted Contest: Sino–Indian Rivalry in the Twentieth Century*. Seattle: University of Washington Press.

Geertz, Clifford. 1973. *The Interpretation of Cultures*. New York: Basic Books.

———. 1985. *Local Knowledge: Further Essays in Interpretive Anthropology*. New York: Basic Books.

Germano, David. 1998. "Re-membering the Dismembered Body of Tibet: Contemporary Tibetan Visionary Movements in the People's Republic of China." *Buddhism in Contemporary Tibet: Religious Revival and Cultural Identity*, ed. M. C. Goldstein and M. T. Kapstein, 53–94. Berkeley: University of California Press.

———. 2001. "Encountering Tibet: The Ethics, Soteriology, and Creativity of Cross-Cultural Interpretation." *Journal of the American Academy of Religion* 69(1), 165–82.

Gillis, John, ed. 1994. *Commemorations: The Politics of National Identity*. Princeton: Princeton University Press.

Gluckman, Max. 1963. "Gossip and Scandal." *Current Anthropology* 4(3), 307–16.

Gold, Ann Grodzins, and Bhoju Ram Gujar. 2002. *In the Time of Trees and Sorrow: Nature, Power, and Memory*. Durham: Duke University Press.

Goldstein, Melvyn C. 1971. "The Balance between Centralization and Decentralization in the Traditional Tibetan Political System." *Central Asiatic Journal* 15(3), 170–82.

———. 1978. "Ethnogenesis and Resource Competition among Tibetan Refugees in South India: A New Face to the Indo-Tibetan Interface." *Himalayan Anthropology*, ed. J. Fisher, 395–420. The Hague: Mouton.

———. 1982. "Lhasa Street Songs: Political and Social Satire in Traditional Tibet." *Tibet Journal* 7(1–2), 56–66.

———. 1989. *A History of Modern Tibet, 1913–1951: The Demise of the Lamaist State*. Berkeley: University of California Press.

———. 1990. "Religious Conflict in the Traditional Tibetan State." *Reflections on Tibetan Culture: Essays in Memory of Turrell V. Wylie*, ed. L. Esptein and R. F. Sherburne, 231–47. Lewiston, Me.: Edwin Mellen Press.

———. 1991. "The Dragon and the Snow Lion: The Tibet Question in the 20th Century." *Tibetan Review* (April), 9–26.

———. 2007. *A History of Modern Tibet*. Volume 2: *The Calm Before the Storm, 1951–1955*. Berkeley: University of California Press.

Goldstein, Melvyn C., Dawei Sherap, and William R. Siebenschuh. 2004. *A Tibetan Revolutionary: The Political Life and Times of Bapa Phuntso Wangye*. Berkeley: University of California Press.

Goldstein, Melvyn C., William R. Siebenschuh, and Tashi Tsering. 1997. *The Struggle for Modern Tibet: The Autobiography of Tashi Tsering*. Armonk, N.Y.: M. E. Sharpe.

Gordon, Avery. 1997. *Ghostly Matters: Haunting and the Sociological Imagination*. Minneapolis: University of Minnesota Press.

Gramsci, Antonio. 1971. *Selections from the Prison Notebooks of Antonio Gramsci*. Translated and edited by Q. Hoare and G. N. Smith. New York: International Publishers.

———. 1988. "Hegemony, Relations of Force, Historical Bloc." *An Antonio Gramsci Reader: Selected Writings, 1916–1935*, ed. D. Forgacs, 189–221. New York: Schocken Books.

Grossberg, Lawrence. 2000. "History, Imagination and the Politics of Belonging: Between Death and the Fear of History." *Without Guarantees: In Honour of Stuart Hall*, ed. Paul Gilroy, Lawrence Grossberg, and Angela McRobbie, 148–64. London: Verso.

Grunfeld, A. Tom. 1996. *The Making of Modern Tibet*. Armonk, N.Y.: M. E. Sharpe.

Guha, Ranajit. 1982. "On Some Aspects of the Historiography of Colonial India."

Subaltern Studies I: Writings on South Asian History and Society, ed. Ranajit Guha, 1–8. Delhi: Oxford University Press.

———. 1997. *Dominance without Hegemony: History and Power in Colonial India*. Cambridge: Harvard University Press.

Guha, Ranajit, and Gayatri Spivak, eds. 1988. *Selected Subaltern Studies*. Oxford: Oxford University Press.

Gupta, Akhil. 1994. "The Reincarnation of Souls and the Rebirth of Commodities: Representations of Time in 'East' and 'West.' " *Remapping Memory*, ed. J. Boyarin, 161–83. Berkeley: University of California Press.

Gupta, Akhil, and James Ferguson. 1997. "Beyond 'Culture': Space, Identity, and the Politics of Difference." *Cultural Anthropology* 7(1), 6–23.

Gutschow, Kim. 2004. *Being a Buddhist Nun: The Struggle for Enlightenment in the Himalayas*. Cambridge: Harvard University Press.

Gyatso, Janet. 1986. "Signs, Memory, and History: A Tantric Buddhist Theory of Scriptural Transmission." *Journal of the International Association of Buddhist Studies* 9(2), 7–35.

———. 1989. "Down with the Demoness: Reflections on a Feminine Ground in Tibet." *Feminine Ground: Essays on Women and Tibet*, ed. J. D. Willis, 33–51. Ithaca: Snow Lion.

———. 1996. "Drawn from the Tibetan Treasury: The *gTer ma* Literature." *Tibetan Literature: Studies in Genre*, ed. J. Cabezon and R. Jackson, 147–69. Ithaca: Snow Lion.

———. 1998. *Apparitions of the Self: The Secret Autobiographies of a Tibetan Visionary*. Princeton: Princeton University Press.

———. 2003. "One Plus One Makes Three: Buddhist Gender Conception and the Law of the Non-Excluded Middle." *History of Religions* 43(2), 89–115.

Gyatso, Janet, and Hanna Havnevik, eds. 2005a. *Women in Tibet*. New York: Columbia University Press.

———. 2005b. "Introduction." *Women in Tibet*, 1–25. New York: Columbia University Press.

Gyatso, Tenzin, the 14th Dalai Lama of Tibet. 1962. *My Land and My People: Memoirs of the Dalai Lama of Tibet*. New York: McGraw-Hill.

———. 1990. *Freedom in Exile: The Autobiography of the Dalai Lama*. New York: HarperCollins.

Halbwachs, Maurice. 1992 [1941/1952]. *On Collective Memory*. Translated and edited by L. A. Coser. Chicago: University of Chicago Press.

Hall, Stuart. 1996. "Introduction: Who Needs 'Identity'?" *Questions of Cultural Identity*, ed. S. Hall and P. du Gay, 4. London: Sage.

———. 2000a [1997]. "The Local and the Global: Globalization and Ethnicity." *Culture, Globalization, and the World-System: Contemporary Conditions for the Representation of Identity*, ed. A. D. King, 19–40. Minneapolis: University of Minnesota Press.

———. 2000b [1997]. "Old and New Identities, Old and New Ethnicities." *Culture, Globalization, and the World-System: Contemporary Conditions for the Representation of Identity,* ed. A. D. King, 41–68. Minneapolis: University of Minnesota Press.

Hanna, Span. 1994. "Vast as the Sky: The Terma Tradition in Modern Tibet." *Tantra and Popular Religion in Tibet,* ed. G. Samuel et al., 1–13. New Delhi: International Academy of Indian Culture and Aditya Prakasha.

Hansen, Anne Ruth. 2007. *How to Behave: Buddhism and Modernity in Colonial Cambodia, 1860–1930.* Honolulu: University of Hawai'i Press.

Hansen, Peter H. 1996. "The Dancing Lamas of Everest: Cinema, Orientalism, and Anglo-Tibetan Relations in the 1920s." *American Historical Review* 101(3), 159–78.

———. 2003. "Why Is There No Subaltern Studies for Tibet?" *Tibet Journal* 28(4), 7–22.

Hansen, Thomas Blom, and Finn Stepputat. 2001. "Introduction: States of Imagination." *States of Imagination: Ethnographic Explorations of the Postcolonial State,* 1–38. Durham: Duke University Press.

Haraway, Donna. 1988. "Situated Knowledge: The Science Question in Feminism as a Site of Discourse on the Privilege of Partial Perspective." *Feminist Studies* 14(3), 575–99.

Harris, Clare. 1999. *In the Image of Tibet: Tibetan Painting after 1959.* London: Reaction Books.

Hartley, Lauran, and Patricia Schiaffini-Vedani, eds. 2008. *Modern Tibetan Literature and Social Change.* Durham: Duke University Press.

Havnevik, Hanna. 1989. *Tibetan Buddhist Nuns: History, Cultural Norms and Social Reality.* Oslo: Norwegian University Press.

Herzfeld, Michael. 1997. *Cultural Intimacy: Social Poetics in the Nation-State.* New York: Routledge.

Hess, Julia Meredith. 2006. "Statelessness and the State: Tibetans, Citizenship, and Nationalist Activism in a Transnational World." *International Migration* 44(1), 79–103.

———. 2009. *Immigrant Ambassadors: Citizenship and Belonging in the Tibetan Diaspora.* Stanford: Stanford University Press.

"HM Stresses Unity in Diversity." Electronic document. *Kathmandu Post,* 9 August 2002. http://www.nepalnews.com.

Hobsbawm, Eric J. 1993. *Nations and Nationalisms since 1780: Programme, Myth, Reality.* Cambridge: Cambridge University Press.

Hobsbawm, Eric, and Terence Ranger, eds. 1992 [1983]. *The Invention of Tradition.* Cambridge: Cambridge University Press.

Hoffman, Danny. 2004. "The Submerged Promise: Strategies for Ethnographic Writing in a Time of War." *Anthropological Quarterly* 77(2), 323–30.

Hopkirk, Peter. 1982. *Trespassers on the Roof of the World: The Race for Lhasa.* Oxford: Oxford University Press.

Hovell, Laurie L. 2001. *English in Tibet, Tibet in English: Self-Presentation in Tibet and the Diaspora*. New York: Palgrave.

Huber, Toni. 1994. "Why Can't Women Climb Pure Crystal Mountain? Remarks on Gender, Ritual and Space in Tibet." *Tibetan Studies*, ed. P. Kvaerne, 350–71. Oslo: Institute for Comparative Research in Human Culture.

——. 1999a. *The Cult of Pure Crystal Mountain: Popular Pilgrimage and Visionary Landscape in Southeast Tibet*. Oxford: Oxford University Press.

——. 1999b. "Putting the Gnas Back into Gnas-kor: Rethinking Tibetan Pilgrimage Practice." *Sacred Spaces and Powerful Places in Tibetan Culture*, ed. T. Huber, 771–804. Dharamsala: Library of Tibetan Works and Archives.

——, ed. 1999c. *Sacred Spaces and Powerful Places in Tibetan Culture*. Dharamsala: Library of Tibetan Works and Archives.

——, ed. 2002. *Amdo Tibetans in Transition: Society and Culture in the Post-Mao Era*. Leiden: Brill.

Hughes, Diane, and Thomas R. Trautmann, eds. 1995. *Time: Histories and Ethnologies*. Ann Arbor: University of Michigan Press.

Hutt, Michael, ed. 2004. *Himalayan People's War: Nepal's Maoist Revolution*. London: Hurst.

International Commission of Jurists. 1960. *Tibet and the Chinese People's Republic*. Geneva: International Commission of Jurists.

——. 1997. *Tibet: Human Rights and the Rule of Law*. Geneva: International Commission of Jurists.

Iyer, Pico. 2008. *The Open Road: The Global Journey of the Fourteenth Dalai Lama*. New York: Knopf.

Jackson, Michael. 2002. *The Politics of Storytelling*. Copenhagen: Museum Tusculanum Press.

Jinpa, Thupten. 2002. *Self, Reality and Reason in Tibetan Philosophy: Tsongkhapa's Quest for the Middle Way*. London: RoutledgeCurzon.

Juergensmeyer, Mark, and Michael Jerryson, eds. 2009. *Buddhist Warfare*. Oxford: Oxford University Press.

Kaplan, Caren. 1996. *Questions of Travel: Postmodern Discourses of Displacement*. Durham: Duke University Press.

Kapstein, Matthew T. 1998. "Concluding Reflections." *Buddhism in Contemporary Tibet: Religious Revival and Cultural Identity*, ed. M. C. Goldstein and M. T. Kapstein, 139–49. Berkeley: University of California Press.

——. 2006. *The Tibetans*. Malden, Mass.: Blackwell.

Karmay, Samten G. 1994. "Mountain Cults and National Identity in Tibet." *Resistance and Reform in Tibet*, ed. S. Akiner and R. Barnett, 112–20. Bloomington: Indiana University Press.

——. 2005. *The Arrow and the Spindle: Studies in Histories, Myths, Rituals, and Beliefs in Tibet*. Volume 2. Kathmandu: Mandala Publications.

Katayama, Lisa. 2008. "Brothers First." *Buddhadharma* (Fall 2008). Accessed online: http://www.thebuddhadharma.com/issues/2008/fall/brothers.php.

Klieger, P. Christiaan. 1989. "Ideology and the Framing of Tibetan History." *Tibet Journal* 14(4), 3–16.

———. 1992. *Tibetan Nationalism: The Role of Patronage in the Accomplishment of a National Identity*. Berkeley: Folklore Institute.

Knaus, John Kenneth. 1999. *Orphans of the Cold War: America and the Tibetan Struggle for Survival*. New York: Public Affairs.

Kohli, M. S., and Kenneth Conboy. 2002. *Spies in the Himalayas: Secret Missions and Perilous Climbs*. Lawrence: University of Kansas Press.

Kornman, Robin. 1997. "Gesar of Ling." *Religions of Tibet in Practice*, ed. D. S. Lopez Jr., 39–68. Princeton: Princeton University Press.

Koselleck, Reinhart. 1985 [1979]. *Futures Past: On the Semantics of Historical Time*. Translated by K. Tribe. Cambridge: MIT Press.

Kramer, Mark, ed. 2006. Special Issue on "Great-Power Rivalries, Tibetan Guerrilla Resistance, and the Cold War in South Asia." *Journal of Cold War Studies* 8(3).

Laclau, Ernest, and Chantal Mouffe. 2001. *Hegemony and Socialist Strategy: Towards a Radical Democratic Politics*. London: Verso.

Laird, Thomas. 2002. *Into Tibet: The CIA's First Atomic Spy and His Secret Expedition to Lhasa*. New York: Grove Press.

———. 2006. *The Story of Tibet: Conversations with the Dalai Lama*. New York: Grove Press.

Lamb, Alistair. 1964. *The China–India Border: The Origins of the Disputed Boundaries*. London: Oxford University Press.

———. 1966. *The McMahon Line: A Study in the Relations between India, China, and Tibet, 1904 to 1914*. 2 volumes. London: Routledge and Kegan Paul.

———. 1986 [1960]. *British India and Tibet, 1766–1910*. London: Routledge and Kegan Paul.

Lane, Fred. 1994. "The Warrior Tribes of Kham," *Asiaweek* (March 2), 30–38.

Lau, Timm. 2009. "Tibetan Fears and Indian Foes: Fears of Cultural Extinction and Antagonism as Discursive Strategy." *vis-à-vis: Explorations in Anthropology* 9(1), 81–90.

Leach, Edmund. 1960. "The Frontiers of Burma." *Comparative Studies in Society and History* 3(1), 49–68.

Leary, William M. 1997/1998. "Secret Mission to Tibet." *Air and Space* (December/January), 62–71.

LeGoff, Jacques. 1992. *History and Memory*. Translated by S. Rendall and E. Claman. New York: Columbia University Press.

Lhamo, Rinchen. 1997 [1926]. *We Tibetans*. New Delhi: Shristi.

Li, Tieh-tseng. 1956. *The Historical Status of Tibet*. New York: King's Crown Press, Columbia University.

Lichter, David, and Lawrence Epstein. 1983. "Irony in Tibetan Notions of the Good Life." *Karma: An Anthropological Inquiry*, eds. C. Keyes and E. V. Daniel, 223–260. Berkeley: University of California Press.

Lin, Hsiao-Ting. 2006. *Tibet and Nationalist China's Frontier: Intrigues and Ethnopolitics, 1928–49*. Vancouver: University of British Columbia Press.

Litzinger, Ralph. 1998. "Memory Work: Reconstituting the Ethnic in Post-Mao China." *Cultural Anthropology* 13(2), 224–55.

——. 2000. *Other Chinas: The Yao and the Politics of National Belonging*. Durham: Duke University Press.

Liu, Melinda. 1999. "When Heaven Shed Blood." *Newsweek* (April 19, international edition), accessed online at http://www.newsweek.com/id/88042.

Long, Jeff. 1986. "Going After Wangdu: The Search for a Tibetan Guerrilla Leads to Colorado's Secret CIA Camp." *Mountain People*, ed. M. Tobias, 112–18. Norman: University of Oklahoma Press.

Lopez, Donald S., Jr. 1998. *Prisoners of Shangri-La: Tibetan Buddhism and the West*. Princeton: Princeton University Press.

——. 2001. "Jailbreak: Author's Response." *Journal of the American Academy of Religion* 69(1), 203–14.

——. 2005. *The Madman's Middle Way: Reflections on the Reality of the Tibetan Monk Gendun Chopel*. Chicago: University of Chicago Press.

Ludden, David, ed. 2002. *Reading Subaltern Studies: Critical Histories, Contested Meanings, and the Globalization of South Asia*. London: Anthem Press.

Lutz, Catherine. 2001. *Homefront: A Military City and the American 20th Century*. Boston: Beacon Press.

——. 2006. "Empire Is in the Details." *American Ethnologist* 33(4), 593–611.

Maher, Derek. 2008. "The Rhetoric of War in Tibet: Toward a Buddhist Just War Theory." *Political Theology* 9(2), 179–91.

——. 2009. "Sacralized Warfare: The Fifth Dalai Lama and the Discourse of Religious Violence." *Buddhist Warfare*, ed. M. Juergensmeyer and M. Jerryson, 77–90. Oxford: Oxford University Press.

Makley, Charlene. 1994. "Gendered Practices and the Inner Sanctum: The Reconstruction of Tibetan Sacred Space in 'China's Tibet.'" *Tibet Journal* 19(2), 61–94.

——. 2003. "Gendered Boundaries in Motion: Space and Identity on the Sino–Tibetan Frontier." *American Ethnologist* 30(4), 597–619.

——. 2005a. "The Body of a Nun: Nunhood and Gender in Contemporary Amdo." *Women in Tibet*, ed. J. Gyatso and H. Havnevik, 259–84. New York: Columbia University Press.

——. 2005b. "'Speaking Bitterness': Autobiography, History, and Mnemonic Politics on the Sino–Tibetan Frontier." *Comparative Studies in Society and History* 47(1), 40–78.

——. 2007. *The Violence of Liberation: Gender and Tibetan Buddhist Revival in Post-Mao China*. Berkeley: University of California Press.

——. n.d. *The Olympic Year: Development and State Violence among Tibetans in China*. Unpublished book manuscript.

Malkki, Liisa. 1992. "National Geographic: The Rooting of Peoples and the Territorialization of National Identity among Scholars and Refugees." *Cultural Anthropology* 7(1), 24–44.

——. 1995a. "Refugees and Exile: From 'Refugee Studies' to the National Order of Things." *Annual Review of Anthropology* 24, 495–523.

——. 1995b. *Purity and Exile: Violence, Memory, and National Cosmology among Hutu Refugees in Tanzania*. Chicago: University of Chicago Press.

Mamdani, Mahmood. 2009. *Saviors and Survivors: Darfur, Politics, and the War on Terror*. New York: Pantheon.

March, Kathryn. 2002. *If Each Comes Half Way: Meeting Tamang Women in Nepal*. Ithaca: Cornell University Press.

Marchetti, Victor, and John Marks. 1974. *The CIA and the Cult of Intelligence*. New York: Alfred A. Knopf.

Marcus, George E. 1998 [1995]. "Ethnography in/of the World System: The Emergence of Multi-Sited Ethnography." *Ethnography through Thick and Thin*, 79–105. Princeton: Princeton University Press.

Martin, Dan (in collaboration with Yael Bentor). 1997. *Tibetan Histories: A Bibliography of Tibetan-Language Historical Works*. London: Serindia.

McCarthy, Roger E. 1997. *Tears of the Lotus: Accounts of Tibetan Resistance to the Chinese Invasion, 1950–1962*. Jefferson, N.C.: McFarland.

McConnell, Fiona. 2009. "De Facto, Displaced, Tacit: The Sovereign Articulations of the Tibetan Government-in-Exile." *Political Geography* 28(6), 343–52.

McGranahan, Carole. 1996. "Miss Tibet, or Tibet Misrepresented?: The Trope of Woman-as-Nation in the Struggle for Tibet." *Beauty Queens on the Global Stage: Gender, Contests, and Power*, ed. C. Cohen, R. Wilk, and B. Stoeltje, 161–84. New York: Routledge.

——. 2001. "Arrested Histories: Between Empire and Exile in Twentieth-Century Tibet." Ph.D. diss., University of Michigan.

——. 2002. "*Sa spang mda' gnam spang mda*': Murder, History, and Social Politics in 1920s Lhasa." *Khams pa Histories: Visions of People, Place, and Authority*, ed. L. Epstein, 103–26. Leiden: Brill.

——. 2003a. "Empire and the Status of Tibet: British, Chinese, and Tibetan Negotiations, 1913–1934." *The History of Tibet*. Volume 3: *The Tibetan Encounter with Modernity*, ed. A. McKay, 267–95. Richmond, Surrey: Curzon Press.

——. 2003b. "From Simla to Rongbatsa: The British and the 'Modern' Boundaries of Tibet." *Tibet Journal* 28(4), 39–60.

——. 2005. "Truth, Fear, and Lies: Exile Politics and Arrested Histories of the Tibetan Resistance." *Cultural Anthropology* 20(4), 570–600.

——. 2006. "Tibet's Cold War: The CIA and the Chushi Gangdrug Resistance, 1956–1974." *Journal of Cold War Studies* 8(3), 102–30.

———. 2007. "Empire Out of Bounds: Tibet in the Era of Decolonization." *Imperial Formations*, ed. A. Stoler, C. McGranahan, and P. Perdue, 187–227. Santa Fe: SAR Press.

———. 2010. "Narrative Dispossession: Tibet and the Gendered Logics of Historical Possibility." *Comparative Studies in Society and History*, in press.

McGranahan, Carole, Susan Chen, Sienna Craig, Charlene Makley, Tashi Rabgey, and Chris Vasantkumar. 2010. "Tibet: Anthropology in a Time of Protest" *Himalaya*, in press.

McKay, Alex. 1997. *Tibet and the British Raj: The Frontier Cadre, 1904–1947*. Richmond, Surrey: Curzon Press.

McLagan, Meg. 1996. "Mobilizing for Tibet: Transnational Politics and Diaspora Culture in the Post–Cold War Era." Ph.D. diss., New York University.

———. 1997. "Mystical Visions in Manhattan: Deploying Culture in the Year of Tibet." *Tibetan Culture in the Diaspora*, ed. F. J. Korom, 69–90. Wien: Verlag Osterreichischen Akademie der Wissenschaften.

———. 2002. "Spectacles of Difference: Cultural Activism and the Mass Mediation of Tibet." *Media Worlds: Anthropology on New Terrain*, ed. F. Ginsburg, L. Abu-Lughod, and B. Larkin, 90–111. Berkeley: University of California Press.

McMahon, Robert J. 1994. *The Cold War on the Periphery: The United States, India, and Pakistan*. New York: Columbia University Press.

Mehra, Parshotam. 1974. *The McMahon Line and After: A Study of the Triangular Contest on India's Northeast Frontier between Britain, China, and Tibet, 1904–1947*. Delhi: Macmillan.

———. 2007. *Essays in Frontier History: India, China, and the Disputed Border*. New Delhi: Oxford University Press.

"Memorandum on Genuine Autonomy for the Tibetan People." 2008. Electronic Document. http://www.tibet.net.

Merry, Sally Engle. 1984. "Rethinking Gossip and Scandal." *Toward a General Theory of Social Control*, ed. D. Black, 271–302. New York: Academic Press.

Miller, Beatrice. 1956. "Ganye and Kidu: Two Forms of Mutual Aid among the Tibetans." *Southwestern Journal of Anthropology* 12, 157–70.

Moran, Peter. 2004. *Buddhism Observed: Travelers, Exiles, and Tibetan Dharma in Kathmandu*. New York: Routledge.

Mouffe, Chantal. 2008. "Critique as Counter-Hegemonic Intervention." *Transversaal*, issue on "The Art of Critique." Accessed online http://eipcp.net/transversal/0808/mouffe/en.

Mueggler, Erik. 2001. *The Age of Wild Ghosts: Memory, Violence, and Place in Southwest China*. Berkeley: University of California Press.

Mullin, Chris. 1975. "Tibetan Conspiracy." *Far Eastern Economic Review* (September 5), 30–34.

Mullin, Glenn H. 1988. *Path of the Bodhisattva Warrior: The Life and Teachings of the Thirteenth Dalai Lama*. Ithaca: Snow Lion.

Mumford, Stan Royal. 1989. "Emplotment of Historical Narratives in the Nepal Himalayas." *Social Analysis* 25, 53–63.

Nagai, Yonosuke, and Akira Iriye, eds. 1977. *The Origins of the Cold War in Asia.* New York: Columbia University Press.

Nora, Pierre. 1989. "Between Memory and History: *Les Lieux de Memoire.*" *Representations* 26, 7–25.

Norbu, Dawa. 1974a. "Editorial: Militant Nationalist Movement." *Tibetan Review* 9(6–7), 3–4.

——. 1974b. "Who Aided Khampas and Why?" *Tibetan Review* 9(6–7), 19–23, 29.

——. 1974c. *Red Star over Tibet.* London: Collins.

——. 1975. "G. Tharchin: Pioneer and Patriot." *Tibetan Review* (December), 18–20.

——. 1979. "The 1959 Tibetan Rebellion: An Interpretation." *China Quarterly* 77, 74–93.

——. 1995. "Han Hegemony and Tibetan Ethnicity." *International Studies* 32(3), 297–314.

Norbu, Jamyang. 1986 [1979]. *Warriors of Tibet: The Story of Aten and the Khampas' Fight for the Freedom of Their Country.* London: Wisdom Publications.

——. 1989. *Illusion and Reality: Essays on the Tibetan and Chinese Political Scene from 1978 to 1989.* Dharamsala: TYC Books.

——. 1994. "The Tibetan Resistance Movement and the Role of the C.I.A." *Resistance and Reform in Tibet,* ed. S. Akiner and R. Barnett, 186–96. Bloomington: Indiana University Press.

——. 1998a. "Rite of Freedom: The Life and Sacrifice of Thupten Ngodup." Electronic document. *World Tibet Network News,* 6 August. http://www.tibet.ca.

——. 1998b. "Dances with Yaks: Tibet in Film, Fiction, and Fantasy of the West." *Tibetan Review* 33(1), 18–23.

——. 2001. "Silent Struggle: Tsongkha Lhamo Tsering (1924–1999)." Electronic document. *High Asia Journal.* http://www.amnyemachen.org.

——. 2004[1997]. "Nonviolence or Non-Action: Some Gandhian Truths about the Tibetan Peace Movement." *Shadow Tibet.* New Delhi: Bluejay Books, 151–60.

——. 2006. "Forgotten Anniversary: Remembering the Great Khampa Uprising of 1956." Electronic document. *World Tibet Network News,* 7 December. http://www.tibet.ca.

——. 2007. "Nonviolence and Non-Action." Electronic document. *Tibet Writes,* 27 December. http://www.tibetwrites.org.

——. 2009. "A Not So Special Meeting." Electronic document. *Shadow Tibet,* 4 February. http//www.jamyangnorbu.com.

Nowak, Margaret. 1984. *Tibetan Refugees: Youth and the New Generation of Meaning.* New Brunswick: Rutgers University Press.

Oberoi, Pia. 2006. *Exile and Belonging: Refugees and State Politics in South Asia.* New Delhi: Oxford University Press.

Okawa, Kensaku. 2007. "Lessons from Tibetans in Taiwan: Their History, Current Situation, and Relationships with Taiwanese Nationalism." University of Tokyo Repository. Issued 19 December 2007. Accessed at http://repository.dl.itc.u-to kyo.ac.jp.

Ong, Aihwa. 1999. *Flexible Citizenship: The Cultural Logics of Transnationality.* Durham: Duke University Press.

Ortner, Sherry B. 1984. "Theory in Anthropology since the Sixties." *Comparative Studies in Society and History* 26(1), 372–411.

——. 1989. *High Religion: A Cultural and Political History of Sherpa Buddhism.* Princeton: Princeton University Press.

——. 1996. *Making Gender: The Politics and Erotics of Culture.* Boston: Beacon Press.

——. 2006. *Anthropology and Social Theory: Culture, Power, and the Acting Subject.* Durham: Duke University Press.

Pachen, Ani, and Adelaide Donnelley. 2000. *Sorrow Mountain: The Journey of a Tibetan Warrior Nun.* New York: Kodansha International.

Pandey, Gyanendra. 1990. *The Construction of Communalism in Colonial North India.* Delhi: Oxford University Press.

——. 1992. "In Defense of the Fragment: Writing about Hindu–Muslim Riots in India Today." *Representations* 37, 7–55.

——. 1995. "Voices from the Edge: The Struggle to Write Subaltern Histories." *Ethnos* 60 (3–4), 224–42.

——. 1996. "The Prose of Otherness." *Subaltern Studies VIII.* Delhi: Oxford University Press.

——. 2001. *Remembering Partition: Violence, Nationalism, and History in India.* Cambridge: Cambridge University Press.

——. 2006. *Routine Violence: Nations, Fragments, Histories.* Stanford: Stanford University Press.

Papailias, Penelope. 2005. *Genres of Recollection: Archival Poetics and Modern Greece.* New York: Palgrave.

Patterson, George. 1968. "Ambush on the Roof of the World." *Reader's Digest* (March), 59–64.

——. 1970. *A Fool at Forty.* Waco, Tex.: Word Books.

——. 1974. "Raid across the Border." *Tibetan Review* 9(6–7), 17–18, 33.

Peissel, Michel. 1972. *The Secret War in Tibet [The Cavaliers of Kham].* Boston: Little, Brown.

Peteet, Julie. 2005. *Landscape of Hope and Despair: Palestinian Refugee Camps.* Philadelphia: University of Pennsylvania Press.

Powers, John. 2004. *History as Propaganda: Tibetan Exiles versus the People's Republic of China.* Oxford: Oxford University Press.

Prakash, Gyan. 1994. "Subaltern Studies as Postcolonial Criticism." *American Historical Review* 99(5), 1475–1990.

Prescott, J. R. V. 1987. *Political Frontiers and Boundaries.* London: Allen and Unwin.

Price, Richard. 2008. *Travels with Tooy: History, Memory, and the African American Imagination.* Chicago: University of Chicago Press.

Rabgey, Tashi, and Tsering Wangchuk. 2004. *Sino–Tibetan Dialogue in the Post-Mao Era: Lessons and Prospects.* Washington, D.C.: East–West Center.

Ramble, Charles. 2002. "Temporal Disjunction and Collectivity in Mustang, Nepal." *Current Anthropology* 43 (supplement):s75–s84.

———. 2007. *The Navel of the Demoness: Tibetan Buddhism and Civil Religion in Highland Nepal.* New York: Oxford University Press.

Renan, Ernest. 1996 [1882]. "What Is a Nation?" *Becoming National: A Reader,* ed. G. Eley and R. G. Suny, 41–55. New York: Oxford University Press.

Richards, Thomas. 1992. "Archive and Utopia." *Representations* 37, 104–35.

———. 1993. *The Imperial Archive: Knowledge and the Fantasy of Empire.* London: Verso.

Richardson, Hugh E. 1984 [1962]. *Tibet and Its History.* 2d ed. Boston: Shambala.

———. 1998 [1945]. *Tibetan Precis. High Peaks, Pure Earth: Collected Writings on Tibetan History and Culture,* ed. M. Aris, 519–666. London: Serindia.

Richardus, Peter, ed. 1998. *Tibetan Lives: Three Himalayan Autobiographies.* Richmond, Surrey: Curzon Press.

Ricoeur, Paul. 1984. *Time and Narrative.* Volume 1. Translated by K. McLaughlin and D. Pellauer. Chicago: University of Chicago Press.

———. 2004. *Memory, History, Forgetting.* Translated by K. Blamey and D. Pellauer. Chicago: University of Chicago Press.

Roberts, John B. III. 1997a. "The Dalai Lama's Great Escape." *George* (October), 130–33.

———. 1997b. "The Secret War over Tibet." *American Spectator* (December), 31–35, 85.

Robbins, Christopher. 1979. *Air America: The True Story of the CIA's Mercenary Fliers in Covert Operations From Pre-War China to Present-Day Nicaragua.* London: Corgi Books.

Roemer, Stephanie. 2008. *The Tibetan Government-in-Exile: Politics at Large.* London: Routledge.

Rosaldo, Renato. 1980. "Doing Oral History." *Social Analysis* 4, 89–99.

———. 1989. "Grief and a Headhunter's Rage." *Culture and Truth: The Remaking of Social Analysis,* 1–21. Boston: Beacon Press.

Rosen, Steven. 2001. "Unmade Movie Had CIA, Colorado Ties." *Denver Post,* 30 May, 1F, 6F.

Ross, Robert S., and Jiang Changbin, eds. 2001. *Re-examining the Cold War: US–China Diplomacy, 1954–1973.* Cambridge: Harvard University Asia Center.

Rudolph, Susanne Hoeber, and Lloyd I. Rudolph. 1984. *Essays on Rajputana: Reflections on History, Culture, and Administration.* New Delhi: Concept Publishing.

Rutherford, Danilyn. 2003. *Raiding the Land of the Foreigners: The Limits of the Nation on an Indonesian Frontier.* Princeton: Princeton University Press.

Sahlins, Marshall. 1981. *Historical Metaphors and Mythical Realities: Structure in the*

Early History of the Sandwich Island Kingdom. Ann Arbor: University of Michigan Press.

——. 1985. *Islands of History.* Chicago: University of Chicago Press.

——. 1991. "The Return of the Event, Again: With Reflections on the Beginnings of the Great Fijian War of 1843 to 1855 between the Kingdoms of Bau and Rewa." *Clio in Oceania: Toward a Historical Anthropology,* ed. Aletta Biersack, 37–99. Washington: Smithsonian Institution Press.

——. 2004. *Apologies to Thucydides: Understanding History as Culture and Vice Versa.* Chicago: University of Chicago Press.

Said, Edward. 1978. *Orientalism.* New York: Vintage Books.

——. 1984. "Reflections on Exile." *Granta* 13, 159–72.

Salopek, Paul. 1997. "How the CIA Helped Tibet Fight Their Chinese Invaders." *Chicago Tribune.* 25 January.

Samten, Ngawang, and Jay Garfield, trans. 2006. *Ocean of Reasoning: A Great Commentary on Nagarjuna's Mulamadhyamikakarika.* New York: Oxford University Press.

Samuel, Geoffrey. 1982. "Tibet as a Stateless Society and Some Islamic Parallels." *Journal of Asian Studies* 41(2), 215–29.

——. 1989. "Gesar of Ling: The Origins and Meanings of the East Tibetan Epic." *Proceedings of the 5th International Seminar on Tibetan Studies,* 711–22. Narita, Japan.

——. 1993. *Civilized Shamans: Buddhism in Tibetan Societies.* Washington: Smithsonian Institution Press.

——. 1994. "Gesar of Ling: Shamanic Power and Popular Religion." *Tantra and Everyday Religion,* ed. G. Samuel et al, 53–78. New Delhi: International Academy of Indian Culture and Aditya Prakashan.

Sangay, Lobsang. 2003. "Tibet: Exiles' Journey." *Journal of Democracy* 14(3), 119–30.

Schwarcz, Vera. 1994. "Strangers No More: Personal Memory in the Interstices of Public Commemoration." *Memory, History, and Opposition under State Socialism,* ed. R. S. Watson, 45–64. Santa Fe: SAR Press.

Schwartz, Ronald D. 1994. *Circle of Protest: Political Ritual in the Tibetan Uprising.* New York: Columbia University Press.

Scott, Joan. 1988. *Gender and the Politics of History.* New York: Columbia University Press.

Sewell, William H., Jr. 2005. *Logics of History: Social Theory and Social Transformation.* Chicago: University of Chicago Press.

Shain, Yossi, ed. 1991. *Governments-in-Exile in Contemporary World Politics.* New York: Routledge.

Shakabpa, Tsepon W. D. 1967. *Tibet: A Political History.* New Haven: Yale University Press.

Shakya, Tsering. 1991. "Tibet and the Occident: The Myth of Shangri-la." *Lungta,* 20–25.

——. 1993. "Whither the Tsampa Eaters?" *Himal* 6(5), 8–11.

——. 1994. "Introduction: The Development of Modern Tibetan Studies." *Resistance and Reform in Tibet*, ed. R. Barnett and S. Akiner, 1–14. London: Hurst.

——. 1999. *The Dragon in the Land of Snows: A History of Modern Tibet since 1947*. London: Pimlico.

——. 2001. "Who Are the Prisoners?" *Journal of the American Academy of Religion* 69(1), 183–90.

——. 2002. "Blood in the Snows: Reply to Wang Lixiong." *New Left Review* 15 (May–June), 39–60.

——. 2008. "Tibetan Questions." *New Left Review* 51 (May–June), 5–26.

Sheng, Michael. 2006. "Mao, Tibet, and the Korean War." *Journal of Cold War Studies* 8(3), 15–32.

Shneiderman, Sara. 2006. "Barbarians at the Border and Civilizing Projects: Analyzing Ethnic and National Identities in the Tibetan Context." *Tibetan Borderlands*, ed. P. C. Klieger, 9–34. Leiden: Brill.

"Shugden in Kham." 30 May 2009. TibetInfoNet Update. Web document, accessed at http://www.tibetinfonet.net/content/update/145.

Sider, Gerald, and Gavin Smith, eds. 1997. *Between History and Histories: The Making of Silences and Commemorations*. Toronto: University of Toronto Press.

Simmel, Georg. 1950. "The Secret and the Secret Society." *The Sociology of Georg Simmel*, trans. and ed. K. H. Wolff, 307–76. New York: Free Press.

Smith, Robert. 1998. "A History of Baba Yeshe's Role in the Tibetan Resistance." B.A. thesis, Johns Hopkins University.

Smith, Warren W., Jr. 1996. *Tibetan Nation: A History of Tibetan Nationalism and Sino–Tibetan Relations*. Boulder: Westview Press.

——. 2008. *China's Tibet?: Autonomy or Assimilation*. Lanham, Md.: Rowman and Littlefield.

——. 2010. *Tibet's Last Stand?: The Tibetan Uprising of 2008 and China's Response*. Lanham, Md.: Rowman and Littlefield.

Sonam, Tenzing, and Ritu Sarin. 1998. *The Shadow Circus*. White Crane Films.

Sperling, Elliot. 1976. "The Chinese Venture in K'am, 1904–1911, and the Role of Chao Erh-feng." *Tibet Journal* 1(2), 10–36.

——. 1994. "The Rhetoric of Dissent: Tibetan Pamphleteers." *Resistance and Reform in Tibet*, ed. S. Akiner and R. Barnett, 238–58. Bloomington: Indiana University Press.

——. 2001. " 'Orientalism' and Aspects of Violence in the Tibetan Tradition." *Imagining Tibet: Perceptions, Projections, and Fantasies*, ed. T. Dodin and H. Räther, 317–30. Boston: Wisdom Publications.

——. 2008. "The Politics of History and the Indo–Tibetan Border (1987–1988)." *India Review* 7(3), 223–39.

——. 2009. "China Digs in Its Heels in Tibet." Electronic document. *Far Eastern Economic Review*, 3 April.

Spiegel, Gabrielle. 2002. "Memory and History: Liturgical Time and Historical Time." *History and Theory* 41, 149–62.

Starks, Richard, and Miriam Murcutt. 2004. *Lost in Tibet: The Untold Story of Five American Airmen, a Doomed Plane, and the Will to Survive*. Guilford, Conn.: Lyons Press.

Stoddard, Heather. 1985. *Le Mendiant d'Amdo*. Paris: Société d'Ethnographie.

———. 1994. "National Publications and National Identity." *Resistance and Reform in Tibet*, ed. S. Akiner and R. Barnett, 120–56. Bloomington: Indiana University Press.

Stoler, Ann Laura. 1989. "Rethinking Colonial Categories: European Communities and the Boundaries of Rule." *Comparative Studies in Society and History* 31(1), 134–61.

———. 1992a. " 'In Cold Blood': Hierarchies of Credibility and the Politics of Colonial Narratives." *Representations* 37, 151–89.

———. 1992b. "Sexual Affronts and Racial Frontiers: European Identities and the Politics of Exclusion in Colonial Southeast Asia." *Comparative Studies in Society and History* 34(3), 514–51.

———. 1995. *Race and the Education of Desire: Foucault's History of Sexuality and the Colonial Order of Things*. Durham: Duke University Press.

———. 2002. *Carnal Knowledge and Imperial Power: Race and the Intimate in Colonial Rule*. Berkeley: University of California Press.

———. 2008. "Imperial Debris: Reflections on Ruins and Ruination." *Cultural Anthropology* 23(2), 191–219.

———, ed. 2006. *Haunted by Empire: Geographies of Intimacy in North American History*. Durham: Duke University Press.

Stoler, Ann Laura, and Carole McGranahan. 2007. "Introduction: Refiguring Imperial Terrain." *Imperial Formations*, ed. A. Stoler, C. McGranahan, and P. Perdue, 3–47. Santa Fe: SAR Press.

Stoler, Ann Laura, and Karen Strassler. 2000. "Castings for the Colonial: On Memory-Work in 'New Order' Java," *Comparative Studies in Society and History* 42(1), 4–48.

Strang, David. 1996. "Contested Sovereignty: The Social Construction of Colonial Imperialism." *State Sovereignty as a Social Construct*, ed. T. J. Biersteker and C. Weber, 22–49. Cambridge: Cambridge University Press.

Takeda, Pete. 2006. *An Eye at the Top of the World: The Terrifying Legacy of the Cold War's Most Daring CIA Operation*. New York: Thunder's Mouth Press.

Tapontsang, Adhe, with Joy Blakeslee. 1997. *Ama Adhe, the Voice that Remembers: The Heroic Story of a Woman's Fight to Free Tibet*. Boston: Wisdom Publications.

Taussig, Michael. 1984. "Culture of Terror—Space of Death: Roger Casement's Putumayo Report and the Explanation of Torture." *Comparative Studies in Society and History* 26, 467–97.

——. 1986. *Shamanism, Colonialism, and the Wild Man: A Study in Terror and Healing*. Chicago: University of Chicago Press.

——. 1991. *The Nervous System*. New York: Routledge.

——. 1993. *Mimesis and Alterity*. New York: Routledge.

——. 1999. *Defacements: Public Secrets and the Labor of the Historical Negative*. Stanford: Stanford University Press.

——. 2006. *Walter Benjamin's Grave*. Chicago: University of Chicago Press.

Tefft, Stanton K., ed. 1980. *Secrecy: A Cross-Cultural Perspective*. New York: Human Sciences Press.

Teichman, Sir Eric. 1922. *Travels of a Consular Officer in Eastern Tibet (Together with a History of Relations between China, Tibet, and India)*. Cambridge: Cambridge University Press.

Terrone, Antonio. 2002. "Visions, Arcane Claims, and Hidden Treasures: Charisma and Authority in a Present-Day Gter Ston." *Tibet, Self, and the Tibetan Diaspora: Voices of Difference*, ed. P. C. Klieger, 213–28. Leiden: Brill.

Tethong, Wangpo. 2000. *Der Wandel in der politischen Elite der Tibeter im Exil: Integrations unt Desintegratinsprozese in der politischen Führungsschicht 1950–1979* (Change in the political elite of the exile Tibetans: Processes of integration and disintegration in the political ruling classes, 1950–1979). Rikon-Zurich: Tibet-Institut.

Thonden, Phintso. 1991. "On the Dragon's Side of the Tibet Question." *Tibetan Review*, May 1991, 12–20.

Thondup, Tulku Rinpoche. 1986. *Hidden Teachings of Tibet: An Explanation of the Terma Tradition of the Nyingma School of Buddhism*. Edited by H. Talbott. London: Wisdom Publications.

Thongchai, Winichakul. 1994. *Siam Mapped: A History of the Geo-Body of a Nation*. Honolulu: University of Hawai'i Press.

Thurman, Robert A. F. 2001. "Critical Reflections on Donald S. Lopez Jr.'s *Prisoners of Shangri-la: Tibetan Buddhism and the West*." *Journal of the American Academy of Religion* 69(1), 191–202.

Trouillot, Michel-Rolph. 1995. *Silencing the Past: Power and the Production of History*. Boston: Beacon Press.

Tsering, Diki. 2000. *Dalai Lama, My Son: A Mother's Story*. Edited by Khedroob Thondup. New York: Viking Arkana.

Tsering, Tashi. 1985. "Nyag-rong mgom-po rnam-rgyal: A 19th Century Khams-pa Warrior." *Soundings in Tibetan Civilization*, ed. B. N. Aziz and M. Kapstein, 196–214. Delhi: Manohar.

——. 1997. "Themes and Perspectives on Tibetan History with Emphasis on nGolog and Preliminary Remarks on Some New Sources." Paper presented at "The History of Tibet: New Resources and Perspectives" Conference, Oxford University. 23–24 May.

Tsing, Anna Lowenhaupt. 1993. *In the Realm of the Diamond Queen*. Princeton: Princeton University Press.

Tuttle, Gray. 2005. *Tibetan Buddhists in the Making of Modern China*. New York: Columbia University Press.

van Beek, Martijn. 2001a. "Beyond Identity Fetishism: 'Communal' Conflict in Ladakh and the Limits of Autonomy." *Cultural Anthropology* 15(4), 525–69.

———. 2001b. "Public Secrets, Conscious Amnesia, and the Celebration of Autonomy for Ladakh." *States of Imagination: Ethnographic Explorations of the Postcolonial State*, ed. T. B. Hansen and F. Stepputat, 365–90. Durham: Duke University Press.

van der Kuijp, Leonard. 1996. "Tibetan Historiography." *Tibetan Literature: Studies in Genre*, ed. J. C. Cabezon and R. Jackson, 39–56. Ithaca: Snow Lion.

Vine, David A. 2009. *Island of Shame: The Secret History of the U.S. Military Base on Diego Garcia*. Princeton: Princeton University Press.

Vostrikov, A. I. 1970. *Tibetan Historical Literature*. Translated by H. C. Gupta. Calcutta: Indian Studies, Past and Present.

Wang, Ban. 2004. *Illuminations from the Past: Trauma, Memory, and History in Modern China*. Stanford: Stanford University Press.

Wang, Lixiong. 2002. "Reflections on Tibet." *New Left Review* 14(March-April), 79–111.

Wanggyal, Phuntsok. 2002. *Liquid Water Does Exist on the Moon*. Beijing: Foreign Languages Press.

Watson, Rubie, ed. 1994. *Memory, History, and Opposition under State Socialism*. Santa Fe: SAR Press.

White, Hayden. 1987. *The Content of the Form: Narrative Discourse and Historical Representations*. Baltimore: Johns Hopkins University Press.

———. 1973. *Metahistory: The Historical Imagination in Nineteenth-Century Europe*. Baltimore: Johns Hopkins University Press.

White, Luise. 1994. "Between Gluckman and Foucault: Historicizing Rumor and Gossip." *Social Dynamics* 20(1), 75–92.

———. 2000a. *Speaking with Vampires: Rumor and History in Colonial Africa*. Berkeley: University of California Press.

———. 2000b. "Telling More: Lies, Secrets, and History." *History and Theory* 39(4), 11–22.

Williams, Raymond. 1977. *Marxism and Literature*. Oxford: Oxford University Press.

Willner, Albert Siegfried. 1995. "The Eisenhower Administration and Tibet, 1953–1961: Influence and the Making of U.S. Foreign Policy." Ph.D. diss., University of Virginia.

Wilson, Thomas M., and Hastings Donnan, eds. 1998. *Border Identities: Nation and State at International Frontiers*. Cambridge: Cambridge University Press.

Wise, David. 1973. *The Politics of Lying: Government Deception, Secrecy, and Power*. New York: Random House.

Yeh, Emily T. 2007a. "Exile Meets Homeland: Politics, Performance and Authenticity in the Tibetan Diaspora." *Environment and Planning D: Society and Space* 25(4), 648–67.

———. 2007b. "Tropes of Indolence and the Cultural Politics of Development in Lhasa, Tibet. Association of American Geographers." *Annals of the Association of American Geographers* 97(3), 593–612.

———. 2008. "Living Together in Lhasa: Ethnic Relations, Coercive Amity, and Subaltern Cosmopolitanism." *The Other Global City*, ed. Shail Mayaram, 54–85. New York: Routledge.

———. 2009. "Tibet and the Problem of Radical Reductionism." *Antipode* 41(5), 983–1010.

Yeh, Emily T., and Kunga T. Lama. 2006. "Hip-Hop Gangsta or Most Deserving of Victims?: Transnational Migrant Identities and the Paradox of Tibetan Racialization in the US." *Environment and Planning A* 38, 809–29.

Yoneyama, Lisa. 1999. *Hiroshima Traces: Time, Space, and the Dialectic of Memory*. Berkeley: University of California Press.

Young, James E. 1993. *The Texture of Memory: Holocaust Memorials and Meaning*. New Haven: Yale University Press.

Yu, Xue. 2005. *Buddhism, War, and Nationalism: Chinese Monks in the Struggle against Japanese Aggressions*. New York: Routledge.

Zablocki, Abraham. 2005. "The Global Mandala: The Transnational Transformation of Tibetan Buddhism." Ph.D. diss., Cornell University.

INDEX

Page numbers in italics refer to illustrations.

China (*continued*)

by, 21–22, 36, 45–51, 67–68, 71–84, 92–98, 113, 172; secret PLA pouch and, 149–53. *See also* People's Liberation Army

Chow, Rey, 238n64

Chushi Gangdrug, 2, 3, 9, 21–23, 27–29, 53, 56–58, 77–91, 97–100, 109–12, 118–25, 127, 132, 176–81, 189–91, 202–3, 208–9, 214–15, 221–23, 258n32; CIA and, 132–36, 163–78; conflict (1994), 28–29, 209–10; government of Tibet and, 93–97, 101–3; history of, 9–10, 111–16, 119–21, 130–32, 203–4, 208–12; as Khampa army, 60–66, 148, 251n54; as pan-Tibetan movement, 55–58, 63–66, 100–101; resistance and (1955–56), 67–88, 93–101; resistance and (1958–60), 104–7; Thirteen Group/United Party Conflict and, 147–49, 155, 177, 260n13, 260. *See also* June 16

class, 17, 57, 68, 86, 101, 121. *See also* social hierarchy

Cold War, 152, 166, 261n23, 263n8

Cole, Jennifer, 119

colonialism, 43–44, 144, 168; dominance and hegemony and, 235n5

Connerton, Paul, 115, 117

contradiction, culture as, 4–5, 11, 17–19, 23, 34, 51–52, 116, 166, 186, 200

critique, politics of, 17–19, 22–23, 28, 33–35, 60, 172–75, 192

Curzon, George Nathaniel Lord, 42–43, 241n21

Dadhag, 220, 224, 231

Dalai Lama, 15, 20, 31–32, 35, 37, 40, 58, 66, 86, 89, 121–24, 140, 160, 169, 182, 205–6, 221, 227, 236n18; Chushi Gangdrug and, 10, 13, 96–99, 101–3, 106, 109–15, 139, 150, 152, 154, 158–59, 174, 208–10, 214–16, 222–25, 265n48; fourteenth (Tenzin Gyatso), 2–5, 7, 9–10, 13, 16, 23–24, 38, 45–47, 51, 55, 65, 79, 91, 93, 105, 127, 141, 144–45, 149, 170, 172, 179, 198, 200, 220, 226, 232–33, 249n42; historical arrest and, 24–26; lineage of, 14–15, 41–43, 76, 245n8, 236n18; Middle-Way modernity

and, 59–60; nonviolence and, 18, 21, 183, 185–97, 199, 268n2; thirteenth, 8, 21, 69, 299; Tibetans' relationships to, 4–5, 9–10, 13–14, 18–19, 24, 76, 111, 172–75, 192, 199–200, 210, 226, 229

Darjeeling, 32, 56, 128–33, 136, 144, 146, 149, 152, 154, 160, 178, 193

Das, Veena, 3, 53, 58, 116

Dawa Norbu, 62, 178, 251n54

decolonization, 6, 38–40, 47, 166

Delhi, 31–32, 78, 80, 93, 115, 136, 140–41, 155–57, 160, 177–78, 193–98, 208, 210, 214–15

Demton Khang (Museum of Tibet), 212

Dharamsala, 3, 13, 18, 24, 32–33, 49, 79, 113–16, 132, 140, 146–47, 156, 160, 174–78, 180, 190, 202, 209–12, 215, 221, 223. *See also* Tibet, government-in-exile of

Dhargye Gonpa, 7, 61, 63, 76

difference, politics of, 3–4, 17–19, 22, 34, 39, 42, 48, 63, 65, 80, 144, 148, 154, 169, 205, 215, 244n20

Dirks, Nicholas, 205, 235n15

Dorje Shugden, 98–99, 221, 249n39, 249n42, 250n43

Dorje Yudon, 80–85, 120–22, 124, 207, 227

Drepung Monastery, 41, 92, 102, 106, 236n18, 246n6

Dreyfus, Georges, 41, 249n42, 268n3

Du Bois, W. E. B., 4

Dulles, Allen, 149

Establishment 22/SFF, 139–41, 186, 220, 259n45

exile. *See* refugees

fear, 20, 26, 28, 38, 105, 112, 123–24, 144, 156, 192, 195, 199, 201–8, 211, 215–17

forgetting, 3, 5, 6, 19, 22, 35, 117–20, 187–89, 199–200, 217, 221. *See also* memory

Fortun, Kim, 29

Foucault, Michel, 19, 21–22, 25, 175, 202

Free Tibet movement, 10, 187–89, 191

Freedom in Exile, 112, 179, 190

Ganden Monastery, 41, 92, 102, 106, 236n18, 246n6

Roosevelt, Franklin D., 165, 241n33
Rosaldo, Renato, 201

Sahlins, Marshall, 116
Samuel, Geoffrey, 40
secrets, 164–65, 176–83, 202; as public, 11.
    See also truth
Sera Monastery, 41, 55, 92, 102, 105–6, 132,
    232, 236n18, 246n6
Shakya, Tsering, 202
Shangri-La, Tibet as, 34, 164, 186
Sikkim, 130, *131*, 144
silences, 18–19, 25, 60, 138, 176, 201–4, 216
social hierarchy, 145–46, 169–72. *See also*
    class
Sonam Gelek, 102, 106–7, 233
sovereignty, 9, 37, 39–40
Spiegel, Gabrielle 238n77
states: boundaries of, 15, 38–44, 48–52;
    sovereignty of Tibetan state and, 37–42
Stepputat, Finn, 15
Stoler, Ann, 58
subaltern studies, 2, 22, 33, 69, 72, 188,
    237n62
subjectivity, 3, 5, 13, 19, 23, 27, 44, 52–57,
    119–20, 175, 202, 246n32. *See also*
    identity
Surkhang Wangchen Gelek, 146, 157–58,
    233

Taiwan, 24, 38, 93, 130, 141, 145–46, 157–59,
    209–10, 213, 222, 225, 260n15
Taklha Phuntsok Tashi, 156, 158, 233
Tashi Tsering, 49, 180, 233
Taussig, Michael, 11, 203, 212
Testimonio, 72–73
Tharchin Babu, 69–72, 78, 154
Thirteen Group, 147–49, 155, 177,
    260nn13–15
Thongchai, Winichakul, 39
Thubten Ngodup, 185–87, 195–200. *See
    also* Unto Death Hunger Strike
Tibet, 48–52; *Chol kha gsum* model,
    242n38, 242n40; history of, 8–9, 201–3;

relations of, with China, 8–9, 37–39, 67;
    territory of, 37–44
Tibet, government-in-exile of, 13–17, 101–
    3, 144–50, 222, 236nn27–28; control
    over history and, 9, 22, 26, 115, 177, 179,
    202, 259n7, 265n39, 270nn4–5
Tibetan Uprising Day (March 10), 113–16,
    118
Tibetan Volunteer Army for Defense of
    Religion, 89, 104. *See also* Chushi
    Gangdrug
Tibetan Youth Congress (TYC), 191–92,
    195–98, 200, 271n21
Tibet Mirror, 69–72, 91, 129, 154, 165
treasure teachings (*gter*), 25–27, 31, 123,
    239n82
Trijang Rinpoche, 96–97, 233
Trouillot, Michel-Rolph, 3, 120
truth, 3, 22, 26–27, 111, 133, 175–76, 188, 191,
    198, 201–16, 223, 228; verification of, 112,
    115–16, 202–12
Tsering Wangmo Dhompa, 176
Tsing, Anna, 153

United Nations, 16, 38, 40, 45, 47, 92–93,
    149–92, 197, 240n3, 269n32
United Party, 146–49, 155, 177
United States–Tibet relations, 2, 38, 45–
    47, 95, 101, 130, 145, 149–51, 157, 165–69,
    241n33, 242n35, 263n11, 264n12. *See also*
    Central Intelligence Agency; Dulles,
    Allen; Kennedy, John F.; Roosevelt,
    Franklin D.
Unto Death Hunger Strike (1998), 185,
    191–97. *See also* Thubten Ngodup

Van Beek, Martijn, 244n20
veterans. *See* Chushi Gangdrug

White, Hayden, 115, 188
White, Luise, 164–65, 202, 204
Wllliams, Raymond, 18

Yonru Pön, 75, 233, 247n17

Carole McGranahan is associate professor of
anthropology at the University of Colorado, Boulder.
She is the co-editor, with Ann Laura Stoler and
Peter C. Perdue, of *Imperial Formations* (2007) and,
with Ann Forbes, of *Developing Tibet?: A Survey of
International Development Projects* (1992).

10 a.m. pr Giuliani

Library of Congress Cataloging-in-Publication Data
McGranahan, Carole.
Arrested histories : Tibet, the CIA, and memories of
a forgotten war / Carole McGranahan.
p. cm.
Includes bibliographical references and index.
ISBN 978-0-8223-4751-4 (cloth : alk. paper)
ISBN 978-0-8223-4771-2 (pbk. : alk. paper)
1. Tibet (China)—History—Autonomy and
independence movements. 2. Memory—Political
aspects—China—Tibet. 3. United States. Central
Intelligence Agency. I. Title.
DS786.M3865 2010
951.05′5—dc22   2010017150

E Main & Presley Way
10 6!
park in back

Nov 28th
10 a.m.

overlooking
golf course